T0176978

SERVICE QUALITY OF CLOUD-BASED APPLICATIONS

SERVICE QUALITY OF CLOUD-BASED APPLICATIONS

Eric Bauer
Randee Adams

IEEE PRESS

WILEY

Library of Congress Cataloging-in-Publication Data:

Bauer, Eric.
  Service quality of cloud-based applications / Eric Bauer, Randee Adams.
    pages cm
  ISBN 978-1-118-76329-2 (cloth)
  1. Cloud computing. 2. Application software–Reliability. 3. Quality of service (Computer networks) I. Adams, Randee. II. Title.
  QA76.585.B3944 2013
  004.67'82–dc23

                           2013026569

Printed in the United States of America

10 9 8 7 6 5 4 3 2 1

CONTENTS

Figures   **xv**

Tables and Equations   **xxi**

1 INTRODUCTION   **1**
   1.1   Approach   1
   1.2   Target Audience   3
   1.3   Organization   3

I CONTEXT   **7**

2 APPLICATION SERVICE QUALITY   **9**
   2.1   Simple Application Model   9
   2.2   Service Boundaries   11
   2.3   Key Quality and Performance Indicators   12
   2.4   Key Application Characteristics   15
       2.4.1   Service Criticality   15
       2.4.2   Application Interactivity   16
       2.4.3   Tolerance to Network Traffic Impairments   17
   2.5   Application Service Quality Metrics   17
       2.5.1   Service Availability   18
       2.5.2   Service Latency   19
       2.5.3   Service Reliability   24
       2.5.4   Service Accessibility   25
       2.5.5   Service Retainability   25

	2.5.6	Service Throughput	25
	2.5.7	Service Timestamp Accuracy	26
	2.5.8	Application-Specific Service Quality Measurements	26
2.6	Technical Service versus Support Service	27
	2.6.1	Technical Service Quality	27
	2.6.2	Support Service Quality	27
2.7	Security Considerations	28

3 CLOUD MODEL   **29**

3.1	Roles in Cloud Computing	30
3.2	Cloud Service Models	30
3.3	Cloud Essential Characteristics	31
	3.3.1	On-Demand Self-Service	31
	3.3.2	Broad Network Access	31
	3.3.3	Resource Pooling	32
	3.3.4	Rapid Elasticity	32
	3.3.5	Measured Service	33
3.4	Simplified Cloud Architecture	33
	3.4.1	Application Software	34
	3.4.2	Virtual Machine Servers	35
	3.4.3	Virtual Machine Server Controllers	35
	3.4.4	Cloud Operations Support Systems	36
	3.4.5	Cloud Technology Components Offered "as-a-Service"	36
3.5	Elasticity Measurements	36
	3.5.1	Density	37
	3.5.2	Provisioning Interval	37
	3.5.3	Release Interval	39
	3.5.4	Scaling In and Out	40
	3.5.5	Scaling Up and Down	41
	3.5.6	Agility	42
	3.5.7	Slew Rate and Linearity	43
	3.5.8	Elasticity Speedup	44
3.6	Regions and Zones	44
3.7	Cloud Awareness	45

4 VIRTUALIZED INFRASTRUCTURE IMPAIRMENTS   **49**

4.1	Service Latency, Virtualization, and the Cloud	50
	4.1.1	Virtualization and Cloud Causes of Latency Variation	51
	4.1.2	Virtualization Overhead	52
	4.1.3	Increased Variability of Infrastructure Performance	53
4.2	VM Failure	54
4.3	Nondelivery of Configured VM Capacity	54

4.4	Delivery of Degraded VM Capacity	57
4.5	Tail Latency	59
4.6	Clock Event Jitter	60
4.7	Clock Drift	61
4.8	Failed or Slow Allocation and Startup of VM Instance	62
4.9	Outlook for Virtualized Infrastructure Impairments	63

II ANALYSIS   65

5 APPLICATION REDUNDANCY AND CLOUD COMPUTING   67

5.1	Failures, Availability, and Simplex Architectures	68
5.2	Improving Software Repair Times via Virtualization	70
5.3	Improving Infrastructure Repair Times via Virtualization	72
	5.3.1 Understanding Hardware Repair	72
	5.3.2 VM Repair-as-a-Service	72
	5.3.3 Discussion	74
5.4	Redundancy and Recoverability	75
	5.4.1 Improving Recovery Times via Virtualization	79
5.5	Sequential Redundancy and Concurrent Redundancy	80
	5.5.1 Hybrid Concurrent Strategy	83
5.6	Application Service Impact of Virtualization Impairments	84
	5.6.1 Service Impact for Simplex Architectures	85
	5.6.2 Service Impact for Sequential Redundancy Architectures	85
	5.6.3 Service Impact for Concurrent Redundancy Architectures	87
	5.6.4 Service Impact for Hybrid Concurrent Architectures	88
5.7	Data Redundancy	90
	5.7.1 Data Storage Strategies	90
	5.7.2 Data Consistency Strategies	91
	5.7.3 Data Architecture Considerations	92
5.8	Discussion	92
	5.8.1 Service Quality Impact	93
	5.8.2 Concurrency Control	93
	5.8.3 Resource Usage	94
	5.8.4 Simplicity	94
	5.8.5 Other Considerations	95

6 LOAD DISTRIBUTION AND BALANCING   97

6.1	Load Distribution Mechanisms	97
6.2	Load Distribution Strategies	99

6.3   Proxy Load Balancers   99
6.4   Nonproxy Load Distribution   101
6.5   Hierarchy of Load Distribution   102
6.6   Cloud-Based Load Balancing Challenges   103
6.7   The Role of Load Balancing in Support of Redundancy   103
6.8   Load Balancing and Availability Zones   104
6.9   Workload Service Measurements   104
6.10   Operational Considerations   105
       6.10.1   Load Balancing and Elasticity   105
       6.10.2   Load Balancing and Overload   106
       6.10.3   Load Balancing and Release Management   107
6.11   Load Balancing and Application Service Quality   107
       6.11.1   Service Availability   107
       6.11.2   Service Latency   108
       6.11.3   Service Reliability   108
       6.11.4   Service Accessibility   109
       6.11.5   Service Retainability   109
       6.11.6   Service Throughput   109
       6.11.7   Service Timestamp Accuracy   109

7 FAILURE CONTAINMENT   111
7.1   Failure Containment   111
       7.1.1   Failure Cascades   112
       7.1.2   Failure Containment and Recovery   112
       7.1.3   Failure Containment and Virtualization   114
7.2   Points of Failure   116
       7.2.1   Single Points of Failure   116
       7.2.2   Single Points of Failure and Virtualization   117
       7.2.3   Affinity and Anti-affinity Considerations   119
       7.2.4   No SPOF Assurance in Cloud Computing   120
       7.2.5   No SPOF and Application Data   121
7.3   Extreme Solution Coresidency   122
       7.3.1   Extreme Solution Coresidency Risks   123
7.4   Multitenancy and Solution Containers   124

8 CAPACITY MANAGEMENT   127
8.1   Workload Variations   128
8.2   Traditional Capacity Management   129
8.3   Traditional Overload Control   129
8.4   Capacity Management and Virtualization   131
8.5   Capacity Management in Cloud   133

8.6	Storage Elasticity Considerations	135
8.7	Elasticity and Overload	136
8.8	Operational Considerations	137
8.9	Workload Whipsaw	138
8.10	General Elasticity Risks	140
8.11	Elasticity Failure Scenarios	141
8.11.1	Elastic Growth Failure Scenarios	141
8.11.2	Elastic Capacity Degrowth Failure Scenarios	143

9 RELEASE MANAGEMENT — **145**

9.1	Terminology	145
9.2	Traditional Software Upgrade Strategies	146
9.2.1	Software Upgrade Requirements	146
9.2.2	Maintenance Windows	148
9.2.3	Client Considerations for Application Upgrade	149
9.2.4	Traditional Offline Software Upgrade	150
9.2.5	Traditional Online Software Upgrade	151
9.2.6	Discussion	153
9.3	Cloud-Enabled Software Upgrade Strategies	153
9.3.1	Type I Cloud-Enabled Upgrade Strategy: Block Party	154
9.3.2	Type II Cloud-Enabled Upgrade Strategy: One Driver per Bus	156
9.3.3	Discussion	157
9.4	Data Management	158
9.5	Role of Service Orchestration in Software Upgrade	159
9.5.1	Solution-Level Software Upgrade	160
9.6	Conclusion	161

10 END-TO-END CONSIDERATIONS — **163**

10.1	End-to-End Service Context	163
10.2	Three-Layer End-to-End Service Model	169
10.2.1	Estimating Service Impairments via the Three-Layer Model	171
10.2.2	End-to-End Service Availability	172
10.2.3	End-to-End Service Latency	173
10.2.4	End-to-End Service Reliability	174
10.2.5	End-to-End Service Accessibility	175
10.2.6	End-to-End Service Retainability	176
10.2.7	End-to-End Service Throughput	176
10.2.8	End-to-End Service Timestamp Accuracy	177
10.2.9	Reality Check	177

10.3 Distributed and Centralized Cloud Data Centers 177
    10.3.1 Centralized Cloud Data Centers 178
    10.3.2 Distributed Cloud Data Centers 178
    10.3.3 Service Availability Considerations 179
    10.3.4 Service Latency Considerations 181
    10.3.5 Service Reliability Considerations 182
    10.3.6 Service Accessibility Considerations 182
    10.3.7 Service Retainability Considerations 182
    10.3.8 Resource Distribution Considerations 182
10.4 Multitiered Solution Architectures 183
10.5 Disaster Recovery and Geographic Redundancy 184
    10.5.1 Disaster Recovery Objectives 184
    10.5.2 Georedundant Architectures 185
    10.5.3 Service Quality Considerations 186
    10.5.4 Recovery Point Considerations 187
    10.5.5 Mitigating Impact of Disasters with
          Georedundancy and Availability Zones 189

III RECOMMENDATIONS 191

11 ACCOUNTABILITIES FOR SERVICE QUALITY 193
11.1 Traditional Accountability 193
11.2 The Cloud Service Delivery Path 194
11.3 Cloud Accountability 197
11.4 Accountability Case Studies 200
    11.4.1 Accountability and Technology Components 201
    11.4.2 Accountability and Elasticity 203
11.5 Service Quality Gap Model 205
    11.5.1 Application's Resource Facing Service
          Gap Analysis 206
    11.5.2 Application's Customer Facing Service
          Gap Analysis 208
11.6 Service Level Agreements 210

12 SERVICE AVAILABILITY MEASUREMENT 213
12.1 Parsimonious Service Measurements 214
12.2 Traditional Service Availability Measurement 215
12.3 Evolving Service Availability Measurements 217
    12.3.1 Analyzing Application Evolution 218
    12.3.2 Technology Components 223
    12.3.3 Leveraging Storage-as-a-Service 224

12.4   Evolving Hardware Reliability Measurement   226
      12.4.1   Virtual Machine Failure Lifecycle   226
12.5   Evolving Elasticity Service Availability Measurements   228
12.6   Evolving Release Management Service Availability Measurement   229
12.7   Service Measurement Outlook   231

13 APPLICATION SERVICE QUALITY REQUIREMENTS   **233**
13.1   Service Availability Requirements   234
13.2   Service Latency Requirements   237
13.3   Service Reliability Requirements   237
13.4   Service Accessibility Requirements   238
13.5   Service Retainability Requirements   239
13.6   Service Throughput Requirements   239
13.7   Timestamp Accuracy Requirements   240
13.8   Elasticity Requirements   240
13.9   Release Management Requirements   241
13.10 Disaster Recovery Requirements   241

14 VIRTUALIZED INFRASTRUCTURE MEASUREMENT AND MANAGEMENT   **243**
14.1   Business Context for Infrastructure Service Quality Measurements   244
14.2   Cloud Consumer Measurement Options   245
14.3   Impairment Measurement Strategies   247
      14.3.1   Measurement of VM Failure   247
      14.3.2   Measurement of Nondelivery of Configured VM Capacity   249
      14.3.3   Measurement of Delivery of Degraded VM Capacity   249
      14.3.4   Measurement of Tail Latency   249
      14.3.5   Measurement of Clock Event Jitter   250
      14.3.6   Measurement of Clock Drift   250
      14.3.7   Measurement of Failed or Slow Allocation and Startup of VM Instance   250
      14.3.8   Measurements Summary   251
14.4   Managing Virtualized Infrastructure Impairments   252
      14.4.1   Minimize Application's Sensitivity to Infrastructure Impairments   252
      14.4.2   VM-Level Congestion Detection and Control   252
      14.4.3   Allocate More Virtual Resource Capacity   253

14.4.4	Terminate Poorly Performing VM Instances	253
14.4.5	Accept Degraded Performance	253
14.4.6	Proactive Supplier Management	254
14.4.7	Reset End Users' Service Quality Expectations	254
14.4.8	SLA Considerations	254
14.4.9	Changing Cloud Service Providers	254

15 ANALYSIS OF CLOUD-BASED APPLICATIONS   **255**

15.1	Reliability Block Diagrams and Side-by-Side Analysis	256
15.2	IaaS Impairment Effects Analysis	257
15.3	PaaS Failure Effects Analysis	259
15.4	Workload Distribution Analysis	260
	15.4.1 Service Quality Analysis	261
	15.4.2 Overload Control Analysis	261
15.5	Anti-Affinity Analysis	262
15.6	Elasticity Analysis	263
	15.6.1 Service Capacity Growth Scenarios	264
	15.6.2 Service Capacity Growth Action Analysis	264
	15.6.3 Service Capacity Degrowth Action Analysis	265
	15.6.4 Storage Capacity Growth Scenarios	265
	15.6.5 Online Storage Capacity Growth Action Analysis	266
	15.6.6 Online Storage Capacity Degrowth Action Analysis	266
15.7	Release Management Impact Effects Analysis	267
	15.7.1 Service Availability Impact	267
	15.7.2 Server Reliability Impact	267
	15.7.3 Service Accessibility Impact	267
	15.7.4 Service Retainability Impact	267
	15.7.5 Service Throughput Impact	267
15.8	Recovery Point Objective Analysis	268
15.9	Recovery Time Objective Analysis	270

16 TESTING CONSIDERATIONS   **273**

16.1	Context for Testing	273
16.2	Test Strategy	274
	16.2.1 Cloud Test Bed	275
	16.2.2 Application Capacity under Test	275
	16.2.3 Statistical Confidence	276
	16.2.4 Service Disruption Time	276
16.3	Simulating Infrastructure Impairments	277
16.4	Test Planning	278
	16.4.1 Service Reliability and Latency Testing	279
	16.4.2 Impaired Infrastructure Testing	280

16.4.3   Robustness Testing   280
16.4.4   Endurance/Stability Testing   282
16.4.5   Application Elasticity Testing   284
16.4.6   Upgrade Testing   285
16.4.7   Disaster Recovery Testing   285
16.4.8   Extreme Coresidency Testing   286
16.4.9   PaaS Technology Component Testing   286
16.4.10   Automated Regression Testing   286
16.4.11   Canary Release Testing   286

17   CONNECTING THE DOTS   287

17.1   The Application Service Quality Challenge   287
17.2   Redundancy and Robustness   289
17.3   Design for Scalability   292
17.4   Design for Extensibility   292
17.5   Design for Failure   293
17.6   Planning Considerations   294
17.7   Evolving Traditional Applications   296
       17.7.1   Phase 0: Traditional Application   298
       17.7.2   Phase I: High Service Quality on Virtualized
                 Infrastructure   298
       17.7.3   Phase II: Manual Application Elasticity   299
       17.7.4   Phase III: Automated Release Management   299
       17.7.5   Phase IV: Automated Application Elasticity 300
       17.7.6   Phase V: VM Migration   300
17.8   Concluding Remarks   301

Abbreviations   303

References   307

About the Authors   311

Index   313

FIGURES

Figure 1.1.   Sample Cloud-Based Application.   2
Figure 2.0.   Organization of Part I: Context.   8
Figure 2.1.   Simple Cloud-Based Application.   10
Figure 2.2.   Simple Virtual Machine Service Model.   10
Figure 2.3.   Application Service Boundaries.   11
Figure 2.4.   KQIs and KPIs.   12
Figure 2.5.   Application Consumer and Resource Facing Service Indicators.   14
Figure 2.6.   Application Robustness.   14
Figure 2.7.   Sample Application Robustness Scenario.   15
Figure 2.8.   Interactivity Timeline.   16
Figure 2.9.   Service Latency.   19
Figure 2.10.   Small Sample Service Latency Distribution.   22
Figure 2.11.   Sample Typical Latency Variation by Workload Density.   22
Figure 2.12.   Sample Tail Latency Variation by Workload Density.   23
Figure 2.13.   Understanding Complimentary Cumulative Distribution Plots.   23
Figure 2.14.   Service Latency Optimization Options.   24
Figure 3.1.   Cloud Roles for Simple Application.   30
Figure 3.2.   Elastic Growth Strategies.   32
Figure 3.3.   Simple Model of Cloud Infrastructure.   34
Figure 3.4.   Abstract Virtual Machine Server.   35
Figure 3.5.   Provisioning Interval (T_{Grow}).   38
Figure 3.6.   Release Interval T_{Shrink}.   39
Figure 3.7.   VM Scale In and Scale Out.   40
Figure 3.8.   Horizontal Elasticity.   40

Figure 3.9.   Scale Up and Scale Down of a VM Instance.   41
Figure 3.10.   Idealized (Linear) Capacity Agility.   42
Figure 3.11.   Slew Rate of Square Wave Amplification.   43
Figure 3.12.   Elastic Growth Slew Rate and Linearity.   43
Figure 3.13.   Regions and Availability Zones.   45
Figure 4.1.   Virtualized Infrastructure Impairments Experienced by
                Cloud-Based Applications.   50
Figure 4.2.   Transaction Latency for Riak Benchmark.   52
Figure 4.3.   VM Failure Impairment Example.   55
Figure 4.4.   Simplified Nondelivery of VM Capacity Model.   55
Figure 4.5.   Characterizing Virtual Machine Nondelivery.   56
Figure 4.6.   Nondelivery Impairment Example.   56
Figure 4.7.   Simple Virtual Machine Degraded Delivery Model.   57
Figure 4.8.   Degraded Resource Capacity Model.   58
Figure 4.9.   Degraded Delivery Impairment Example.   58
Figure 4.10.   CCDF for Riak Read Benchmark for Three Different Hosting
                Configurations.   59
Figure 4.11.   Tail Latency Impairment Example.   60
Figure 4.12.   Sample CCDF for Virtualized Clock Event Jitter.   61
Figure 4.13.   Clock Event Jitter Impairment Example.   61
Figure 4.14.   Clock Drift Impairment Example.   62
Figure 5.1.   Simplex Distributed System.   68
Figure 5.2.   Simplex Service Availability.   68
Figure 5.3.   Sensitivity of Service Availability to MTRS (Log Scale).   70
Figure 5.4.   Traditional versus Virtualized Software Repair Times.   71
Figure 5.5.   Traditional Hardware Repair versus Virtualized Infrastructure
                Restoration Times.   72
Figure 5.6.   Simplified VM Repair Logic.   73
Figure 5.7.   Sample Automated Virtual Machine Repair-as-a-Service Logic. 74
Figure 5.8.   Simple Redundancy Model.   75
Figure 5.9.   Simplified High Availability Strategy.   76
Figure 5.10.   Failure in a Traditional (Sequential) Redundant Architecture. 76
Figure 5.11.   Sequential Redundancy Model.   77
Figure 5.12.   Sequential Redundant Architecture Timeline with No Failures. 77
Figure 5.13.   Sample Redundant Architecture Timeline with Implicit Failure. 78
Figure 5.14.   Sample Redundant Architecture Timeline with Explicit Failure. 79
Figure 5.15.   Recovery Times for Traditional Redundancy Architectures.   80
Figure 5.16.   Concurrent Redundancy Processing Model.   81
Figure 5.17.   Client Controlled Redundant Compute Strategy.   82
Figure 5.18.   Client Controlled Redundant Operations.   83
Figure 5.19.   Concurrent Redundancy Timeline with Fast but
                Erroneous Return.   83
Figure 5.20.   Hybrid Concurrent with Slow Response.   84
Figure 5.21.   Application Service Impact for Very Brief Nondelivery Events. 86
Figure 5.22.   Application Service Impact for Brief Nondelivery Events.   86

Figure 5.23.   Nondelivery Impact to Redundant Compute Architectures.   88
Figure 5.24.   Nondelivery Impact to Hybrid Concurrent Architectures.   89
Figure 6.1.   Proxy Load Balancer.   98
Figure 6.2.   Proxy Load Balancing.   100
Figure 6.3.   Load Balancing between Regions and Availability Zones.   104
Figure 7.1.   Reliability Block Diagram of Simplex Sample System
               (with SPOF).   116
Figure 7.2.   Reliability Block Diagram of Redundant Sample System
               (without SPOF).   117
Figure 7.3.   No SPOF Distribution of Component Instances across
               Virtual Servers.   118
Figure 7.4.   Example of No Single Point of Failure with
               Distributed Component Instances.   118
Figure 7.5.   Example of Single Point of Failure with Poorly Distributed
               Component Instances.   119
Figure 7.6.   Simplified VM Server Control.   120
Figure 8.1.   Sample Daily Workload Variation (Logarithmic Scale).   128
Figure 8.2.   Traditional Maintenance Window.   129
Figure 8.3.   Traditional Congestion Control.   130
Figure 8.4.   Simplified Elastic Growth of Cloud-Based Applications.   134
Figure 8.5.   Simplified Elastic Degrowth of Cloud-Based Applications.   135
Figure 8.6.   Sample of Erratic Workload Variation (Linear Scale).   138
Figure 8.7.   Typical Elasticity Orchestration Process.   139
Figure 8.8.   Example of Workload Whipsaw.   139
Figure 8.9.   Elastic Growth Failure Scenarios.   141
Figure 9.1.   Traditional Offline Software Upgrade.   150
Figure 9.2.   Traditional Online Software Upgrade.   151
Figure 9.3.   Type I, "Block Party" Upgrade Strategy.   154
Figure 9.4.   Application Elastic Growth and Type I,
               "Block Party" Upgrade.   155
Figure 9.5.   Type II, "One Driver per Bus" Upgrade Strategy.   156
Figure 10.1.   Simple End-to-End Application Service Context.   164
Figure 10.2.   Service Boundaries in End-to-End Application Service Context.   165
Figure 10.3.   Measurement Points 0–4 for Simple End-to-End Context.   166
Figure 10.4.   End-to-End Measurement Points for Simple
               Replicated Solution Context.   167
Figure 10.5.   Service Probes across User Service Delivery Path.   168
Figure 10.6.   Three Layer Factorization of Sample End to End Solution.   170
Figure 10.7.   Estimating Service Impairments across the Three-Layer Model.   171
Figure 10.8.   Decomposing a Service Impairment.   172
Figure 10.9.   Centralized Cloud Data Center Scenario.   178
Figure 10.10. Distributed Cloud Data Center Scenario.   179
Figure 10.11. Sample Multitier Solution Architecture.   184
Figure 10.12. Disaster Recovery Time and Point Objectives.   185
Figure 10.13. Service Impairment Model of Georedundancy.   187

Figure 11.1.   Traditional Three-Way Accountability Split: Suppliers,
                Customers, External.   195
Figure 11.2.   Example Cloud Service Delivery Chain.   195
Figure 11.3.   Service Boundaries across Cloud Delivery Chain.   196
Figure 11.4.   Functional Responsibilities for Applications Deployed on IaaS. 198
Figure 11.5.   Sample Application.   201
Figure 11.6.   Service Outage Accountability of Sample Application.   201
Figure 11.7.   Application Elasticity Configuration.   203
Figure 11.8.   Service Gap Model.   205
Figure 11.9.   Service Quality Zone of Tolerance.   206
Figure 11.10.   Application's Resource Facing Service Boundary.   207
Figure 11.11.   Application's Customer Facing Service Boundary.   208
Figure 12.1.   Traditional Service Operation Timeline.   216
Figure 12.2.   Sample Application Deployment on Cloud.   217
Figure 12.3.   "Network Element" Boundary for Sample Application.   218
Figure 12.4.   Logical Measurement Point for Application's
                Service Availability.   218
Figure 12.5.   Reliability Block Diagram of Sample Application (Traditional
                Deployment).   219
Figure 12.6.   Evolving Sample Application to Cloud.   220
Figure 12.7.   Reliability Block Diagram of Sample Application on Cloud. 220
Figure 12.8.   Side-by-Side Reliability Block Diagrams.   221
Figure 12.9.   Accountability of Sample Cloud Based Application.   221
Figure 12.10.   Connectivity-as-a-Service as a Nanoscale VPN.   222
Figure 12.11.   Sample Application with Database-as-a-Service.   224
Figure 12.12.   Accountability of Sample Application with
                Database-as-a-Service.   224
Figure 12.13.   Sample Application with Outboard RAID Storage Array.   225
Figure 12.14.   Sample Application with Storage-as-a-Service.   225
Figure 12.15.   Accountability of Sample Application with
                Storage-as-a-Service.   226
Figure 12.16.   Virtual Machine Failure Lifecycle.   227
Figure 12.17.   Elastic Capacity Growth Timeline.   229
Figure 12.18.   Outage Normalization for Type I "Block Party"
                Release Management.   230
Figure 12.19.   Outage Normalization for Type II "One Driver per
                Bus" Release Management.   231
Figure 13.1.   Maximum Acceptable Service Disruption.   235
Figure 14.1.   Infrastructure impairments and application impairments.   244
Figure 14.2.   Loopback and Service Latency.   246
Figure 14.3.   Simplified Measurement Architecture.   251
Figure 15.1.   Sample Side-by-Side Reliability Block Diagrams.   256
Figure 15.2.   Worst-Case Recovery Point Scenario.   268
Figure 15.3.   Best-Case Recovery Point Scenario.   269
Figure 16.1.   Measuring Service Disruption Latency.   277

Figure 16.2.   Service Disruption Latency for Implicit Failure.   277
Figure 16.3.   Sample Endurance Test Case for Cloud-Based Application.   283
Figure 17.1.   Virtualized Infrastructure Impairments Experienced
                by Cloud-Based Applications.   288
Figure 17.2.   Application Robustness Challenge.   289
Figure 17.3.   Sequential (Traditional) Redundancy.   290
Figure 17.4.   Concurrent Redundancy.   290
Figure 17.5.   Hybrid Concurrent with Slow Response.   291
Figure 17.6.   Type I, "Block Party" Upgrade Strategy.   293
Figure 17.7.   Sample Phased Evolution of a Traditional Application.   296

TABLES AND EQUATIONS

TABLES

TABLE 2.1.   Mean Opinion Scores [P.800]   26
TABLE 13.1.   Service Availability and Downtime Ratings   236

EQUATIONS

Equation 2.1.   Availability Formula   18
Equation 5.1.   Simplex Availability   68
Equation 5.2.   Traditional Availability   69
Equation 10.1. Estimating General End-to-End Service Impairments   171
Equation 10.2. Estimating End-to-End Service Downtime   172
Equation 10.3. Estimating End-to-End Service Availability   173
Equation 10.4. Estimating End-to-End Typical Service Latency   173
Equation 10.5. Estimating End-to-End Service Defect Rate   175
Equation 10.6. Estimating End-to-End Service Accessibility   175
Equation 10.7. Estimating End to End Service Retainability (as DPM)   176
Equation 13.1. DPM via Operations Attempted and Operations Successful   238
Equation 13.2. DPM via Operations Attempted and Operations Failed   238
Equation 13.3. DPM via Operations Successful and Operations Failed   238
Equation 14.1. Computing VM FITs   248
Equation 14.2. Converting FITs to MTBF   249

1

INTRODUCTION

Customers expect that applications and services deployed on cloud computing infrastructure will deliver comparable service quality, reliability, availability, and latency as when deployed on traditional, native hardware configurations. Cloud computing infrastructure introduces a new family of service impairment risks based on the virtualized compute, memory, storage, and networking resources that an Infrastructure-as-a-Service (IaaS) provider delivers to hosted application instances. As a result, application developers and cloud consumers must mitigate these impairments to assure that application service delivered to end users is not unacceptably impacted. This book methodically analyzes the impacts of cloud infrastructure impairments on application service delivered to end users, as well as the opportunities for improvement afforded by cloud. The book also recommends architectures, policies, and other techniques to maximize the likelihood of delivering comparable or better service to end users when applications are deployed to cloud.

1.1   APPROACH

Cloud-based application software executes within a set of virtual machine instances, and each individual virtual machine instance relies on virtualized compute, memory,

Service Quality of Cloud-Based Applications, First Edition. Eric Bauer and Randee Adams.
© 2014 The Institute of Electrical and Electronics Engineers, Inc. Published 2014 by John Wiley & Sons, Inc.

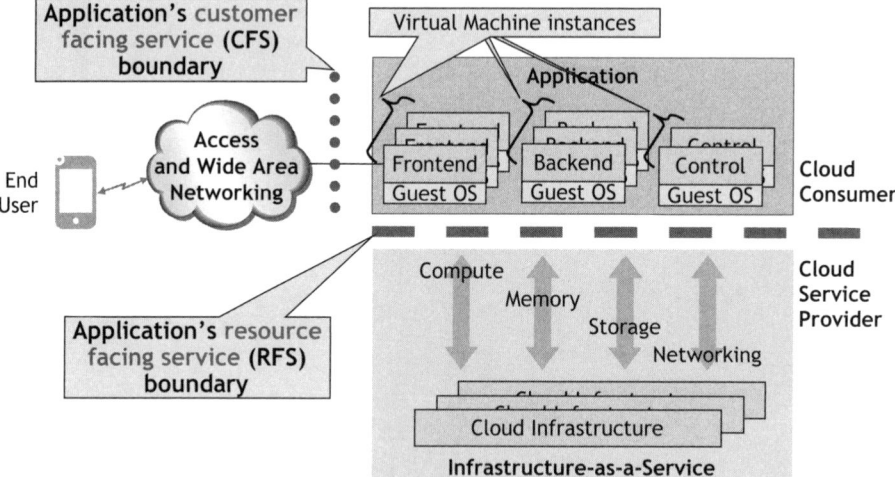

Figure 1.1. Sample Cloud-Based Application.

storage, and networking service delivered by the underlying cloud infrastructure. As shown in Figure 1.1, the application presents **customer facing service** toward end users across the dotted service boundary, and consumes virtualized resources offered by the Infrastructure-as-a-Service provider across the dashed **resource facing service** boundary. The application's service quality experienced by the end users is primarily a function of the application's architecture and software quality, as well as the service quality of the virtualized infrastructure offered by the IaaS across the resource facing service boundary, and the access and wide area networking that connects the end user to the application instance. This book considers both the new impairments and opportunities of virtualized resources offered to applications deployed on cloud and how user service quality experienced by end users can be maximized. By ignoring service impairments of the end user's device, and access and wide area network, one can narrowly consider how application service quality differs when a particular application is hosted on cloud infrastructure compared with when it is natively deployed on traditional hardware.

The key technical difference for application software between native deployment and cloud deployment is that native deployments offer the application's (guest) operating system direct access to the physical compute, memory, storage, and network resources, while cloud deployment inserts a layer of hypervisor or virtual machine management software between the guest operating system and the physical hardware. This layer of hypervisor or virtual machine management software enables sophisticated resource sharing, technical features, and operational policies. However, the hypervisor or virtual machine management layer does not deliver perfect hardware emulation to the guest operating system and application software, and these imperfections can adversely impact application service delivered to end users. While Figure 1.1 illustrates application deployment to a single data center, real world applications are often deployed to multiple data centers to improve user service quality by shortening transport latency to end users, to support business continuity and disaster recovery, and for other business reasons. Application service quality for deployment across multiple data centers is also considered in this book.

This book considers how application architectures, configurations, validation, and operational policies should evolve so that the acceptable application service quality can be delivered to end users even when application software is deployed on cloud infrastructure. This book approaches application service quality from the end users perspective while considering standards and recommendations from NIST, TM Forum, QuEST Forum, ODCA, ISO, ITIL, and so on.

1.2 TARGET AUDIENCE

This book provides application architects, developers, and testers with guidance on architecting and engineering applications that meet their customers' and end users' service reliability, availability, quality, and latency expectations. Product managers, program managers, and project managers will also gain deeper insights into the service quality risks and mitigations that must be addressed to assure that an application deployed onto cloud infrastructure consistently meets or exceeds customers' expectations for user service quality.

1.3 ORGANIZATION

The work is organized into three parts: context, analysis, and recommendations. **Part I: Context** frames the context of service quality of cloud-based applications via the following:

- *"Application Service Quality"* (Chapter 2). Defines the application service metrics that will be used throughout this work: service availability, service latency, service reliability, service accessibility, service retainability, service throughput, and timestamp accuracy.
- *"Cloud Model"* (Chapter 3). Explains how application deployment on cloud infrastructure differs from traditional application deployment from both a technical and an operational point of view, as well as what new opportunities are presented by rapid elasticity and massive resource pools.
- *"Virtualized Infrastructure Impairments"* (Chapter 4). Explains the infrastructure service impairments that applications running in virtual machines on cloud infrastructure must mitigate to assure acceptable quality of service to end users. The application service impacts of the impairments defined in this chapter will be rigorously considered in Part II: Analysis.

Part II: Analysis methodically considers how application service defined in Chapter 2, "Application Service Quality," is impacted by the infrastructure impairments enumerated in Chapter 4, "Virtualized Infrastructure Impairments," across the following topics:

- *"Application Redundancy and Cloud Computing"* (Chapter 5). Reviews fundamental redundancy architectures (simplex, sequential redundancy, concurrent redundancy, and hybrid concurrent redundancy) and considers their ability to mitigate application service quality impact when confronted with virtualized infrastructure impairments.
- *"Load Distribution and Balancing"* (Chapter 6). Methodically analyzes work load distribution and balancing for applications.
- *"Failure Containment"* (Chapter 7). Considers how virtualization and cloud help shape failure containment strategies for applications.
- *"Capacity Management"* (Chapter 8). Methodically analyzes application service risks related to rapid elasticity and online capacity growth and degrowth.
- *"Release Management"* (Chapter 9). Considers how virtualization and cloud can be leveraged to support release management actions.
- *"End-to-End Considerations"* (Chapter 10). Explains how application service quality impairments accumulate across the end-to-end service delivery path. The chapter also considers service quality implications of deploying applications to smaller cloud data centers that are closer to end users versus deploying to larger, regional cloud data centers that are farther from end users. Disaster recovery and georedundancy are also discussed.

Part III: Recommendations covers the following:

- *"Accountabilities for Service Quality"* (Chapter 11). Explains how cloud deployment profoundly changes traditional accountabilities for service quality and offers guidance for framing accountabilities across the cloud service delivery chain. The chapter also uses the service gap model to review how to connect specification, architecture, implementation, validation, deployment, and monitoring of applications to assure that expectations are met. Service level agreements are also considered.
- *"Service Availability Measurement"* (Chapter 12). Explains how traditional application service availability measurements can be applied to cloud-based application deployments, thereby enabling efficient side-by-side comparisons of service availability performance.
- *"Application Service Quality Requirements"* (Chapter 13). Reviews high level service quality requirements for applications deployed to cloud.
- *"Virtualized Infrastructure Measurement and Management"* (Chapter 14). Reviews strategies for quantitatively measuring virtualized infrastructure impairments on production systems, along with strategies to mitigate the application service quality risks of unacceptable infrastructure performance.

- *"Analysis of Cloud-Based Applications"* (Chapter 15). Presents a suite of analysis techniques to rigorously assess the service quality risks and mitigations of a target application architecture.
- *"Testing Considerations"* (Chapter 16). Considers testing of cloud-based applications to assure that service quality expectations are likely to be met consistently despite inevitable virtualized infrastructure impairments.
- *"Connecting the Dots"* (Chapter 17). Discusses how to apply the recommendations of Part III to both existing and new applications to mitigate the service quality risks introduced in Part I: Basics and analyzed in Part II: Analysis.

As many readers are likely to study sections based on the technical needs of their business and their professional interest rather than strictly following this work's running order, cross-references are included throughout the work so readers can, say, dive into detailed Part II analysis sections, and follow cross-references back into Part I for basic definitions and follow references forward to Part III for recommendations. A detailed index is included to help readers quickly locate material.

ACKNOWLEDGMENTS

The authors acknowledge the consistent support of Dan Johnson, Annie Lequesne, Sam Samuel, and Lawrence Cowsar that enabled us to complete this work. Expert technical feedback was provided by Mark Clougherty, Roger Maitland, Rich Sohn, John Haller, Dan Eustace, Geeta Chauhan, Karsten Oberle, Kristof Boeynaems, Tony Imperato, and Chuck Salisbury. Data and practical insights were shared by Karen Woest, Srujal Shah, Pete Fales, and many others. Bob Brownlie offered keen insights into service measurements and accountabilities. Expert review and insight on release management for virtualized applications was provided by Bruce Collier. The work benefited greatly from insightful review feedback from Mark Cameron. Iraj Saniee, Katherine Guo, Indra Widjaja, Davide Cherubini, and Karsten Oberle offered keen and substantial insights. The authors gratefully acknowledge the external reviewers who took time to provide through review and thoughtful feedback that materially improved this book: Tim Coote, Steve Woodward, Herbert Ristock, Kim Tracy, and Xuemei Zhang.

The authors welcome feedback on this book; readers may e-mail us at Eric .Bauer@alcatel-lucent.com and Randee.Adams@alcatel-lucent.com.

I

CONTEXT

Figure 2.0 frames the context of this book: cloud-based applications rely on virtualized compute, memory, storage, and networking resources to provide information services to end users via access and wide area networks. The application's primary quality focus is on the user service delivered across the application's customer facing service boundary (dotted line in Figure 2.0).

- *Chapter 2, "Application Service Quality,"* focuses on application service delivered across that boundary. The application itself relies on virtualized computer, memory, storage, and networking delivered by the cloud service provider to execute application software.
- *Chapter 3, "Cloud Model,"* frames the context of the cloud service that supports this virtualized infrastructure.
- *Chapter 4, "Virtualized Infrastructure Impairments,"* focuses on the service impairments presented to application components across the application's resource facing service boundary.

Service Quality of Cloud-Based Applications, First Edition. Eric Bauer and Randee Adams.
© 2014 The Institute of Electrical and Electronics Engineers, Inc. Published 2014 by John Wiley & Sons, Inc.

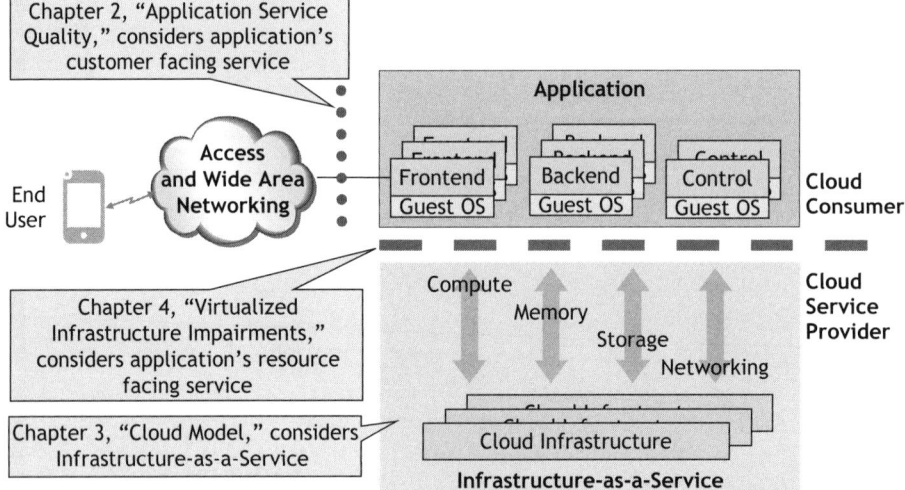

Figure 2.0. Organization of Part I: Context.

2

APPLICATION SERVICE QUALITY

This section considers the service offered by applications to end users and the metrics used to characterize the quality of that service. A handful of common service quality metrics that characterize application service quality are detailed. These user service key quality indicators (KQIs) are considered in depth in Part II: Analysis.

2.1 SIMPLE APPLICATION MODEL

Figure 2.1 illustrates a simple cloud-based application with a pool of frontend components distributing work across a pool of backend components. The suite of frontend and backend components is managed by a pair of control components that provide management visibility and control for the entire application instance. Each of the application's components, along with their supporting guest operating systems, execute in distinct virtual machine instances served by the cloud service provider. The Distributed Management Task Force (DMTF) defines *virtual machine* as:

> the complete environment that supports the execution of guest software. A virtual machine is a full encapsulation of the virtual hardware, virtual disks, and the metadata associated with it. Virtual machines allow multiplexing of

Service Quality of Cloud-Based Applications, First Edition. Eric Bauer and Randee Adams.
© 2014 The Institute of Electrical and Electronics Engineers, Inc. Published 2014 by John Wiley & Sons, Inc.

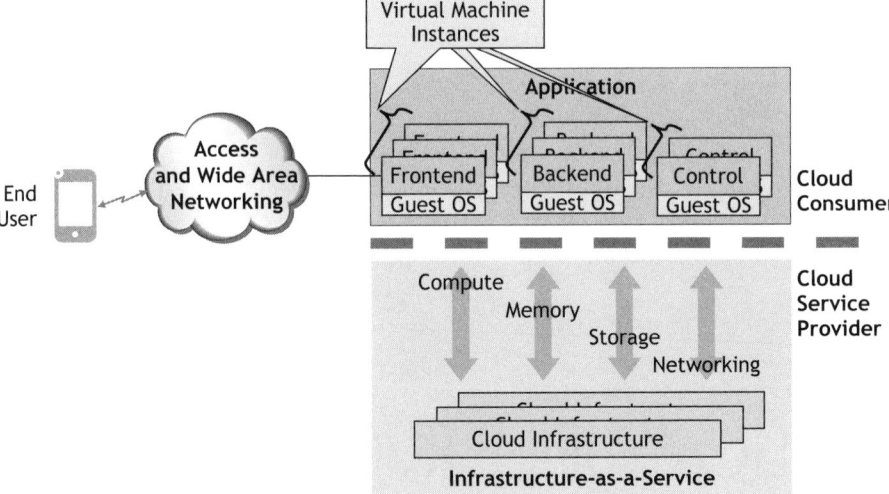

Figure 2.1. Simple Cloud-Based Application.

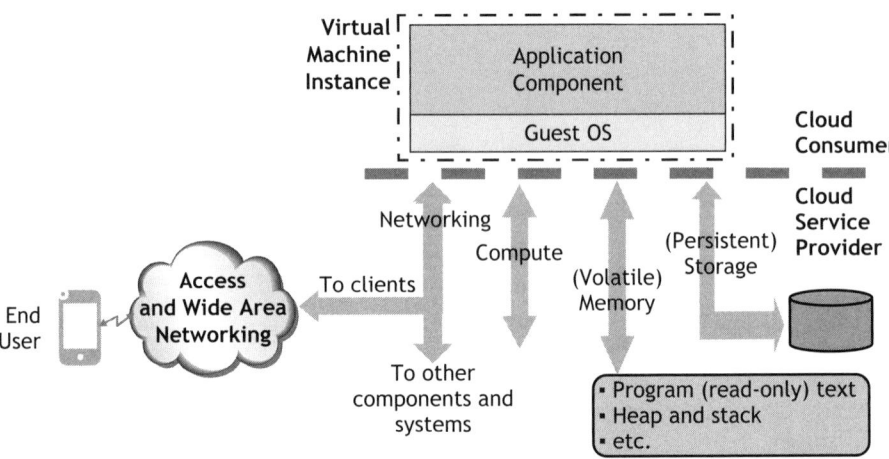

Figure 2.2. Simple Virtual Machine Service Model.

the underlying physical machine through a software layer called a hypervisor. [DSP0243]

For simplicity, this simple model ignores systems that directly support the application, such as security appliances that protect the application from external attack, domain name servers, and so on.

Figure 2.2 shows a single application component deployed in a virtual machine on cloud infrastructure. The application software and its underlying operating system—referred to as a *guest* OS—run within a virtual machine instance that emulates a dedicated physical server. The cloud service provider's infrastructure delivers the following resource services to the application's guest OS instance:

- *Networking.* Application software is networked to other application components, application clients, and other systems.
- *Compute.* Application programs ultimately execute on a physical processor.
- *(Volatile) Memory.* Applications execute programs out of memory, using heap memory, stack storage, shared memory, and main memory to maintain dynamic data, such as application state
- *(Persistent) Storage.* Applications maintain program executables, configuration, and application data on persistent storage in files and file systems.

2.2 SERVICE BOUNDARIES

It is useful to define boundaries that demark applications and service offerings to better understand the dependencies, interactions, roles, and responsibilities of each element in overall user service delivery. This work will focus on the two high-level application service boundaries shown in Figure 2.3:

- Application's **customer facing service** (CFS) boundary (dotted line in Figure 2.3), which demarks the edge of the application instance that faces users. User service reliability, such as call completion rate, and service latency, such as call setup, are well-known service quality measurements of telecommunications customer facing service.

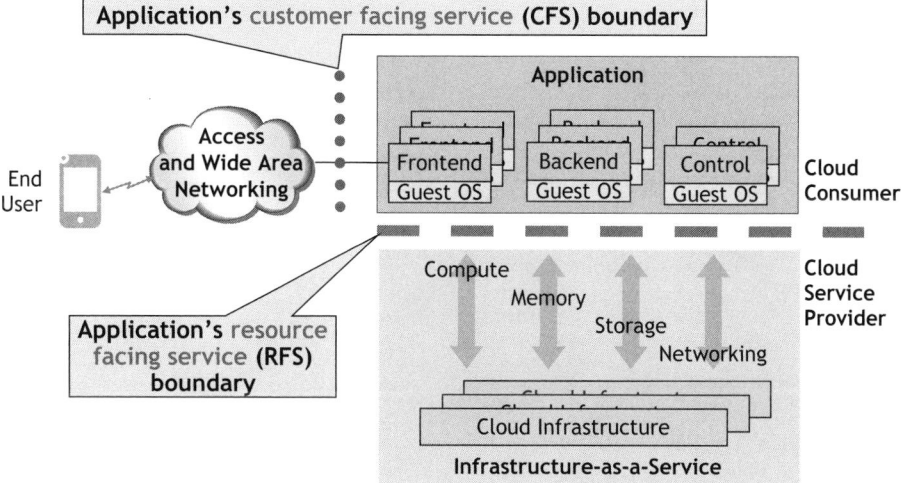

Figure 2.3. Application Service Boundaries.

- Application's **resource facing service** (RFS) boundary (dashed line in Figure 2.3), which demarks the boundary between the application's guest OS instances executing in virtual machine instances and the virtual compute, memory, storage, and networking provided by the cloud service provider. Latency to retrieve desired data from persistent storage (e.g., hard disk drive) is a well-known service quality measurement of resource facing service.

Note that customer facing service and resource facing service boundaries are relative to a particular entity in the service delivery chain. Figure 2.3, and this book, consider these concepts from the perspective of a cloud-based application, but these same service boundary notions can be applied to an element of the cloud Infrastructure-as-a-Service or technology component offered as "as-a-Service" like Database-as-a-Service.

2.3 KEY QUALITY AND PERFORMANCE INDICATORS

Qualities such as latency and reliability of service delivered across a service boundary can be quantitatively measured. Technically useful service measurements are generally referred to as key performance indicators (KPIs). As shown in Figure 2.4, a subset of KPIs across the customer facing service boundary characterize key aspects of the customer's experience and perception of quality, and these are often referred to as key *quality* indicators (KQIs) [TMF_TR197]. Enterprises routinely track and manage these KQIs to assure that customers are delighted. Well-run enterprises will often tie staff bonus payments to achieving quantitative KQI targets to better align the financial interests of enterprise staff to the business need of delivering excellent service to customers.

In the context of applications, KQIs often cover high-level business considerations, including service qualities that impact user satisfaction and churn, such as:

- *Service Availability* (Section 2.5.1). The service is online and available to users;
- *Service Latency* (Section 2.5.2). The service promptly responds to user requests;

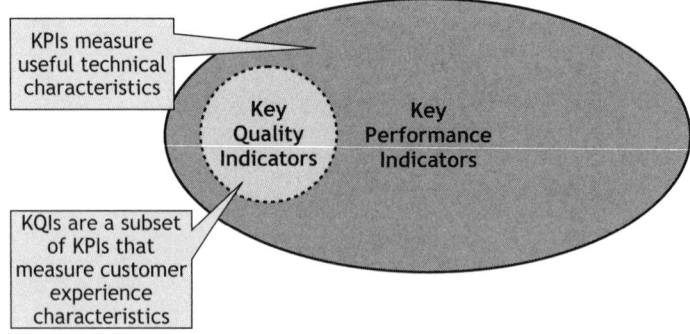

Figure 2.4. KQIs and KPIs.

- *Service Reliability* (Section 2.5.3). The service correctly responds to user requests;
- *Service Accessibility* (Section 2.5.4). The probability that an individual user can promptly access the service or resource that they desire;
- *Service Retainability* (Section 2.5.5). The probability that a service session, such as a streaming movie, game, or call, will continuously be rendered with good service quality until normal (e.g., user requested) termination of that session;
- *Service Throughput* (Section 2.5.6). Meeting service throughput commitments to customers;
- *Service Timestamp Accuracy* (Section 2.5.7). Meeting billing or regulatory compliance accuracy requirements.

Different applications with different business models will define KPIs somewhat differently and will select different KQIs from their suite of application KPIs.

A primary resource facing service risk experienced by cloud-based applications is the quality of virtualized compute, memory, storage, and networking delivered by the cloud service provider to application components executing in virtual machine (VM) instances. Chapter 4, "Virtualized Infrastructure Impairments," considers the following:

- *Virtual Machine Failure* (Section 4.2). Like traditional hardware, VM instances can fail
- *Nondelivery of Configured VM Capacity* (Section 4.3). For instance, VM instance can briefly cease to operate (aka "stall")
- *Degraded Delivery of Configured VM Capacity* (Section 4.4). For instance, a particular virtual machine server may be congested, so some application IP packets are discarded by the host OS or hypervisor.
- *Excess Tail Latency on Resource Delivery* (Section 4.5). For instance, some application components may occasionally experience unusually long resource access latency.
- *Clock Event Jitter* (Section 4.6). For instance, regular clock event interrupts (e.g., every 1 ms) may be tardy or coalesced.
- *Clock Drift* (Section 4.7). Guest OS instances' real-time clocks may drift away from true (UTC) time.
- *Failed or Slow Allocation and Startup of VM Instances* (Section 4.8). For instance, newly allocated cloud resources may be nonfunctional (aka dead on arrival [DOA])

Figure 2.5 overlays common customer facing service KQIs with typical resource facing service KPIs on the simple application of Section 2.1.

As shown in Figure 2.6, the robustness of an application's architecture characterizes how effectively the application can maintain quality across the application's customer facing service boundary despite impairments experienced across the resource facing service boundary and failures within the application itself.

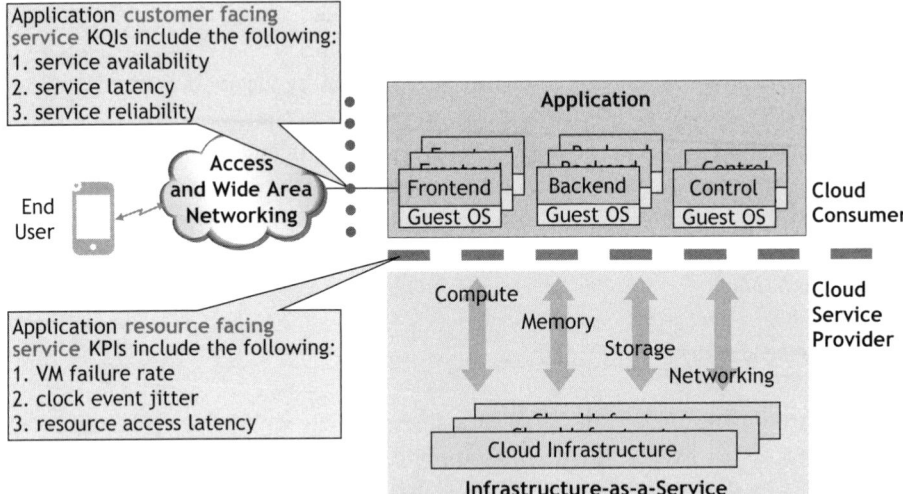

Figure 2.5. Application Consumer and Resource Facing Service Indicators.

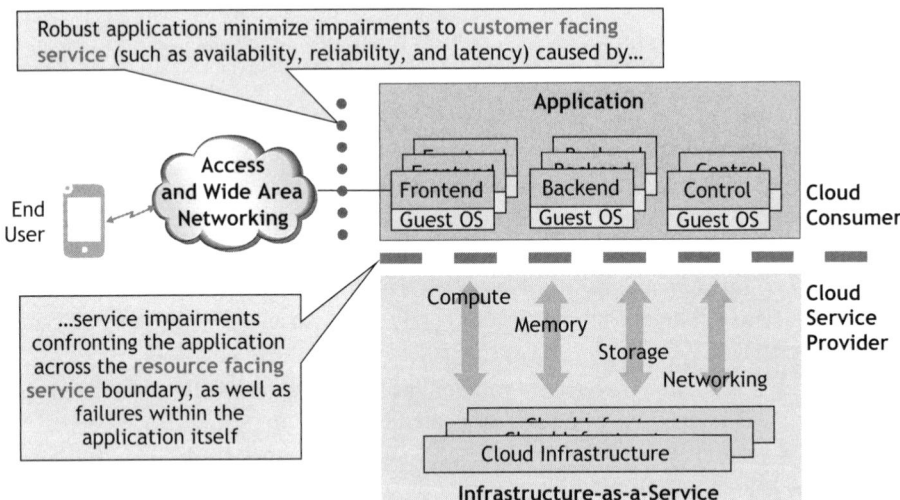

Figure 2.6. Application Robustness.

Figure 2.7 illustrates a concrete robustness example: if the cloud infrastructure stalls a VM that is hosting one of the application backend instances for hundreds of milliseconds (see Section 4.3, "Nondelivery of Configured VM Capacity"), then is the application's customer facing service impacted? Do some or all user operations take hundreds of milliseconds longer to complete, or do some (or all) operations fail due to timeout expiration? A robust application will mask the customer facing service impact of this service impairment so end users do not experience unacceptable service quality.

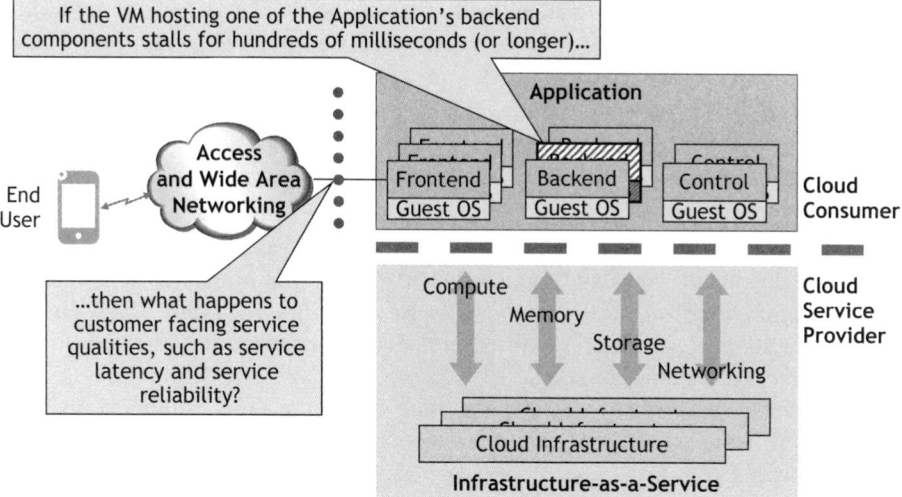

Figure 2.7. Sample Application Robustness Scenario.

2.4 KEY APPLICATION CHARACTERISTICS

Customer facing service quality expectations are fundamentally driven by application characteristics, such as:

- Service criticality (Section 2.4.1)
- Application interactivity (Section 2.4.2)
- Tolerance to network traffic impairments (Section 2.4.3).

These characteristics influence both the quantitative targets for application's service quality (e.g., critical applications have higher service availability expectations) and specifics of those service quality measurements (e.g., maximum tolerable service downtime influences the minimum chargeable outage downtime threshold).

2.4.1 Service Criticality

Readers will recognize that different information services entail different levels of criticality to users and the enterprise. While these ratings will vary somewhat based on organizational needs and customer expectations, the criticality classification definitions from the U.S. Federal Aviation Administration's National Airspace System's reliability handbook are fairly typical:

- *ROUTINE* (Service Availability Rating of 99%). "*Loss of this capability would have a minor impact on the risk associated with providing safe and efficient operations*" [FAA-HDBK-006A].

- *ESSENTIAL* (Service Availability Rating of 99.9%). *"Loss of this capability would significantly raise the risk associated with providing safe and efficient operations"* [FAA-HDBK-006A].
- *CRITICAL* (Service Availability Rating of 99.999%). *"Loss of this capability would raise to an unacceptable level, the risk associated with providing safe and efficient operations"* [FAA-HDBK-006A].

There is also a "Safety Critical" category, with service availability rating of seven 9s for life-threatening risks and services where *"loss would present an unacceptable safety hazard during the transition to reduced capacity operations"* [FAA-HDBK-006A]. Few commercial enterprises offer services or applications that are safety critical, so seven 9's expectations are rare.

The higher the service criticality the more the enterprise is willing to invest in architectures, policies, and procedures to assure that acceptable service quality is continuously available to users.

2.4.2 Application Interactivity

As shown in Figure 2.8, there are three broad classifications of application service interactivity:

- *Batch or Noninteractive Type* for nominally "offline" applications, such as payroll processing, offline billing, and offline analytics, which often run for minutes or hours. Aggregate throughput (e.g., time to complete an entire batch job) is usually more important to users of an offline application than the time to complete a single transaction. While a batch job may consist of hundreds, thousands, or more individual transactions that may each succeed or fail individually, each failed transaction will likely require manual action to correct resulting in an increase in the customer's OPEX to perform the repairs. While interactivity expectations for batch operations may be low, service reliability expectations (e.g., low transaction fallout rate to minimize the cost of rework) are often high.

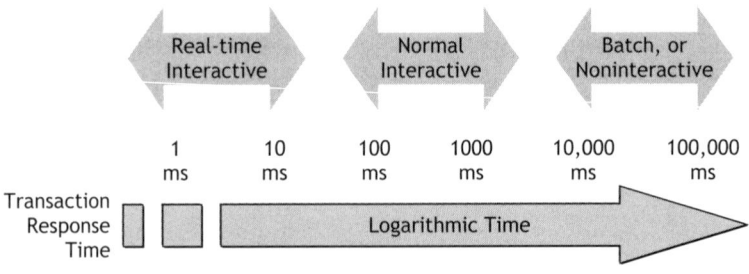

Figure 2.8. Interactivity Timeline.

- *Normal Interactive Type* for nominally online applications with ordinary inter-activity expectations, such as routine web traffic (e.g., eCommerce), and com-munications signaling. There is a broad range of interactivity expectations based on application types, service providers, and other factors. For example, most users will wait no more than a few seconds for ring back after placing a telephone call or for the video on their IP TV to change after selecting a different channel, but may wait longer for web-based applications, such as completing an eCom-merce transaction. Interactive transaction response times are nominally measured in hundreds or thousands of milliseconds.
- *Real-Time Interactive Type* for applications that are extremely interactive with strict response time or service latency expectations. Interactive media content (e.g., audio or video conferencing), gaming (e.g., first-party shooter games), and data or bearer plane applications (e.g., firewalls and gateways) all have strict real-time service expectations. Transaction response times for real-time applica-tions are often measured in milliseconds or tens of milliseconds.

2.4.3   Tolerance to Network Traffic Impairments

Data networks are subject to three fundamental types of service impairments:

- *Packet Loss.* Individual data packets can be discarded by intermediate systems due to network congestion, corrupted in transit, or otherwise lost between the sender and receiver.
- *Packet Delay.* Electrical and optical signals propagate at a finite velocity, and their flow through intermediate systems, such as routers and switches, takes finite time. Thus, there is always some latency between the instant one party transmits a packet and the moment that the other party receives the packet.
- *Packet Jitter.* Variation in packet latency from packet to packet in a single data stream is called jitter. Jitter is particularly problematic for isochronous data streams, such as conversational audio or video, where the receiving device must continuously render streaming media to an end user. If a packet has not arrived in time to be smoothly rendered to the end user, then the end user's device must engage some lost packet compensation mechanism, which is likely to somewhat compromise the fidelity of the service rendered and thus degrade the end user's quality of experience.

[RFC4594] characterizes tolerance to packet loss, delay, and jitter for common classes of applications.

2.5   APPLICATION SERVICE QUALITY METRICS

While different applications offer different functionality to end users, the primary service KQIs across the application's customer facing service boundary for end users of applications generally include one or more of the following:

- Service availability (Section 2.5.1)
- Service latency (Section 2.5.2)
- Service reliability (Section 2.5.3)
- Service accessibility (Section 2.5.4)
- Service retainability (Section 2.5.5)
- Service throughput (Section 2.5.6)
- Service timestamp accuracy (Section 2.5.7)
- Application specific service quality measurements (Section 2.5.8).

Note that consistency of service quality is also important to users; measured service quality performance should be consistent and repeatable from hour to hour and day to day. Service consistency of branded information and communication services are likely to be as important to end users as consistency of any other branded product.

2.5.1 Service Availability

Availability is defined as the *"ability of an IT service or other configuration item to perform its agreed function when required"* [ITIL-Availability]. Availability is mathematically expressed in Equation 2.1, the availability formula:

$$\text{Availability} = \frac{\text{Agreed Service Time} - \text{Outage Downtime}}{\text{Agreed Service Time}}. \tag{2.1}$$

Agreed Service Time is the period during the measurement window that the system should be up. For so-called 24 × 7 × Forever systems (sometimes awkwardly called "24 × 7 × 365"), Agreed Service Time is every minute of every day; for systems that are permitted planned downtime, the planned and scheduled downtime can be excluded from Agreed Service Time. *OutageDowntime* is defined as: *"the sum, over a given period, of the weighted minutes, a given population of a systems, network elements or service entities was unavailable divided by the average in-service population of systems, networks element or service entities"* [TL_9000]. Note that modern applications often provide several different functions to different users simultaneously, so partial capacity and partial functionality outages are often more common than total outages; partial capacity or functionality outages are often prorated by portion of capacity or primary functionality impacted.

Service availability measurements and targets generally reflect the service criticality of the affected applications (see Section 2.4.1, "Service Criticality"). For example, consider the availability-related definitions used by popular IaaS supplier targeting enterprise applications of nominally "essential" and "routine" criticality in which the minimum chargeable downtime is at least 5 minutes: *"Unavailable" means that all of your running instances have **no external connectivity during a five minute period and*** *you are unable to launch replacement instances.** Critical services will generally have much stricter service measurements and performance targets. For example, the telecom industry's quality standard TL 9000 uses the following outage definition: *"all outages shall be counted that result in a complete loss of primary functionality . . . for all or part of the system for a duration greater than 15 seconds during the operational window, whether the outage was unscheduled or scheduled"* [TL_9000]. Obviously, minimum chargeable outage duration of 15 seconds is far more stringent than minimum chargeable outage duration of 5 minutes. In addition to stricter service performance targets, critical services will often include more precise measurements, such as prorating of partial capacity or functionality impairments, rather than all-or-nothing measurements (e.g., *"no connectivity during a five minute period"*). Outage events tend to be rare acute events, with weeks, months, or years of outage-free operation punctuated by an event lasting tens of minutes or even hours. Thus, availability or outage downtime is often tracked on a 6-month rolling average to set outage events into an appropriate context.

Requirements for this measurement are discussed in Section 13.1, "Service Availability Requirements."

2.5.2   Service Latency

As shown in Figure 2.9, service latency is the elapsed time between a request and the corresponding response. Most network-based services execute some sort of transactions on behalf of client users: web applications return web pages in response to HTTP GET requests (and update pages in response to HTTP PUT requests); telecommunications networks establish calls in response to user requests; gaming servers respond to user inputs; media servers stream content based on user requests; and so on.

In addition to detailed service latency measurements, such as time to load a web page, some applications have service latency measurement expectations for higher level

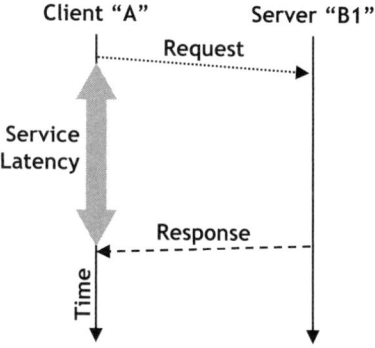

Figure 2.9. Service Latency.

* "Amazon EC2 Service Level Agreement," effective date: October 23, 2008, http://aws.amazon.com/ec2-sla/ accessed on December 14, 2012.

operations that include many discrete transactions, such as how many seconds or minutes it takes to activate a new smartphone, or how long it takes to provision application service for a new user. Well-engineered solutions will cascade the high-level latency application expectations down to lower-level expectations to enable methodical management of overall service latency.

Requirements for this measurement are discussed in Section 13.2, "Service Latency Requirements."

2.5.2.1 Traditional Causes of Latency Variations. The latency between the time a client sends a request and the time the client receives the response will inevitably vary for reasons including:

- *Request Queuing.* Rather than immediately rejecting requests that arrive the instant when a resource is busy, queuing those requests increases the probability that those requests will be served successfully, albeit with slightly greater service latency. Assuming that the system is engineered properly, request queuing enables the offered load to be served promptly (although not instantaneously) without having to deploy sufficient system hardware to serve the busiest traffic instant (e.g., the busiest millisecond or microsecond). In essence, request queuing enables one to trade a bit of system hardware capacity for occasionally increased service latency.
- *Caching.* Responses served from cached memory are typically much faster than requests that require one or more disk reads or network transactions.
- *Disk Geometry.* Unlike random access memory (RAM), in which it takes the same amount of time to access any memory location, disk storage inherently has nonuniform data access times because of the need to move the disk head to a physical disk location to access stored data. Disk heads move in two independent directions:
  - Rotationally as the disk storage platters spin
  - Track-to-track, as the disk heads seek between concentric data storage rings or tracks.
  The physical layout of file systems and databases are often optimized to minimize latency for rotational and track-to-track access to sequential data, but inevitably some data operations will require more time than others due to physical layout of data on the disk.
- *Disk Fragmentation.* Disk fragmentation causes data to be stored in noncontiguous disk blocks. As reading noncontiguous disk blocks requires time-consuming disk seeks between disk reads or writes, additional latency is introduced when operating on fragmented portions of files.
- *Variations in Request Arrival Rates.* There is inevitably some randomness in the arrival rates of service requests, and this moment to moment variation is superimposed over daily, weekly, and seasonal usage patterns. When offered load is higher, request queues will be deeper, and hence queuing delays will be greater.

* *Garbage Collection.* Some software technologies require periodic garbage collection to salvage resources that are no longer required. When garbage collection mechanisms are active, resources may be unavailable to serve application user requests.
* *Network Congestion or Latency.* Bursts or spikes in network activity can cause the latency for IP packets traversing a network to increase.
* *Unanticipated Usage and Traffic Patterns.* Database and software architectures are configured and optimized for certain usage scenarios and traffic mixes. As usage and traffic patterns vary significantly from nominal expectations, the configured settings may no longer be optimal, and thus performance may degrade.
* *Packet Loss and Corruption.* Occasionally IP packets are lost or damaged when traveling between the client device and application instance, or between components within the solution. It takes time to detect lost packets and then to retransmit them, thus introducing latency.
* *Resource Placement.* Resources that are held locally offer better performance than resources held in a nearby data center, and resources held in a nearby data center generally are accessible with lower latency than resources held in data centers on distant continents.
* *Network Bandwidth.* As all web users know, web pages load slower over lower bandwidth network connections; DSL is better than dialup, and fiber to the home is better than DSL. Likewise, insufficient network bandwidth between resources in the cloud—as well as insufficient access bandwidth to users—causes service latency to increase.

Application architectures can impact an application's vulnerability to these latency impairments. For example, applications that factor functionality so that more networked transactions or disk operations are required are often more vulnerable to latency impairments than applications with fewer of those operations.

2.5.2.2 Characterizing Service Latency. Figure 2.10 shows the service latency distribution of 30,000 transactions of one sample application. While the median (50th percentile) service latency is 130 ms, there is a broad range of responses; the slowest response in this data set (1430 ms) is more than 10 times slower than the 50th percentile. As one can see from this cumulative distribution, the latency "tail" includes a few outliers (sometimes called "elephants") that are significantly slower than the bulk of the population. As these tail values can be far slower than typical (e.g., 50th or 90th percentile) latency, it is useful to methodically characterize the latency statistics of the tail across millions of transactions, rather than the thousands of samples in the data set of Figure 2.10.

Individually recording the service latency of each transaction and then directly analyzing hundreds of thousands, millions or more data points is often infeasible, and thus it is common for service latency measurements to be recorded in measurement buckets or bins (e.g., less than 30 ms, 30–49 , and 50–69 ms). Figure 2.11 shows service latency based on binned measurements for a real-time Session Initiation Protocol (SIP)

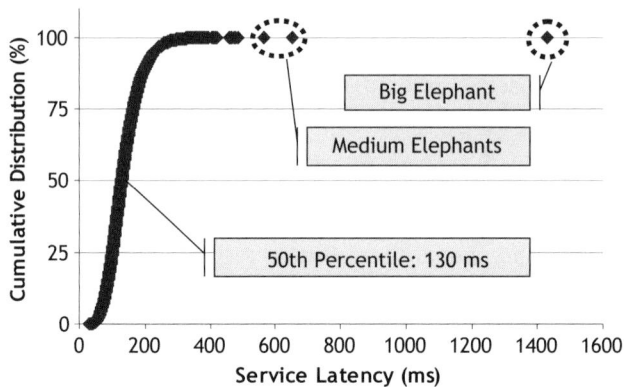

Figure 2.10. Small Sample Service Latency Distribution.

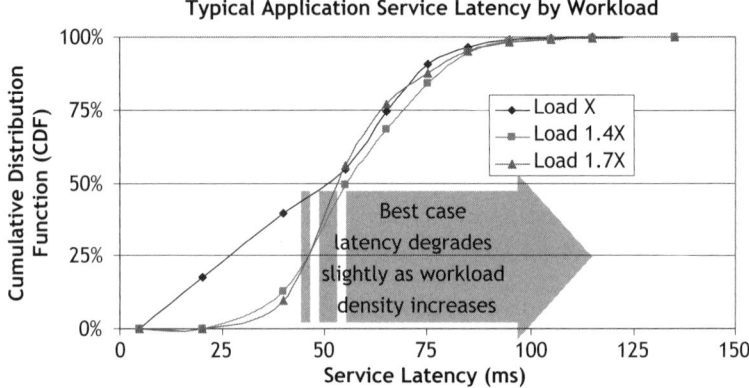

Figure 2.11. Sample Typical Latency Variation by Workload Density.

application running on virtualized infrastructure. Figure 2.11 gives service latency at three different workload densities—"X," 1.4 times "X," and 1.7 times "X"—and one can see that typical (e.g., 50th percentile and 90th percentile) latencies are consistent, while the best case latency (e.g., fastest 25%) degrades slightly as workload density increases.

As the linear cumulative distribution function (CDF) of Figure 2.11 obscures the latency tail along the "100%" line, a logarithmic complementary cumulative distribution function (CCDF) is the best way to visualize the latency tail. Note that while the CDF uses a linear scale for distribution on the *y*-axis, the CCDF uses a logarithmic scale on the *y*-axis to better visualize the extreme end of the tail. Figure 2.12 gives a CCDF of the same application's latency data set of Figure 2.11, and the tail behaviors for nominally the slowest 1 in 50,000 operations are radically different, with the slowest 1 in 100,000 operations of the 1.7 times "X" density being several times greater than at density 1.4 times "X." Thus, if the quality of service criteria considered only typical

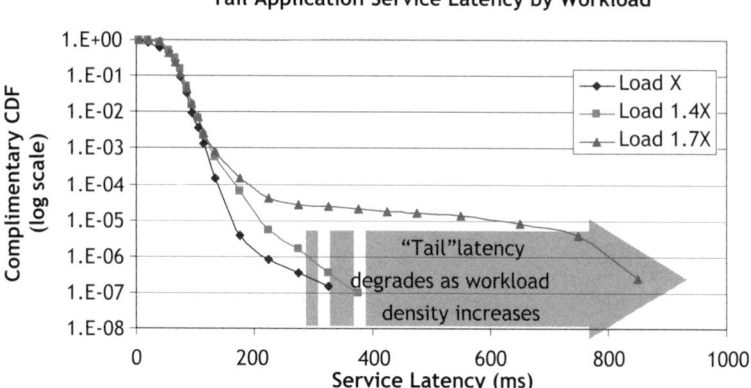

Figure 2.12. Sample Tail Latency Variation by Workload Density.

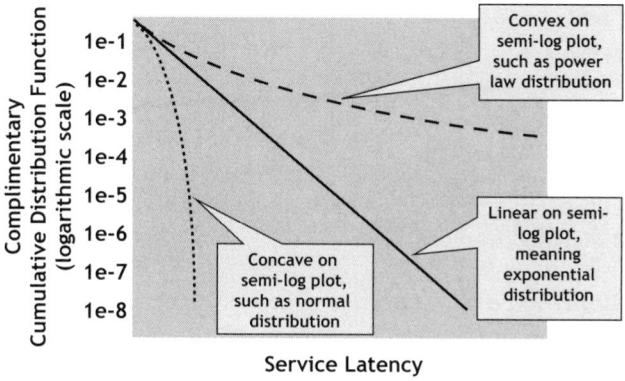

Figure 2.13. Understanding Complimentary Cumulative Distribution Plots.

(e.g., 50th percentile and 90th percentile) service latency, then the density of 1.7 times X workload—or perhaps even higher—might be acceptable. However, if the QoS criteria considered tail (e.g., 99.999th percentile or 10^{-5} on the CCDF) service latency, then the 1.4 times X workload might determine the maximum acceptable density.

While actual measured latency data often produces rather messy CCDFs, the results can be analyzed by considering the statistical distribution of the data. Figure 2.13 overlays three classes of statistical distributions onto a CCDF:

- *Concave (e.g., normal) distributions* fall off very quickly on semi-log CCDF plots. For example, the slowest one in 10^5 might be only three times slower than the slowest one in 10 operations.
- *Exponential distributions* plot as straight lines on semi-log CCDFs, so the slowest one in 10^5 might be five times slower than the slowest one in 10 operations.

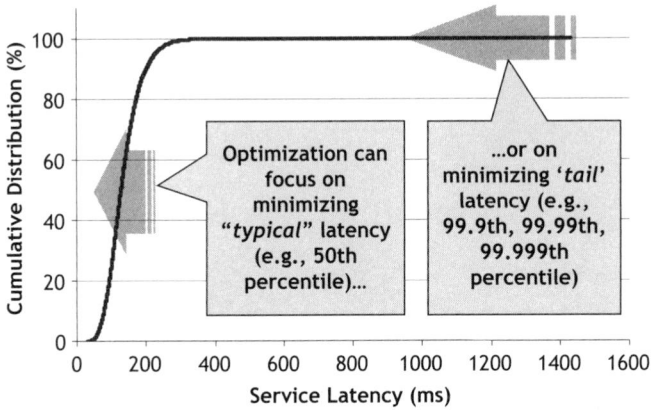

Figure 2.14. Service Latency Optimization Options.

- *Convex (e.g., power law) distributions* fall off slower than exponential distributions, so the slowest one in 10^5 operations might be several tens of times slower than the slowest one in 10 operations.

As one can see from Figure 2.12, real distributions might blend several classes of theoretical distributions, such as having a normal distribution to the slowest one in 10^4 operations, and becoming power law farther out in the tail (perhaps starting around the slowest one in 50,000 operations).

2.5.2.3 Optimizing Service Latency. There are two broad service latency related characteristics that one can attempt to optimize (visualized in Figure 2.14):

- *Minimizing "typical" latency*, to shave milliseconds (or microseconds) off the typical or 50th percentile latency to improve median performance
- *Minimizing "tail" latency*, to reduce the number of operations that experience service latencies far beyond "typical," thereby shrinking the latency "tail" to reduce distribution variance by eliminating elephants.

As the root causes of typical and tail latency are often different, it is important to agree on exactly what characteristic to optimize so the applicable root causes can be identified and proper corrective actions deployed.

2.5.3 Service Reliability

Reliability is defined by [TL_9000] as "*the ability of an item to perform a required function under stated conditions for a stated time period.*" Service reliability is the ability of an application to correctly process service requests within a maximum acceptable time. Service reliability impairments are sometimes called defective, failed, or fallout operations. While service reliability can be measured as a probability of success (e.g., 99.999% probability of success), probabilistic representations are not easy for many people to understand and are mathematically difficult to work with. Instead, sophisticated customers and suppliers often measure service reliability as defective (or failed) operations per million attempts (DPM). For example, seven defective operations per million attempts is much easier for most people to grasp than 99.9993% service reliability. In addition, DPM can often be combined by simply summing the DPM values along the critical service delivery path. Requirements for this measurement are discussed in Section 13.3, "Service Reliability Requirements."

2.5.4 Service Accessibility

Application service accessibility is the probability of a user successfully establishing a new application service session or connection, such as to begin streaming video content or to begin an audio call or start an interactive game. Applications often have specific service accessibility metrics, such as telephony service accessibility impairments, which are sometimes called "failed call attempts." Service accessibility is sometimes used as a proxy for service availability, such as in " 'Availability' or 'Available' means that Customer is able to log on to the Application. . . ." Note that this work does not consider accessibility of application service for users with physical disabilities who may require modified service input, rendering of output, or operation. Requirements for this measurement are discussed in Section 13.4, "Service Accessibility Requirements."

2.5.5 Service Retainability

It is important to users of session-oriented services—like streaming video—that their session continue to operate uninterrupted with acceptable service quality until the session terminates normally (e.g., the streaming video completes). Service retainability is the probability that an existing service session will remain fully operational until the end user requests the session be terminated. Applications often have application-specific service retainability metrics, such as "dropped calls" or "premature releases" for tele-phony service retainability impairments. As the risk of a service retention failure increases with the duration of the service session, retainability is often either explicitly normalized by time (e.g., risk per minute of service session) or implicitly (e.g., retention risk for a 90-minute movie or a 10-minute online game or a 3-minute telephone call). For example, the risk of abnormal service disconnection during a 30-minute video call is nominally 10 times higher than the risk of disconnection for a 3-minute video call. Thus, retainability is the probability that an unacceptable service impacting event will affect a single user's active service session during the normalization window (e.g., per minute of user session). Requirements for this measurement are discussed in Section 13.5, "Service Retainability Requirements."

2.5.6 Service Throughput

Service throughput is the sustained rate of successful transaction processing, such as number of transactions processed per hour. Service throughput is generally considered a service capacity indicator, but failure to meet service throughput expectations for a (nominally) properly engineered configuration is often seen as a service quality problem. Service throughput is coupled to service reliability, since customers care most about successfully processed operations—sometimes called "goodput"—rather than counting unsuccessful or failed operations. For example, an application in overload may successfully return properly formed TOO BUSY responses to many user service requests to prevent application collapse, but few users would consider those TOO BUSY responses as successful throughput or goodput. Thus, sophisticated customers may specify throughput with a maximum acceptable transaction or fallout rate. Requirements for this measurement are discussed in Section 13.6, "Service Throughput Requirements."

2.5.7 Service Timestamp Accuracy

Many applications must carefully record timestamps for billing, regulatory compliance, and operational reasons, such as fault correlation. Some applications and management systems use timestamps to record—and later reconstruct—sequence and chronology of operations, so erroneous timestamps may produce a faulty chronology of the sequence of operations/events. While regulatory compliance and operational considerations may not be concerns of end users, operations and compliance staff are special users of many applications, and they may rely on accurate timestamps to do their jobs. As will be discussed in Section 4.7, "Clock Drift," virtualization can impact the accuracy of real time perceived by application and guest OS software executing in a virtual machine instance relative to universal coordinated time (UTC) compared with execution on native hardware. Requirements for this measurement are discussed in Section 13.7, "Timestamp Accuracy Requirements."

2.5.8 Application-Specific Service Quality Measurements

Classes of applications often have application-specific service quality measurements that are tailored to the specific application, such as:

- *Mean Opinion Score* characterizes the overall quality of experience as perceived by end users, especially for streaming services, such as voice calling, interactive video conferencing, and streaming video playback. Mean opinion scores (MOS) [P.800] are typically expressed via the five-point scale in Table 2.1.

TABLE 2.1. Mean Opinion Scores [P.800]

MOS	Quality	Impairment
5	Excellent	Imperceptible
4	Good	Perceptible but not annoying
3	Fair	Slightly annoying
2	Poor	Annoying
1	Bad	Very annoying

Service quality metrics of streaming applications are primarily impacted by the coding and decoding (aka codec) algorithm and implementation, packet loss, packet latency and packet jitter. Sophisticated client applications can mask service quality impairments from the user by implementing dejitter buffers to mitigate minor packet delivery variations and implementing lost packet compensation algorithms when individual data packets are not available in time. Service quality impairments result in a worse overall quality of experience for the end user. High service quality for many applications requires low latency, low jitter, and minimal packet loss, although the degree of tolerance for jitter and packet loss is application and end user dependent. Service quality is primarily considered at the end user's physical rendering interface, such as the audio played to user's ear or the video rendered before the user's eyes. Rendering of audio, video, and other service to users inherently integrates service impairments of the application itself along with packet latency, loss, and jitter across the access and wide area networking, as well as the quality and performance of the devices that both encoded and decoded the content. For example, the voice quality of wireless calls is limited by the voice coder/decoder (aka codec) used, the latency, jitter, and packet loss of the wireless access network, as well as the presence or absence of audio transcoding. The overall service quality impact of any individual component in the service delivery path (e.g., a cloud based application) is generally difficult to quantitatively characterize. End-to-end service quality is considered in Chapter 10, "End to End Considerations."

- *Audio/Video Synchronization* (aka "lip sync"), Synchronization of audio and video is a key service quality for streaming video because if speech is shifted by more than about 50 ms relative to video images of the speaker's lips moving, then the viewers' quality of experience is degraded.

2.6 TECHNICAL SERVICE VERSUS SUPPORT SERVICE

The term "service quality" associated with applications is often used in two rather different contexts: *technical service quality* (Section 2.6.1) of an application instance or *support service quality* (Section 2.6.2) offered by a supplier or service provider to their customers. Throughout this book, the term "service quality" shall refer to ***technical*** service quality, not support service quality.

2.6.1 Technical Service Quality

Technical service quality characterizes the application service delivered to users across the customer facing service boundary, such as service availability (Section 2.5.1), service latency (Section 2.5.2), and service reliability (Section 2.5.3).

2.6.2 Support Service Quality

Both suppliers and service providers routinely offer technical ***support services*** to their customers. Many readers will be familiar with traditional helpdesks or customer support service arrangements. As with technical service KQIs, support service KQIs vary based on the type of application or service being supported. Support service KQIs generally include three metrics:

- *Respond.* How quickly the provider is able to respond to the customer's request for assistance. For example, the time to answer a telephone call for assistance is a common response time metric; customers may expect different response times when calling 911 to request emergency assistance compared with calling their credit card company to address a billing issue. The start and stop points for support service respond times will vary based on industry practices and supplier policies.
- *Restore.* How quickly service is restored. Note that service is sometimes restored via a workaround, such as a temporary configuration change or restarting a hung process.
- *Resolve.* Problems are typically resolved by correcting the true root cause(s), such as installing a software patch that corrects a residual defect that escaped into production software. Industry practices and supplier policies will dictate exactly when a problem is considered resolved, such as upon a patch or fix being scheduled for delivery, or a patch or fix actually being delivered, or a patch or fix actually being installed and verified in the production environment.

Only aspects of support service that directly relate to addressing technical service quality outages and impairments are considered in this work.

2.7 SECURITY CONSIDERATIONS

Security attacks are a chronic risk for both traditional and cloud-based applications. Quality and reliability diligence is concerned with assuring that legitimate traffic is served with acceptable quality; security diligence addresses rejecting nonlegitimate traffic and myriad other security risks. Security attacks can directly impact the availability, accessibility, throughput, and quality of an application service via Distributed Denial of Service (DDoS) attacks, or impact service reliability and correctness by tampering with application data or configuration information. Security processes and practices are separable from quality and reliability processes, but should be worked in parallel. Computer security in general, and cloud security in particular, are active and important topics that are beyond the scope of this work. Readers are encouraged to consult security resources like [CSA] for more information on this crucial topic.

3

CLOUD MODEL

Cloud computing is fundamentally a business model that enables organizations and individuals to outsource the ownership and operation of the compute, memory, storage, and networking of the hosts that support the organizations' and individuals' applications to cloud service providers. This shifts computing to a utility model, such as electricity, water, telephony, broadband internet, and so on, in that that a service provider owns and operates the necessary equipment and facilities to deliver computing service and consumers are able to use service on demand. NIST [NIST] defines cloud computing as:

> a model for enabling ubiquitous, convenient, on-demand network access to a shared pool of configurable computing resources (e.g., networks, servers, storage, applications, and services) that can be rapidly provisioned and released with minimal management effort or service provider interaction. This cloud model is composed of five essential characteristics, three service models, and four deployment models. [SP800-145]

This chapter reviews the standard roles, service models, and essential characteristics of cloud computing. The chapter concludes with a brief description of cloud regions and availability zones.

Service Quality of Cloud-Based Applications, First Edition. Eric Bauer and Randee Adams.
© 2014 The Institute of Electrical and Electronics Engineers, Inc. Published 2014 by John Wiley & Sons, Inc.

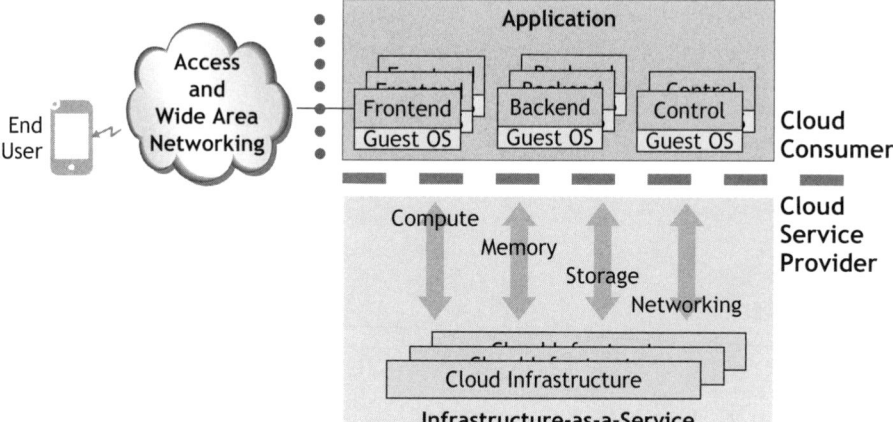

Figure 3.1. Cloud Roles for Simple Application.

3.1 ROLES IN CLOUD COMPUTING

Figure 3.1 visualizes the cloud consumer and cloud provider roles on the simple application model used in Chapter 2, "Application Service Quality." This work focuses on cloud consumers because they often have primary responsibility for application service quality, and on cloud service providers, because they often have primary responsibility for the infrastructure service quality.

The cloud consumer offers application service to end users by selecting and integrating software components from application suppliers that are hosted on compute infrastructure provided by one or more cloud service providers. One or more cloud or IP carriers provide network connectivity between cloud data centers and end users.

3.2 CLOUD SERVICE MODELS

NIST defines three cloud service models:

- *Infrastructure as a Service (IaaS).* The capability provided to the consumer is to provision processing, storage, networks, and other fundamental computing resources where the consumer is able to deploy and run arbitrary software, which can include operating systems and applications [SP800-145].
- *Platform as a Service (PaaS).* The capability provided to the consumer is to deploy onto the cloud infrastructure consumer-created or acquired applications created using programming languages, libraries, services, and tools supported by the provider [SP800-145].
- *Software as a Service (SaaS).* The capability provided to the consumer is to use the provider's applications running on a cloud infrastructure. The applications

are accessible from various client devices through either a thin client interface, such as a web browser (e.g., web-based email), or a program interface [SP800-145].

The customer facing service boundary of the IaaS or PaaS service provider is the resource facing service boundary of the cloud-based application. As this work focuses on cloud-based applications, this work will consider the IaaS/PaaS-to-application service boundary as the application's resource facing service boundary.

3.3 CLOUD ESSENTIAL CHARACTERISTICS

The five essential characteristics of cloud computing [SP800-145] are:

1. On-demand self-service (Section 3.3.1)
2. Broad network access (Section 3.3.2)
3. Resource pooling (Section 3.3.3)
4. Rapid elasticity (Section 3.3.4)
5. Measured service (Section 3.3.5).

The highest level application service quality risk of each essential characteristic is considered separately.

3.3.1 On-Demand Self-Service

On-demand self-service is defined as "a consumer can unilaterally provision computing capabilities, such as server time and network storage, as needed automatically without requiring human interaction with each service provider" [SP800-145]. On-demand self-service enables cloud-based applications to be vastly more dynamic than traditional applications because new resources can be allocated and deallocated on-the-fly by cloud consumers. This naturally results in more configuration and capacity changes being executed, and many of these on-demand changes will happen during moderate to heavy usage periods when it is convenient for cloud consumers rather than deliberately postponing the changes to low usage maintenance periods (e.g., in the middle of the night). Thus, provisioning actions must become more reliable for cloud-based applications to maintain high service availability and quality despite more frequent on-demand configuration changes happening during moderate to heavy application usage periods.

3.3.2 Broad Network Access

Broad network access is defined as "capabilities are available over the network and accessed through standard mechanisms that promote use by heterogeneous thin or thick client platforms" [SP800-145]. End users consume cloud-based applications via IP access and wide area networks. End-to-end service quality is considered in Chapter 10, "End-to-End Considerations."

3.3.3   Resource Pooling

Resource pooling is defined as "the provider's computing resources are pooled to serve multiple consumers using a multi-tenant model, with different physical and virtual resources dynamically assigned and reassigned according to consumer demand. . . . Examples of resources include storage, processing, memory, and network bandwidth" [SP800-145]. Traditionally, applications and their supporting operating systems are deployed directly onto native hardware, so nominally the full capacity of the compute, memory, storage, and networking resources offered by the hardware are constantly available to the application subject to timesharing by the operating system. Sharing pooled resources across multiple consumers inevitably increases the risk of resource contention, including "Delivery of Degraded VM Capacity" (Section 4.4), increased "Tail Latency" (Section 4.5), and "Clock Event Jitter" (Section 4.6). The application service quality risks caused by the infrastructure due to resource-sharing policies and technologies (e.g., virtualization) are a focus of this work.

3.3.4   Rapid Elasticity

Rapid elasticity is defined as "capabilities can be elastically provisioned and released, in some cases automatically, to scale rapidly outward and inward commensurate with demand. To the consumer, the capabilities available for provisioning often appear to be unlimited and can be appropriated in any quantity at any time" [SP800-145]. Figure 3.2 illustrates the three fundamental elastic growth strategies:

- *Horizontal Growth.* Adding more resource instances (e.g., VMs and virtual disk volumes to an existing application instance). "Scale out" refers to horizontal growth actions, such as adding more VM instances; "scale in" refers to horizontal degrowth (i.e., shrink) operations.
- *Vertical Growth.* Increasing the resource allocation for existing resource instances to an existing application instance (e.g., increasing memory allocation

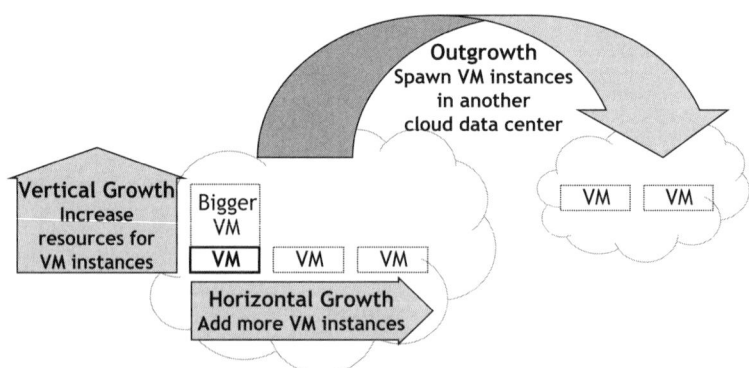

Figure 3.2. Elastic Growth Strategies.

of an existing VM instance or maximum disk allocation of an existing virtual storage device). "Scale up" refers to vertical growth actions, such as growing the size of a previously allocated virtual disk partition; "scale down" refers to vertical degrowth (i.e., shrink) operations. Note that an option for vertical growth is to replace a previously allocated VM with a larger instance.

- *Outgrowth.* Typically means instantiating a new application instance in another cloud data center.

Elastic measurements are discussed in Section 3.5, and elasticity growth and degrowth is analyzed in detail in Chapter 8, "Capacity Management."

3.3.5 Measured Service

Measured service is defined as "cloud systems automatically control and optimize resource use by leveraging a metering capability at some level of abstraction appropriate to the type of service (e.g., storage, processing, bandwidth, and active user accounts). Resource usage can be monitored, controlled, and reported, providing transparency for both the provider and consumer of the utilized service" [SP800-145]. Combining measured service with on demand elasticity enables cloud consumers to proactively manage how much application capacity is online across time. Chapter 8, "Capacity Management," considers how the errors and failures encountered while managing the application capacity online can lead to insufficient capacity being provided to serve the offered workload with acceptable service quality.

3.4 SIMPLIFIED CLOUD ARCHITECTURE

PaaS is inherently less well-defined than either IaaS (at the bottom of the cloud service model stack) or SaaS (at the top of the cloud service model stack). Rather than focusing on where the IaaS : PaaS or PaaS : SaaS dividing line should be, this work considers a simplified cloud model comprised of five logical components:

- Application software (Section 3.4.1)
- Virtual machine servers (Section 3.4.2)
- Virtual machine server controllers (Section 3.4.3)
- Cloud operations support systems (Section 3.4.4)
- Cloud technology components offered "as-a-Service" (Section 3.4.5).

Figure 3.3 illustrates how the first four simplified component types interact. Technology components offered "as-a-Service"— such as Database-as-a-Service—are logically black boxes that applications can configure and use and can be considered PaaS components.

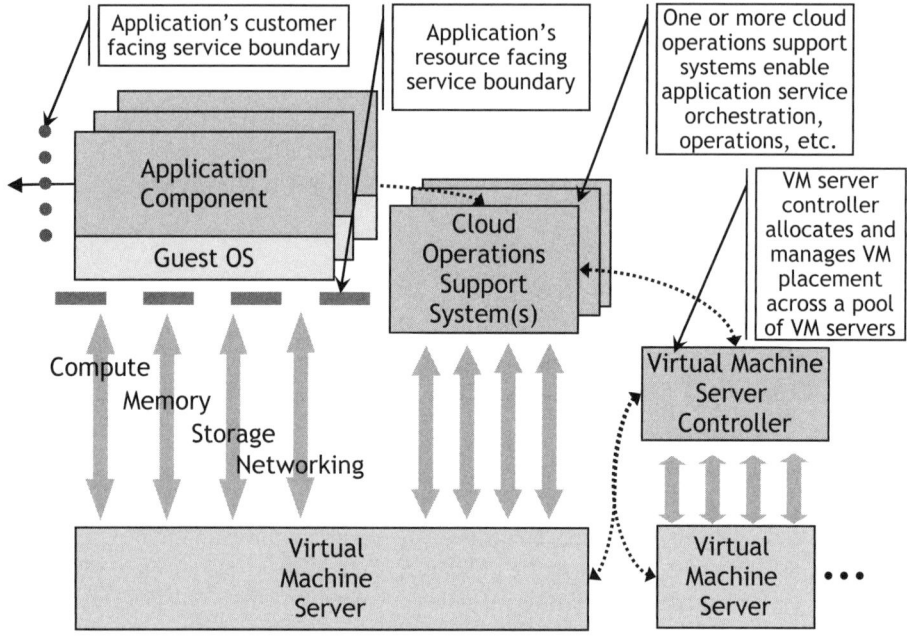

Figure 3.3. Simple Model of Cloud Infrastructure.

3.4.1 Application Software

The application instance is an entity that includes the application software components and their guest OSs instantiated in a suite of virtual machines. Traditionally, application quality measurements are normalized against either network element or system instances. The standard definitions of network element and system* do not fit perfectly to cloud deployment, but Chapter 12, "Service Availability Measurement," offers a parsimonious adaptation of these concepts to cloud-based application deployment.

---

* "System" is defined by [TL_9000] as: "A collection of hardware and/or software items located at one or more physical locations where all of the items are required for proper operation. No single item can function by itself." "*Network Element*" (NE) is defined by [TL_9000] as: "A system device, entity or node including all relevant hardware and/or software components located at one location. The Network Element (NE) must include all components required to perform the primary function of its applicable product category. If multiple FRUs, devices, and/or software components are needed for the NE to provide its product category's primary function, then none of these individual components can be considered an NE by themselves. The total collection of all these components is considered a single NE. Note: While an NE may be comprised of power supplies, CPU, peripheral cards, operating system and application software to perform a primary function, no individual item can be considered an NE in its own right."

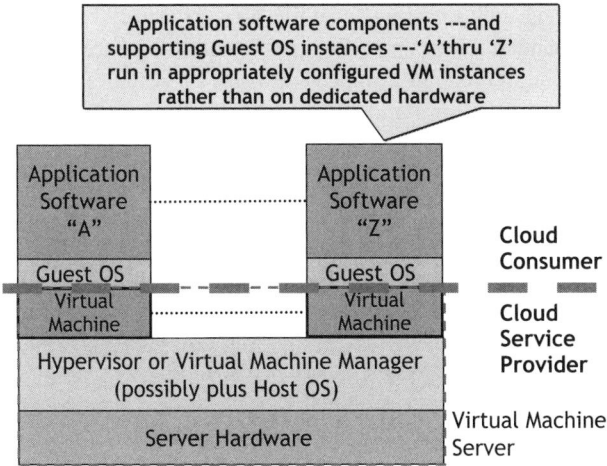

Figure 3.4. Abstract Virtual Machine Server.

3.4.2 Virtual Machine Servers

Virtual machine servers physically host virtual machine instances. Figure 3.4 illustrates a virtual machine server consisting of a number of virtual machine instances hosted by a virtual machine manager or hypervisor software executing on some server or general purpose computer. Virtual machine server elements will often be built from large pools of rack-mounted servers (RMS) and delivered as preconfigured racks—or even shipping containers—of equipment. Note that VM instances are ephemeral and likely to be created on the fly and be active for hours, days, weeks, or months before being deallocated. The physical hardware supporting the virtual machine server is expected to be in service for years.

3.4.3 Virtual Machine Server Controllers

Virtual machine servers enable efficient resource sharing to permit many applications to be consolidated onto far less hardware than with traditional, dedicated hardware configurations. Increasing the scale of application consolidation and resource sharing drives down operational expenditure (OPEX), and ultimately gave rise to so-called warehouse-scale computing. To efficiently operate pools of virtual machine servers, specialized online critical operations support systems (OSSs) referred to in this work as virtual machine server controllers are required. Virtual machine server controllers allocate, manage, and control virtual machine instances—including the corresponding hardware resources—hosted across one or more virtual machine servers. These controllers play a critical role in minimizing user service impact to applications running on the virtual machine servers, such as enforcing application specific anti-affinity rules to assure that no individual virtual machine server becomes a single point of failure for applications (see Section 7.2.4, "No Single Point of Failure Assurance in Cloud Computing"). These controllers will be involved in service orchestration and federated to support cloud bursting. While virtual machine servers naturally focus on individual virtual machine instances, virtual machine server controllers are likely to control the mapping of individual application instances into sets of virtual machine instances that are likely to be distributed across multiple virtual machine servers.

3.4.4   Cloud Operations Support Systems

Operations support systems (OSSs) provide myriad support functions to operate, administer, maintain, and provision applications running on virtual machine servers, and to support the cloud infrastructure itself. For example, OSSs support orchestration of on boarding of applications, elastic growth, cloud bursting, and related service management functions. OSS functionality is often distributed across multiple types and instances of interworking support systems. For instance, executing application outgrowth to another cloud data center inevitably requires careful coordination by one or more OSSs, with the virtual machine server controllers managing the virtual machine servers in the applicable cloud data centers.

3.4.5   Cloud Technology Components Offered "as-a-Service"

Cloud computing encourages customers and service providers to treat common standard technology components as services rather than software products. Thus, rather than being forced to purchase a technology component, such as a database management system or load balancer outright, then install, operate, and maintain it to enable another application to operate, cloud encourages a service provider to offer the technology component "as-a-Service." The technology component as-a-service offering reduces both CAPEX and OPEX for most cloud consumers, and enables them to focus on adding value for the enterprise rather than investing in maintenance and operation of industry standard technology components. For this analysis, these technology components offered "as-a-Service" will simply be treated as component instances that interwork with application components to deliver application service to end users.

3.5   ELASTICITY MEASUREMENTS

Rapid elasticity of online capacity offers fundamentally new functionality beyond what was traditionally supported for native applications, and thus new service metrics are appropriate to measure the key quality characteristics of an application's rapid elasticity. The cloud computing industry has not yet formally standardized a complete suite of elasticity metrics, so the authors will use the following elasticity measurement concepts in this work:

- Density (Section 3.5.1)
- Provisioning interval (Section 3.5.2)
- Release interval (Section 3.5.3)

- Scaling in and out (Section 3.5.4)
- Scaling up and down (Section 3.5.5)
- Agility (Section 3.5.6)
- Slew rate and linearity (Section 3.5.7)
- Elasticity speedup (Section 3.5.8).

3.5.1 Density

[SPECOSGReport] proposes a density measurement for cloud that *"measures how many instances of the workload can be run on the* [unit under test] *before performance degrades below a specified* [quality of service]." Different cloud service providers' virtualized infrastructures will support somewhat different densities (e.g., workload per VM instance) for the same application based on factors such as:

- The underlying hardware components and architecture
- The hypervisor and host software
- The cloud service provider's operational policies and infrastructure configuration.

VM density is impacted by both the application's architecture, as well as the quality of virtualized infrastructure delivered by the cloud service provider. Figure 2.12 showed how tail latency behavior can be significantly influenced by workload density. Degraded delivery of virtualized resources (see Section 4.4, "Delivery of Degraded VM Capacity") may reduce the workload that can be consistently served with acceptable service quality. For example, as the workload increases, the cloud infrastructure may begin to discard IP packets at the busiest moments; timeout expiration and retransmission of those discarded packets adds directly to the tail of the application's service latency distribution. If a cloud service provider's virtualized infrastructure does not consistently deliver sufficient resource throughput with acceptable quality to the application, then the application will typically need to grow horizontally to decrease density so the application latency (especially the tail) is less degraded.

3.5.2 Provisioning Interval

Traditionally, it took days or weeks for customers to order and take delivery of physical compute, memory, networking, or storage hardware, which could then be manually installed before application software could be reconfigured to use the additional resource capacity. Cloud computing dramatically reduces that logistical delay for acquiring resources from days or weeks to minutes or less. [SPECOSGReport] proposes a *provisioning interval* measurement for cloud, which is *"the time between initiating the request to bring up a new resource or to relinquish it, and when the resource is either ready to serve the first request or when it serves the first request."* Figure 3.5 visualizes provisioning interval T_{Grow} for horizontal growth of online capacity. The interval begins when a cloud OSS, human, or other entity initiates elastic growth of online application capacity. The interval includes the following:

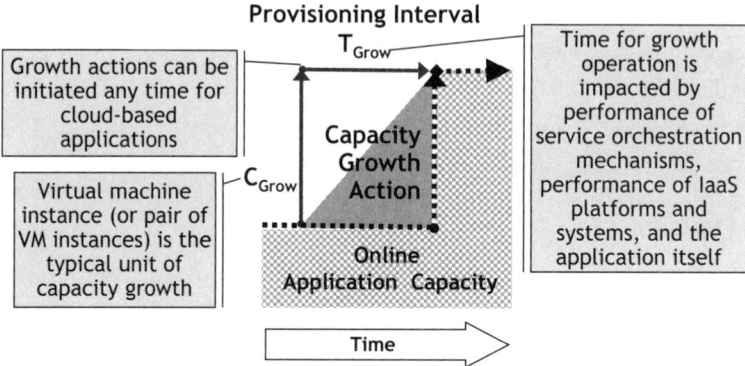

Figure 3.5. Provisioning Interval (T_{Grow}).

1. Cloud OSS requesting additional virtual resources (e.g., VM instances) from cloud infrastructure.
2. Cloud service provider successfully allocating additional virtual resources and assigning them to the cloud consumer.
3. Initializing application software into newly allocated or grown virtual resources.
4. Verifying the new application component works properly, such as via test traffic or other operational readiness verification.
5. Synchronizing and assimilating the new or grown virtual resource(s) with preexisting application components.

The interval ends when the new application capacity is available to serve user traffic. Note that the provisioning interval can be applied to growth of both VM instances and to persistent storage.

Elastic growth is quantized into discrete units of application capacity driven by the quanta of resource offered by the cloud service provider, typically VM instance. Figure 3.5 shows application capacity increasing by C_{Grow}. One can thus define a logical *growth density* measurement by considering the unit of application capacity (C_{Grow}) per quanta of virtualized cloud resource (e.g., virtual machine instance). For example, an application may add capacity for 100 additional active users (i.e., C_{Grow} = 100 users) per virtual machine instance grown.

Provisioning interval is largely determined by the application's architecture and elastic growth procedures, but the interval needed by the cloud service provider to allocate additional virtual resources as well as the availability of sufficient resources is in the critical path and thus impacts the overall interval. Note that elastic growth actions routinely happen when the application instance is under heavy and growing load, so application performance may be more sluggish than when the application instance is under light or moderate load.

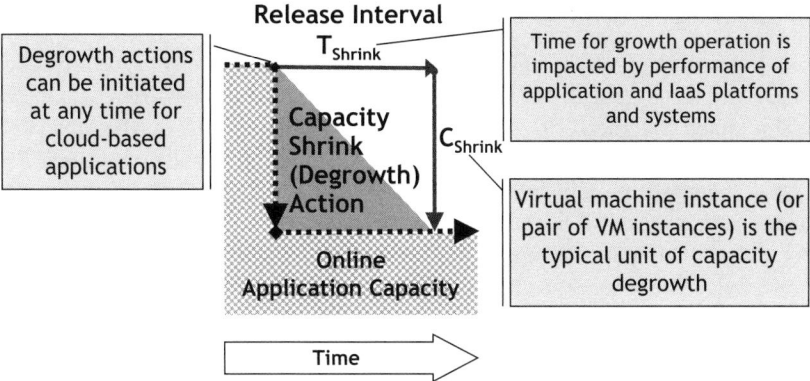

Figure 3.6. Release Interval T$_{\text{shrink}}$.

3.5.3 Release Interval

Since workloads shrink as well as grow, elastic applications should be engineered to gracefully release resources when they are no longer required. While the time required to release excess application capacity is not likely to impact user service, this measurement may be important when the offered workload whipsaws (see Section 8.9, "Workload Whipsaw"). Figure 3.6 visualizes a timeline for resource release. The release interval ($\mathbf{T}_{\text{Shrink}}$) begins when the cloud OSS, human, or other entity decides to initiate a capacity degrowth action and includes:

1. Selecting virtualized resource(s) to release.
2. Blocking new traffic from being assigned to selected resource(s).
3. Draining or migrating active traffic away from the selected resource(s). Note that if traffic does not naturally drain away from the selected resource(s) fast enough, then traffic may be terminated.
4. Releasing selected resource(s) back to cloud service provider.

C_{Shrink} is the unit of application capacity that is diminished by the release action. C_{Grow} and C_{Shrink} will often be equal (e.g., an application can both grow and shrink online capacity one VM instance at a time). As resources are often billed on an hourly basis, there is seldom much business value in shaving seconds or minutes off of $\mathbf{T}_{\text{Shrink}}$ because it has no impact on user service, and if resource usage is billed by the hour, then small reductions in $\mathbf{T}_{\text{Shrink}}$ will likely produce negligible OPEX savings.

The release interval may be dominated by the time required to drain or migrate traffic from the resource to be released. The nature of the application (e.g., stateful and session oriented vs. stateless) along with the role of the target resource in service delivery and the cloud consumer's willingness to impact users' service drives also impact how aggressively traffic can be drained from resources being released.

3.5.4   Scaling In and Out

Figure 3.7 illustrates scale in and scale out for horizontal elasticity. Typically, applications have a fixed overhead for supervisory and control functions ($R_{Overhead}$ in Figure 3.7). This fixed overhead $R_{Overhead}$ must be instantiated before the first unit of user service-capacity R_{Grow} can be instantiated to serve the application instance's first user. Thus, the application instance requires $R_{Overhead}$ plus one unit of R_{Grow} to serve the first user.

As shown in Figure 3.8, application resource usage can grow by units of R_{Grow} (e.g., discrete VM instances) to increase online service capacity by units of C_{Grow}.

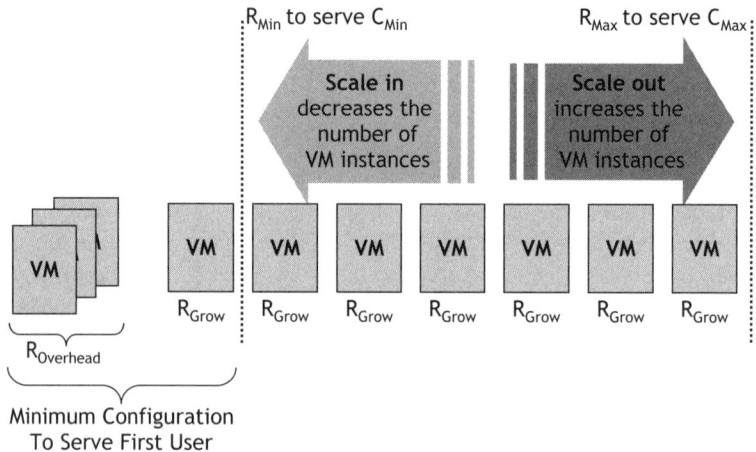

Figure 3.7. VM Scale In and Scale Out.

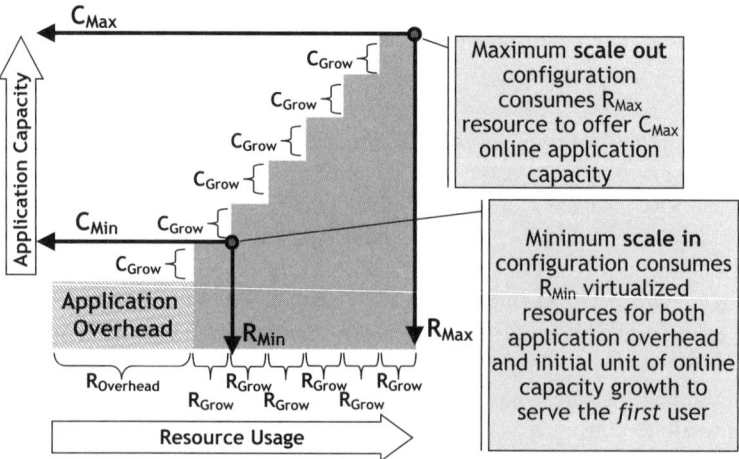

Figure 3.8. Horizontal Elasticity.

The maximum supported online capacity for an application instance is often limited by:

- *Internal Algorithms.* For example, linear searching across unsorted datasets becomes impractical when the dataset becomes too large, so more powerful data arrangements are necessary before the maximum capacity limit can be increased.
- *Static Allocations.* If a nonelastic data structure is statically allocated for the application at startup time (e.g., table of active user sessions, open files, worker VM instances, etc), then that allocation can limit the maximum capacity of the application instance.
- *License Limit.* For commercial reasons, applications may deliberately limit capacity growth. For example, if a cloud consumer has licensed only "X" simultaneous user sessions of capacity for a technology component used by the application, then the application should prohibit capacity growth beyond that licensed capacity.
- *External Constraints.* The maximum useful capacity of an application instance may be limited by the capacity of supporting systems, such as payment gateway request processing from a credit card payment processor.
- *Financial Constraints.* The cloud consumer may constrain the maximum permitted application capacity to prevent overrunning the organization's budget.

3.5.5 Scaling Up and Down

Figure 3.9 illustrates scale up and scale down with vertical elastic growth. Theoretically, one could scale up or down resources, such as RAM allocation, number of CPU cores, size of disk partitions, CPU clock rate, and I/O bandwidth. Taking advantage of elastic online vertical growth of some resources (e.g., CPU cores) may be infeasible or impractical for most guest OSs and applications, but online vertical growth of other resources (e.g., CPU clock rate and I/O bandwidth) is often very natural. Thus, applications may support online vertical growth (scale up) of some resources (e.g., CPU clock rate), but not of other resources (e.g., CPU cores).

Note that horizontal growth need not always grow by the same size resource. For example, an application could theoretically start by growing one size virtual machine

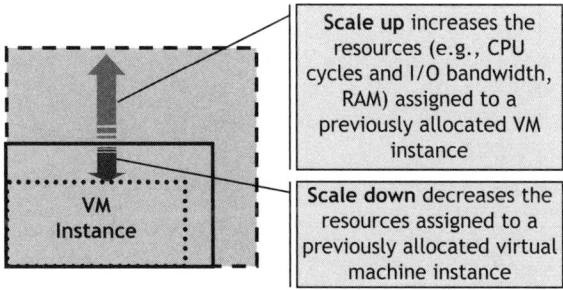

Figure 3.9. Scale Up and Scale Down of a VM Instance.

(e.g., two-CPU core) and as the application continued to grow horizontally, it could potentially scale up the unit of growth (e.g., growing by four-CPU core VM instances).

3.5.6 Agility

[SPECOSGReport] proposes a capacity **agility** measurement for cloud that "characterizes the ability to scale the workload and the ability of a system provisioned to be as close to the needs of the workload as possible." Essentially, this characterizes how closely online application capacity can track with the offered workload, and this is fundamentally limited by the unit of capacity growth (C_{Grow} from Figure 3.5) and capacity degrowth (C_{Shrink} from Figure 3.6) that are supported by the application. The linkage of capacity growth quanta and capacity agility is easily understood from the visualization in Figure 3.10. Each growth action adds C_{Grow} extra capacity; the smaller that unit of growth, the closer the online capacity can track to offered workload.

Note that like physical inventory for a retailer, spare online capacity is not inherently a bad thing. The trick is to carefully manage the "inventory" of spare online capacity so that fluctuations in offered workload can efficiently be served with acceptable service quality while minimizing both the cloud consumer's user service quality risk and their OPEX. Thus, capacity agility is an important application characteristic, but the cloud consumer's operational policies, as well as the application's provisioning interval T_{Grow}, will determine how much spare online capacity is actually maintained.

C_{Grow} is fundamentally determined by both how cloud service providers quantize resources (e.g., offering VM instances with whole numbers of CPUs and fixed RAM allocations), as well as the application's architecture. Chapter 8, "Capacity Management," considers this topic in more detail, but the trade-off often comes down to balancing the smallest unit of C_{Grow} without consuming too much resource in overhead (e.g., guest OS instances along with management and control functionality), as well as the increased OPEX and complexity associated with managing more small component instances rather than fewer large component instances.

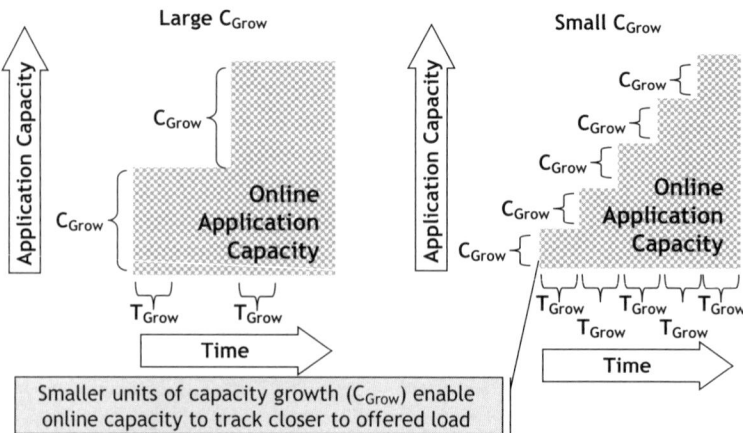

Figure 3.10. Idealized (Linear) Capacity Agility.

3.5.7 Slew Rate and Linearity

Electrical engineers use the concept of slew rate to characterize how quickly the output of an amplifier can track with a dramatic change in the input, as shown in Figure 3.11.

As with amplifiers, rapid elasticity is incapable of instantaneously tracking workload swings. Instead, slew rate characterizes the unit of capacity growth (C_{Grow}) that can be added in a provisioning interval T_{Grow} (Section 3.5.2, "Provisioning Interval"). Thus, an application's maximum capacity slew rate is the maximum C_{Grow} divided by T_{Grow}. As shown in Figure 3.12, slew rate captures the "bulk" behavior application elasticity, such as how much application capacity can grow in one or more hours.

Linearity of elastic growth considers the rate of C_{Grow} divided by T_{Grow} (i.e., the slope or slew rate) across the application's entire elastic range from C_{Min} to C_{Max}. For example, does the typical value of T_{Grow} remain constant across the application's entire elastic range, or does T_{Grow} increase (or decrease) as online capacity approaches C_{Max}? Likewise, the linearity of elastic degrowth is considered by examining C_{Shrink} divided by T_{Shrink} from C_{Max} to C_{Min}. If elasticity is not linear across the application's entire

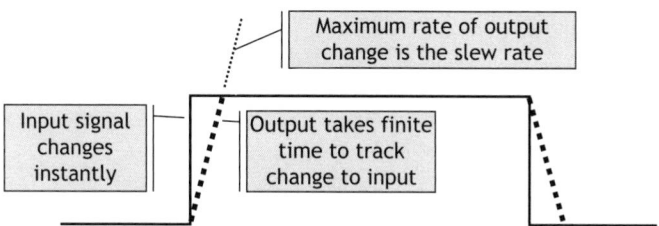

Figure 3.11. Slew Rate of Square Wave Amplification.

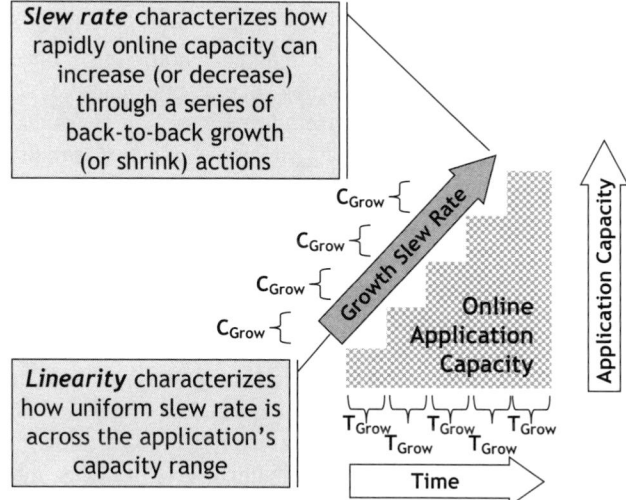

Figure 3.12. Elastic Growth Slew Rate and Linearity.

capacity range, then the elasticity policies will need to assure that automated application elasticity policies can track varying workloads even when traffic surges while the application is at the most sluggish point on its elasticity growth curve.

3.5.8   Elasticity Speedup

[SPECOSGReport] proposes an elasticity *speedup* measurement for cloud characterizing any performance improvement from increasing resources. In essence, if allocated resources are increased by "X" then will application throughput increase substantially? An example of a process that enjoys elasticity speedup is cleaning a house: the more people who pitch in, the faster the house is cleaned. The canonical example of a process that does not enjoy an elasticity speedup is having a baby: while one woman can make a baby in 9 months, nine women cannot make a baby in 1 month. An example cloudbased application that might experience elasticity speed up is building application software binaries because individual software modules can be compiled in separate VM instances in parallel. For instance, if a software application includes 1000 source code files that must be compiled, then instantiating more VM instances to simultaneously compile those files should shorten overall job completion time.

Elasticity speedup is driven by the application's architecture. Elasticity speedup benefits may be linear for incremental resource growth after discounting resources consumed by application overhead, including coordination and control of user traffic.

3.6   REGIONS AND ZONES

Traditionally, enterprises arranged for geographically distant data centers to be promptly available to enable business continuity following a disaster event that renders a data center unavailable or inaccessible. Cloud computing makes it simpler to arrange for disaster recovery service at a cloud data center that is physically far enough from the primary data center that no single event will impact both sites. Cloud changes the economics of application deployment so it may become practical to deploy application instances to multiple geographically dispersed data centers, all of which actively serve traffic rather than relying on a single primary site and a cold or warm disaster recovery site.

Some cloud service providers implement availability zones within their data centers to create "virtual" data centers that each rely on independent infrastructure to contain the impact of infrastructure failures. Consider Figure 3.13, which shows two hypothetical cloud data center sites ("North" and "South") that are physically separated by 1000 miles so no single disaster event like an earthquake can simultaneously impact both sites. Within each of the data centers are three completely independent availability zones: North-1, North-2, and North-3 within the north data center, and South-1, South-2, and South-3 within the southern data center. It is prudent to partition each data center into independent physical infrastructure and administrative domains to assure that the impact of any infrastructure failure or administrative error will be contained to a single partition, rather than impacting all consumers hosted in the warehouse scale data center;

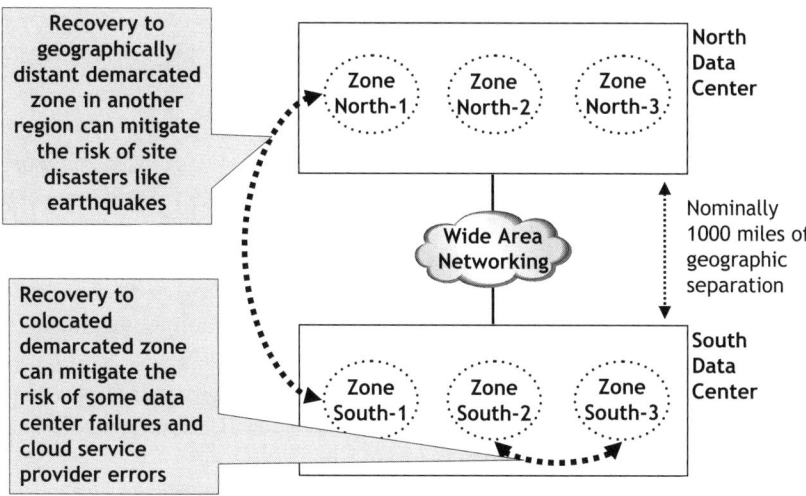

Figure 3.13. Regions and Availability Zones.

each of these partitions is called an "availability zone." For example, if a fire broke out in the data center, then the emergency power off (EPO) impact should be limited to a single availability zone (hopefully, only a single rack or row of equipment within that availability zone). Thus, collocated availability zones should mitigate the risks of some cloud infrastructure failures and administrative errors, but geographically separated (i.e., regional) data centers are required to mitigate the risk of force majeure events like earthquakes.

3.7   CLOUD AWARENESS

Simply deploying an application onto cloud infrastructure does not make it "cloud aware." The Open Data Center Alliance (ODCA) frames the notion of "*cloud awareness*" as follows:

> Cloud-aware applications have been designed and built with the sole intent of running in a cloud environment. They are both free of the dependencies and assumptions which burden traditional or legacy applications, while simultaneously able to fully exploit the inherent advantages of cloud. [ODCA_CIaaS]

An application that is not cloud aware is called *traditional*, defined by ODCA as follows:

> Simply put, a program or system that has not been specifically designed (or remediated) to transparently leverage the unique capabilities of cloud computing. Rather, such applications may be migrated to run in a cloud context, but the value realization from such instances will be limited. [ODCA_CIaaS]

ODCA offers eight attributes of cloud awareness [ODCA_CIaaS] [Freemantle] [ODCA_DCCA]; let us consider the customer facing service quality risks of each of these attributes:

- *Composable: "Applications are distributed and dynamically wired"* [ODCA_ CIaaS]. Distribution of functionality introduces the risks of communication impairments between the distributed components; wide area distribution exposes greater risk of communication latency, packet loss, and jitter than local area distribution. The dynamic nature of composability raises further risks because each configuration action, like redirecting an IP packet flow or a service relationship between distributed components carries the risk of failure that impacts user service.

- *Elastic: "The ability to scale up but also to scale down based on the load"* [ODCA_CIaaS]. Chapter 8, "Capacity Management," considers the service quality risks of elasticity in detail.

- *Evolvable: "This is related to portability, and suggests the ability to replace existing underlying technology or vendor decisions with others, as the needs of the business or market change, with minimal impact to the business"* [ODCA_ CIaaS]. All information systems evolve from one generation of technology, standards, and product releases to the next; successful businesses must learn to manage their systems through these evolutionary cycles. Cloud computing accelerates the pace of evolution across the ICT ecosystem, and practices such as continuous delivery and DevOps (i.e., a collaboration between development and operations) may encourage even faster adoption of newer technologies as they become available. Cloud encourages the development and adoption of technology components offered as a service so suppliers and service providers can independently evolve individual application components to facilitate the evolutionary path for cloud consumers. Application architectures that treat "everything" as a service via appropriate standard interfaces can evolve more easily than brittle monolithic architectures. Not only are popular technology components offered as-a-service likely to be more stable because of extensive usage that will have exposed and repaired virtually all residual defects, but those components should natively support rapid elasticity. New applications can accelerate time to market by leveraging existing PaaS technology components like load balancers, message queues, database management servers, and so on. A business challenge is to leverage enough platform services to shorten time to market and boost service quality by using proven components while not making the application tightly coupled to a specific cloud service provider's platform or components.

- *Extensible: "Applications are incrementally deployed and tested"* [ODCA_ CIaaS]. Incremental development and continuous delivery lead to far more frequent software release changes than traditional development models. The service quality risks of release management are considered in Chapter 9, "Release Management."

- *Granular Metering and Billing.* Resource pricing in general, including granularity of metering and billing, will influence how aggressively cloud consumers manage the spare online application capacity that they maintain to cope with traffic swings and failure events. As each capacity management action carries a tiny risk of failure, fewer capacity management operations yield a slightly lower service risk than more frequent capacity management actions. Likewise, maintaining more spare online capacity has a slightly lower service quality risk than keeping spare capacity to the consumer's policy minimum, especially if the cloud consumer's policy fails to accurately anticipate actual traffic growth, resource failure or elasticity reliability, and latency performance.

- *Multitenant: "Multiple cloud subscribers may be using the same underlying resources and infrastructure from the cloud provider, with reliability, security, and consistent performance"* [ODCA_CIaaS]. Sharing cloud infrastructure resources contributes to the risks of Chapter 4, "Virtualized Infrastructure Impairments."

- *Portable: "Applications can run almost anywhere, any cloud provider and from any device"* [ODCA_CIaaS]. Software portability is not a new concept, and cloud computing does not materially change the user service quality risks associated with application portability.

- *Self-Service.* Cloud computing relies on self-service to both reduce cloud consumer's OPEX via automation and to improve customer satisfaction by giving customers greater control over their service experience. Self-service is likely to increase the rate of configuration changes requested of the application because it will be far easier for each user to click a few buttons on a website themselves to tailor their service experience than it was to request a change to their service via the technical support helpdesk or other traditional channel. In addition to far more frequent configuration changes, the self-service interface mechanisms must be extremely robust because users will inevitably make mistakes when attempting self-service changes. Creative and inquisitive users may even try seemingly odd configurations in attempts to mash up or tailor service to better fit their unique work style, need or taste. Thus, self-service means that the application's configuration mechanisms must be super robust to mitigate the impact of unexpected and even pathological configurations that users may accidentally or deliberately set via self service mechanisms.

4

VIRTUALIZED INFRASTRUCTURE IMPAIRMENTS

This chapter considers the resource facing service impairments experienced by a cloud-based application for virtualized compute, memory, storage, and networking. As shown in Figure 4.1, these impairments are:

- *VM Failure* (Section 4.2). A virtual machine instance can terminate or cease to operate for some reason other than explicit request of the cloud consumer or the application instance itself.
- *Nondelivery of Configured VM Capacity* (Section 4.3). The cloud service provider's infrastructure platform can fail to give a VM instance any resources for a period of time (such as during a live migration event), thereby preventing the application component nominally running in that VM instance from doing any useful work.
- *Delivery of Degraded VM Capacity* (Section 4.4). The cloud service provider's infrastructure can fail to give a VM instance enough of their nominally configured compute, memory, storage, or networking capacity to adequately serve the application's offered workload, such as when heavy demand from other

Service Quality of Cloud-Based Applications, First Edition. Eric Bauer and Randee Adams.
© 2014 The Institute of Electrical and Electronics Engineers, Inc. Published 2014 by John Wiley & Sons, Inc.

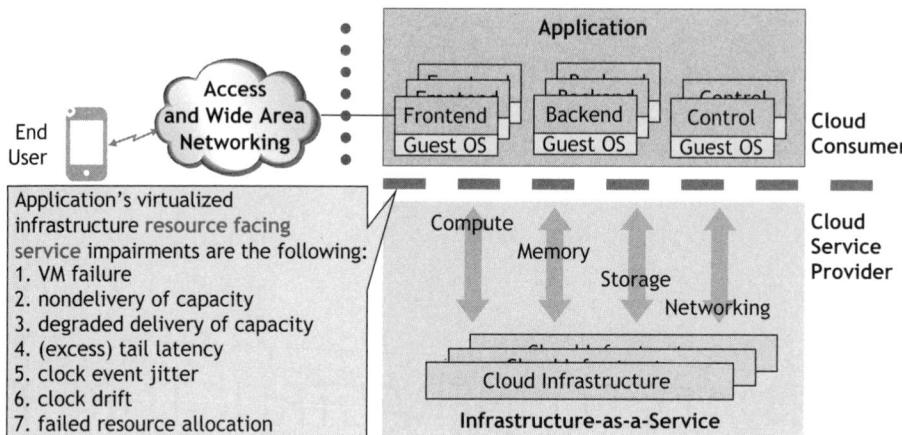

Figure 4.1. Virtualized Infrastructure Impairments Experienced by Cloud-Based Applications.

applications' VM instances running on the same VM server host cause contention and queuing for shared infrastructure resources.

- *"Tail" Latency* (Section 4.5). Hypervisors and increased resource sharing often cause resource access latencies to be worse than on native hardware, especially for occasional outlier events in the statistical "tail." The chapter begins with a discussion of service latency, virtualization, and cloud computing.
- *Clock Event Jitter* (Section 4.6). Strict real-time applications, such as those that handle bearer traffic, such as interactive video, often rely on consistent clock events to minimize jitter in application packets delivered to end users. Jitter introduced by tardy, lost, or coalesced clock interrupt events can directly impact the quality of service delivered to end users.
- *Clock Drift* (Section 4.7). Real-time clocks for guest OS instances supporting application components may drift away from standard (UTC) time due to virtualization.
- *Failed or Slow Allocation and Startup of VM Instance* (Section 4.8). Occasionally, the cloud service provider may be unable to successfully allocate and configure a VM instance and start up the guest OS and application software promptly.

4.1 SERVICE LATENCY, VIRTUALIZATION, AND THE CLOUD

Virtualization and cloud add additional service latency risks beyond those discussed in Section 2.5.2, "Service Latency"; Section 4.1.1 considers "Virtualization and Cloud Causes of Latency Variation," Section 4.1.2 discusses "Virtualization Overhead," and Section 4.1.3 covers "Increased Variability of Infrastructure Performance."

4.1.1   Virtualization and Cloud Causes of Latency Variation

Virtualization explicitly decouples application software from the underlying hardware resources and helps enable the essential cloud characteristic of resource sharing. With greater resource sharing comes the risk of greater resource contention that could increase an application's latency in accessing a shared resource, such as CPU, networking, or storage, especially when that or another coresident application component is under stress. The incremental latency risk of virtualization comes from several sources:

- *Resource Utilization and Contention Latency.* A primary goal of both virtualization and cloud computing is to increase utilization of physical resources. Although there are resource utilization concerns with traditional systems, virtualized systems exacerbate the concern. Increased utilization of finite resources inherently means that more requests will queue for access rather than enjoying instantaneous access available when applications have dedicated physical resources. Any resource sharing increases the risk of resource contention, which is typically addressed via some form of serialization via queuing, and queuing entails a wait period, thus accruing latency. Resource contention is more likely to occur as the traffic load on the system increases. Carefully tuned queuing/scheduling strategies are essential to assure that application instances receive timely access to resources so they can deliver acceptable service latency to users. The more aggressive the Infrastructure-as-a-Service (IaaS) supplier is about resource sharing (aka application/workload consolidation or "oversubscription"), the greater the risk of resource contention and hence increased resource access latency and even the possibility of putting a coresident application into overload.
- *Real-Time Notification Latency.* While access to physical resources such as compute cycles, disk storage, or networking are likely to be randomly distributed across time, real-time clock interrupt notifications are inherently synchronized. If multiple application instances request notification for the same real-time clock interrupt event, then some executions may be serialized and thus implicitly shift the real time understood by the applications that are notified later. If the application requires periodic or synchronous real-time notification, such as for streaming media, then any variations in execution timing of application instances can introduce clock event jitter. While the virtualized application may or may not be inherently aware of any notification jitter, end users will directly experience this jitter; if this jitter is severe enough, then the users' quality of experience will degrade. Clock event jitter is discussed further in Section 4.6.
- *Virtualization and Emulation Overhead Latency.* System calls made by application software may pass through the additional layer of hypervisor software in virtualized deployment to access hardware resources, and the additional layer of software may add some latency. Beyond simply proxying access by VM instances to physical resources, virtual machine managers also emulate physical hardware devices, and perhaps even processors and instruction sets; the more elaborate the emulation, the greater the incremental runtime latency. For example, emulating

a processor or instruction set architecture requires far more runtime processing than natively executing application instructions on the target VM server host. Note that the virtualization overhead latency is dramatically shortened as virtualization-enabled processors are deployed and hypervisors evolve to fully leverage hardware support for virtualization.

- *Separating/Decomposing Resources Can Defeat Some Optimizations.* Modern computer and operating system architectures have evolved sophisticated performance optimizations, such as advanced caching strategies. Introducing additional networking latency when storage is not locally accessible to processors and main memory may compromise performance optimizations that were designed for locally accessible mass storage. Likewise, communications between application components executing in VM instances on hosts at opposite sides of a data center may have higher latency (and perhaps lower throughput) than for native compute blades hosted in the same chassis. One can reduce this impact when both optimal affinity rules are fully specified and the cloud service provider is able to honor those rules.
- *CPU Interrupt Response Time Variation and Loading.* As the CPU becomes busier, it takes longer to get around to handling scheduled tasks
- *Live Migration.* Execution of "live" migration events impacts operation of VM instances between the moment the VM instance is paused on one VM server host and the time it is resumed on another VM server host.

4.1.2 Virtualization Overhead

Figure 4.2 overlays service latency data for a sample application ([Riak], an open source NoSQL [NoSQL] distributed database) deployed both with and without virtualization on the same server hardware. The CCDF makes two points instantly apparent:

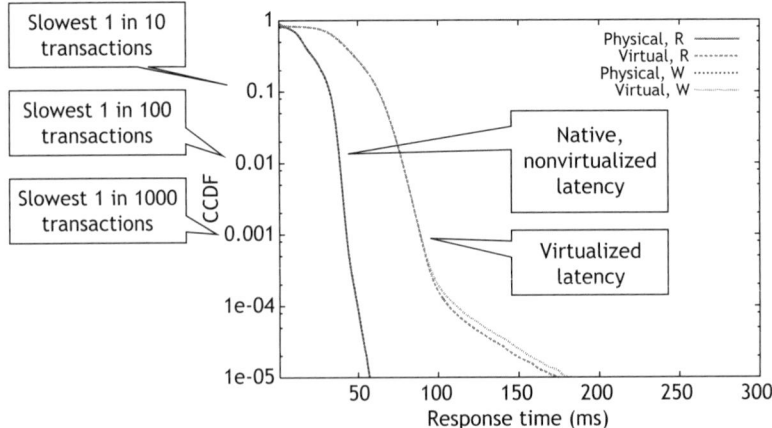

Figure 4.2. Transaction Latency for Riak Benchmark.

- Service latency of the virtualized configuration is substantially greater (i.e., worse) than for native at all points on the statistical distribution.
- The latency tail of the virtualized configuration is far more substantial than the tail of the native distribution.

The authors do not suggest that either the virtualization platform under test or the application of Figure 4.2 are typical, but merely that application service latency on virtualized and cloud-based applications can be materially different from native deployments. The choice and configuration of the underlying hypervisor technology, as well as the architecture of the physical resources and the operational policies of the cloud service provider (e.g., resource utilization factors and scheduling priorities) will all impact the service latency of actual application deployments. The reader's target application will inevitably experience rather different latency curves on native and virtualized deployments.

4.1.3   Increased Variability of Infrastructure Performance

Traditionally deployed applications generally enjoy fairly consistent compute, memory, storage, and local networking performance because once the application software is instantiated on the physical infrastructure, there are often few configuration or operational changes that materially impact the application's access to the resources of the underlying hardware. In contrast, the essential characteristics of resource sharing and rapid elasticity drive cloud service providers to manage their virtualized infrastructure more aggressively to maximize utilization of the underlying physical infrastructure resources. In particular, the cloud service provider controls VM placement, resource scheduling policies, and subsequent migration of individual VM instances, and placement impacts the instantaneous quality and quantity of virtualized resources to an applications' VM instances because coresident application's VM instances are likely to be placing independent demands on shared resources. The service provider's operational policies and architecture will determine how instantaneous resource contention and scheduling issues are resolved, but resource sharing inevitably results in some time- and/or capacity-sharing arrangements for virtualized and cloud-based applications that are not present when applications are deployed directly on unshared native hardware.

To comply with anti-affinity rules, an application's virtual machine instances are likely to be placed across several virtual machine servers, and individual VM instances are likely to be placed on different CPU cores within each virtual machine server based on availability of capacity. As the instantaneous workload of each of the VM instances for each of the applications that are running on each of the VM servers varies from moment to moment, the instantaneous quality and capacity of virtualized infrastructure resources available to each of an application's VM instances will vary, so applications are more likely to experience throughput variations across pools of nominally identical (even identically loaded) application instances when running on cloud infrastructure than when running directly on native hardware.

4.2 VM FAILURE

Applications experience IaaS service via virtual machine instances, which emulate the servers or single-board computers that application software components would traditionally execute on. Virtualization is a complex software technology, so occasional software failures are inevitable. Virtual machine instances ultimately execute on physical servers that will eventually fail. Operationally, a VM failure is any situation that causes the VM instance to cease functioning properly for a cause other than one of the following "normal" VM termination triggers:

1. Explicit request by the cloud consumer (e.g., request via self-service GUI)
2. Explicit "shutdown" request by the application instance itself
3. Explicit termination by IaaS provider for predefined policy reasons, such as nonpayment of bill or executing a lawful takedown order.

Any cause of VM termination that is not attributable to the cloud consumer, the application itself, or for predefined policy reasons is considered a VM failure, including:

- VM termination for the convenience of the IaaS provider rather than for the cloud consumer
- Failure of virtual machine server hardware hosting a VM instance
- Failure of hypervisor or host OS (e.g., crash or panic) hosting a VM instance
- Hardware maintenance error resulting in a failure of resident VMs
- Power failure.

Figure 4.3 illustrates a sample manifestation of VM failure on the sample application of Chapter 2, in which one of the VM instances hosting one of the application's backend components fails. The high-level service quality question becomes exactly what is the customer facing service quality impairment associated with this VM failure? Are pending user operations delayed or completely lost? Is any state information lost?

Measurement of this impairment is considered in Section 14.3.1, "Measurement of VM Failure."

4.3 NONDELIVERY OF CONFIGURED VM CAPACITY

The hypervisor is responsible for providing temporal isolation among VMs, that is, "the capability of isolating the temporal behavior (or limiting the temporal interferences) of multiple VMs among each other, despite them running on the same physical host and sharing a set of physical resources such as processors, memory, and disks" [Wikipedia-TI]. However, it is possible that for a period of time, a particular VM instance will be denied access to virtualized compute, memory, storage, or networking due to live migration, resource sharing/contention, wait time in the scheduling queue, or some other reason. This nondelivery event can be perceived as a VM "stall" or "hiccup" or a loss of processing continuity. Figure 4.4 gives a simplified visualization of a nondelivery of VM

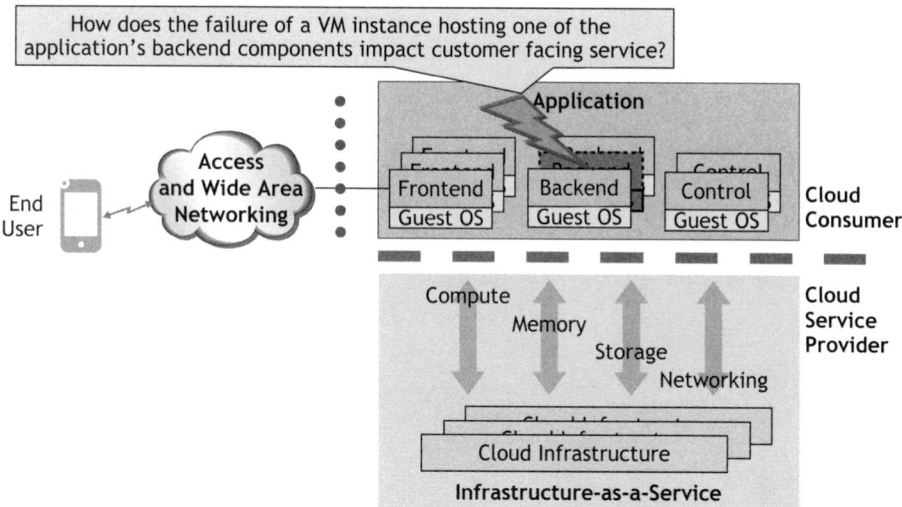

Figure 4.3. VM Failure Impairment Example.

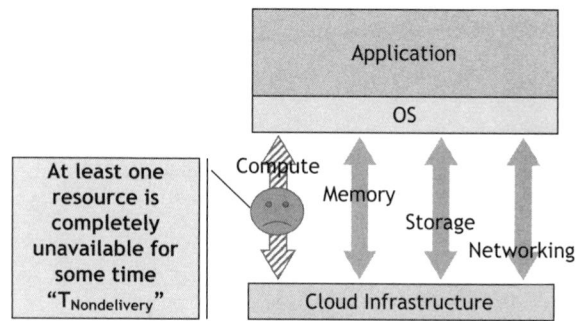

Figure 4.4. Simplified Nondelivery of VM Capacity Model.

capacity scenario: the hypervisor blocks access for a particular virtual machine to one or more resource types for a period of time, in this case compute resource for a time $T_{Nondelivery}$. Obviously, when a VM instance is temporarily denied access to a required resource (e.g., during a live migration event), application service will be impacted because the application component hosted in that VM instance is unable to perform useful work during $T_{Nondelivery}$.

Nondelivery events are easily understood in the context of live VM migration. A nondelivery incident is experienced during live migration when a nominally running (aka "live") VM instance is migrated to another host. Technically, the VM instance is running on $\textbf{Host}_{Source}$ until time $\textbf{T}_{Pause}$, at which point volatile state information and control is transferred to $\textbf{Host}_{Destination}$, and then $\textbf{Host}_{Destination}$ activates the VM instance so it resumes execution at time $\textbf{T}_{Resume}$. $\textbf{T}_{Nondelivery}$ is then the elapsed time between $\textbf{T}_{Resume}$ and $\textbf{T}_{Pause}$, as shown in Figure 4.5. Nondelivery "hiccup" or "stall" events can also occur due to congestion or other reasons. Note that (e.g., VM "stall") events can also cause the VM instance's perception of real time to skew; real-time clock drift within VM instances is considered in Section 4.7, "Clock Drift."

Figure 4.6 illustrates a manifestation of this impairment in which the VM instance hosting one of the application's backend components stalls for hundreds of milliseconds. Does the end user experience much slower service, or do impacted operations fail outright (after timeout), or does user service hang, or is there some other user visible impact across the application's customer facing service boundary?

Measurement of this impairment is considered in Section 14.3.2, "Measurement of Nondelivery of Configured VM Capacity."

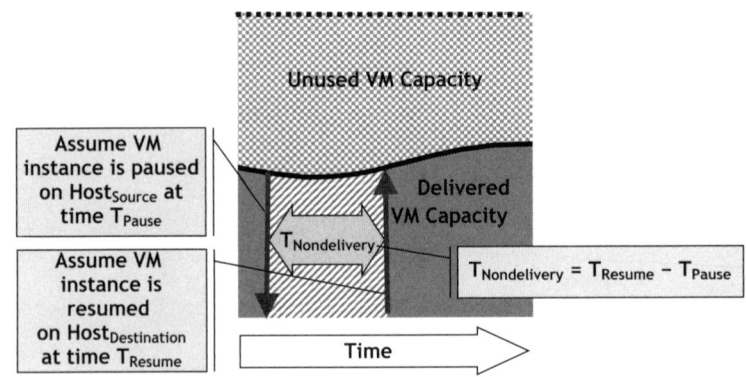

Figure 4.5. Characterizing Virtual Machine Nondelivery.

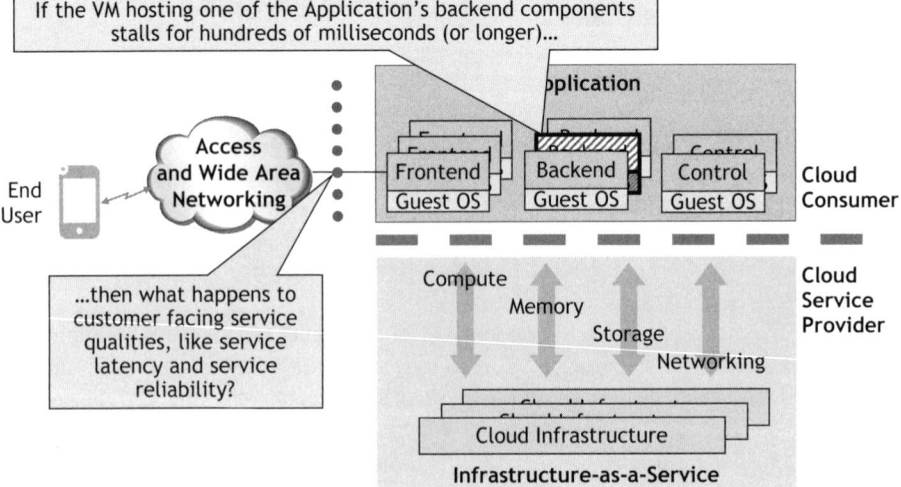

Figure 4.6. Nondelivery Impairment Example.

4.4   DELIVERY OF DEGRADED VM CAPACITY

Resource sharing is an essential characteristic of cloud computing, and IaaS service providers rely on virtual machine managers and other mechanisms to implement policies to manage resource access, sharing, and contention. Figure 4.7 gives a simple visualization of a degraded delivery of VM capacity scenario: storage bandwidth available to a particular application in a VM instance is restricted for a period $T_{Degraded}$ when diminished resource capacity is delivered to the VM instance because one or more other applications in other virtual machine instances are making heavy demands on shared storage resources so the hypervisor delivers less storage bandwidth to the application's VM instance than usual. When resource requests by applications approach or exceed the physical capacity of the shared infrastructure, some requests will be deferred (e.g., queued) and others will be flow controlled (e.g., bandwidth/rate limited). Figure 4.8 visualizes the timeline of a degraded VM capacity event: the resource capacity delivered to the VM instance is diminished by $C_{Degraded}$ for some period $T_{Degraded}$.

Another example of degraded delivery could arise based on CPU frequency scaling. To reduce power consumption when utilization is low, the CPU frequency of VM server hosts may be reduced. This will increase the latency of processing requests, as the CPU will run slower and take longer to complete any request. This can produce the paradoxical result of potentially delivering higher latency when the system is mostly idle. The system may experience periods of degraded delivery of disk resources due to inefficient disk space allocation or insufficient resources allocated resulting in system performance issues or failures. The system may experience higher networking latency if congestion leads the infrastructure to discard IP packets, which triggers retransmission after some timeout interval has elapsed. Other reasons for periods of degraded delivery include lumpy scheduling, interrupt coalescence, and jitter-related artifacts, all of which could hinder provision of sufficient resources to the VM(s) to meet capacity needs.

Figure 4.9 illustrates a scenario in which the VM hosting one of the application's backend components delivers degraded networking capacity (i.e., dropped IP

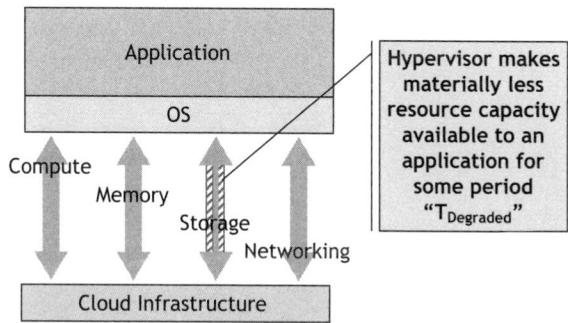

Figure 4.7. Simple Virtual Machine Degraded Delivery Model.

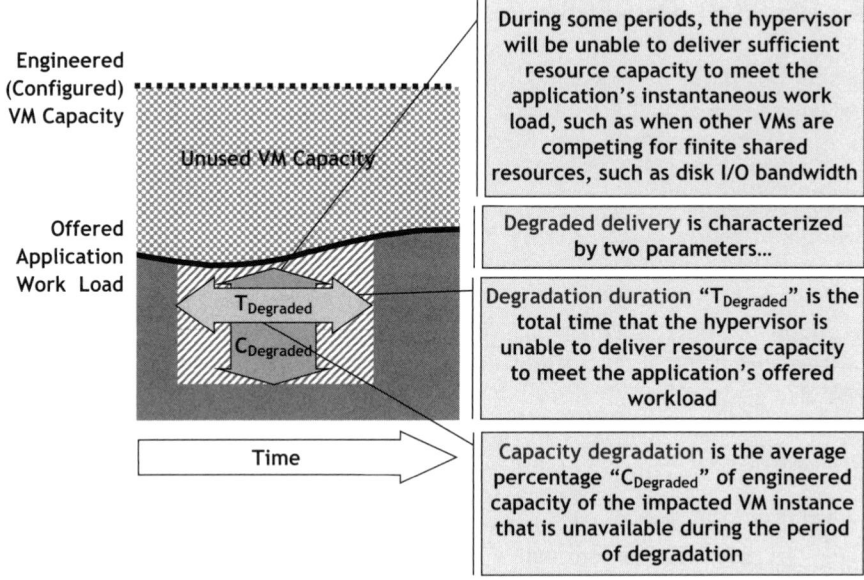

Figure 4.8. Degraded Resource Capacity Model.

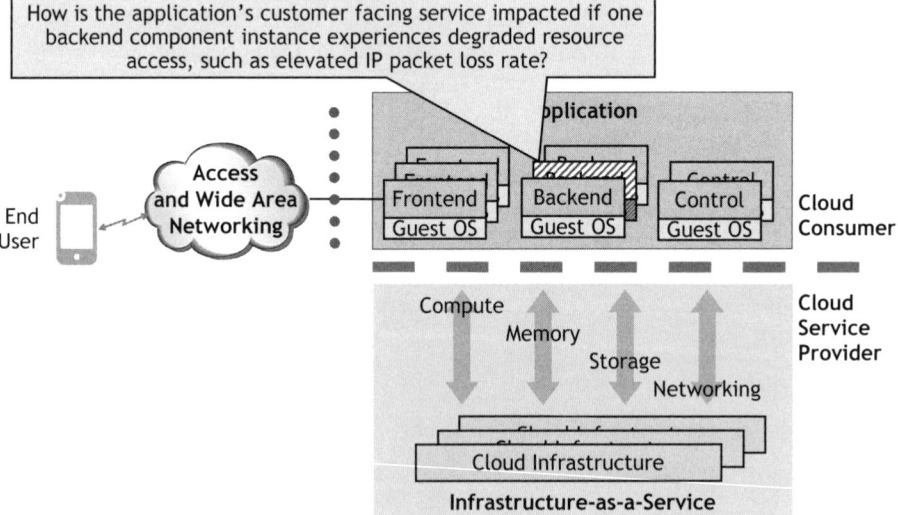

Figure 4.9. Degraded Delivery Impairment Example.

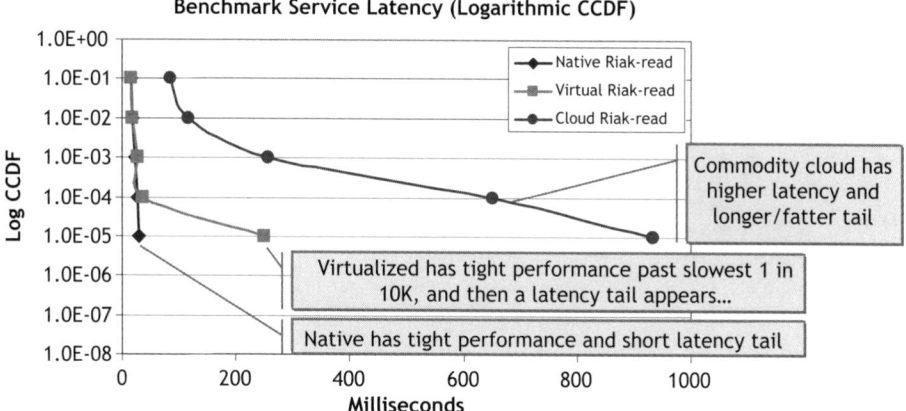

Figure 4.10. CCDF for Riak Read Benchmark for Three Different Hosting Configurations.

packets) due to resource contention by other VM instances. The service quality question then becomes what happens to the application's customer facing service if tens or hundreds of IP packets per million are dropped before reaching the backend component?

Measurement of this impairment is considered in Section 14.3.3 "Measurement of Delivery of Degraded VM capacity."

4.5   TAIL LATENCY

As discussed in Section 4.1, "Service Latency, Virtualization, and the Cloud," virtualization machine managers and increased resource sharing often cause resource access latencies to be worse than on native hardware, especially for occasional outlier events in the statistical "tail" [Dean]. Figure 4.10 shows a CCDF for a read benchmark against the Riak open source database running either natively (i.e., no virtualization) or under virtualization on the same dedicated hardware, or running on a commercial cloud. The CCDF clearly shows that while tail latency of native (nonvirtualized) hosts is very close to typical latency read benchmark, virtualization for this configuration adds a material latency tail to the slowest few samples per hundred thousand, and cloud-hosting causes a significant latency tail that materially slows at least a few requests per thousand.

Figure 4.11 illustrates a manifestation of this impairment in which the slowest one in several thousand backend requests are, perhaps 20 times slower than the slowest 1 in 10 operations. The question becomes, what happens to the latency, reliability, and overall quality of application service delivered to end users?

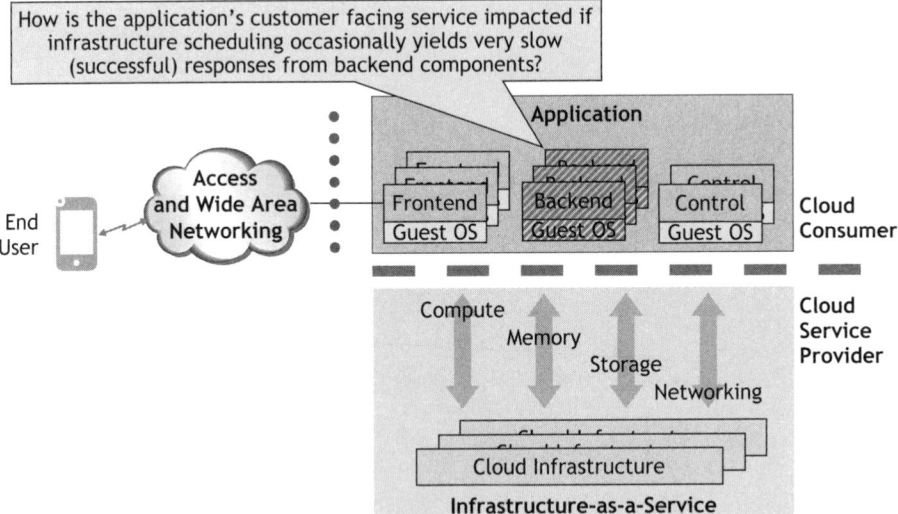

Figure 4.11. Tail Latency Impairment Example.

Measurement of this impairment is considered in Section 14.3.4, "Measurement of Tail Latency."

4.6 CLOCK EVENT JITTER

Strict real-time applications, such as those that handle bearer traffic, such as interactive video, often rely on consistent clock events to minimize jitter in application packets delivered to end users. Jitter introduced by tardy or coalesced clock interrupt events can directly impact the quality of service delivered to end users. Hypervisor overhead and other factors associated with virtualization and cloud can introduce clock event jitter impairments beyond what native deployments experience. Figure 4.12 gives a CCDF of test results illustrating clock event jitter across hundreds of millions of 1-ms clock events on tuned infrastructure.

The impact of this impairment is easily understood in the context of a conferencing bridge, which combines real-time streaming media from multiple end users into a seamless audio/video teleconference. As shown in Figure 4.13, each user's device sends streaming media (e.g., RTP) to the conferencing bridge, and during every timer interrupt, the conferencing bridge combines the live streams sent from each of the participants' devices into a single merged stream, which is sent back to all of the participants. If a clock event for the conferencing bridge is late, then the conference bridge is unable to deliver a consistent isochronous stream of media to end users' devices so packets arrive too late to be smoothly rendered to users requiring devices to engage lost packet compensation mechanisms (e.g., replaying stale packets and freezing video image) to minimize user service quality impact.

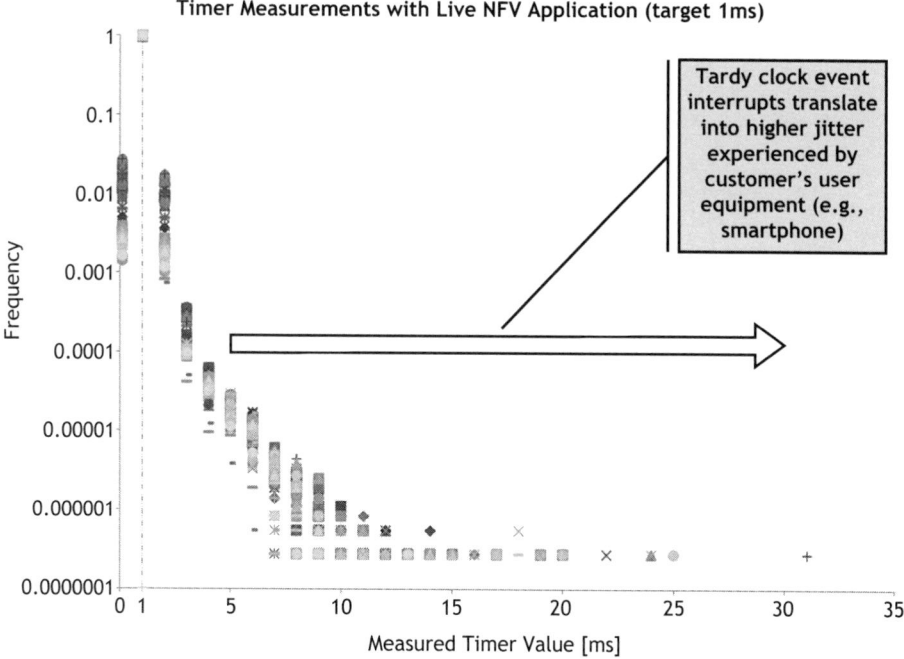

Figure 4.12. Sample CCDF for Virtualized Clock Event Jitter.

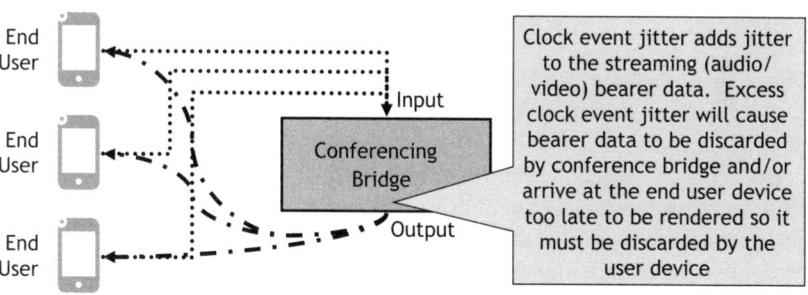

Figure 4.13. Clock Event Jitter Impairment Example.

4.7 CLOCK DRIFT

Coordinated universal time (UTC) is the standard time reference against which clock accuracy is measured. Host computers periodically synchronize their local clocks with a known accurate reference clock (often synchronized to NIST.gov, GPS, etc.) via the network time protocol (NTP, RFC 5905) or the precision time protocol (PTP, IEEE 1588). Application components generally rely on the underlying guest operating system to maintain an accurate clock for time stamping event records and for other uses.

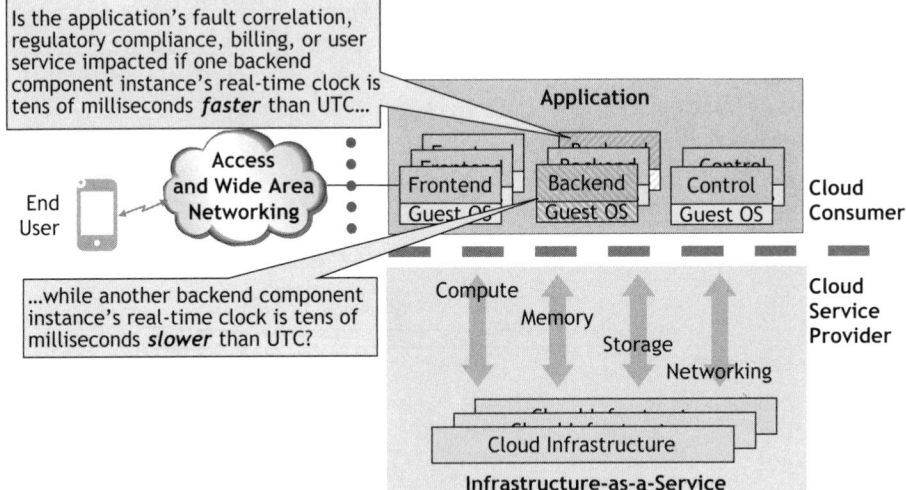

Figure 4.14. Clock Drift Impairment Example.

Decoupling the guest OS from the underlying hardware via virtualization and live migration, which can surreptitiously move an application and guest OS instance between hardware hosts, creates risks that additional clock drift (error) will confront applications deployed to cloud. While this drift is unlikely to be large (e.g., seconds or minutes), some applications may be sensitive to even small clock drifts (e.g., microseconds or milliseconds).

Figure 4.14 illustrates a scenario in which the real-time clocks of the application's backend component instances drift from UTC by several milliseconds so one backend instance is somewhat faster than UTC and one is somewhat slower. This clock drift means that requests served by some backend component instances will be stamped with incorrect times, so subsequent attempts to reconstruct the order of actions that occurred almost simultaneously across different backend components may be missequenced.

Measurement of this impairment is considered in Section 14.3.6, "Measurement of Clock Drift."

4.8 FAILED OR SLOW ALLOCATION AND STARTUP OF VM INSTANCE

VM allocation, configuration, and startup of application component instances is critical to "on boarding" applications, growing online capacity, and software release management. Allocation and configuration of a VM instance followed by guest OS plus application software within that allocated VM instance is a complex, multistep process that is susceptible to many risks that can either cause the operation to fail outright or to be too slow and thus fail to complete within the maximum acceptable time. The impact of failed or slow allocation and startup of VM instances is considered in Chapter 8, "Capacity Management." Measurement of this impairment is considered in Section 14.3.7, "Measurement of Failed or Slow Allocation and Startup of VM Instance."

4.9 OUTLOOK FOR VIRTUALIZED INFRASTRUCTURE IMPAIRMENTS

As the popularity of virtualization and cloud computing grows, infrastructure hardware and software suppliers will focus on improving the performance of their virtualized infrastructure offerings. These improvements, along with the benefits of Moore's Law, will improve the quality and consistency of virtualized compute, memory, storage, and networking delivered to applications' virtual machine instances. In the long run, the frequency and severity of at least some of these infrastructure impairments should materially decrease, but as John Maynard Keynes wrote in 1927:

> The long run is a misleading guide to current affairs. In the long run we are all dead. Economists [and engineers] set themselves too easy, too useless a task if in tempestuous seasons they can only tell us that when the storm is past the ocean is flat again. [Keynes]

Thus, Part II: Analysis considers how these virtualized infrastructure impairments are likely to impact applications in the medium and short run, and Part III: Recommendations offers guidance on how to mitigate the risk of application service impact due to virtualized infrastructure impairments.

II

ANALYSIS

This part of the book analyzes how qualities of the customer facing service offered by cloud based applications are impacted by both the benefits and the risks of cloud deployment.

- *Chapter 5, "Application Redundancy and Cloud Computing,"* reviews fundamental redundancy architectures (simplex, sequential redundancy, concurrent redundancy and hybrid concurrent redundancy) and considers their ability to mitigate application service quality impact when confronted with virtualized infrastructure impairments.
- *Chapter 6, "Load Distribution and Balancing,"* methodically analyzes work load distribution and balancing for applications.
- *Chapter 7, "Failure Containment,"* considers how virtualization and cloud impact failure containment strategies for applications.
- *Chapter 8, "Capacity Management,"* methodically analyzes application service risks related to elastic online capacity growth and degrowth.
- *Chapter 9, "Release Management,"* considers how virtualization and cloud impact release management actions to patch, update, upgrade, and retrofit application software.

Service Quality of Cloud-Based Applications, First Edition. Eric Bauer and Randee Adams.
© 2014 The Institute of Electrical and Electronics Engineers, Inc. Published 2014 by John Wiley & Sons, Inc.

- *Chapter 10, "End-to-End Considerations,"* explains how application service quality impairments accumulate across the service delivery path. The chapter also considers service quality implications of deploying applications to smaller cloud data centers that are closer to end users versus deploying to larger, regional cloud data centers that are farther from end users. Disaster recovery and geo-redundancy are also discussed.

5

APPLICATION REDUNDANCY AND CLOUD COMPUTING

Component redundancy is deployed to mitigate the service impact of inevitable failures. This chapter considers how simplex, traditional (sequential) redundancy and nontraditional (concurrent) redundancy architectures mitigate the application service impacts of virtualized infrastructure impairments. Section 5.2 explains how virtualization technology can improve software restore times, and Section 5.3 explains how virtualization and cloud can improve infrastructure restore times. Section 5.4 explains how redundant architectures improve service availability by rapidly recovering service to a redundant component rather than requiring a failure to be repaired before user service can be restored. Section 5.5 compares and contrasts sequential redundancy with concurrent redundancy arrangements. Section 5.6 methodically considers the application service impact of virtualized infrastructure impairments on simplex, sequential redundant, concurrent redundant, and hybrid concurrent redundant architectures. Section 5.7 discusses the role of data in redundancy. Section 5.8 discusses overall redundancy considerations.

Service Quality of Cloud-Based Applications, First Edition. Eric Bauer and Randee Adams.
© 2014 The Institute of Electrical and Electronics Engineers, Inc. Published 2014 by John Wiley & Sons, Inc.

5.1 FAILURES, AVAILABILITY, AND SIMPLEX ARCHITECTURES

Failures are inevitable, so applications must be prepared to cope with components that fail. Distributed systems are also vulnerable to transient events, such as dropped IP packets, as well as more persistent failures, such as crashed software processes (see Section 16.4.3, "Robustness Testing," for a broad list of common failure scenarios). Consider the simple distributed system of Figure 5.1 with a client application "A" that interacts with a server "B1." Traditional simplex operation entails one and only one application instance (e.g., "B1") serving any particular user instance (e.g., "A"). Thus, when an application component "B1" (in Figure 5.1) fails, all state and volatile information held by the server is lost, as well as all networking context (e.g., sessions with client devices). Note that persistent storage should remain intact, because that is what "persistent" means.

Figure 5.2 illustrates a service availability timeline for a simplex system in which the server "B1" is "up" (available to serve client "A") until the server fails (nominally after the Mean Time between Failures or MTBF), and the server is down until the failure is repaired and service is restored (nominally after the Mean Time to Restore Service or MTRS). MTRS is sometimes called maintainability.

As explained in Section 2.5.1, "Service Availability," availability is the portion of total time that a service is up. For simplex systems, one can compute service availability via Equation 5.1, simplex availability:

$$\text{Availability} = \frac{\text{MTBF}}{\text{MTBF} + \text{MTRS}}. \qquad (5.1)$$

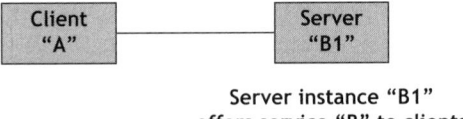

Server instance "B1"
offers service "B" to clients

Figure 5.1. Simplex Distributed System.

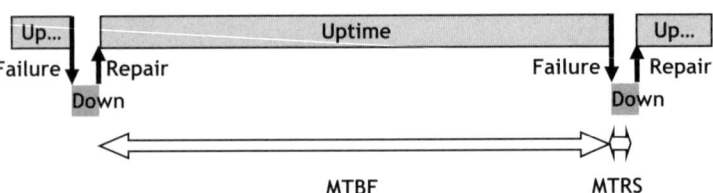

Figure 5.2. Simplex Service Availability.

Note that for simplex systems, the Mean Time to Repair (MTTR) is generally equal to the MTRS, and thus the simplex availability of Equation 5.1 is equivalent to the traditional availability formula of Equation 5.2 that most readers will be familiar with.

$$\text{Availability} = \frac{\text{MTBF}}{\text{MTBF} + \text{MTTR}}. \tag{5.2}$$

Maintainability is a measure of how quickly and effectively a configuration item or IT service can be restored to normal working order after a failure, and is often measured and reported as MTRS. Maintainability for a simplex system includes three steps:

1. *Failure Detection.* Automatic failure detection is often fairly prompt (nominally minutes or seconds), but if the system relies on manual failure detection (e.g., end-users reporting trouble through customer support processes), then it might take tens of minutes or longer for the application service provider's maintenance engineers to realize that a component instance is not properly serving users. As a practical matter, client "A" distinguishes two classes of failures:
   a. *Explicit failures* are explicitly signaled to the client "A," typically via an error response, such as 500 Server Internal Error. Upon receipt of an explicit failure indication, the client unambiguously knows that the server is currently unable to properly service the client's request, so the client "A" must somehow address the failure condition (e.g., returning failure indication to the end user) and a maintenance engineer must resolve the failure condition of server "B1."
   b. *Implicit failures* occur when the client "A" infers that a request failed because no response is received in a reasonable time.
2. *Troubleshooting* the failure to identify the failed component and determine what repair action must be taken to restore service. Troubleshooting the cause of failure is typically at least partially manual, and thus may take time.
3. *Repairing the Failed Unit and Restoring Service.* Repair actions, such as restarting an application, rebooting a system, replacing failed hardware, reinstalling software, and restoring backed up data, can take minutes to hours, or longer if necessary spare parts or backup media is not physically on site at the time of the failure. Since restoring service of traditional simplex systems requires human involvement, logistical delays associated with notifying and scheduling appropriately trained staff, as well as transportation time of staff and/or replacement hardware, can prolong outage duration.

Service for simplex systems is unavailable to users until all three of these tasks are accomplished. Overall, outage durations for simplex (nonredundant) systems often stretch to hours or even longer on traditional systems. Improving maintainability, thereby shortening MTRS, improves service availability. Figure 5.3 shows service availability as a function of MTRS by solving Equation 5.1 with a constant failure rate.

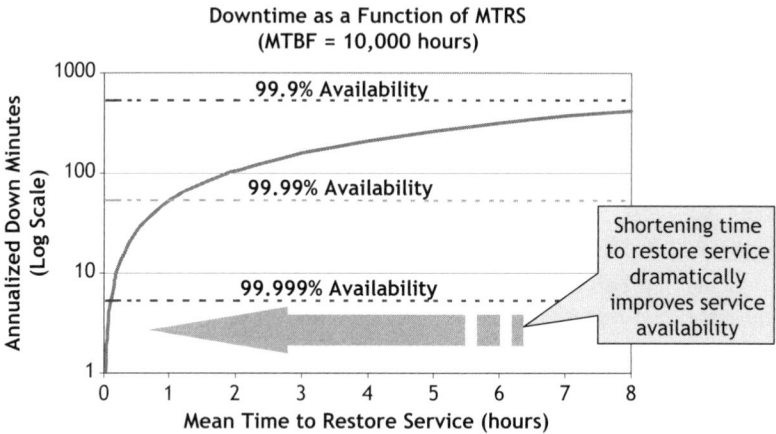

Figure 5.3. Sensitivity of Service Availability to MTRS (Log Scale).

5.2 IMPROVING SOFTWARE REPAIR TIMES VIA VIRTUALIZATION

Software failures of traditionally deployed simplex application components are typically repaired via one of two options:

1. Application software is restarted.
2. Operating system is rebooted.

Software repair typically covers "rejuvenating" the application to return the software to an operational state rather than correcting the true root cause of failure. Resolv-
ing the true root cause of a software failure often requires installing a software patch
that corrects the residual defect that produced the failure event.

As Figure 5.4 shows, virtualization offers several new repair options for software
failures. From slowest to fastest, the virtualized restoration options are the following:

- *Virtual Machine (VM) Reset.* A VM can be reset by causing a transition from
  deactivate to activate (a hard VM boot) without a corresponding deallocation
  and reallocation of virtual resources. It is disruptive—like turning off and on a
  computer—and thus state information will be lost. A VM reset has longer latencies than a reboot of the VM.
- *VM Reboot.* Guest OS and application software can be rebooted without resetting the entire virtual machine instance.
- *Activate VM Snapshot.* VM snapshot is a mechanism that preserves a copy of a
  VM image at a certain instant in time that includes the VM's memory contents,
  settings, and virtual disk state. Once the snapshot has been successfully created,

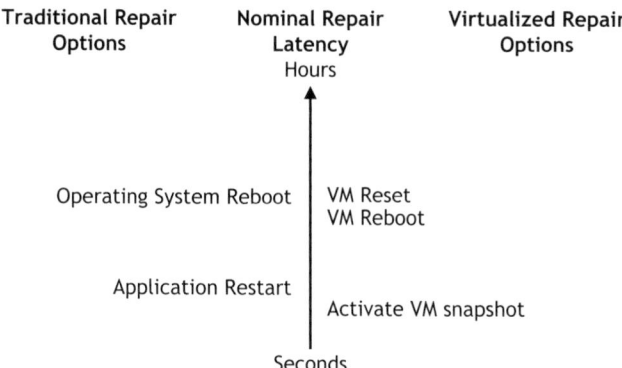

Figure 5.4. Traditional versus Virtualized Software Repair Times.

it may be immediately activated or stored for later activation. A VM snapshot is a useful repair mechanism, as it provides a means of recovering from a failure in one version of the VM to a more stable (i.e., prefailure) version. Following a failure, a previously recorded VM snapshot can be restored from disk and activated faster than a traditional cold restart because the snapshot activation bypasses time-consuming application startup actions, since those tasks would have been performed before the snapshot was taken and thus do not need to be repeated. Snapshots may be taken:

○ *Of a Freshly Booted Application Instance.* Activating a fresh boot snapshot can significantly reduce recovery time by skipping OS and application startup times.
○ *Periodically.* Note that if the periodic snapshot captured the evolving failure, like a memory leak shortly before total heap exhaustion, then the periodic snapshot would not reliably clear the failure. Thus, periodic snapshot recoveries should always be prepared to fall back to a fresh boot snapshot or an OS restart, if the periodic snapshot recovery is unsuccessful.

Since it represents an older version of the VM, snapshot activation may not offer seamless service recovery for the user in the event of a failure since it will not likely have the most recent state and session information.

To shorten the duration of service impact, both human and automatic mechanisms will generally trigger the fastest recovery mechanism that is likely to clear the failure rather than completing an exhaustive troubleshooting analysis to pinpoint the true root cause of failure. If the fastest recovery action fails to resolve the problem, then a more aggressive—and presumably slower and/or more impactful—recovery action can be executed. For example, if an application component hangs, then the first recovery action might be to activate a fresh boot snapshot of the application component. If that fails to restore service, then the VM instance might reset.

5.3 IMPROVING INFRASTRUCTURE REPAIR TIMES VIA VIRTUALIZATION

As shown in Figure 5.5, virtualization and cloud computing enable traditional, manual hardware repair processes to be replaced with offline VM migration, which can be automated to dramatically shorten infrastructure repair times. Section 5.3.1 explains traditional hardware repair; Section 5.3.2 explains automatic VM Repair-as-a-Service (RaaS); and Section 5.3.3 discusses the implications of these mechanisms.

5.3.1 Understanding Hardware Repair

MTTR is a mature and widely used concept. This chapter will use the ITILv3 definition of MTTR [ITILv3MTTR]: *"the average time taken to repair a Configuration Item or IT Service after a Failure. MTTR is measured from when the CI or IT Service fails until it is Repaired. MTTR does not include the time required to Recover or Restore."* MTTR for computers and information systems hardware is often assumed to be 4 hours for equipment in locations with staff and spare hardware units on-site. Rigorous training and sophisticated operational policies can shorten hardware MTTR, or more generous support arrangements can be made with slower respond/restore/resolve requirements with longer hardware MTTR targets and lower costs. Note that MTRS is a related measurement that is often confused with MTTR. The ITILv3 definition of MTRS [ITILv3MTRS] is *"the average time taken to Restore a Configuration Item or IT Service after a Failure. MTRS is measured from when the CI or IT Service fails until it is fully Restored and delivering its normal functionality."*

5.3.2 VM Repair-as-a-Service

As virtualization and cloud technology eliminate the need for physical maintenance actions to repair application components impacted by infrastructure failures, it becomes practical to deploy automated "VM RaaS" mechanisms rather than relying on manual actions by application maintenance engineers to return an application to normal

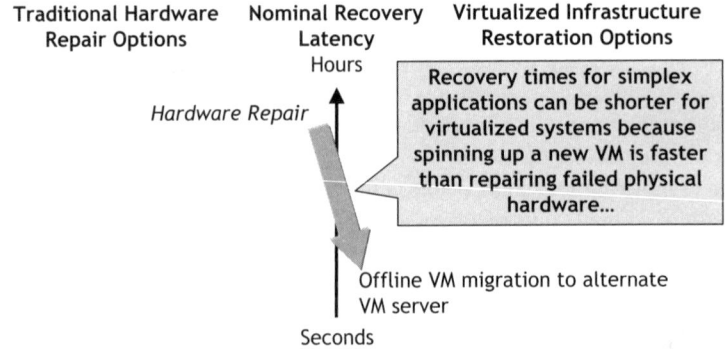

Figure 5.5. Traditional Hardware Repair versus Virtualized Infrastructure Restoration Times.

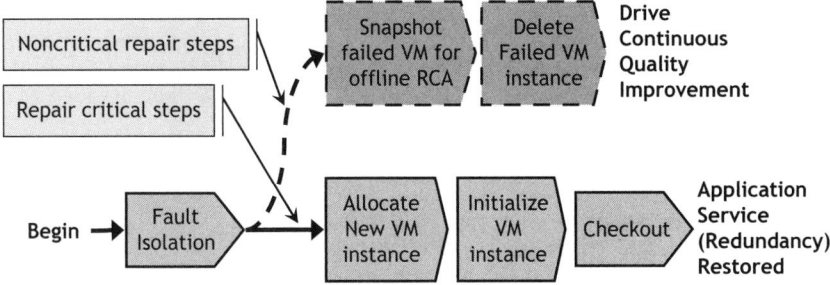

Figure 5.6. Simplified VM Repair Logic.

operation following an infrastructure failure. After identifying the faulty VM instance to be repaired, the automated VM repair logic splits into two parallel procedures shown in Figure 5.6:

- *Repair Critical Steps.* This replaces the failed VM instance and returns the application to full operational status (e.g., redundant operation). This procedure consists of:
  ○ Automated allocation and configuration of replacement vm instance
  ○ Automated initialization and startup of replacement vm instance or activation of vm snapshot
  ○ Automated checkout of replacement VM instance.

This procedure concludes when the replacement VM instance is properly integrated with the running application component instance. Note that this activity must not interfere with service recovery activities provided by the application.

- *Noncritical Procedure.* Includes tasks that are not in the critical repair path of replacing the failed VM instance, so these noncritical tasks can be executed in parallel to the repair critical procedure. The primary noncritical tasks are:
  ○ Capture VM failure, configuration, and snapshot data for offline analysis.
  ○ Release and cleanup (e.g., delete) failed and no longer needed resources.

The cloud consumer and/or cloud service provider can decide which VM failure events to analyze to true root cause as a means to identify proper corrective actions so service quality can be continuously improved.

As these automated actions are likely to complete in minutes rather than nominally hours for traditional hardware repairs, it is important to recognize that the failure detection process, which activates the automated VM repair process, can also be automated to further shorten MTTR. For instance, if the application's management and control function automatically signals the automated VM repair mechanisms about the failure after it has recovered service, then the VM repair can begin seconds after the VM failure event occurs. Fully automating failure detection and activation of repair service process is obviously much faster than traditional processes, in which a hardware failure alarm

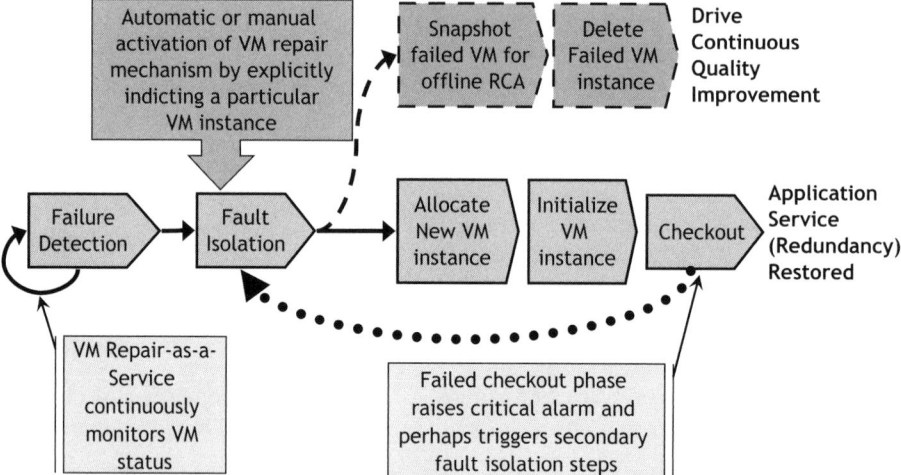

Figure 5.7. Sample Automated Virtual Machine Repair-as-a-Service Logic.

causes a maintenance engineer to create a trouble ticket that is dispatched to initiate the traditional hardware repair process.

The VM repair logic of Figure 5.6 can be integrated into a fully automated VM RaaS, which implements the service logic illustrated in Figure 5.7. VM RaaS adds the following key features to the basic logic of Figure 5.6:

- RaaS can implement a surveillance mechanism to proactively detect VM instance failures. When the automated VM instance failure detection mechanism indicts a VM instance, that instance is reported to the fault isolation element to begin the VM repair process.
- Faulty VM instance can be explicitly reported to the RaaS offering. For example, the application's management and control infrastructure can explicitly identify a faulty VM instance to be repaired immediately after the application's high availability mechanism successfully restores user service after failure. VM instances to be repaired can also be manually identified via appropriate GUI or command line mechanisms.
- Checkout phase raises a critical alarm if the automated repair action failed to recover service so that a human maintenance engineer can troubleshoot the problem. Some RaaS offerings may be smart enough to support secondary fault isolation and recovery logic if the primary repair action fails to resolve the problem.

5.3.3   Discussion

Virtualization and cloud computing enable cloud consumers to treat virtual machines as "disposable" rather than repairable units. While traditional disassemble/interchange/

reassemble procedures are impractical to automate, replacement (nominally "repair") of VM instances can largely be automated, which enables both cycle time reduction, reduced risk of procedural errors during repair action, and lower cost per failure event. Shorter repair times dramatically improve the service availability of simplex (i.e., nonredundant) applications and components, and actual repair times are likely to vary based on efficiency and effectiveness of automated VM RaaS offerings, so more sophisticated availability models should be used for simplex applications protected by VM RaaS offerings. Shorter repair times due to automating "VM RaaS" offers the potential to reduce the window of simplex or reduced capacity exposure following virtual machine failure of redundant and highly available applications.

5.4 REDUNDANCY AND RECOVERABILITY

Figure 5.8 illustrates the simplified redundancy model that will be used throughout this work: client instance "A" can access service "B" from a pool of application server instances "B1" thru "B*n*." If "B1" is unable to serve client "A"s request promptly, then service is recovered to another server instance (e.g., "B2"), and the request is retried to that redundant server instance. As explained in Section 5.1, real distributed applications often include multiple tiers of interacting components so a component may logically be a server when interacting with some software entities and a client when interacting with other entities.

In contrast to a simplex architecture that typically required at least some manual troubleshooting and repair to recover service, redundant architectures enable the entire recovery process to be automated, as shown in Figure 5.9. Following a failure (1), the system should rapidly, automatically detect the failure (2), then isolate the failure to a recoverable unit (3), and rapidly, automatically recover service to a redundant component (4), thereby restoring service for users (5). The objective of high availability, mechanisms is to automatically detect a failure, isolate/identify the failed component and recover user service to an operational component as fast as possible to minimize

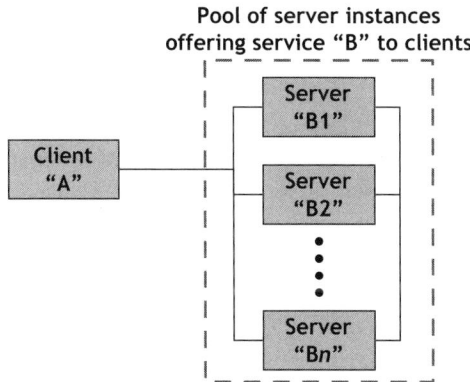

Figure 5.8. Simple Redundancy Model.

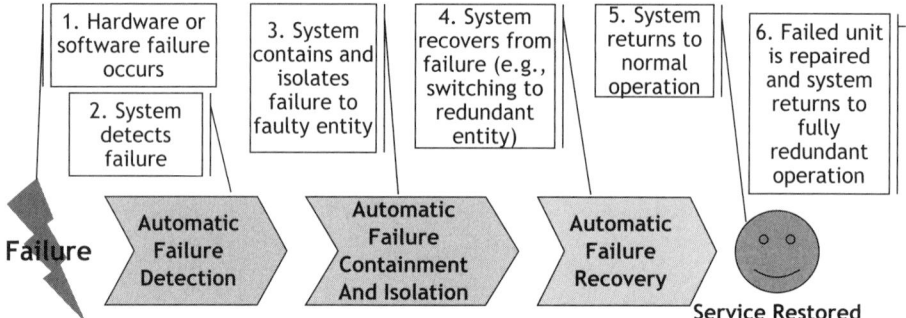

Figure 5.9. Simplified High Availability Strategy.

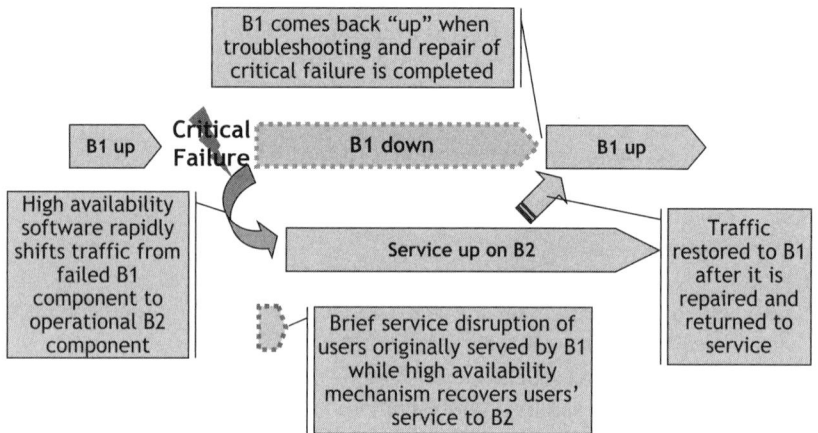

Figure 5.10. Failure in a Traditional (Sequential) Redundant Architecture.

user impact. While it is infeasible for this all to be instantaneous, the goal is for this to be faster than the maximum acceptable service disruption time so that failure events only impact service reliability metrics (e.g., failed transactions per million attempts) rather than accruing chargeable service downtime and thus also impacting service availability metrics (e.g., service downtime). Although repairing a failure requires careful troubleshooting of the root cause of failure (e.g., which hardware component or software module failed), in redundant architectures, one must merely isolate the failure to the correct redundant unit so that the appropriate automatic recovery mechanism can be activated. Traditional highly available systems with redundancy routinely mitigate user service disruptions due to failure in seconds or less. Note that the true root cause of the primary failure must still be repaired to return the system to protected full redundancy, but that repair can be completed as a nonemergency maintenance action.

As shown in Figure 5.10, the primary serving unit ("B1") is down for essentially the same time as with a simplex architecture, yet user service can be restored quickly by redirecting user traffic to a redundant unit "B2," which can assume new and existing traffic. Thus, the duration of user service impact is far shorter (nominally seconds) than for simplex architectures.

As shown in Figure 5.11 traditional high availability is implemented via redundant hardware and software (e.g., a redundant server instance "B2" to protect "B1"), and requests are unicast to one and only one of the redundant server instances at a time (i.e., either "B1" or "B2," not both). This architecture depends heavily on fast detection and recovery from failures. Note that proxy load balancing technologies discussed in Chapter 6, "Load Distribution and Balancing," can shield the client from complexities of server redundancy.

Figure 5.12 shows a timeline of normal user service of a sequential redundancy system when no failure exists: client "A" sends a request to server instance "B1"; and "B1" successfully processes the request and sends a response back to client "A." Server instance "B2" is not involved in the transaction because "B1" successfully served client "A."

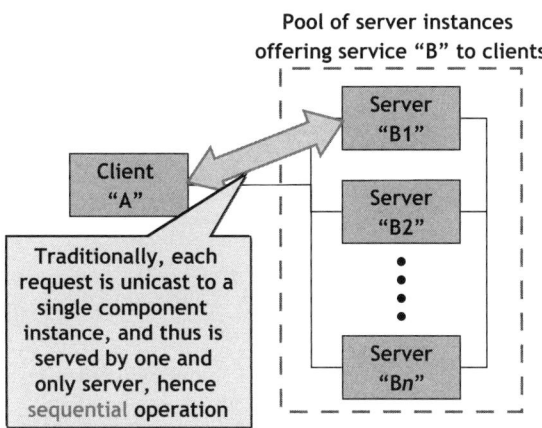

Figure 5.11. Sequential Redundancy Model.

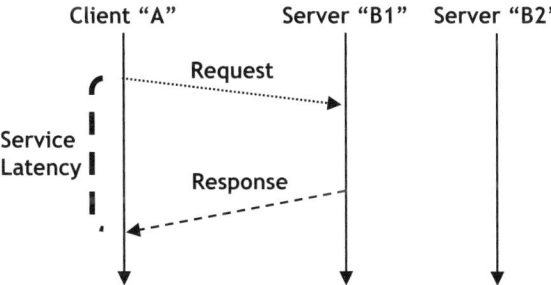

Figure 5.12. Sequential Redundant Architecture Timeline with No Failures.

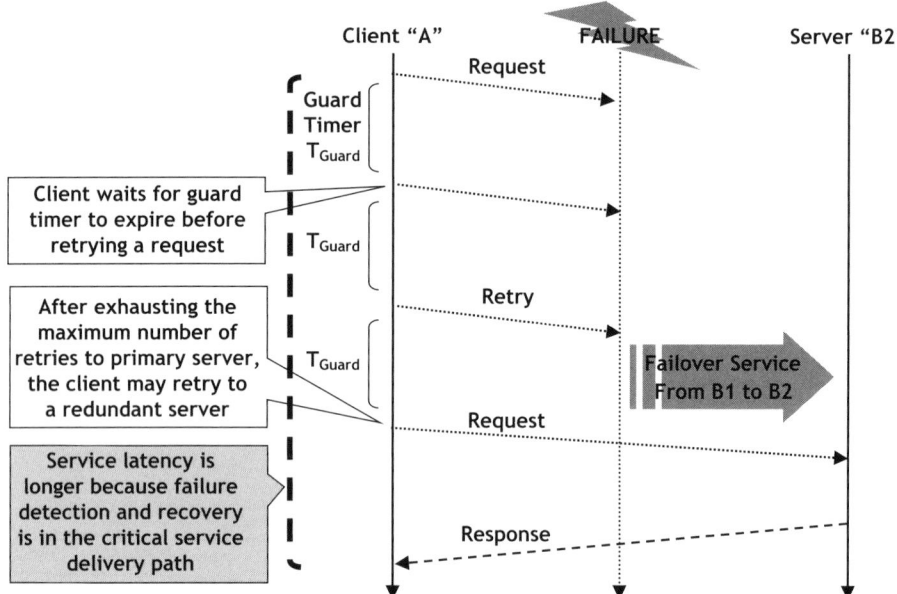

Figure 5.13. Sample Redundant Architecture Timeline with Implicit Failure.

Figure 5.13 shows a user service timeline of recovery from a major component failure for a sequential redundancy system:

- Client "A" sends a request to server instance "B1."
- As server instance "B1" has experienced a major failure, it is incapable of returning any explicit failure indication to client "A."
- Guard timer maintained by client "A" expires without a response from server instance "B1" being received, so client "A" retries the request to "B1."
- Additional guard timeout periods expire, followed by retries until client "A" reaches its MaximumRetryCount value, and service is failed over from server instance "B1" to "B2."
- Client "A" sends the service request to server instance "B2."
- Server instance "B2" promptly returns a successful reply to client "A."

Note that failover might be controlled by monitoring software implemented in the application's high availability infrastructure rather than via client software.

In some cases, the primary serving unit "B1" remains sufficiently functional to return an explicit failure response to client "A," so "A" can failover to "B2" as soon as explicit failure response is received rather than waiting for repeated requests to "B1" to time out. As shown in Figure 5.14, user service recovery is faster when the primary unit rapidly and explicitly signals failure to client "A" via a response, such as 500 Server Internal Error.

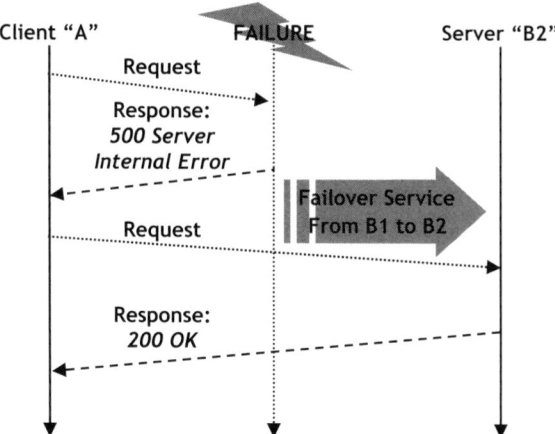

Figure 5.14. Sample Redundant Architecture Timeline with Explicit Failure.

5.4.1 Improving Recovery Times via Virtualization

Redundant units can be configured across a range of states of readiness, which affect how quickly the redundant unit can recover user service, and thus directly impact service outage duration. While the exact meaning (i.e., state of readiness) of "cold," "warm," and "hot" standby vary from industry to industry, generally the hotter the standby, the faster the service recovery. For example, a fully booted standby application instance can recover service faster than a server that has booted the operating system but not started the application, and both of those arrangements can recover service faster than a standby server that is not even powered on.

Virtualization introduces several new recovery options that consume less physical resources than traditional redundancy configurations. Figure 5.15 gives a side-by-side timeline of both traditional and virtualized recovery strategies for redundant architectures and their associated nominal recovery latency. From slower to faster, the new virtualized recovery options are:

- *Activate Suspended VM.* VMs in the "suspended state" are disabled from performing tasks. The state of the virtual machine and its resources are saved to nonvolatile storage, and virtual resources may be deallocated. Application component instances can be started up in VMs, and those VM instances can be suspended; following failure, a suspended VM instance can be activated, resynchronized, and begin serving users. Suspended VM instances are sleeping "deeply," so there is more incremental recovery latency compared with activating a "paused" VM instance, and even more latency compared to active or hot standby VM redundancy; however, even fewer virtualized platform resources are consumed to support suspended VM redundancy.
- *Activate Paused VM.* In the "paused" state, a virtual machine and its virtual resources are instantiated, but they are not enabled to execute tasks. Since these

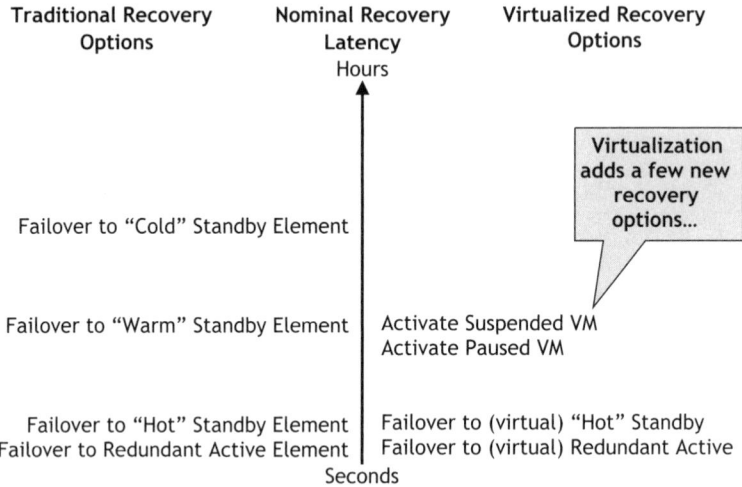

Figure 5.15. Recovery Times for Traditional Redundancy Architectures.

paused VM instances are already instantiated and resources are allocated, they can be activated and made available to recover service quickly. Paused VM instances are sleeping "lightly" so there is additional service recovery latency compared to a switchover to a redundant active or hot standby VM instance, but it has the advantage that fewer platform (e.g., CPU) resources are consumed to maintain paused VMs than for online active VM instances.

- *Failover to Active, Virtual Redundant Unit.* Traditional redundant units (e.g., active/standby redundancy) can be configured, kept in synch, and maintained as (activated) virtual machines rather than being traditionally deployed on dedicated hardware. Failovers to redundant units in virtual machine instances should have the same latency as native redundant deployment. Note that standby redundant units are lightly utilized when the active unit is operational, so virtualization enables the redundant unit's compute, memory, and networking resources that would be mostly idle for traditional deployments to be used by or shared by other applications when virtualized, which can lower the cloud consumer's OPEX.

5.5 SEQUENTIAL REDUNDANCY AND CONCURRENT REDUNDANCY

As shown in Figure 5.16, concurrent redundancy architectures entail client instance "A" logically multicasting service requests to two or more server instances "B1," "B2," and so on.

Having two or more server instances process the exact same client request simultaneously increases the probability that the correct response will be rapidly delivered to the client. However, this architecture has several drawbacks:

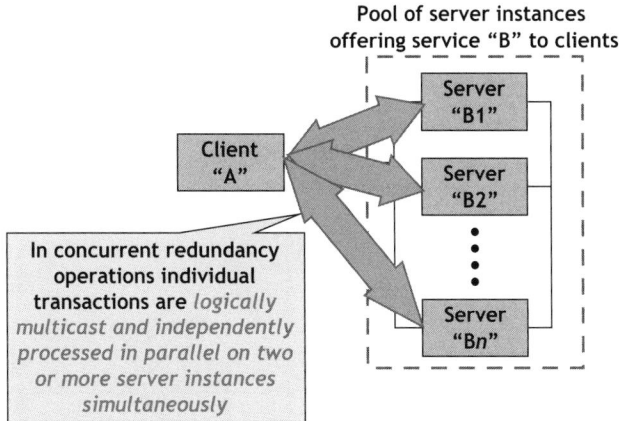

Figure 5.16. Concurrent Redundancy Processing Model.

- *Concurrent redundancy materially increases the complexity of client software* which must both manage the (logically) multicast requests and responses, as well as decide which response to use; sometimes, delayed responses (because some server instances might be slow) or conflicting responses (some server instances might be faulty or data may not be in synch) are returned, further complicating the logic.
- *Concurrent redundancy increases the challenge of synchronization* because each operation is expected to occur simultaneously on two or more independent server instances accessing the same logical application data, and thus synchronization mechanisms must be designed to cope with literally constant data contention.
- *Concurrent redundancy materially increases server resources consumed* because at least twice the resources are consumed since each request is processed at least twice compared with simplex or traditional sequential redundancy arrangements.

Figure 5.17 gives a timeline of how a concurrent redundancy arrangement operates:

- Client "A" logically multicasts each request to multiple server instances ("B1," "B2," and "B3" in this case).
- Each server instance responds to client "A" independently; inevitably, the response latencies will be somewhat different from each server.
- Client "A" applies a selection strategy to the responses to determine which result to use, and when. To mask failures of individual server instances, the client's selection strategy might not wait for responses from all server instances. Each server instance returns its response independently, and client "A" selects a response based on an algorithm, such as:

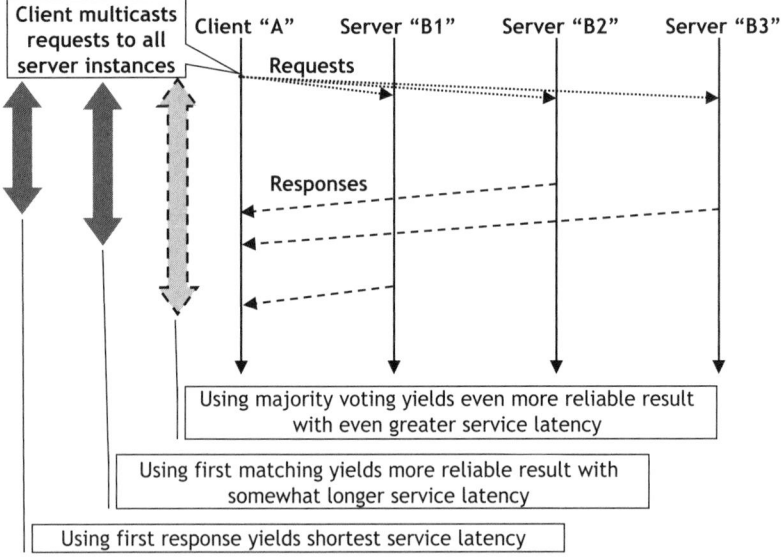

Figure 5.17. Client Controlled Redundant Compute Strategy.

- First (i.e., fastest) successful (i.e., nonerror) response
- First pair of matching responses
- Majority of successful responses received within a fixed time period.

Figure 5.18 shows a concurrent redundancy operation when server instance "B2" fails. Since both "B1" and "B3" promptly provide successful responses to "A," service latency impact due to failure of "B2" is negligible, regardless of whether "B2" explicitly signaled failure (e.g., returning 500 Server Internal Error) or implicitly signaled failure (e.g., via timeout expiration).

Note that using the first response inherently produces shorter service latency than for simplex or redundant architectures, but creates the risk that a single software failure may compromise service for all users. For example, Figure 5.19 illustrates the case of a software failure that causes one server instance to always return "404 Not Found"* before other server instances can return correct results; in this case, that erroneous result would automatically be used. Thus, clients of concurrent redundancy architectures often use selection algorithms, such as the first pair of matching responses to both minimize the risks of using a fast but wrong response and mask critical failures of individual server instances that preclude any response from the other server instances. [Dean] introduces the notion of "*tied requests,*" it which requests are sent to multiple servers tagged with the identity of those other servers. The first server that responds to the request issues a cancelation to the other servers so that multiple responses are not returned.

---

* "404 Not Found" is defined as "*The server has not found anything matching the Request-URI*" [RFC2616].

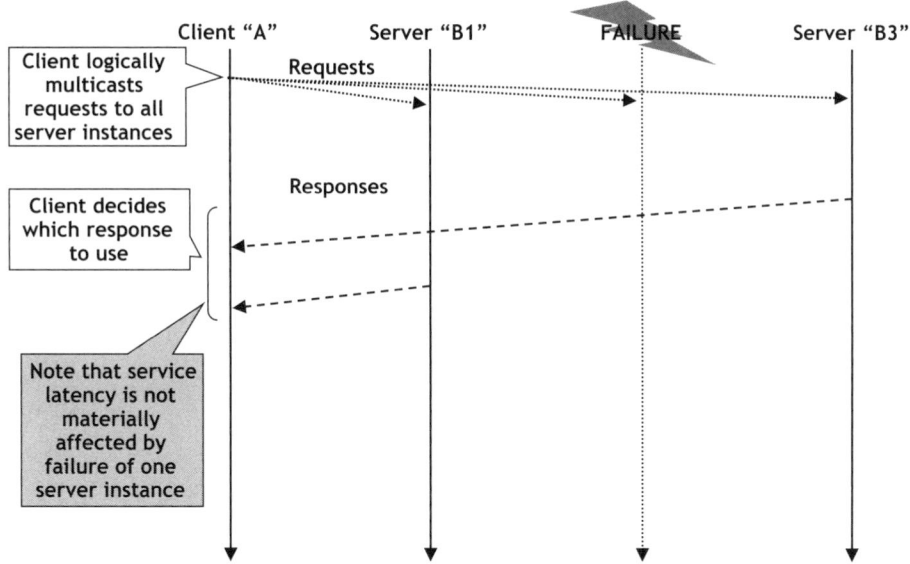

Figure 5.18. Client Controlled Redundant Operations.

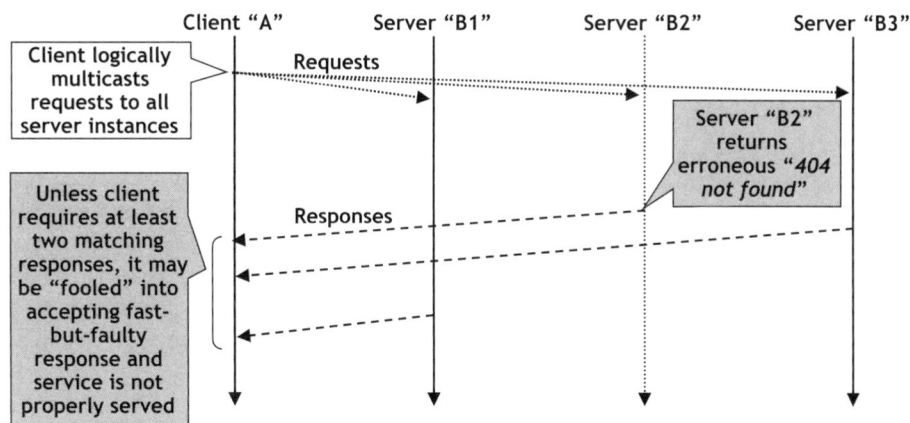

Figure 5.19. Concurrent Redundancy Timeline with Fast but Erroneous Return.

5.5.1 Hybrid Concurrent Strategy

Concurrent redundancy arrangements offer better user service quality than sequential redundancy arrangements by effectively eliminating the latency of failure detection and recovery from user service delivery, but consuming far more resources. As most applications may not require the full service latency, reliability and availability benefits

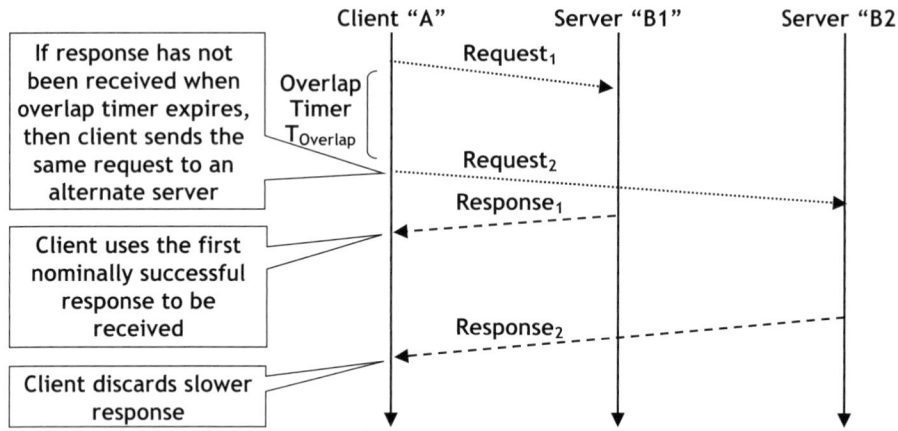

Figure 5.20. Hybrid Concurrent with Slow Response.

offered by concurrent redundancy architectures, one can achieve much of the service quality benefit with vastly lower resource consumption with a hybrid concurrent model. The hybrid model sends each request to a single server instance initially, and a successful response from that server instance will be used when it is provided within an overlap timeout. If the selected server instance does not reply within that overlap timeout (e.g., within the 99th, 99.9th, or 99.99th percentile service latency time), then the request is sent to another server instance. Whichever response is received first will be used by the client. The hybrid concurrency strategy is very similar to the "*hedged request*" strategy discussed in [Dean]. Figure 5.20 shows the timeline for hybrid concurrent operation: client "A" sends a request to "B1," and if no response is received before T_{Guard}, then client "A" sends the same request to server "B2" and uses the first successful response from either B1 or B2. While it is certainly possible that "B1" will respond to the original request late or that a retry to "B1" might succeed (as shown in Figure 5.20), it should be at least as likely that "B2" will respond promptly. But if "B1" has failed, then by promptly overlapping the request to "B2," the client should receive a timely response despite the failure of "B1."

5.6 APPLICATION SERVICE IMPACT OF VIRTUALIZATION IMPAIRMENTS

This section considers how well each of the application service impacts (Section 2.5, "Application Service Quality") of infrastructure impairments (Chapter 4, "Virtualized Infrastructure Impairments") are mitigated by the four redundancy architectures reviewed in this chapter:

- Simplex (nonredundant) architectures (Section 5.1)
- Traditional, sequential redundant architectures (Section 5.4)

- Concurrent redundancy architectures (Section 5.5)
- Hybrid concurrent architectures (Section 5.5.1).

5.6.1   Service Impact for Simplex Architectures

Since simplex architectures feature only a single serving component and service recovery or repair has a significant user service impact, application service impact of simplex deployments often directly endure the full impact of noncatastrophic virtualized infrastructure impairments until service is so heavily impacted that the impact of a service impacting recovery action is justified. Service impact for simplex architectures is the performance baseline that other arrangements are compared to.

5.6.2   Service Impact for Sequential Redundancy Architectures

User service impact of traditional, sequential redundant architectures when confronted with virtualized infrastructure impairments are considered as the following:

- Impact of VM Failure (Section 5.6.2.1)
- Impact of Nondelivery Events (Section 5.6.2.2)
- Impact of Degraded Delivery Events (Section 5.6.2.3)
- Impact of Tail Latency (Section 5.6.2.4)
- Impact of Clock Event Jitter (Section 5.6.2.5)
- Impact of Clock Drift (Section 5.6.2.6)
- Impact of VM Allocation and Startup Impairments (Section 5.6.2.7).

5.6.2.1 Impact of VM Failure. VM failure appears to traditional redundancy mechanisms as a hardware failure. Assuming spare VM capacity is available from the IaaS, then offline migration can be used to "repair" failed components faster than native deployments can be repaired, thereby reducing the application's simplex exposure time. While duplex failures caused by second failures occurring while the system is simplex exposed are rare events, minimizing simplex exposure is a best practice.

5.6.2.2 Impact of Nondelivery Events. Figure 5.21 illustrates the timeline for service delivery with a very brief $T_{\text{Nondelivery}}$ event so that the sum of $T_{\text{Nondelivery}}$ and T_{Normal} is less than T_{Guard}. In this case the service impact for a traditional redundant architecture is the same as for a simplex architecture.

Figure 5.22 illustrates a timeline for service delivery when $T_{\text{NonDelivery}}$ plus T_{Normal} is somewhat longer than T_{Guard} so the client issues retries for transactions that were not responded to before the guard time expired. As $T_{\text{Nondelivery}}$ approaches and exceeds the maximum acceptable service latency, users will deem transactions to have failed, thus impacting service reliability and service accessibility, and perhaps service retainability. Nondelivery of VM capacity directly impacts application service latency for traditional/ sequential application architectures. The user service impact for a traditional redundant architecture on brief nondelivery events is the same as for a simplex architecture, since

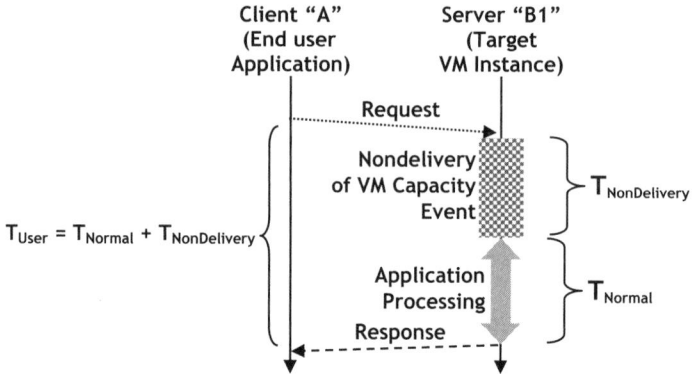

Figure 5.21. Application Service Impact for Very Brief Nondelivery Events.

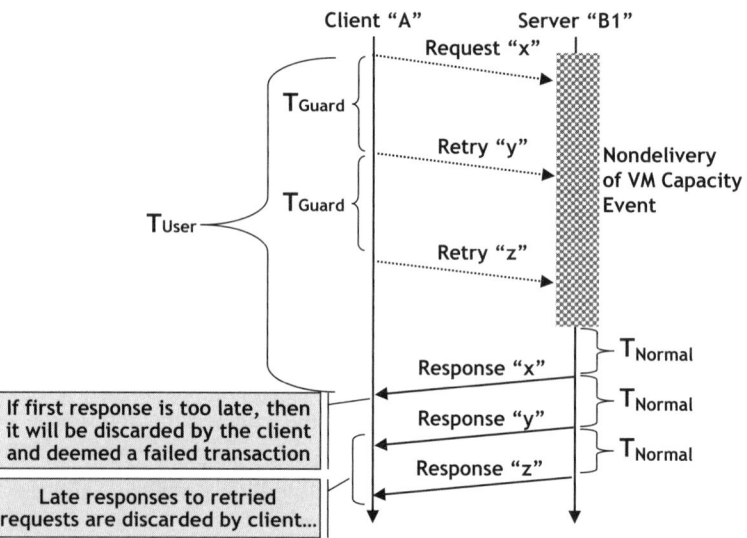

Figure 5.22. Application Service Impact for Brief Nondelivery Events.

redundancy mechanisms should not activate. Longer delays may result in application failover.

5.6.2.3   Impact of Degraded Delivery Events. Degraded resource capacity will directly impact service latency by increasing service latency for at least some operations due to queuing for resource access, but traditional redundancy mechanisms should not activate so the user service will be the same as with simplex architectures.

5.6.2.4   Impact of Tail Latency. As excess tail latency events are unlikely to impact both the initial request and all subsequent retries traditional redundancy mechanisms will not activate so the user service impact will be the same as with simplex architectures.

5.6.2.5 Impact of Clock Event Jitter. As only a single component instance is serving each user request in traditional redundancy architectures, the user service impact of clock event jitter is the same for traditional redundancy as for simplex architectures.

5.6.2.6 Impact of Clock Drift. System clocks can drift between redundant components so that two or more redundant instances (e.g., "B1" and "B2") have different views of the current time. As a result, clients may experience (slight) apparent temporal shifts when service fails over from one server instance (e.g., "B1") to another (e.g., "B2").

5.6.2.7 Impact of VM Allocation and Startup Impairments. While VM allocation and startup is in the critical path of user service recovery for simplex architectures, it is not in the critical path of user service recovery of traditional redundancy architectures. VM allocation and startup is necessary to restore full redundancy following failure in a traditional architecture, so failed or slow VM allocation and startup prolongs the period of simplex exposure following failure with traditional redundancy architectures, but this impairment has little impact on user service.

5.6.3 Service Impact for Concurrent Redundancy Architectures

Concurrent redundancy architectures are better at mitigating user service impacts of virtualized infrastructure impairments than either sequential redundancy or simplex architectures, as discussed in the next sections.

5.6.3.1 Impact of VM Failure. As shown in Figure 5.18, concurrent redundancy architectures can completely mask the user service impact of VM failure.

5.6.3.2 Impact of Nondelivery Events. As shown in Figure 5.23, concurrent redundancy architectures effectively mitigate nondelivery impairment events.

5.6.3.3 Impact of Degraded Delivery Events. Concurrent redundancy architectures effectively mitigate degraded resource delivery events in the same way they mitigate nondelivery events.

5.6.3.4 Impact of Tail Latency. Concurrent redundancy architectures fully mitigate the user service impact of tail latency events because successful timely responses will mask tardy responses.

5.6.3.5 Impact of Clock Event Jitter. Concurrent redundancy architectures mitigate the user service impact of clock jitter events by using a successful low jitter response and discarding high jitter responses.

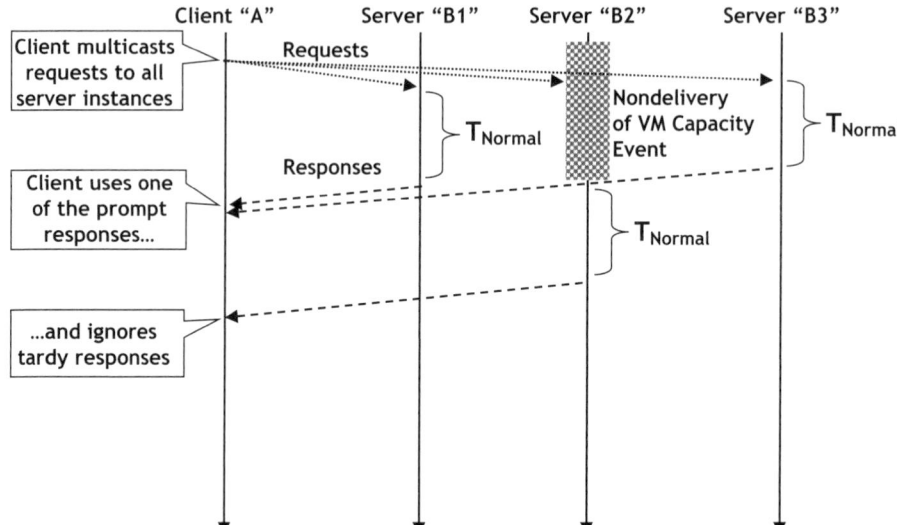

Figure 5.23. Nondelivery Impact to Redundant Compute Architectures.

5.6.3.6 Impact of Clock Drift. If the real-time clocks of servers in the concurrent redundancy pool drift out of sync, then both clients and cloud consumers may become confused about the sequence and chronology of transactions that were served by different server instances. While this hazard is fundamentally the same, as with sequential redundancy, concurrent redundancy means that actual responses sent to clients can alternate between server components so clients might experience slightly differing timestamps between any two transactions, while with sequential redundancy, the client is only exposed to server clock drift following failover or switchover events.

5.6.3.7 Impact of VM Allocation and Startup Impairments. VM allocation and startup impairments are not in the user service delivery or recovery path, so these impairments have no impact on user service for concurrent redundancy architectures.

5.6.4 Service Impact for Hybrid Concurrent Architectures

Hybrid concurrent redundant architectures mitigate virtualized infrastructure impairments better than traditional, sequential redundancy arrangements, but not quite as well as concurrent redundancy arrangements.

5.6.4.1 Impact of VM Failure. Hybrid redundant architectures yield a slight increase (i.e., degradation) in user service latency for operations initially sent to a failed VM instance compared with concurrent redundancy arrangements, but the overall service latency impact is likely to be much smaller than for traditional redundancy architectures.

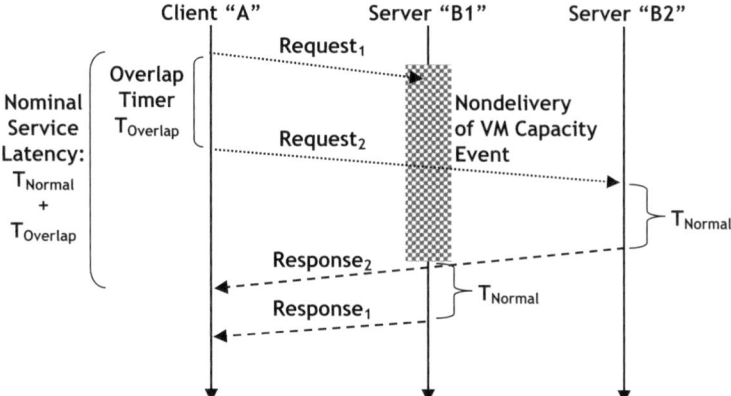

Figure 5.24. Nondelivery Impact to Hybrid Concurrent Architectures.

5.6.4.2 Impact of Nondelivery Events. As shown in Figure 5.24, hybrid redundant architectures should limit service latency due to nondelivery events to approximately $T_{Overlap}$ plus T_{Normal}.

5.6.4.3 Impact of Degraded Delivery Events. Hybrid redundant architectures will effectively mitigate the user service impact of degraded delivery events like they mitigate nondelivery events. As shown in Figure 5.24, hybrid redundant architectures should limit service latency due to uncorrelated degraded delivery events to approximately $T_{Overlap}$ plus T_{Normal}.

5.6.4.4 Impact of Tail Latency. Hybrid redundant architectures should mitigate extreme tail latency events because expiration of $T_{Overlap}$ will cause requests to be retried to another server component instance so clients should receive responses within $T_{Overlap}$ plus T_{Normal}. The more aggressive (i.e., shorter) $T_{Overlap}$ is set, the smaller the service latency tail should be.

5.6.4.5 Impact of Clock Event Jitter. Hybrid concurrent architectures are generally ineffective at mitigating clock event jitter that is significantly shorter than $T_{Overlap}$ because a redundant request will not be sent and served fast enough to mask most clock jitter events.

5.6.4.6 Impact of Clock Drift. Clients are somewhat more likely to experience server clock drift with hybrid redundant architectures than with sequential redundancy because individual transactions will occasionally be served by alternate servers with hybrid arrangements, while alternate servers are only used in sequential redundancy arrangements following failover or switchover.

5.6.4.7 Impact of VM Allocation and Startup Impairments. VM allocation and startup impairments are not in the user service delivery or recovery path, so these impairments have no impact on user service for hybrid redundant architectures.

5.7 DATA REDUNDANCY

At the highest level, distributed applications deliver service by executing programs on processors that respond to inputs based on data. Earlier sections of this chapter considered redundancy arrangements of processors to mitigate failed component instances and retry strategies to mitigate lost input requests. Program files are static, so they are easy to replicate in advance. That brings one to the question of data that is not completely static, which covers a diverse family such as:

- Application instance configuration data, such as IP addresses and DNS names
- User data, such as user names, passwords, and preferences
- Application data, such as inventory databases
- Session data, such as users currently logged on and last transaction executed
- Transaction data, such as the input parameters for the pending client request
- Variables and processor registers, such as the current value of the stack pointer.

The impact of recovering service after data have been lost varies dramatically across this range: without a DNS name, an application component may not even be able to start successfully, but losing the contents of automatic variables when a process crashes may not even be noticed. Thus, architects must carefully catalog what data are acceptable to lose on failure (e.g., contents of automatic variables in main memory) and what data must be retained across failure events. The validation of the essential data should be in the form of executable tests that accompany the application software. Retaining data that rarely changes (e.g., DNS names) is relatively easy via writing information to persistent (disk) storage and periodic replication. Retaining highly volatile data is much harder because of the volatility forces higher bandwidth for replication and greater risk of concurrency issues when maintaining consistency with replicated values. However, if volatile data can be stored in a shared redundant repository, replication is simplified, and more components can provide recovery for another failed component by accessing its volatile data from the shared storage, although at a possible latency cost for data retrieval.

5.7.1 Data Storage Strategies

Application architects have three broad options for locating application data:

- *Store It in Application RAM Memory.* This offers the fastest access and highest cost option. RAM is inherently a volatile storage medium; when power goes away, so does the data. As a practical matter, RAM is generally tightly coupled with a particular application instance on a (virtual) machine. One accesses and manipulates the content of that RAM via a particular application instance, and if/when that application instance fails, then the contents of that RAM is generally lost. Thus, one can refer to RAM-based storage as "volatile" because failure of the application or virtual machine using that RAM will cause the contents of that "volatile" RAM storage to be lost. Because RAM offers extremely low access latencies, it is ideal for storing volatile data (e.g., processor stacks), as well as frequently accessed data (e.g., executable instructions).

- *Store It on Persistent Media.* Hard disk drives, FLASH memory, and optical disks are called persistent media because the data stored on those devices is persistent across typical power and application failures. Persistent storage devices generally offer very large capacities, and while the cost per device may be moderate to high, the cost per unit of storage is cheap. Persistent storage has inherently slower access latencies, and thus it is more awkward to store extremely dynamic data on persistent media; in the extreme case the dynamic data might change faster than the persistent media can record those changes, and thus latency performance of the persistent media becomes the limiting factor on application performance.
- *Store It in the Client Application/Device*, so the cost and maintenance of the data is the responsibility of the client user rather than the application component architect. While pushing data from the application itself to the client device does not eliminate the risk of user service impact on failure, it does transfer accountability to the end user, and thus beyond the scope of this document.

Note that the contents of RAM storage is often initialized (or cached) by copying data from persistent media, like when an executable program is copied from persistent hard disk into main memory to execute. Note also that cache memory (e.g., L2 cache on microprocessor chips) is not considered in the context of data storage because the contents of cache are explicitly synchronized to one of the fundamental storage options earlier.

One of the principles of data storage advocated by Amazon Web Service is: "Keep dynamic data closer to the compute and static data closer to end-user" [Varia]. Dynamic data is a good candidate for RAM storage as a result, while copies of static data should be stored and made available to application instances that can best serve the end user. Note that for large-scale systems, it is much easier to move compute than to move data.

Just as "no single point of failure" requirements prohibit singleton application process or VM instances, no single RAM or persistent storage device may be a single point of failure for critical applications either. Generally, this means that all data must be maintained in two physically independent instances so if a failure impacts one storage device then service can be rapidly recovered to another storage device. Placement of the independent data instances and their ability to synchronize and provide reliable storage with low latency for accessing applications is an important consideration in configuring an application's data needs.

5.7.2 Data Consistency Strategies

Data management is complex in the cloud environment since transactions can span multiple application instances and be stored in multiple locations. There are two types of mechanisms generally used to keep data synchronized: ACID and BASE.

Mechanisms that possess ACID (atomicity, consistency, isolation, and durability) properties ensure transactional reliability [Wikipedia-DB]. Many relational database systems (e.g., SQL based) provide ACID capabilities. These mechanisms should be used when transactional reliability and immediate consistency are essential to meet customer needs, as these mechanisms can be very resource intensive and may introduce latency into transactions.

BASE (basically available, soft state, eventual consistency) mechanisms ensure eventual consistency, that is, transactions do not require all copies to be immediately consistent to succeed. By loosening this requirement a simpler, less resource intensive, more fault tolerant solution is supported that is well suited for scalability. Many web and e-mail services that require scalability can take advantage of the less-complex BASE properties because they do not have to be instantly up to date.

5.7.3   Data Architecture Considerations

Applications should be architected to back up or replicate persistent application, user and enterprise data so that failure of a persistent storage device can be mitigated either by recovering to a component instance hosting a replica of the data or restoring data from a backup. Volatile state information should be stored in RAM and replicated across redundant components. Alternatively, volatile data should be pushed out of application server component instances either back to the client (if possible) or into a shared and highly available registry server to minimize user service disruption on component failure. For highly distributed databases, weaker eventual consistency (BASE) should be considered instead of ACID arrangements to improve scalability. While ACID ensures data consistency across all copies of the data as part of successful completion of a transaction, BASE decouples the updating of the data from the transaction, allowing the transaction to complete before all of the copies of the data have been updated. For example, if a particular data store is not available due to a network problem, the rest of the system is available to continue functioning and the data is updated in that data store once it is available.

5.8   DISCUSSION

This section summarizes the advantages and drawbacks of the four redundancy architectures across several dimensions:

- Service Quality Impact (Section 5.8.1)
- Concurrency Control (Section 5.8.2)
- Resource Usage (Section 5.8.3)
- Simplicity (Section 5.8.4).

Application architects must pick the option that best fits the design goals and constraints of their project.

5.8.1 Service Quality Impact

In descending order of feasible service quality (i.e., best to worst), the four architectures are the following:

1. *Concurrent Redundancy* architectures effectively mitigate the user service impact of VM failure, nondelivery of virtualized resource, degraded delivery of virtualized resource, tail latency, clock event jitter, and VM allocation and startup impairments. Note that concurrent redundancy and hybrid concurrent architectures are somewhat more vulnerable to clock drift because if different servers have different clock times, then the chronology of events may become confused, which can create service, billing, troubleshooting, and other errors.

2. *Hybrid Concurrent* architectures mitigate all of the impairments addressed by concurrent redundancy but with slightly increased service latency for some transactions.

3. *Sequential Redundancy* architectures should effectively mitigate VM failures because these appear like the hardware failures that traditional mechanisms were designed to mitigate. If nondelivery of virtual resource events are very long relative to guard timeouts, then sequential redundancy mechanisms may activate to limit user service impact; otherwise, the user service impact will be the same as with simplex architectures. The impact of degraded resource delivery, tail latency, and clock drift are likely to be the same as with simplex architectures. Note that user service is not impacted by VM allocation and startup impairments on service recovery with redundant architectures, although these impairments do directly prolong user service recovery times for simplex architectures.

4. *Simplex* architectures are the baseline against which service impact of virtualized infrastructure impairments should be compared. Deploying simplex configurations protected by VM RaaS (aka self-healing) mechanisms can boost service availability compared with native deployment by significantly shortening service recovery times.

5.8.2 Concurrency Control

Parallel and concurrent programming is hard because synchronization of shared resources across concurrent processes or threads must be carefully controlled to prevent one instance from damaging (e.g., overwriting) another instance's changes. With inadequate concurrency controls, one risks having data values erroneously overwritten, leading to inaccurate operations and compromised data integrity. With excessive concurrency controls, one risks performance bottlenecks due to excessive serialization and deadlock. In order of increasing concurrency risk (i.e., low risk to high risk), the four architectures are:

1. *Simplex* has the least concurrency risk, and thus the simplest (and thus most likely to be defect free) concurrency controls can be implemented. After all, data that is not directly shared by other software components does not require synchronization mechanisms to maintain consistency across components.

2. *Sequential Redundancy* has modest concurrency risk because, by design, concurrent operations are limited.

3. *Hybrid Concurrent* redundancy has elevated concurrency risk because by design, slow operations will be overlapped by concurrently executing operations on other component instances. The shorter the overlap timer ($T_{Overlap}$), the more likely operations are to be simultaneously pending with multiple server instances. When $T_{Overlap}$ is large, then the concurrency risk is only slightly greater than for sequential redundancy; as $T_{Overlap}$ shrinks the frequency of concurrency—and hence the risk of exposing concurrency control defects—rises.

4. *Concurrent Redundancy* has maximum concurrency risk because by design, all operations will execute simultaneously and in parallel on at least two component instances. As concurrent redundancy architectures are intended to actually execute the same operation in parallel, traditional synchronization schemes, such as coarse grained mutual exclusion (mutex) locks, are likely to defeat the service quality benefits. After all, there is little value in sending requests simultaneously to two or three component instances if service by those components will be serialized by a single mutex lock, which assures that the response from the component instance that successfully acquired the mutex first will be used, and the responses from component instances that had to wait for the mutex will be slower and thus be discarded.

5.8.3   Resource Usage

As measured usage is an essential characteristic of cloud computing, lower resource usage should yield lower OPEX for the cloud consumer. In increasing order of resource usage—and thus presumably increasing OPEX—the four architectures are:

1. Simplex
2. Sequential redundancy
3. Hybrid concurrent redundancy. Note that hybrid concurrent implementations are likely to consume only slightly more resources than sequential redundancy (e.g., only for transactions slower than $T_{Overlap}$).
4. Concurrent redundancy implementation will consume significantly more resources than sequential and hybrid concurrent redundancy architectures as each transaction will be processed at least twice.

5.8.4   Simplicity

Simple systems are easier to build right the first time and thus tend to be more reliable. In descending order of simplicity (i.e., simplest to most complex), the four architectures are:

1. Simplex
2. Sequential redundancy
3. Concurrent redundancy, because of complex concurrency controls

4. Hybrid concurrent, because the actual concurrency risk varies based on the configured value of $T_{Overlap}$.

5.8.5 Other Considerations

Enthusiasm for the service quality benefits of concurrent redundancy should be tempered by several practical considerations, as well as the fact that different components will likely evolve at different speeds based on a cost/benefit analysis for that component:

1. *Accruing the full benefits of concurrent redundancy requires fine grained concurrency controls* so that multiple component instances can effectively serve identical requests in parallel. Poorly architected and coarse-grained concurrency controls can produce worse service performance than simplex or sequential redundancy arrangements.
2. *Existing application protocols may not properly support full concurrent operation.* For example, existing application protocols may not support issuing multiple identical requests to separate component instances simultaneously, and later canceling or aborting tardy responses.
3. *Client software must change* to support concurrent operation.
4. *Debugging concurrent programming problems is harder* than debugging problems in simplex or traditional (sequential) architectures.

   As a thought experiment, imagine that your bank has decided to implement concurrent redundancy for their automated teller machines so that each ATM will send every transaction to both of the bank's data centers simultaneously. Consider the case of a withdrawal request: the ATM will send identical withdrawal transactions to both data centers, and then send a cancel request to the slower data center after the first successful response is received. What can possibly go wrong with this service arrangement, and what might happen to your bank account balance?

6

LOAD DISTRIBUTION
AND BALANCING

Wikipedia defines load balancing as "*a computer networking method to distribute workload across multiple computers or a computer cluster, network links, central processing units, disk drives, or other resources, to achieve optimal resource utilization, maximize throughput, minimize response time, and avoid overload*" [Wikipedia-LB]. This chapter reviews the architectural, operational and service quality considerations of both proxy and nonproxy load balancing technologies.

6.1 LOAD DISTRIBUTION MECHANISMS

Load balancing can be implemented either by positioning an intermediate system in the service delivery path as a proxy or via mechanisms that do not rely on an intermediate system in the service delivery path.

- *Proxy Load Balancers* (Figure 6.1). With proxy load balancing the client "A" sees the IP address of the proxy load balancer. The proxy load balancer is responsible for the distribution of client requests across the pool of servers "B1," "B2," and "Bn." As proxy load balancers are in the critical service delivery path, their

Service Quality of Cloud-Based Applications, First Edition. Eric Bauer and Randee Adams.
© 2014 The Institute of Electrical and Electronics Engineers, Inc. Published 2014 by John Wiley & Sons, Inc.

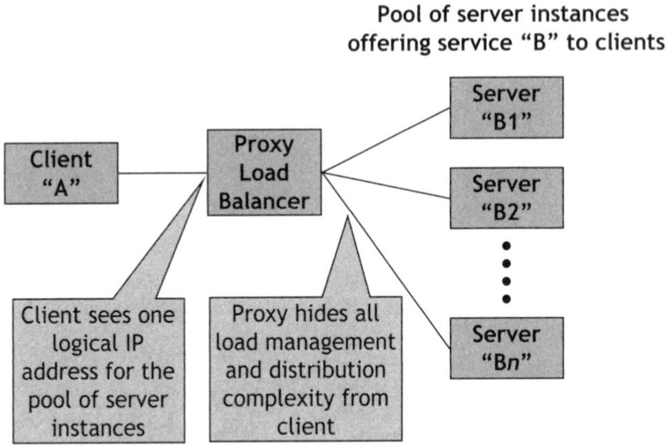

Pool of server instances
offering service "B" to clients

Figure 6.1. Proxy Load Balancer.

downtime contributes to service downtime; however, because a proxy load balancer is in the service delivery path, it can gather metrics on offered workload and performance of all server instances in its pool. Note that while message queue servers provide a load balancing function, message queue servers are not explicitly considered in this chapter. Proxy load balancing can be provided using software modules or computer appliances with special purpose hardware and integrated firmware to provide the load balancing capabilities.

• *Nonproxy Load Distributors* are mechanisms that do not insert an additional component into the service delivery path. While nonproxy mechanisms generally do not add service downtime because they are not in the critical service delivery path, they are not able to produce the rich service measurements that proxy mechanisms can, precisely because they are not in the service delivery path. Nonproxy load distribution or balancing mechanisms include:

   ○ *Static Client Configuration.* Each client "A" can be configured with the IP address of a primary server instance (e.g., "B1"). One or more secondary instances (e.g., "B2") can also be configured for client "A" to use if the primary instance is unavailable.

   ○ *DNS.* Clients retrieve the IP address for one or more server instances from DNS. The DNS server can act as a load balancer by providing clients with one or more IP addresses based on a given domain name. Round robin distribution is one technique for how DNS responds to those domain name requests. When a client sends a domain name request to DNS, the DNS server provides an ordered list of IP addresses corresponding to that domain name. The order of the list changes with each client request in an attempt to balance traffic to be sent to the components supporting the service identified by the domain name. Note that clients can decide to select any IP address in that list so it does not guarantee how client work load is actually distributed.

   ○ *Multicast IP Addressing.* Clients can use multicast IP addressing to send requests to multiple servers simultaneously, and then wait for the first server

to respond. This mechanism works well in certain contexts (e.g., DHCP), but limitations on multicast support across WANs temper the usefulness of this mechanism.
- ○ *Anycast.* Clients can use anycast to route to a single node within a group of potential servers all identified by the same destination address.
- ○ *Representation State Transfer (REST).* Clients maintain any state information they need and communicate with the servers using a standard interface exchanging representations of the resources rather than the resources themselves.

6.2 LOAD DISTRIBUTION STRATEGIES

Client workload distribution across a pool of server or application component instances can be driven via several basic strategies including:

- • *Static Configuration.* Each client "A" is statically mapped to one primary instance (e.g., "B1"). Optionally, one or more secondary server instances can be configured.
- • *Round Robin.* requests can be uniformly distributed across the pool of available servers on the fly.
- • *Random Choices.* Requests can be randomly distributed across the pool of available servers.
- • *Performance Based.* Requests can be distributed based on observed performance of server component instances, such as biasing distribution to server instances with shorter service latency and away from instances with greater service latency.
- • *Status Based.* Server instances that are not active or have failed will not be included in the pool of available servers until they are once again active.
- • *Orchestration Enabled.* Workload distribution can be integrated with both cloud consumer and cloud service provider operations, such as planned maintenance, release management and elasticity to gracefully drain traffic away from server instances prior to starting operations impacting those instances, and begin flowing traffic to server instances after maintenance actions have completed. Orchestration enabled workload distribution can minimize the user service disruption of elastic degrowth, release management, and elastic growth actions.

6.3 PROXY LOAD BALANCERS

As shown in Figure 6.2, load balancing via proxy has the following basic steps:

1. Client sends request to proxy load balancer.
2. Load balancer selects a server instance to serve the client's request.

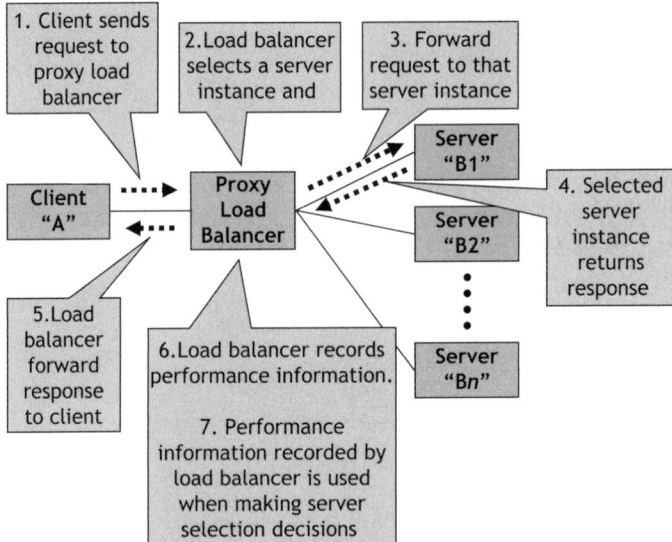

Figure 6.2. Proxy Load Balancing.

3. Load balancer forwards client's request to selected server instance.
4. Selected server instance returns response to client's request to load balancer.
5. Load balancer forwards response to client.
6. Load balancer records performance information, such as service response latency for the selected server instance.
7. Performance information recorded by load balancer is used when making server selection decisions for future requests and as input for operations support systems.

Load distribution algorithms implemented by proxy load balancers include simple methods discussed in Section 6.2, "Load Distribution Strategies," such as round robin or random choice. More complex algorithms can take into account one or more of the following factors:

- *Session "Stickiness."* Some requests must be sent to the same component/instance that has handled other requests for the same session. In Figure 6.2, if server "B1" is providing service to client "A", then all messages associated with that session will continue to be sent to server "B1" as long as "B1" is available and any of its critical downstream components.
- *Component Availability.* Components that are out of service or otherwise unavailable must be removed from the pool of available components.
- *Component Resource Utilization.* Traffic should be spread in a way to maximize usage of available resources.

- *Resource Availability.* Server components with the most available resources (e.g., CPU, memory) based on application needs (e.g., as specified in a service-level agreement [SLA]) may be chosen.
- *Current Load on the Component.* Although traffic should be spread so as to maximize usage of resources it should not cause components to exceed their resources and trigger overload conditions.
- *Latency.* Requests should be distributed to minimize response latency for the end user. This may include prioritizing component selection based on closest location to the end user to minimize transport latency.

As proxy load balancers are in the critical service delivery path they are often designed to be highly available, and thus are typically deployed with some form of sequential redundancy.

6.4 NONPROXY LOAD DISTRIBUTION

DNS is probably the most common nonproxy load distribution strategy used by applications. Load balancing via DNS has the following basic steps:

1. Client sends DNS server a domain name (e.g., www.wikipedia.org) and receives one or more IP addresses assigned to that domain name.
2. Client caches the address(es).
3. Client sends request for service using one of the IP addresses provided by DNS.
4. If the server does not successfully return a response to the client, then the client may either retry the request to another IP address provided by DNS in the original response or the client may request another IP address from DNS to use.
5. Selected server instance returns response to client
6. Client continues to use that server to send other messages associated with that session or transaction.

Static configuration of distributed applications is also common. Load balancing via static configuration has the following basic steps:

1. IP address of one (or more) server is explicitly written into a registry or configuration file on the client device.
2. Client sends request for service to the statically configured IP address associated with the service.
3. Selected server instance returns response to client, and client continues to use that address for other messages associated with that session or transaction.
4. If primary configured server fails to respond to the client within the guard timeout and subsequent retries to the primary fail, then the client can use a secondary

server if one was configured or return an error to the end user until the primary server is returned to service

Other nonproxy load-balancing mechanisms such as multicast and anycast are used less frequently than either DNS or static configuration. Unlike proxy load balancers, nonproxy load distribution is not generally in the critical delivery path particularly in the case of static configuration. However, there is no load balancer collecting metrics on server behavior to help support decisions such as growth.

6.5 HIERARCHY OF LOAD DISTRIBUTION

Complex applications are generally architected with several tiers of service and functionality, and load distribution mechanisms and policies are generally implemented at each tier. Consider the architectural tiers of load distribution for a hypothetical web application:

- *Data Center Tier.* Assuming the application is deployed to multiple data centers (perhaps for disaster recovery), clients must select which data center to direct each client request to. This tier of load distribution is generally via DNS (nonproxy load distribution).
- *Application Instance Tier.* If multiple application instances exist within a single data center—perhaps in different availability zones within a single data center— then the client must be directed to a specific application instance. This tier of load distribution is generally via DNS (nonproxy load distribution).
- *Application Frontend.* A single application instance is likely to have a pool of frontend servers that actually terminate HTTP traffic, so each client request must be distributed to a particular frontend server instance. This tier of load distribution is frequently done via proxy mechanisms, such as conventional load balancers or application distribution controllers.
- *Application Backend.* Backend component instances are likely to implement business logic, database functionality, and so on. As there are likely to be multiple instances of backend components for capacity, performance, and resilience, some load distribution mechanism must be deployed to enable frontend components (as "clients") to get service from backend component instances (as "servers"). While message queue servers are a common architecture for managing workloads between frontend and backend server components (and are not considered in this chapter), nonproxy load balancing mechanisms will be used for many applications.

Note that even a single application may require workload distribution across geographically separated data centers, as well as across different types of component instances within the same data center. Each workload distribution step may have somewhat different selection criteria and constraints, and thus require different data and different implementation architectures.

6.6 CLOUD-BASED LOAD BALANCING CHALLENGES

Workload distribution across applications deployed to cloud is more complex than for traditional deployments because:

- Rapid elasticity produces dynamic application configurations as workload grows and shrinks so load balancers must distribute workloads across this dynamic server pool
- Usage-based pricing and rapid elasticity encourage larger pools of smaller-sized server instances to enable resource usage to track more closely with offered load.
- Virtualized infrastructure will potentially deliver less consistent server instance throughput and latency than traditionally deployed application components, so load balancers must address more variable server performance.
- Virtualization and support for vertical growth means that application component instances with different typical throughput can coexist in a pool of application server components, so load balancers must recognize asymmetric server component capacity.

Later sections will discuss these topics in more detail and how the challenges are met in the cloud environment.

6.7 THE ROLE OF LOAD BALANCING IN SUPPORT OF REDUNDANCY

Chapter 5, "Application Redundancy and Cloud Computing," discussed four fundamental redundancy strategies: simplex, sequential redundancy, concurrent redundancy, and hybrid concurrent redundancy.

- *Simplex.* By definition, load distribution is trivial for a simplex component because there is only a single serving unit; nonproxy methods, such as DNS, are generally used to enable clients to find the simplex server instance.
- *Sequential Redundancy.* Intelligent proxy load balancers implement basic sequential redundancy by automatically detecting failed or otherwise unavailable server instances and sending traffic only to available server instances. Complexity arises in the following cases:
  1. Server instance fails while one or more client requests are pending.
  2. Silent failure of server instance means that load balancer is unaware of component failure.

     To mitigate the complexity the load balancer can set a guard timer. If the response is not received within the timer interval, it can retry the request several times or return an error message to the requesting client. The load balancer can collect metrics on the length of the nonresponse by the server instance and send an alarm indicating server instance failure and remove the server instance from its pool of available instances.

- *Concurrent Redundancy.* For concurrent redundancy, the proxy load balancer can assume the role of the client and take on the responsibility for sending requests to multiple server instances and choosing the "best" response to return to the client that made the original request. As explained in Section 5.5, selection of the "best" response can sometimes be complicated by delayed responses or conflicting responses.
- *Hybrid Concurrent Redundancy.* For hybrid concurrent redundancy the proxy load balancer could assume the role of sending each client request to a single server instance initially. If a successful response is received within the overlap timeout ($T_{Overlap}$) from that server instance, then it will be sent back to the requesting client. If the selected server instance does not reply within that overlap timeout ($T_{Overlap}$), then the load balancer sends the request to another server instance. Whichever response is received first by the load balancer will be sent to the client.

6.8   LOAD BALANCING AND AVAILABILITY ZONES

As shown in Figure 6.3, DNS is typically used to distribute workloads across a suite of data centers and availability zones. If an entire data center is unavailable (e.g., as a result of a disaster event), then traffic can be directed to another data center by reconfiguring DNS. See Section 10.5, "Disaster Recovery and Geographic Redundancy," for more details on disaster recovery.

6.9   WORKLOAD SERVICE MEASUREMENTS

Proxy load balancers are well positioned to monitor and collect data about offered workload from clients and performance of the server instances in its pool. These data can be used to make better load distribution decisions to:

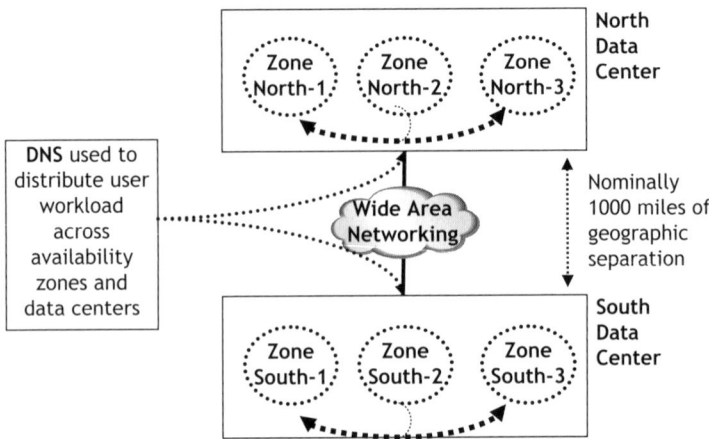

Figure 6.3. Load Balancing between Regions and Availability Zones.

- *Mitigate performance impairments* of individual server components (see Section 6.10.3).
- *Trigger elastic growth* when offered load increases (see Section 8.5).
- *Trigger elastic degrowth* when offered load decreases (see Section 8.5).

In order to measure the effectiveness of the load balancing, the following performance measurements should be collected by the load balancer for a given interval (e.g., 5, 15, and 30 minutes) for each server instance in the pool:

- Number of requests sent by the load balancer to a server instance
- Number of failure responses returned by a server instance to the load balancer
- Number of implicit failures detected by load balancer as timeout expirations
- Response latency between the client and server instance, generally both typical (e.g., mean) and some tail variance latency (see Section 2.5.2.2, "Characterizing Service Latency")
- Portion of requests that meet latency requirements (e.g., as set by policies).

The load balancer should provide metrics to an operational support system (OSS) or a virtual machine server controller (VMSC) because:

1. Metrics are used by a proxy load balancer to drive decisions of how to distribute client requests.
2. Metrics are used to trigger threshold crossing alarms to trigger elastic growth and so on.
3. Metrics are used as performance management data to OSSs to enable better network/capacity planning and operations.

Note that the growth and degrowth activities may be manual or automatically triggered through policies and service orchestration. Metrics can be pushed to or pulled from the OSS based on the required interface between the components.

6.10 OPERATIONAL CONSIDERATIONS

6.10.1 Load Balancing and Elasticity

Proxy load balancing and elasticity are interrelated in several ways:

- As indicated in Section 6.9, load balancers can collect and forward metrics to an OSS or VMSC, indicating the amount of traffic the server instances are handling. This coupled with capacity forecasting can trigger resource growth or degrowth activities.
- When server instances are added to the load balancer's pool during elastic growth, the load balancer should be notified of the change and start sending

traffic to the new server instance(s). This addition will result in the rebalancing of the workload across the updated pool

- As part of degrowth, the load balancer can support this activity by draining traffic from the server instance to be degrown and directing new traffic to the remaining server instances in the pool. Once the traffic has been successfully drained from the server instance, it is removed from the server instance pool as part of the degrowth procedure and the load balancer will no longer send traffic to that server instance. Note that this method of draining traffic from the server instance is similar to the method used to support release management as explained in Section 6.10.3.
- In support of outgrowth, the load balancer may be involved in transferring traffic to another load balancer in a different data center.

Chapter 8, "Capacity Management," considers elasticity in detail.

6.10.2   Load Balancing and Overload

Each VM instance has a finite service capacity, and the primary function of the proxy load balancer is to assure that workload is distributed across the pool of available server instances that the load balancer itself controls. If the load balancer's pool of resources is at or beyond its engineered capacity, then the load balancer instance has the following options for subsequent client requests:

- Continue to distribute requests to the active server instances in the pool and let them execute their overload mechanisms.
- Silently drop requests until the overload condition has ended.
- Respond back to the client with an error message indicating overload (e.g., "TOO BUSY").

In addition to managing an overloaded pool of server instances, a proxy load balancer can mitigate overload situations by:

- Directing traffic away from overloaded server instances and using alternate service instances.
- Raising an overload alarm to the cloud OSS so elastic capacity growth and/or rebalancing workload across other application instances can be initiated.

Note that the load balancer itself may go into overload. TCP sockets are known to misbehave if there is huge throughput running through a single socket and even exponential backoff does not work well to resolve this. Overload control mechanisms must be introduced into the load balancer itself in order to keep it functioning properly.

6.10.3 Load Balancing and Release Management

As discussed in Section 9.5, proxy load balancers may be useful in supporting release management operations to support the following:

- Proactively balancing the workload served by each application release.
- When draining traffic from the old release, load balancers must keep track of existing sessions on the old release, direct new traffic to server instances running the new release, and send any traffic associated with the existing sessions to the active server instance currently handling those sessions even if it is still on the old release. Note that this same draining procedure can be used during degrowth.
- In coordination with block party-type software upgrade (see Section 9.3.1), load balancing will distribute workload taking into account policies and version information when multiple versions of the application instance are active and available for traffic.
- In coordination with one driver per bus type software upgrade (see Section 9.3.2), load balancing will distribute workload to the active application instances. Although only one version will be active at a time, there may be a period of draining traffic in which multiple releases are active and traffic needs to be controlled for distribution to the correct release.

6.11 LOAD BALANCING AND APPLICATION SERVICE QUALITY

The potential impact of proxy load balancing on application service quality is considered for the following:

- Service Availability (Section 6.11.1)
- Service Latency (Section 6.11.2)
- Service Reliability (Section 6.11.3)
- Service Accessibility (Section 6.11.4)
- Service Retainability (Section 6.11.5)
- Service Throughput (Section 6.11.6)
- Service Timestamp Accuracy (Section 6.11.7).

Note that in cases where nonproxy load balancing may provide support, it will be explicitly noted below.

6.11.1 Service Availability

Proxy load balancing has a positive impact on service availability by:

- Monitoring the availability of the server instances in its pool and directing traffic to active server instances.

- Monitoring the health of server instances based on resource availability metrics collected and directing traffic to server instances with sufficient resources to manage the workload.
- Rerouting failed requests to an alternate server instance. The requests may have failed explicitly with an error message or implicitly based on timers maintained by the load balancer.

A proxy load balancer can have a negative impact on service availability because:

- The load balancer becomes another critical element in the service path and must be included in the availability calculation for the application service.
- The load balancer becomes a single point of failure so it must be redundant to provide high availability.
- The load balancer goes into overload.

If elastic growth fails to activate or execute promptly and correctly, then user traffic may experience overload control (e.g., TOO BUSY errors) rather than being served normally. Accountability for this service impact is complex and is discussed in Section 11.4, "Accountability Case Studies."

6.11.2   Service Latency

Proxy load balancing can have a positive impact on service latency by:

- Collecting metrics on response latency measured for each server instance in the pool and using that data to direct workload to servers that can meet response requirements (as dictated by policies).
- Support concurrent redundancy (if implemented) to make sure a timely response is provided to the client.

Nonproxy load balancing can have a positive impact on service latency by specifically configuring server instances to be those closest in location to the requesting client (e.g., based on transmission times). It can also add latency in retrieving the data.

6.11.3   Service Reliability

Proxy load balancing can have a positive impact on service reliability by monitoring resource usage on the servers and directing traffic to servers that have sufficient resources available to process requests (e.g., based on SLA specifications) and not overload those servers that are already at capacity.

Proxy load balancing can have a negative impact on service reliability by introducing failures into the service itself.

6.11.4   Service Accessibility

Proxy load balancing has a similar positive impact on service accessibility as service availability:

- Monitoring the availability of the server instances in its pool and directing traffic to active server instances.
- Monitoring the health of server instances based on resource availability metrics collected and directing traffic to server instances with sufficient resources to manage the workload.
- Rerouting failed requests to an alternate server instance. The requests may have failed explicitly with an error message or implicitly based on timers maintained by the load balancer.

Proxy load balancing can have a negative impact on service accessibility by becoming inaccessible itself.

6.11.5   Service Retainability

Proxy load balancing can have a positive impact on service retainability by providing session "stickiness"—sending all requests associated with the same session or transaction to the same server. If that server is not available, the load balancer should keep track of and direct requests to an alternate server that has access to the session data and can retain the service.

Proxy load balancing can have a negative impact on service retainability by failing itself, thereby impacting user service delivery. Note that some load balancers may not be able to maintain session information for long-lasting sessions (e.g., lasting for days).

6.11.6   Service Throughput

Proxy load balancing can have a positive impact on service throughput by managing the workload in a way that mitigates overload conditions, such as:

- Routing workload to servers that have sufficient capacity, that is, that are not themselves in overload.
- Providing metrics to an OSS or service orchestration mechanism indicating the need to:
  - Grow additional instance to provide additional capacity.
  - Move an instance to a server with more resources available.

Proxy load balancing can have a negative impact on service throughput by becoming a bottleneck and not being able to handle the traffic being presented to it.

6.11.7   Service Timestamp Accuracy

Neither proxy nor nonproxy load balancing has any impact on service timestamp accuracy.

7

FAILURE CONTAINMENT

High availability systems are designed so that no single failure causes an unacceptable user service disruption by automatically detecting, containing, and recovering from inevitable failures. Virtualization technology and cloud computing not only create options for failure containment architectures that are more powerful than with traditional architectures, but also introduce new risks. Section 7.1, "Failure Containment," gives a thorough treatment of failure containment, and Section 7.2, "Points of Failure," gives a thorough treatment of traditional deployment risks and cloud mitigation techniques. The chapter concludes with Section 7.3, "Extreme Solution Coresidency," and Section 7.4, "Multitenancy and Solution Containers."

7.1 FAILURE CONTAINMENT

Failure containment is like watertight compartments on a ship: it limits the impacts of a failure (i.e., a hole in the ship's hull) to give management and control functions (i.e., captain and crew for a ship and high availability middleware for an application) a stable platform to direct service recovery actions from. One can unpack failure containment into the following concepts:

Service Quality of Cloud-Based Applications, First Edition. Eric Bauer and Randee Adams.
© 2014 The Institute of Electrical and Electronics Engineers, Inc. Published 2014 by John Wiley & Sons, Inc.

- *Failure Cascades* (Section 7.1.1). Containment stops failure cascades.
- *Failure Containment and Recovery* (Section 7.1.2). A failure container generally defines a unit for failure recover.
- *Failure Containment and Virtualization* (Section 7.1.3). Virtualization technology enables more flexibility in failure container sizes than what traditional hardware deployments offer.

7.1.1 Failure Cascades

Fault is defined as "*(1) A defect in a hardware device or component; for example, a short circuit or broken wire. (2) An incorrect step, process, or data definition in a computer program*" [IEEE610]. *Error* is primarily defined as "*the difference between a computed, observed, or measured value or condition and the true, specified, or theoretically correct value or condition. For example, a difference of 30 meters between a computed result and the correct result*" [IEEE610]. *Failure* is defined as "*the inability of a system or component to perform its required functions within specified performance requirements*" [IEEE610]. Faults are said to be *activated*, leading to errors, and errors can lead to failures. For example, a software defect (**fault**) in the stopping condition of a *do/while* loop is activated, leading to an infinite loop **error**, which prevents the system from replying to a user's request within the specified time and thus produces a service **failure**.

If a system does not contain the initial failure promptly, then a cascade of secondary failures may be triggered. These concepts are easily illustrated via the example of watertight compartments on a ship. A hole in the ship's hull is a fault that is activated when the hole is below the waterline (e.g., the fault is not a problem when the ship is in dry dock); water flooding into the ship is the error. Well-designed ships will contain the flooding to a single watertight compartment, which prevents the flooding from sinking the ship because even with a single flooded watertight compartment, the vessel maintains sufficient buoyancy to remain afloat. If the flooding is not successfully contained to a single watertight compartment, then flooding will eventually compromise so much buoyancy that the ship sinks (a catastrophic failure). Thus, an improperly contained failure can cascade from a potentially small event to a catastrophic failure over time. Failure containment for applications should strictly limit the extent of service impact. For example, just as a single hole in a ship should not cause it to sink, a single bug, such as a memory leak, should not cascade to produce a total service outage for all users.

7.1.2 Failure Containment and Recovery

Failure containment is crucial to the following:

- *Prevent failure cascades* by providing a barrier to contain a failure's impact.
- *Enable limited service recovery actions* so that partial capacity or functionality impairments can be corrected without requiring service impact to all users or functionality. For example, while most software failures can be cleared by

restarting the entire application (thereby impacting 100% of active users), failures that are rigidly contained to a particular module or process can be cleared by recovering that particular module, thereby nominally impacting only the portion of users or functionality tied to that failed and recovered module. As service downtime is generally prorated by capacity lost or impacted, an architecture that enables a failure event to be recovered by impacting, say, 10% of active users, is far better than an architecture that requires 100% of active users to be impacted on recovery.

- *Provide a fallback mechanism.* Netflix introduced the notion of a circuit breaker mechanism, in which if a critical failure is detected, connections to the failed component are broken and a fallback mechanism is initiated. The fallback mechanism can be something like using local data if the connection to an external data store has been broken or failing fast and returning an error message to the client. The fallback options can be customized to the application based on providing some type of acceptable service or notification to the client. In many cases, failing fast and recovering to another instance or instantiating a new instance may be the easiest option.

- *Maintain availability requirements* by making sure that sufficient application capacity remains online to meet service availability commitments despite a single component failure. For example, if the application's service level agreement specifies that outage time is accrued when more than 10% of service has been lost due to a failure, then containing a failure's impact to less than 10% of user capacity can prevent the failure from escalating into a chargeable service outage.

Distributed applications have traditionally been built with the following hierarchy of failure containment (from smallest to largest):

- *Transaction.* Transactions traditionally offer rigid containment for database operations. Aborting a pending transaction wipes away all traces of the aborted operation, thereby elegantly containing failure events.

- *Client Request.* Clients and servers of distributed applications are generally designed so that individual requests can fail without compromising the client session. For example, an individual application programming interface (API) call can fail for myriad reasons (e.g., user not authorized, resource not found, and system too busy), and the application will continue to operate properly despite an error being returned via an API. The request failure generally flows back to the client—and perhaps the user—where it can be revised and resubmitted to the server. The cancel and reload functions on a web browser leverage failure containment at the client request level.

- *Client Session.* If a user session becomes damaged, then the user will often abandon it and start a fresh session. For example, if the service quality of a streaming movie or telephone call becomes unacceptable, then the user will often terminate the session and restart the movie or redial the call.

- *Software Process.* Severe software problems are generally contained within a single software process. Readers will undoubtedly be familiar with PC applications that hang and must be terminated via the operating system's task manager so the application can be restarted to restore normal operation.
- *Application Component.* An application is generally made up of several components (e.g., frontend, application, and database); a component level failure can generally be contained to that component, and it can recover using its own redundancy mechanism without adversely impacting the application service.
- *Operating System Instance.* More severe software problems may require the entire operating system to be rebooted. Undoubtedly, many readers are familiar with rebooting their cable modem's operating system by power cycling the unit to restore residential broadband service to proper operation.
- *Distributed Application Instance.* The most severe failures of distributed systems may require all operating systems and/or components in the application instance to be rebooted, possibly after some repair action (e.g., reloading or repairing compromised configuration data).
- *Availability Zone or Data Center.* Availability zones or data centers are the largest unit of failure containment that is generally supported, and they are engineered to contain the service impact of disaster events, such as earthquakes, that could render a data center unavailable or inaccessible. Disaster recovery mechanisms are designed to rigidly contain a failure to a single availability zone or cloud data center to assure that application service can be promptly restored despite all application software and data hosted in the impacted site or zone being indefinitely unavailable or inaccessible. Geographic redundancy, or georedundancy, relies on vast physical separation of data centers to assure that no individual force majeure event, such as an earthquake, can impact more than one data center.

The flip side of rigidly containing a failure within a transaction, session, or process is that all other components must be capable of continuing to operate acceptably well despite the failure. Netflix gave this robust operation the colorful name of "Rambo architecture," which they describe as *"Each system has to be able to succeed, no matter what, even all on its own . . . each distributed system* [must] *expect and tolerate failure from other systems on which it depends"* [Netflix10]. After all, a partial functionality outage gives the user the option of accepting degraded functionality or not; a total outage leaves the user stranded.

7.1.3 Failure Containment and Virtualization

Virtualization can enable even more powerful failure containment than native deployment because the resource configuration of the virtual machine (VM) is no longer strictly defined by the underlying hardware. Virtualization enables architects more flexibility to select the size of VM instances to use with an application than native hardware. Consider the example of a hypothetical simplex application that can be configured to serve 100 users, either with a single "big" VM instance or with 10 "little" VM instances.

Assume that identical application and guest OS software run in both big and little VM instances, and the software failure rate is the same regardless of the VM size. Assume further that the application software has a mean time between failures (MTBF) of 1 year and that the failure events have a mean time to restore service (MTRS) of 20 minutes. Thus, the typical big VM instance configuration experiences one outage per year with 20 minutes of service downtime for all 100 users. The typical small VM instance configuration experiences 10 outages per year (one outage for each of the 10 small VM instances), and each of those events accrues 20 minutes of service downtime for the 10 users served by the impacted small VM instance. However, since 10 impacted users is only 10% of the 100 users served by the application, the outage of a single small VM instances is prorated to be a 10% capacity loss event, and 10% capacity loss for 20 minutes is equivalent to 2 minutes of total service downtime. Ten small VM instance outages per year (each accruing the equivalent of 2 minutes of total service downtime) has the same total service downtime of a single big VM instance, which accrues 20 minutes of total service downtime in a single event per year. Thus, changing the capacity (size) of the failure containment does not generally impact service availability, although the complexity may increase, introducing a possibility of a slight decrease in MTBF.

While containment size is unlikely to materially impact failure rate, recovery time, or prorated service availability, it does affect the number of users impacted by each outage event, sometimes called the "footprint of failure." Footprint of failure is actually an important attribute that has very practical implications in the real world. If a small number of users (perhaps only one) are impacted by a service outage, then service recovery is often worked with ordinary priority. If a large or very large number of users are impacted by a failure event, then service recovery will be worked on an emergency basis. Certain types of services in some localities may even be obligated to formally disclose details of the outage event to government regulators (e.g., telecommunications outage reporting to the U.S. Federal Communications Commission), which both adds expense and regulatory risks for the service provider.

Just as children are advised not to put all of their eggs into one basket, application service providers are advised not to put all of their users into a single failure group. Unfortunately, the opposite extreme of putting each subscriber into an individual failure group (e.g., served by a single, dedicated VM instance) requires massive resource overhead and may not be architecturally feasible for large classes of applications. Thus, architects must balance simultaneously minimizing the footprint of failure and resource consumption when determining containment size.

Note that component size (e.g., maximum number of users, sessions, and transactions served per component instance) may also influence recovery latency. For example, if per user/session/transaction auditing and/or recovery actions are required to complete a failover or other service recovery action, then a component supporting "$10X$" users/sessions/transactions is likely to take somewhat longer to failover than a component supporting a maximum of only "X" users/sessions/transactions. If the difference in failover latency is material compared with the maximum acceptable service latency, then architects should consider the failover latency budget when engineering application component capacity onto VM instances.

7.2 POINTS OF FAILURE

7.2.1 Single Points of Failure

As explained in Section 5.4, "Redundancy and Recoverability," redundancy and high availability architectures are designed to enable a single failure event to be rapidly detected and service recovered to a redundant component without accruing unacceptable user service impact. Operationally, this means that any single failure is rigidly contained to a single component instance so service can be rapidly recovered to a redundant component instance. Failure of a nonredundant (i.e., simplex) component in the critical service delivery path impacts service until the failed component can be repaired or replaced and service can be recovered; thus, simplex components in the critical service delivery path whose failure will produce a service outage are said to be "single points of failure." By having redundancy built into the system's design, service can be restored rapidly following failure via a rapid and automatic *failover* from the failed unit rather than requiring a much slower manual hardware replacement or repair activity. Note that platform or application software may be required to activate a failover to move traffic from the failed "side" to the "operational" side.

Single points of failure are generally identified by constructing and analyzing an application's reliability block diagram (RBD). For example, assume that a hypothetical application has a frontend component "A" and a backend component "B" so that instances of both "A" and "B" must be available to deliver service to users, and hence are in the critical service delivery path. Figure 7.1 shows a RBD of this example system with a single frontend component instance "A_1" and three backend component instances "B_1," "B_2," and "B_3" that are necessary to serve the engineered workload with acceptable service quality. In this nonredundant configuration, failure of component

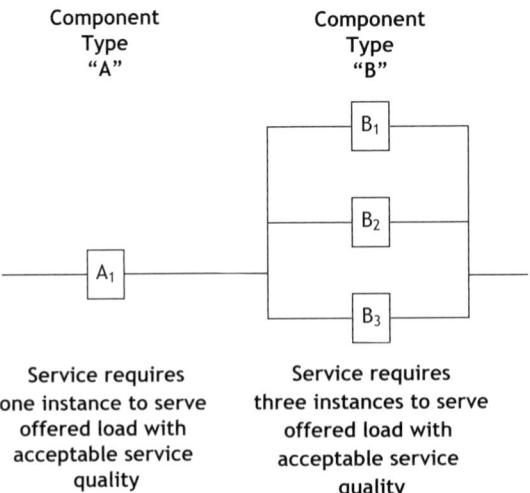

Component
Type
"A"

Component
Type
"B"

B_1

B_2

A_1

B_3

Service requires
one instance to serve
offered load with
acceptable service
quality

Service requires
three instances to serve
offered load with
acceptable service
quality

Figure 7.1. Reliability Block Diagram of Simplex Sample System (with SPOF).

"A_1" produces a 100% capacity loss outage and failure of one backend component instance (e.g., "B_1") produces a 33% capacity loss outage. Thus, component "A_1" is a single point of failure (SPOF) because its unavailability produces a total service outage.

The nonredundant SPOF design of Figure 7.1 can be enhanced to be no SPOF as shown in Figure 7.2 by the following:

1. making simplex component A redundant so that failure of one instance (e.g., A_1) no longer yields a service outage until that component can be repaired or replaced.
2. adding an additional B component instance so that failure of one instance (e.g., B_1) no longer produces a partial capacity loss outage until that component can be repaired or replaced.

7.2.2 Single Points of Failure and Virtualization

The incremental SPOF risk of virtualization is best understood through an example, so let us consider the no SPOF application architecture of Figure 7.2. The optimal distribution of components across virtualized server instances to achieve no SPOF is shown in Figure 7.3: two VM servers host both a single instance of type A and a single instance of type B (i.e., virtual server "S1" hosting A_1 and B_1 and virtual server "S2" hosting A_2 and B_2) and two other virtual servers hosting one instance of type B (i.e., virtual server "S3" hosting B_3 and virtual server "S4" hosting "B_4").

Figure 7.4 illustrates successful operation of this optimal distribution by demonstrating how, although failure of Virtual Server S1 impacts both A_1 and B_1, the service requirement of at least one instance of server type A and at least three instances of type B is still met.

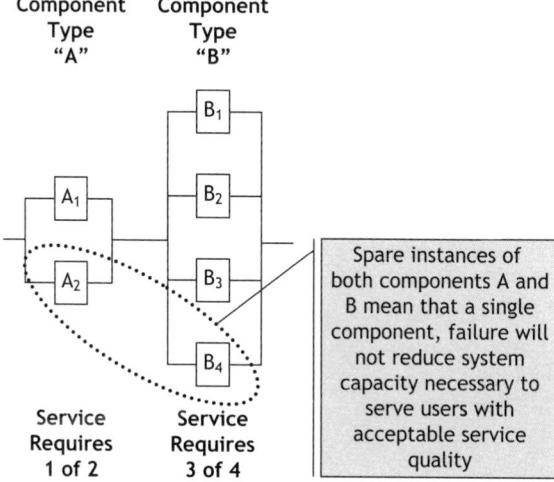

Figure 7.2. Reliability Block Diagram of Redundant Sample System (without SPOF).

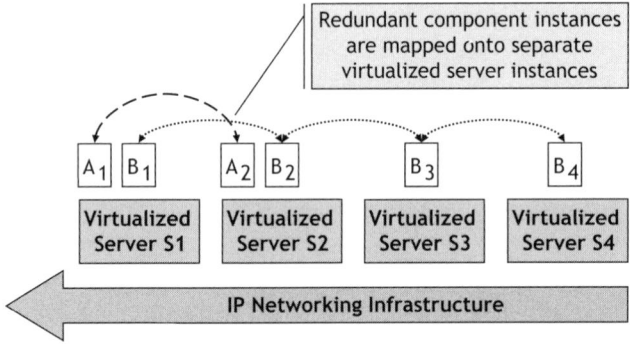

Figure 7.3. No SPOF Distribution of Component Instances across Virtual Servers.

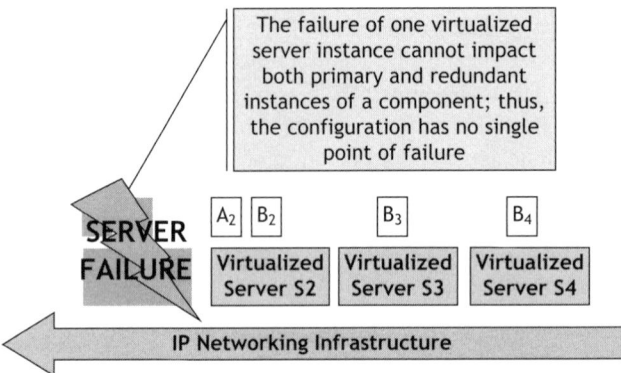

Figure 7.4. Example of No Single Point of Failure with Distributed Component Instances.

In contrast, Figure 7.5 illustrates an alternate mapping of component instances onto virtual servers that creates a SPOF when both A_1 and A_2 are hosted on virtual server S1. The failure of the virtual server S1 breaches the minimum component configuration required to serve the offered load with acceptable service quality, and thus produces an outage. "Anti-affinity" rules enable applications to provide constraint rules to the IaaS implementation so that no SPOF requirements are not breached during the following infrastructure events:

1. Initial allocation of application resources
2. Elastic growth of application resources
3. Elastic degrowth (shrink) of application resources

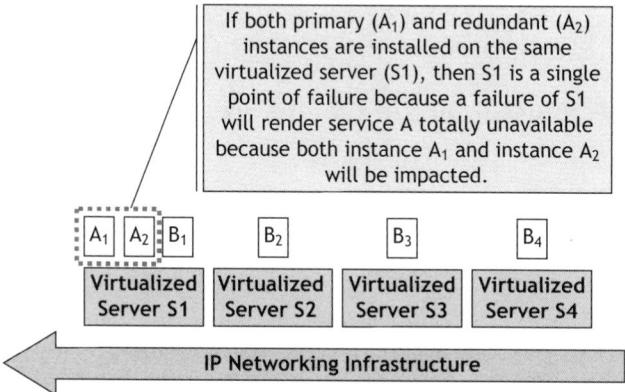

If both primary (A₁) and redundant (A₂) instances are installed on the same virtualized server (S1), then S1 is a single point of failure because a failure of S1 will render service A totally unavailable because both instance A₁ and instance A₂ will be impacted.

Figure 7.5. Example of Single Point of Failure with Poorly Distributed Component Instances.

4. Migrating/reconfiguring cloud resources during IaaS operations, such as when consolidating/balancing VM loads or storage allocations across virtualized disk arrangements

5. Activating or resuming VM snapshots

6. Restarting/recovering/reallocating virtual resources (e.g., VMs, storage) following failure

7. Carrying out uncoordinated administrative actions on the cloud and application layers.

7.2.3 Affinity and Anti-affinity Considerations

When configuring native systems, application architects typically make explicit install time decisions about which server or blade each individual application component instance should run on. System architects carefully balance the performance benefits of having related components in close proximity (e.g., on different compute blades in a single chassis or even on different CPU cores on a single blade or rack mounted server) against the SPOF risk, in which a single hardware failure would disrupt both the primary and redundant instances of any system component. For example, if a high availability system relies on a pair of registry servers to host volatile application data, then a traditional high availability configuration would explicitly install those two registry instances on different hardware servers so that no single hardware server, Ethernet switch, and other failure could simultaneously impact both registry instances. Note that since the pair of registry instances mirror all changes in volatile data to minimize loss of context following failure of one registry instance, there is likely to be significant network traffic between the two registry servers, and hence between the hardware servers supporting each registry instance. While mirroring of volatile data would presumably run significantly faster if both registry server instances were on the same server instance, collocating them on the same server instance would create a SPOF. Thus, architects of high availability systems will explicitly trade-off slightly lower performance and somewhat increased network utilization to eliminate a SPOF from the deployed application.

7.2.4 No SPOF Assurance in Cloud Computing

"Resource pooling" is an essential characteristic of cloud computing motivating the cloud provider to maximize usage of resources. Cloud computing limits the application architect's and cloud consumer's ability to explicitly control the mapping of software component instances onto physical hardware resources because the cloud service provider has control over resource allocation decisions. In addition, hypervisors support online (live) migration of VM instances, which enables cloud service providers to physically move (live) VM instances from one VM server to another. Moreover, those physical placement decisions (i.e., which virtual server instance will host the VM instance requested by any particular application at any particular time) will ultimately be made dynamically by the cloud service provider's VM server controller(s) and their operations support systems. In addition, those placement decisions may change over time based on the cloud service provider's maintenance plans, resource needs of other applications, and even power management policies. This highlights the need for no SPOF rules to be enforced both on resource allocation and whenever VM instances are moved.

Figure 7.6 illustrates simplified VM server control architecture. Requests to instantiate applications or to elastically grow an application are presented to software that orchestrates control across a pool of VM server instances located in one or more data centers. The VM server controller implements the requested application configuration change while simultaneously enforcing both the application's anti-affinity rules and the

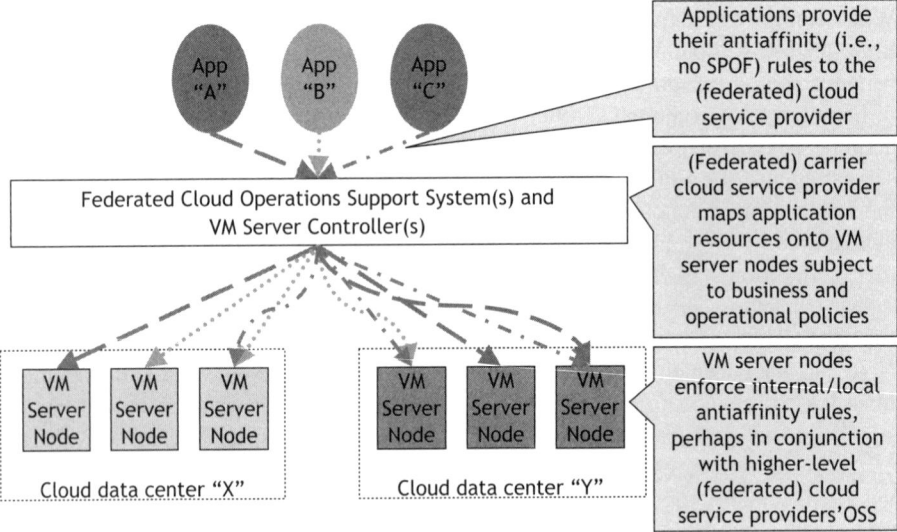

Figure 7.6. Simplified VM Server Control.

cloud service provider's operational policies. The result is commands to one or more VM servers to allocate and configure VM instances. In addition to considering anti-affinity rules, VM server controllers may consider other factors, such as data center utilization, time of day, physical location of actual and anticipated end users, and other factors in their automation tools.

VM server controllers can implement a higher level of no SPOF assurance by distributing instances across independent VM servers, and VM servers themselves will implement some no SPOF assurance. Establishing clear accountability rules for no SPOF assurance is essential as failing to properly enforce no SPOF rules puts applications at risk of extended service outages.

7.2.5   No SPOF and Application Data

Applications maintain volatile information to track active sessions, pending transactions, resource status, recent performance statistics, cached data, program stacks, etc. Application architects are confronted with the classic challenge of balancing duration of service impact following failure against (1) operational expenditure (OPEX) for maintaining redundant application or data instances and (2) development expense for implementing and testing complex data replication, failure detection, and failure recovery mechanisms. As the contents of an application's volatile memory are managed by an application itself, eliminating an SPOF for volatile memory generally means either of the following:

- *Maintaining a copy of application's dynamic memory/storage in another application process instance* (e.g., a standby or mated pair process instance)
- *Having the ability to rapidly rebuild application's volatile memory from persistent* storage (e.g., reloading executable program binaries and user profile data) and/or from nonimpacted software instances (e.g., retrieving user state/context data from client applications)
- *Storing volatile data in a shared data registry server*, which is redundant and stored on servers separate from the application software.

Although the contents of persistent storage can be automatically protected from routine application software and power failures, the contents are vulnerable to physical failure (e.g., disk head crashes), as well as software, human, and other failures that damage the data but not the physical device. Vulnerability to data damage by software, human, or other nonphysical failures is generally mitigated via periodic backups, application data audits, and procedures to restore predamage snapshots of data from those backups. Vulnerability to physical storage device failure is mitigated via physical redundancy as either of the following:

- *Redundancy within the Logical Storage Device.* Redundant array of inexpensive/independent disks (RAIDs) is a common way to eliminate the SPOF for individual hard disk devices by writing data to multiple physical hard disk drives. The RAID storage device automatically writes the data to multiple independent disks so that no single hard disk (or other single component) failure will impact the ability to access data. The RAID storage device guarantees data consistency across the redundant copies of data within the logical storage device. Operationally, applications might access RAID persistent storage via a network protocol such as network file system (NFS), so the application sees a single logical storage device (i.e., file system and files), and detection and mitigation of physical storage failures are managed completely by the RAID storage array.

• *Redundancy across Multiple Logical Storage Devices.* Data redundancy can be maintained by individual application instances across multiple logical storage devices, such as having each application instance maintain the primary persistent storage on a local hard disk device and having changes automatically replicated across the network to another independent storage device. When multiple logical storage devices are used, consistency must be managed by either the application itself or via the file/data replication service. Often data changes will be collected into a batch and replicated asynchronously, such as every 15 minutes. While asynchronous replication has minimal impact on service latency, it does introduce a window of data loss on recovery from that point in time replicas. Synchronous replication across multiple logical storage devices is possible, but that generally impacts service latency as both devices must successfully update persistent storage before responding to application users; however, when one of the logical storage devices fails, the application instance can switch to exclusively use the alternate logical storage device until the failed unit can be repaired/replaced. Note that the application will be exposed to risk of data loss if the alternate disk fails before the other disk can be replaced and restored to service.

7.3   EXTREME SOLUTION CORESIDENCY

Virtualization allows solutions comprised of multiple applications to potentially be taken to the extreme where all of the applications in the solution are consolidated and deployed onto a pair of VM servers. This deployment of multiple high availability (i.e., redundant) application instances across a minimal physical host configuration with no SPOF is referred to by the authors as "extreme solution coresidency." Although all components of all applications are redundant so no SPOF technically exists, each VM server in an extremely coresident configuration represents a massive failure footprint, which has correlated service impact on up to half of each and every one of the solution's high availability components across all application instances. Application's high availability mechanisms must cope not only with a failure event that impacts a possibly huge portion of the application's functionality and/or capacity but also with simultaneous and correlated impact of other applications in the solution that the application itself depends upon. For example, if all of the application instances of an (highly available) eCommerce solution are consolidated onto two VM server hosts and one of the hosts fails completely, then all of the active components on the failed host must recover service on the other host and reconnect with other applications in the solution, such as backend database servers, credit card payment systems, and logistics servers. The added complexity of recovering from simultaneous failure of both components within the application itself, as well as reconnecting with external applications upon which the target application depends, makes service recovery for extreme solution coresidency configurations more complex and possibly slower and less reliable.

Ideally, all application components rapidly and robustly recover user service following failures in extreme solution coresidency configurations; alternately, the cloud consumer or application can treat the failure as catastrophic and rely on disaster recovery mechanisms to restore user service.

7.3.1 Extreme Solution Coresidency Risks

Assuming that each individual application meets high availability and no-single-point-of-failure requirements when configured across two physical hosts, the extreme coresidency question becomes: **How much longer will user service recovery from a host failure be for extreme solution coresidency than for the slowest high availability application configuration deployed standalone?** After all, if solution recovery time for extreme coresidency is simply the maximum of the individual application recovery times, then one simply finds the slowest application and optimizes that application's recovery time. Some extreme coresidency concerns are the following:

1. *If a component failover depends on another server, then the failover might take longer with extreme coresidency.* That is, if during the activation of application "A," it requires application "B" to process a request, then application "A" will not be able to resume service until after application "B" has already recovered.

2. *A deadlock situation could occur that prevents some applications from recovering.* That is, if activation of application "A" depends on application "B" running, and similarly, application "B" depends on application "C" and application "C" depends on application "A," then none of the applications may ever recover.

3. *Multiple applications failing over at the same time could saturate or overload critical resources*, such as the CPU or disk access, thus prolonging service recovery significantly beyond nominal recovery times.

4. If any combination of active/standby instances is allowed on each physical host, then *it is not practical to test every possible configuration.* Development teams may not test the true worst-case scenario extreme coresidency configuration in the lab because they cannot predict it, and thus are forced to discover it in the field.

5. *The use of backoff timers to slow recovery of individual application instances to deal with the worst-case extreme solution coresidency failures may unnecessarily slow recovery for typical failure scenarios.*

6. *If one of the coresident applications is making heavy demands on hardware resources, then a more critical application may experience degraded service.*

When a VM server failure impacts an extremely coresident solution, the nonimpacted VM server(s) will likely experience a correlated workload spike as potentially all nonimpacted application component instances simultaneously initiate recovery actions to mitigate the impact of the extreme coresidency failure event. These overlapping, potentially interdependent recovery actions, coupled with likely short-term performance degradations of virtualized infrastructure as all component instances simultaneously execute recovery actions, increases the risk that overall service recovery will not successfully complete within the maximum acceptable service disruption time. To mitigate the risk, it is necessary to thoroughly analyze and test the extreme solution coresidency configuration and determine if the architecture needs to be modified to more effectively manage any detected risks (see Section 15.5, "Anti-affinity Analysis").

The following architectural strategies are recommended to ensure that applications can recover quickly when a host with extreme coresidency fails:

1. It is preferable for *redundant components to run active/active, load shared rather than active/standby* so that recovering applications do not have to wait for a standby component instance to be promoted. Client applications should establish and maintain sessions for at least two noncoresident instances of load shared servers, so that if half the servers fail simultaneously due to VM server failure, then applications can still maintain service without disruptions. (Note that maintaining multiple sessions to the same service has to be done carefully to avoid state inconsistency across the sessions.)

2. *Circular dependencies must be avoided*, such as A depending on B, which depends on C, which depends on A.

3. *Redundant instances should always be as prepared as possible to take over service from their mate instance(s).* That is, the process should be running, and state data received from the active instance should be properly stored in memory data structures, and so on. This is to minimize the amount of processing needed to activate the redundant unit and avoid critical resource shortages.

4. *Applications should support fault recovery on all of their interfaces independently.* It should not be assumed that any two interfaces will, or will not, fail at the same time.

7.4 MULTITENANCY AND SOLUTION CONTAINERS

Application service providers will often aggregate suites of application instances and technology components into logical solution bundles or "containers," which conveniently separate all configuration and user data of one application user group from another. For example, an application service provider offering online collaboration services to enterprise customers can architect their offering so that the configuration and application data for each enterprise customer are rigidly separated from every other enterprise customer (also known as closed user groups), and each enterprise's container is operated according to that enterprise customer's security and other operational policies. While traditionally these closed user groups might be implemented via complex application logic that programmatically isolate separate user communities, virtualization enables separate application and solution instances to be created in separate virtualized resources and operated independently alongside each other, thus reducing application complexity and minimizing risk of one user community interacting or interfering with another community. This should enable the application service provider to quickly deploy and efficiently operate service containers for individual customers. In addition to rigidly containing the customer's proprietary information, this should also provide another level of failure containment. For example, if one customer accidentally sets a security policy that erroneously denies authenticated users access to data they should be authorized to see, then the application service provider's containers should prevent that error from impacting user service for other enterprises who are "tenants" of that application service provider, even if they are running the same application from the same cloud data center.

8

CAPACITY MANAGEMENT

This chapter considers the service quality risks of online, elastic capacity growth and degrowth of cloud-based applications. Practical aspects of elasticity operations, including overload controls, are discussed. The chapter concludes with a review of the risks of rapid elasticity. Note that elasticity is mentioned in several other sections of this book:

- Elasticity strategies and measurements were introduced in Section 3.5, "Elasticity Measurements."
- Application elasticity requirements are considered in Section 13.8, "Elasticity Requirements."
- Architectural analyses of application elasticity risks are discussed in Section 15.6, "Elasticity Analysis."
- Testing of application elasticity is considered in Section 16.4.5, "Application Elasticity Testing."

Service Quality of Cloud-Based Applications, First Edition. Eric Bauer and Randee Adams.
© 2014 The Institute of Electrical and Electronics Engineers, Inc. Published 2014 by John Wiley & Sons, Inc.

8.1 WORKLOAD VARIATIONS

Application workloads vary for several fundamental reasons:

- *Long-Term Popularity/Usage Growth and Decline Trends.* Popularity will often grow over time or existing customers will often be methodically migrated onto a new application. Methodical migration of users from legacy systems to new systems is often executed with thousands of users migrated per week, and those users can quickly grow usage of the new application week on week. Eventually, older applications become obsolete and less popular, and usage declines. These longer term popularity/usage trends can be explicitly managed when users are methodically migrated or monitored and tracked as "organic" popularity growth and degrowth trends play out over time.
- *Daily, Weekly, and Seasonal Traffic Variations.* Figure 8.1 shows a typical daily workload of a communications application on a logarithmic scale. Note that the peak load (nominally at 10 a.m. local time) is more than 100 times greater than the off-peak load (nominally 5 a.m.). Different applications may see very different workload patterns. Many applications have weekly traffic variations, such as enterprise applications having heavy workload on business days and light workloads on weekends. Seasonality patterns are also common, such as consumer eCommerce applications experiencing higher workloads in the weeks before Christmas.
- *Extreme Popularity Peaks.* Some enterprise applications exhibit extreme seasonality peaks, such as consumer eCommerce traffic volumes on "Black Friday" and "Cyber Monday," release day for a new product or service, or the day of a major entertainment or sporting event.
- *Extraordinary Events.* Promotional, viral (e.g., Slashdot), and other events of regional or national significance (e.g., earthquake and terrorist act) can produce unpredictable workload spikes.

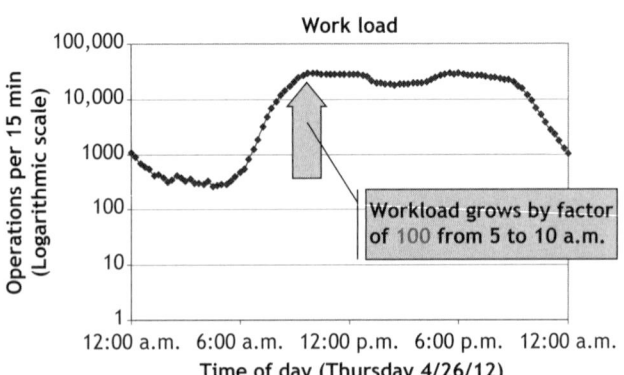

Figure 8.1. Sample Daily Workload Variation (Logarithmic Scale).

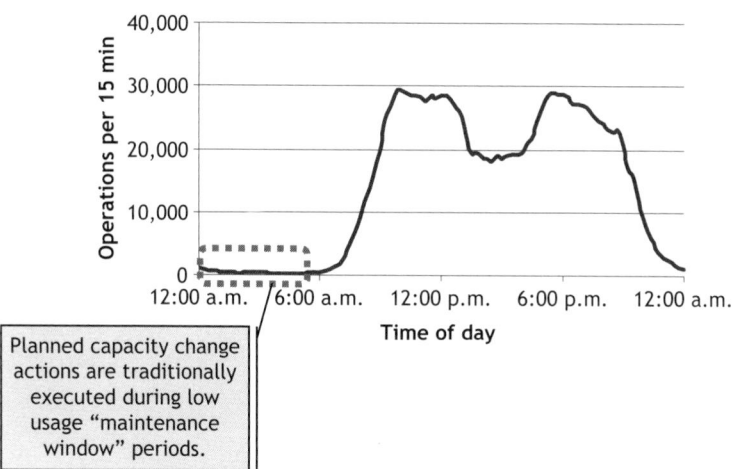

Figure 8.2. Traditional Maintenance Window.

- *Market Trials.* Workload will naturally vary due to market trials when spinning up very limited service capacity to run a user trial or a trial of a new implementation of a service to compare it with the existing implementation, and then spinning down that capacity when the trial is over.

8.2 TRADITIONAL CAPACITY MANAGEMENT

Traditionally, application capacity was directly tied to capital expense because supporting more online service capacity meant buying more physical compute, memory, storage, and networking resources to host application software. Typically, all of that application capacity was maintained online 24 × 7 because it was simpler and had lower service quality risk to leave full capacity online than actively managing online application service capacity. Capacity management events were usually carefully planned and scheduled in advance and executed during low usage maintenance window periods (see Figure 8.2). Industry practice has evolved to treat these scheduled events specially, and in many cases, applications are permitted to experience short planned outages to safely complete capacity management operations. Those customers that use high-quality methods of procedure (MOPs), diligent planning, adequate training and preparation, and careful execution could grow or degrow service for traditional applications with acceptable service risk.

8.3 TRADITIONAL OVERLOAD CONTROL

Well-designed applications detect the overload condition when offered workload exceeds the online engineered service capacity and gracefully reject (or "shape") some

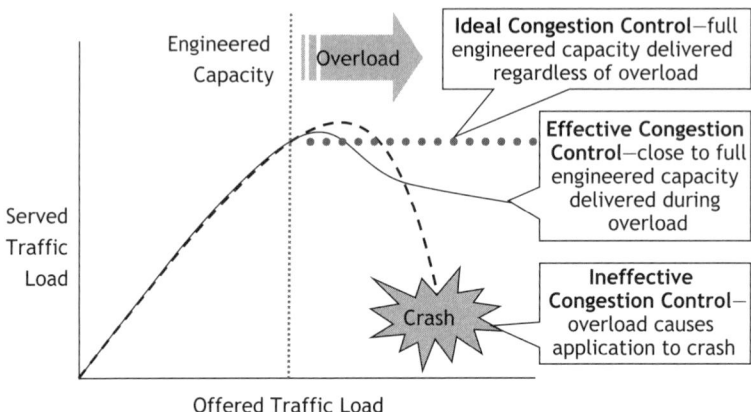

Figure 8.3. Traditional Congestion Control.

traffic, such as by returning appropriate "TOO BUSY" errors to some user requests and rescheduling low priority activities (e.g., measurement reports) until the overload condition has ended. As shown in Figure 8.3, proactively shaping the workload by gracefully declining to serve some offered load is better than letting the application run past saturation to the point of catastrophic failure.

While end users might interpret the result of overload controls (e.g., "all circuits are busy, try your call again later") to indicate service unavailability, methodically rejecting traffic is exactly what well-engineered applications are designed to do, so it is not considered a product-attributable service outage. Instead, the user service impact is attributable to the application service provider who failed to engineer sufficient online capacity to meet offered load. Technically, the customer would have made a procedural error of failing to configure sufficient service capacity to meet offered load.

The best practice has traditionally been to follow rigorous capacity management processes. The capacity management process recommended by IT Infrastructure Library (ITIL) includes the following key activities [ITIL_CM]:

- Performance monitoring
- Workload monitoring
- Application sizing
- Resource forecasting
- Demand forecasting
- Modeling
- Implementing capacity-related changes.

As a practical matter, traditional capacity management often boiled down to predicting the peak user workload for an application and installing capacity to serve a greater workload. This relatively static capacity management strategy presented risks of both wasting capital expenditure (CAPEX) if predicted demand never materializes, and rejecting (or serving poorly) user traffic if offered load exceeds online capacity until more capacity could be engineered, purchased, installed, and brought online. In the typical best case, a traditional application was deployed with 15% excess capacity beyond expected peak demand, so most of the time, there was vastly more available (i.e., wasted) capacity than was necessary to serve offered load. The bottom line was that traditional capacity management forced enterprises to put significant CAPEX at risk to serve possible peak user demand that may never materialize and may eventually decline as consumer tastes and business needs shift.

Note that in reality, degrowth operations were rarely performed, presumably because the value of hardware resources depreciates so rapidly that by the time the customer was confident that capacity could be degrown, the residual value of the unused/underused hardware was too low to justify the operational expenditure (OPEX) of releasing and redeploying the resource and the potential risk of failure and service impact if the shrink operation failed.

8.4 CAPACITY MANAGEMENT AND VIRTUALIZATION

Virtualization makes it far simpler and faster to instantiate new virtual machine (VM) instances to host online application capacity than with traditional hardware resources. Rather than ordering additional hardware resources from a supplier (e.g., compute blades, RAM, and hard disks), waiting days or weeks for the hardware to be delivered, and manually executing a written procedure to physically install the hardware, one can allocate additional virtual resources in minutes or less. In addition, virtualization makes it far simpler to reuse resources that have been deallocated by an application than with traditional application deployments. Note that this does assume good forecasting by both the infrastructure providers to ensure sufficient resources are available to support application growth, as well as by the cloud consumers to ensure their roadmaps on capacity growth are given to the cloud providers.

In addition to the traditional capacity growth implementation model of acquiring new resources (e.g., compute blade or VM instance) and installing application software onto those resources, virtualization technology introduces two novel options:

- *Activating VM Snapshots.* Hypervisors enable a VM snapshot to be created and stored of the configuration and memory contents of a VM instance at a point in time. That saved snapshot can later be activated to create a clone of the original VM instance at the moment that the snapshot was taken. This mechanism can be used to bypass at least some of the traditional procedures—and hence time— associated with loading and configuring (guest) operating system and application software when implementing capacity growth.
- *Activating Suspended VM Instances.* Hypervisors permit VM instances to be suspended, which effectively puts the VM instance into a deep sleep in which it consumes no CPU resources. As a suspended VM instance will not respond to heartbeat messages, use of this mechanism must be carefully coordinated with the application's high availability mechanism to prevent misinterpreting the

suspension of a VM instance for capacity management reasons with a VM instance failure event.

After activating a snapshot or suspended VM instance, both the VM instance itself and the rest of the application's management and control infrastructure must resynchronize state information to properly reintegrate the newly activated VM capacity with the running application instance.

The example of Figure 8.1 showed daily workload of a sample application growing by two orders of magnitude from 5 to 10 a.m. local time. Fortunately, virtualization technology has proven itself in enterprise data center deployments as an efficient tool for workload consolidation, so hypervisors can efficiently share the infrastructure resources that are nominally supporting the target application at 5 a.m. local time when the sample application's offered load is minimal with other applications to optimize overall resource utilization. Thus, virtualization can enable capacity management across a broader pool of applications because the hypervisor—like older timesharing multiuser computer systems—can efficiently share precious resources across pools of applications by implementing predefined policies. Resources unused by a particular application at a particular time (e.g., sample application at 5 a.m.) can be used by another application rather than simply being wasted. Finding applications and users to consume resource capacity at off-peak hours may be somewhat challenging for the infrastructure supplier, but this is a routine problem for myriad businesses, such as airlines and hotels, which have developed sophisticated pricing and promotional models to fill their off-peak capacity.

As described in Section 3.5.4, "Scaling In and Out," and Section 3.5.5, "Scaling Up and Down," virtualization gives great flexibility in the size and configuration of those resources for tracking offered workload. Section 7.1.3, "Failure Containment and Virtualization," discusses failure containment considerations in the VM instance sizing decision. Thus, application architects must select appropriate vertical sizes of its VM instances and appropriate scale out and scale in configurations. Even with flexible resources, multiple application instances will often be deployed by customers across several availability zones and data centers rather than relying on a single enormous application instance. Beyond failure containment, architects will consider the application's slew rate (see Section 3.5.7, "Slew Rate and Linearity") when determining the application's horizontal and vertical scale. This simple notion of maximum application slew rate must consider the following:

- *Concurrency.* Are elastic growth actions strictly serialized by the application— perhaps even rejecting new growth requests received when an elastic growth action is pending—or can multiple growth actions be overlapped?
- *Unit of Capacity Growth (Agility).* Are multiple sizes of C_{Grow} supported (e.g., growing by either a two-CPU core VM instance or a four-CPU core VM instance), or is only a single unit of capacity growth supported?
- *Linearity of Growth.* Is provisioning interval, unit of capacity growth, and concurrency constant across the application's entire capacity range from minimum scale down to maximum scale up?

These factors determine the maximum sustained application slew rate, and the cloud operations support system (OSS) must consider this maximum rate when determining how much spare application online capacity to maintain. Capacity management policy decisions by the cloud consumer must balance the OPEX of maintaining spare online capacity against the service quality risk of having insufficient online capacity available to serve user traffic across a traffic surge and/or failure.

8.5 CAPACITY MANAGEMENT IN CLOUD

Two cloud computing characteristics radically shift capacity management expectations for the cloud consumer by introducing the notion of on-demand growth, provisioning, and release management activities:

- *On-Demand Self-Service.* A consumer can unilaterally provision computing capabilities, such as server time and network storage, as needed automatically without requiring human interaction with each service provider. [SP800-145]
- *Rapid Elasticity.* Capabilities can be elastically provisioned and released, in some cases automatically, to scale rapidly outward and inward commensurate with demand. To the consumer, the capabilities available for provisioning often appear to be unlimited and can be appropriated in any quantity at any time. [SP800-145]

Cloud computing's essential characteristic of rapid elasticity leads to Weinman's *Cloudonomics Law No. 2*:

On-demand trumps forecasting. The ability to rapidly provision capacity means that any unexpected demand can be serviced, and the revenue associated with it captured. The ability to rapidly de-provision capacity means that companies don't need to pay good money for non-productive assets. Forecasting is often wrong, especially for black swans, so the ability to react instantaneously means higher revenues, and lower costs. [Weinman]

Thus, the onus is on the cloud service provider to forecast and assure that sufficient resources are available to meet cloud consumers' needs.

Capacity management in the cloud can be deployed in two basic ways:

- *Manually triggered capacity management events*, in which human beings explicitly initiate (and perhaps execute) elastic growth or degrowth procedures. For example, an enterprise may explicitly trigger significant capacity growth prior to an event that is likely to trigger unusually high offered loads, such as Cyber Monday for eCommerce applications.
- *Automatically triggered capacity management events* when sophisticated elasticity management operations support systems are implemented and configured to autonomously implement elasticity policies. Automatic mechanisms must predict

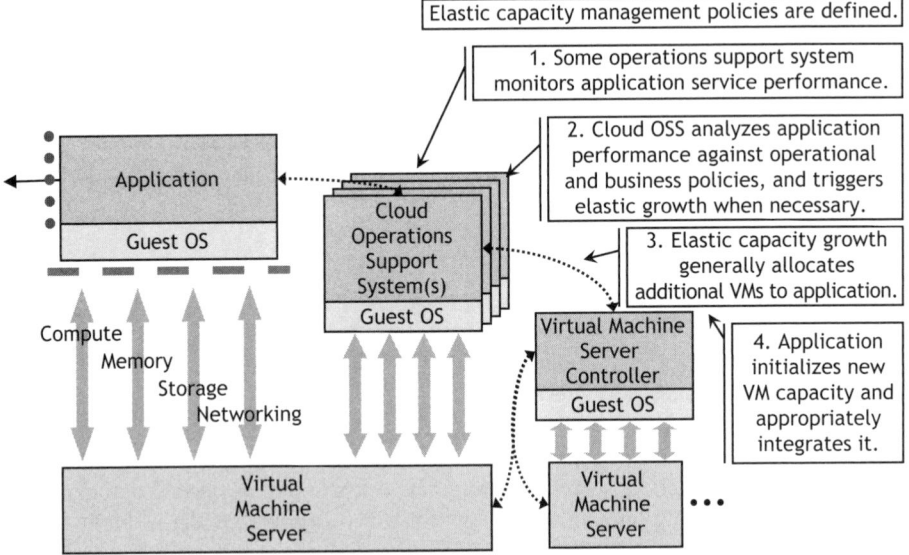

Figure 8.4. Simplified Elastic Growth of Cloud-Based Applications.

offered load into the near future so that additional capacity can be brought online ahead of the growing workload. The policies driving automated growth must also implement hysteresis to prevent elasticity oscillations.

Figure 8.4 tailors the simplified cloud model of Figure 3.3 to give a simple view of elastic capacity management in the cloud. Rapid elastic growth normally begins with some automatic mechanism monitoring the workload offered to an application, based on data collected by a load balancer, the application's own performance metrics (e.g., throughput and number of active sessions), or utilization levels of cloud infrastructure resources (e.g., CPU cycles and free disk space). When a usage measurement passes a threshold (e.g., CPU occupancy is too high for too long), the cloud OSS can automatically initiate the appropriate horizontal, vertical, or outgrowth action. That action begins with a request to the cloud service provider for more resources; then, the cloud OSS coordinates integration of the newly allocated cloud resources with the online application instance; the new application component instance is verified with a set of test sessions to assure it is functioning properly; and finally the newly expanded application capacity is brought online and made available to serve users. Note that cloud consumers' solutions often rely on a suite of interworking application and technology components, so growing capacity of one component (e.g., an application's backend) may imply that other components that support the target component (e.g., database components) should also be grown to minimize the risk of capacity bottlenecks arising after capacity growth events.

Figure 8.4 provides a simplified model of elastic growth; however, much of the complexity lies in choosing the correct measurement thresholds, policies, and triggering

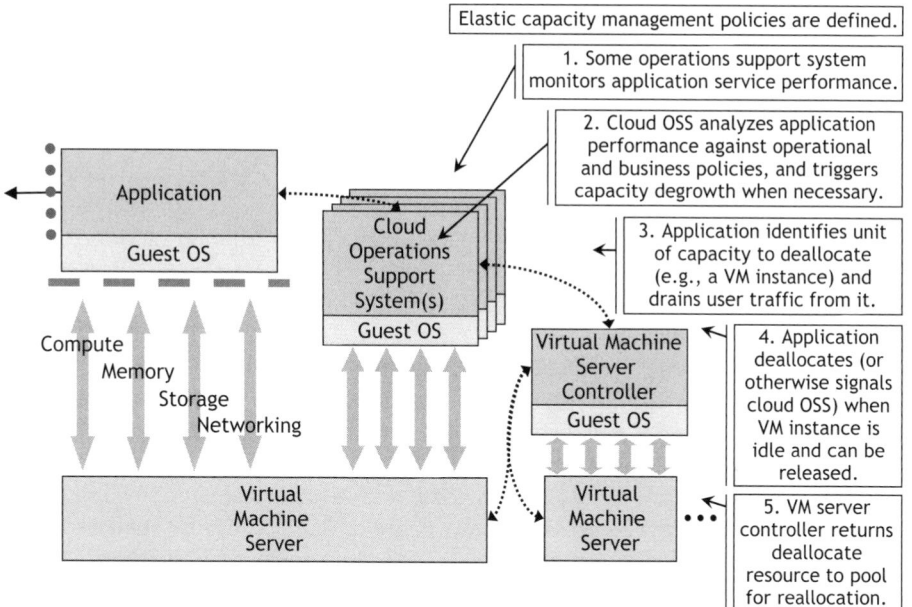

Figure 8.5. Simplified Elastic Degrowth of Cloud-Based Applications.

points for capacity growth. This selection requires an analysis of the particular application's resource needs based on a typical workload and how its usage changes with an increase in workload. There are numerous analysis tools (e.g., Dapper and AppDynamics) that can help monitor resource and work patterns in order to help characterize resource needs that can be fed into the application's forecasting. It is important to analyze the particular application because there are many influential factors that impact resource usage, such as whether the application needs to retrieve and replicate state information.

Figure 8.5 gives a simplified view of typical elastic degrowth. The cloud OSS monitoring the application's workload and resource usage determines that usage has remained below a degrowth threshold for long enough and decides based on application provided policies to shrink resource capacity. The cloud OSS selects a specific resource(s) to be released, directs new traffic to other resources, drains or relocates users from the selected resources, and finally releases the resources back to the infrastructure service provider.

8.6   STORAGE ELASTICITY CONSIDERATIONS

Persistence makes virtualized storage a rather different type of resource to manage than VM instances. For example, while there may be very few active users on a social networking site at 2 a.m. local time, requiring only a few VM instances to serve the user service workload, all of the users' pictures, videos, blogs, and other personal information must still be stored. Persistent storage allocated to cloud-based applications can also grow, but this is typically less frequent. While online capacity demands routinely cycle from high to low usage periods, persistent storage needs typically only grow and are not decreased.

Persistent storage is often factored out of traditional application server configurations into external storage arrays, network attached storage, or external database servers. The mechanisms that have traditionally enabled applications to use outboard persistent storage (e.g. network file system [NFS]) can often be leveraged to grow storage horizontally, such as by mounting a new storage device alongside a preexisting storage device, or reconfiguring the networked storage devices that are mounted from a smaller volume to a larger volume.

In the event that the application does not assimilate sufficient persistent storage capacity when the application instance is online, one might be forced to create a new application instance with a larger persistent storage allocation. For example, if an application does not permit a database instance to be resized after initial installation, then increasing the size of the database instance may require creating a new installation of the application with a larger database instance and importing the contents of the original (smaller) database instance. Fortunately, cloud computing gives new options for software release management that can reduce the user service impact of release management actions; this topic is considered in Chapter 9, "Release Management."

8.7   ELASTICITY AND OVERLOAD

Traditionally, when offered workload exceeds online application capacity, the application would engage congestion control mechanisms, such as returning some "TOO BUSY" indication to clients to reduce the offered workload and pausing low priority, high resource consuming activities. The application would continue to correctly serve some high priority traffic until the overload condition has cleared, and then the application would revert to normal operation.

Rapid elasticity shifts this traditional overload expectation because application capacity can elastically grow to minimize the risk of online application capacity being insufficient to serve the offered workload. If the provisioning interval is short enough and the cloud consumer's operational policies are set up to rapidly detect and trigger elastic growth actions on online spare capacity, then moments when offered load exceeds online capacity should be rare. Inevitably, exceptional events will occasionally cause workload to grow faster than the provisioning interval can track, so the application will have to activate overload control mechanisms in parallel with elastic growth actions as a best effort to serve users until sufficient application capacity can be brought online.

Note that elastic growth during an overload event is more complicated and risky (and hence has a higher likelihood of failure) than normal operation because of the following:

1. Congestion controls are active, so some work will be explicitly rejected. Active congestion controls will cause both the server and clients to behave slightly

differently, including executing somewhat different legs of code, thereby increasing the risk of exposing a residual defect in an error leg somewhere. For example, application architects must be careful to assure that no actions related to elastic growth are rejected by congestion controls during overload periods to prevent a growth deadlock in which insufficient application capacity is online, so requests are blocked and the online capacity growth action cannot complete successfully because critical actions are rejected by overload controls.

2. Overload condition is likely to be accompanied by degraded performance, which delays completion times, so the application may be more sluggish and possibly degrade the application's provisioning interval. Poorly tuned watchdog timers can aggravate the overload condition by causing clients to retry slow operations, thus pushing the application deeper into overload.

3. Overload conditions may trigger VM failures or impairments. For these cases, application service recovery (e.g., failover to another VM instance) or repair (e.g., killing the faulty VM instance and spinning up a new VM instance on another server) techniques should be employed.

4. Elastic growth operations themselves place an additional workload on some application server components, and this additional workload might aggravate overload.

Thus, all aspects of rapid elastic growth should be engineered to function reliably even when the application is in sustained overload. Likewise, application overload control mechanisms should be intelligent enough to deactivate any congestion controls when sufficient online application capacity has been added to serve the offered workload with acceptable service quality.

Although applications should elastically grow up to their maximum licensed capacity to mitigate an overload condition, at least some users may not experience ideal service quality (e.g., receiving "TOO BUSY" is not ideal service for most users). Typically, cloud consumers are responsible for defining operational policies regarding how much spare online capacity to maintain and when to trigger elastic capacity growth actions so sufficient application capacity is online to continuously serve offered workload with acceptable service quality. If user service is impacted because the cloud consumer's policies are too lean, resulting in insufficient spare online capacity being maintained to serve traffic spikes, then user service impact is generally attributable to the cloud consumer. If the cloud consumer's management policies are not properly executed by a cloud OSS, then the user service impact of overload should be attributed to that OSS.

8.8   OPERATIONAL CONSIDERATIONS

Elastic growth actions are likely to be triggered due to one of the following:

- *Application service performance degradation because workload density is too high* (see Sections 2.5.2.2, "Characterizing Service Latency," and 3.5.1, "Density"), so additional online capacity is added to reduce density.

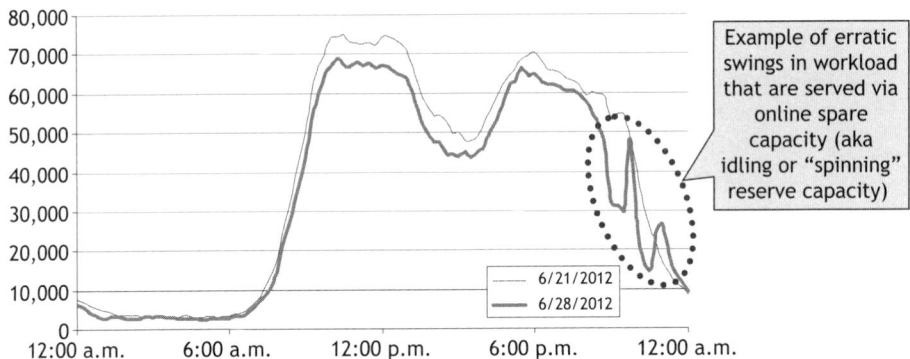

Figure 8.6. Sample of Erratic Workload Variation (Linear Scale).

- *Insufficient spare capacity is online.* The example of Figure 8.1 experienced two orders of magnitude growth in workload between 5 and 10 a.m., so additional online capacity could be brought online somewhat ahead of the daily workload growth to assure that sufficient capacity is available to serve user traffic with acceptable service quality. Note that online spare capacity also supports unexpected traffic spikes, such as shown in Figure 8.6.
- *Engineered capacity exceeds policy thresholds.* Application supplier's and/or cloud consumer's policy might assign no more than "*X*" online users per resource instance, so when the number of online users reaches one more than "*N*" times *X*, then (*N* + 1)th resource instance is elastically grown to avoid exceeding the policy limit.
- *Critical failure event reduced online capacity*, so a capacity growth action to replace the lost service or spare capacity is executed. Redundant (1 + 1) systems are often at elevated service risk (called "simplex exposure") between the time of component failure and the time the failed capacity can be replaced because service is vulnerable to a prolonged outage if a second failure occurs before the capacity impacted by the first failure can be restored.

Typically, an OSS proactively monitors offered load, historic traffic patterns, application performance, and other factors to make a short term prediction of offered load, and initiate an elastic growth action if insufficient application capacity is online to meet that predicted workload and still maintain sufficient "spare" online capacity to mitigate failure and transient workload events. This OSS follows a procedure such as the one shown in Figure 8.7 managed by a single team responsible for capacity management.

8.9   WORKLOAD WHIPSAW

Investors use the term whipsaw to mean "to beset or victimize in two opposite ways at once, by a two phase operation, or by the collusive action of two opponents" [Merriam-Webster]. This notion also applies to dramatic workload changes, such as the

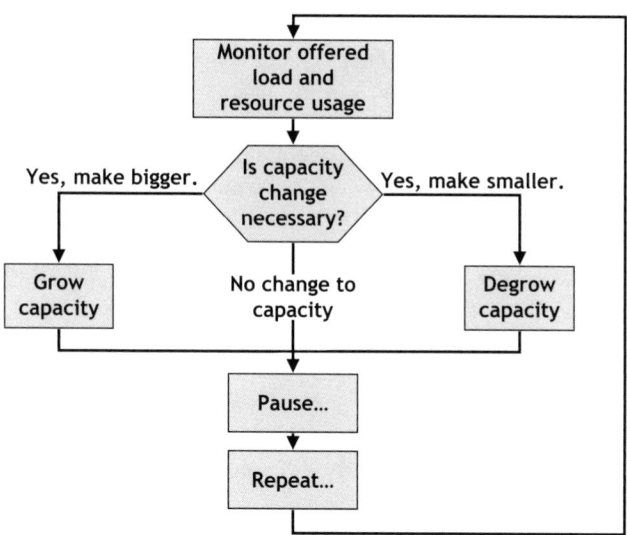

Figure 8.7. Typical Elasticity Orchestration Process.

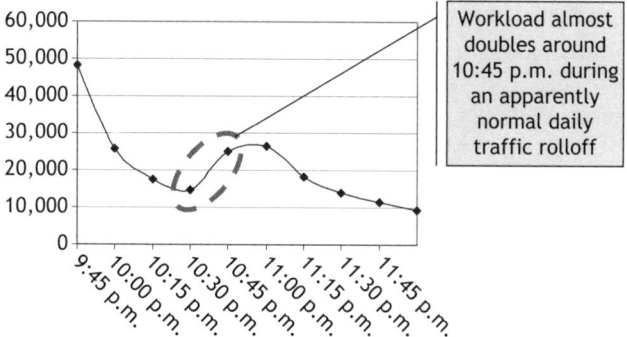

Figure 8.8. Example of Workload Whipsaw.

event around 10:45 PM in Figure 8.8. The elasticity OSS is likely to be gracefully degrowing online capacity when the whipsaw traffic spike begins around 10:45 PM. Ideally, the elasticity OSS and application can instantly cancel any pending degrowth action and then immediately initiate elastic growth to address traffic spikes like this. This leads to three architectural principles.

1. *Rapid cancellation of pending online capacity degrowth actions should be supported.*
2. *Elasticity requests should not be queued* by applications or elasticity OSSs, because by the time the request is dequeued, the elasticity action may no longer be appropriate.

3. *Supporting different units of capacity growth can be useful* when arbitrarily large numbers of growth actions cannot be simultaneously executed. For example, if an application only permits one VM instance of online capacity growth to occur at a time, then having flexibility to size that instance to, say, two, four, or eight CPU cores gives more flexibility to address both ordinary and extraordinary (e.g., whipsaw events) by growing two-CPU core VMs when workload is slowly growing and growing by eight-CPU core VMs when workload is surging. The advantage of this does have to be weighed against the complexity of monitoring resource usage and the introduction of numerous permutations to test.

8.10   GENERAL ELASTICITY RISKS

Growing capacity of an online application that is actively serving traffic is inherently risky, but different growth strategies carry different risks:

- *Horizontal growth is generally the simplest strategy, and hence the lowest risk* because of the following:
  - New resource instances can be created and initialized without impacting service covered by other resource instances.
  - A single application instance can manage the growth action.
- *Outgrowth is more complex than horizontal*, and hence higher risk because of the following:
  - Outgrowth operations often require coordination between two data centers' orchestration frameworks, and thus complexity increases the risk of failure.
  - Outgrowth operations insert a higher latency, lower bandwidth, and somewhat less reliable network connection between preexisting and newly allocated resources.
  - Outgrowth operations will likely have to manage additional security requirements and check if the outgrown resources are in a different network, security, and administrative domain, but this is outside the scope of this study.
- *Vertical growth is generally the most complex* because application and guest OS configuration information changes when the engineered throughput (e.g., number of CPU cores, amount of RAM, and network bandwidth) or persistent storage per component instance changes on the fly. Note that while changing only network bandwidth allocated to a VM instance might technically be considered vertical growth (or degrowth), engineered network capacity is inherently tied to the compute throughput of a component instance, so there is little sense in changing only one type of throughput-related capacity for a well-engineered application. If merely the networking allocation of a VM serving a well-engineered distributed application is increased, then compute or memory capacity is likely to quickly become the bottleneck, so much of the additional network capacity may be wasted; if network allocation is decreased, then networking is likely to become the capacity bottleneck, so some allocated compute capacity is wasted.

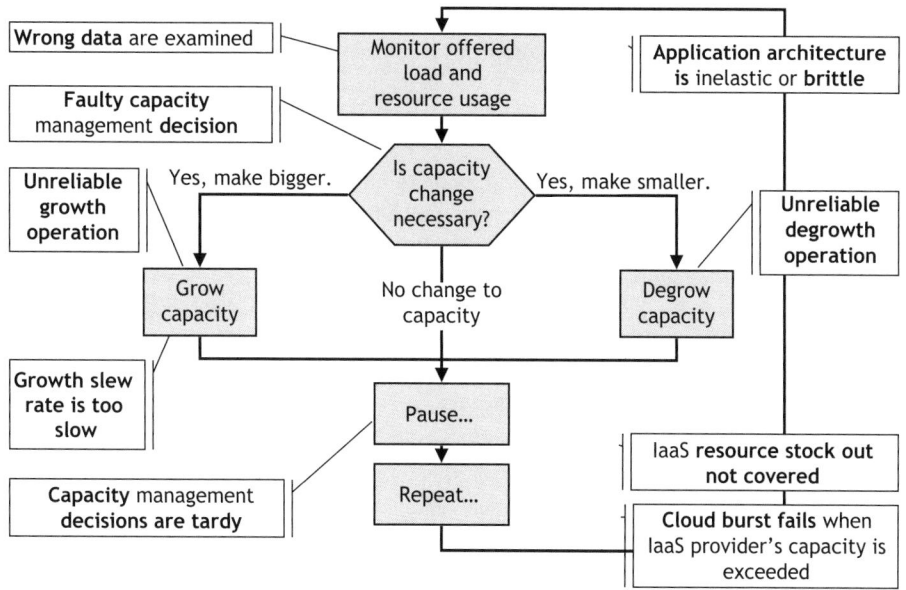

Figure 8.9. Elastic Growth Failure Scenarios.

8.11 ELASTICITY FAILURE SCENARIOS

Elastic capacity operations introduce new failure scenarios to detect and mitigate. As the failure scenarios for growth and degrowth operations are rather different, they will be considered separately. Figure 8.9 overlays high level failure scenarios onto Figure 8.7. Section 15.6, "Elasticity Analysis," offers an analysis methodology to apply when architecting applications to verify acceptable service quality when confronted with inevitable elasticity failures.

8.11.1 Elastic Growth Failure Scenarios

Successful elastic growth adds a unit of online service or storage capacity to an application instance in an acceptable provisioning interval so that sufficient capacity is available to serve the offered workload. This suggests four broad failure scenarios:

1. Elastic growth action fails outright (Section 8.11.1.1, "Elastic Growth Action Failure Scenarios")
2. Elastic growth action (provisioning interval) takes too long (Section 8.11.1.2, "Excess Provisioning Interval Scenarios")
3. Elastic growth action is activated too late (Section 8.11.1.3, "Growth Policy and Operations Failure Scenarios")
4. Workload grows faster than application can grow (Section 8.11.1.4, "Insufficient Online Spare Capacity Maintained").

8.11.1.1 Elastic Growth Action Failure Scenarios. A specific elastic growth action request for a specific application instance can fail to complete successfully for several reasons:

1. *Application Instance's Maximum Capacity Limit Has Been Reached.* While cloud service providers offer the illusion of infinite resources, individual application instances of real applications are not infinitely elastic. When an application instance reaches the maximum licensed or architected limit, then it should prohibit additional capacity growth and gracefully manage excess offered load by activating overload control mechanisms. Ideally, the cloud consumer has policies and procedures to either instantiate a new application instance or shift workload to another application instance that has spare capacity.
2. *Cloud Service Provider Fails to Provide Requested Resources.* The cloud service provider may be unable to provide resources that meet the application's constraints (e.g., resource capacity/size specification, comply with affinity and anti-affinity rules, and within consumer's budget/business constraints), and thus the application instance's growth action will fail.
3. *Application Software Failure.* A software defect in the application or a technology component can occur during the elastic growth action, which prevents successful completion of the action.

8.11.1.2 Excess Provisioning Interval Scenarios. An application's elastic growth action can take longer than expected to complete successfully because of the following:

1. Cloud service provider is slow to provide requested resources because of heavy aggregate workload.
2. Application instance is slow because of heavy user workload.
3. Application instance is slow because of large amounts of data to be processed or configured.

8.11.1.3 Growth Policy and Operations Failure Scenarios. Elastic growth actions nominally take the provisioning interval to complete, and thus growth actions must be initiated at least one provisioning interval before the additional capacity will be required to serve offered load. Cloud consumers will deploy operational policies that maintain sufficient excess capacity to mitigate transient traffic spikes and inevitable failure scenarios. Should the cloud consumer maintain insufficient online spare capacity, then a component failure or transient workload spike could push the application temporarily into overload and thus deliver degraded quality of experience to at least some users until additional application capacity is brought online. Likewise, if the cloud consumer's policies maintain insufficient excess capacity and do not accurately predict near term workloads, then offered load can easily outstrip online application capacity. In essence, cloud consumers bet their ability to accurately predict near-term workloads against spare online capacity; the more accurately consumers can predict future workloads, the less spare capacity (beyond that is required to mitigate inevitable failures) must be kept online.

8.11.1.4 Insufficient Online Spare Capacity Maintained. As discussed in Section 3.5.7, "Slew Rate and Linearity," an application's nominal growth rate is the unit of capacity growth (C_{Grow}) divided by the provisioning interval. If the workload grows faster than that nominal application growth rate for long enough, then there will be insufficient application capacity online to serve the offered load. Cloud consumers are responsible for maintaining sufficient online spare capacity so that even if offered load grows faster than the application's maximum growth rate for a period of time, then sufficient online spare capacity is in place so that user workload does not outstrip online capacity. If offered load does outstrip online application capacity, then the application should engage overload controls, which may reject user traffic.

8.11.2 Elastic Capacity Degrowth Failure Scenarios

Service risks during elastic degrowth arise from the following:

1. *Failures Draining User Traffic from the Resource to Be Released.* Draining traffic is obviously a delicate process, as a failure may directly impact one or more user's quality of experience, such as producing service retainability impairments as active user sessions are abruptly terminated.

2. *Application Fails to Stop Using Released Resource.* If the application does not properly track the resources being released, then additional traffic may be sent to the deactivated—and perhaps even deallocated—resource, only to have the traffic dropped, causing the user to experience degraded service reliability, latency, or overall service quality.

3. *Pending or Failed Elastic Degrowth Action Delays or Deadlocks an Elastic Growth Action.* If traffic surges during the release interval, then an elastic growth action may be triggered. If an elastic growth action cannot overlap a pending release action or the pending release actions cannot be canceled, then the application may be driven into overload until the release can complete and the growth action can begin.

While orderly cancellation of a pending degrowth action is not a failure scenario per se, rapidly and cleanly canceling a pending online capacity degrowth action is a complex operation, so applications should be architected and tested to assure that degrowth events can be rapidly and reliably canceled so that subsequent growth actions can reliably complete. Leakage of released resources, in which the application successfully releases a resource but the resource is not successfully deallocated by the cloud service provider, is also a business risk. While resource leakage should not impact user service, it will contribute to the cloud consumer's OPEX.

9

RELEASE MANAGEMENT

"Release management" is the term used by IT Infrastructure Library (ITIL) to cover planning, executing, and controlling the distribution and installation of new and changed software. A key function of release management is software upgrade. Best practices for release management can be found in ITIL's Service Transition book [ITIL_ST]. This section discusses traditional strategies for software upgrades and proposes alternate strategies that leverage cloud mechanisms to mitigate some of the service quality risks associated with executing software upgrades.

9.1 TERMINOLOGY

Software upgrade entails installation of a new version of software and evolution of the application's data schema (if needed) to introduce new features, bug fixes, and deploy other changes to the software. Note that the term **software upgrade** will be used in this work to encompass the following:

- *Software Patch or Software Update.* Small changes to the software that do not materially change functionality and do not require schema changes to persistent data, such as bug fixes or security patches.

Service Quality of Cloud-Based Applications, First Edition. Eric Bauer and Randee Adams.
© 2014 The Institute of Electrical and Electronics Engineers, Inc. Published 2014 by John Wiley & Sons, Inc.

- *Software Upgrade.* Major changes to the software that changes functionality and may require schema (or other) changes to persistent data.
- *Retrofit.* Traditionally, "retrofit" referred to even more substantial changes to the software and architecture requiring a complete replacement of the software and usually some hardware components. As cloud unbundles hardware from software, the traditional retrofit notion of coordinating hardware/firmware and software changes will not generally apply.

Backout and rollback are mechanisms to undo a "toxic" software upgrade and are defined as follows:

- A software release **backout** entails undoing the software and data changes associated with the new version *before* the new release has been committed.
- A software release **rollback** restores the old version and data *after* the new release has been committed.

Maintenance and synchronization of persistent and dynamic data during software upgrade will also be discussed. Persistent data are data that are preserved beyond a particular session or transaction such as subscriber data. Dynamic data are more transitory information, such as state data, that are only maintained across a session or transaction. Both types of data need to be considered during software upgrade.

9.2   TRADITIONAL SOFTWARE UPGRADE STRATEGIES

Traditional application deployments have finite hardware resources, and thus a software upgrade must complete "in place" on that finite hardware. There are two fundamental software upgrade strategies with finite hardware resources:

- *Offline Software Upgrade.* The application is taken offline for the duration of the upgrade procedure. Thus, the duration of the offline period is a critical parameter, but the procedure can be simpler because service is not operational during the procedure itself.
- *Online Software Upgrade.* Highly available systems often maintain sufficient hardware redundancy that it is possible to logically split the redundant system into two simplex halves, each of which can be upgraded separately. This scheme leaves the application simplex exposed during the upgrade so a failure during the upgrade period could produce a prolonged service outage. This strategy is significantly more complicated than offline software upgrade.

9.2.1   Software Upgrade Requirements

Enterprises often expect software upgrade of critical applications to have minimal user service impact (also known as be "hitless"); practically, this often means user service may be unavailable or disrupted for nominally seconds. Ideally, user sessions or trans-actions will be preserved, but gracefully terminating user sessions and transactions is acceptable for most noncritical applications. As with other service quality expectations, it is unlikely that customers will tolerate greater service impact on upgrade of cloud-based applications than they experience with traditionally deployed versions of those same applications.

Traditional software upgrade requirements also include the following:

- *Ability to "Soak" the New Release to Verify Proper Operation before Committing to Use the New Release.* Occasionally, a software upgrade will prove to be incompatible with existing clients, applications, or other operational character-istics, and thus be unacceptable or toxic in a particular operational environment. Customers generally like to soak or validate the stability of the new release by running traffic on it for a sufficient amount of time (e.g., several days to a week) to make sure it is functioning properly. Note that in traditional high availability architecture, soak may entail running the application without redundancy (i.e., simplex exposed) for the duration of the soak.

- *Ability to Promptly Backout a Toxic Release or Rollback to the Previous Release if Necessary.* If a new release proves to be toxic or otherwise unacceptable, then enterprises want to be able to promptly restore the previous release. Operation-ally, this means that sufficient time must be allocated so that if initial soak testing demonstrates a release to be toxic, then there must be sufficient remaining time in the maintenance window to back out the toxic release or roll back to the previ-ous release before the maintenance window closes.

- *Backward Compatibility between Old Release and New Release Interfaces* to reduce impact of the upgrade on interfacing components. New functionality should be enabled and coordinated with other components.

- *Ability to Skip Releases (e.g., Release "N" to Release "N + 3").* Not every customer will accept every software release for practical reasons (e.g., do not need the new functionality or fixes offered by a new release), commercial reasons (e.g., did not license the new/upgraded release), or operational reasons (e.g., the benefit of installing a particular release does not exceed the expected cost/complexity of installing that particular release). However, at some point, most customers will presumably be enticed to upgrade, and then they will prefer a "skip" upgrade, meaning upgrading from release "N" to release "$N + I$," where $I > 1$ (i.e., the next release). Skipping releases offers enterprises the practical benefit of forgoing the operational expenditure (OPEX) and service disruption associated with actually installing each of the skipped releases, although there is considerable OPEX involved in the skip release itself. For example, a customer may install release 2.0, and then pass on releases 3.0 and 4.0 and then want to accept release 5.0; in this case, the customer would want a skip upgrade that enabled them to go directly from 2.0 to release 5.0 without requiring explicit upgrade transitions through releases 3.0 and 4.0. Note that it is much more difficult to guarantee compatibility of the new and old releases when skipping multiple releases, since external interfaces and data schemas are often enhanced over a period of time with new customer feature requests. Data evolution may have to cycle through each release, requiring a long interval.

Due to cost concerns and potential impact to users, sophisticated customers often require the following:

- *Ability to Complete the Upgrade—and If Necessary, Roll Back to the Previous Release—within a Single Maintenance Window* (See Section 9.2.2, "Maintenance Windows"). Because traditional software upgrade has the potential of causing a large service impact if unsuccessful and may render the application simplex exposed or at reduced capacity, software upgrade is generally performed as a maintenance activity during a low usage period.

In order to provide robust software upgrade, the following requirements will also apply depending on the software upgrade mechanism used:

- Clients shall be able to interface with the new and old version virtual application instances.
- Sufficient resources (e.g., network, disk, CPU, memory, and IP addresses) must be available from the infrastructure-as-a-service (IaaS) service provider to support both the old and new version virtual application instances.
- Software licenses need to be shared by both the old and new versions of the virtual application instance during the interval that they are both active.
- Old version virtual application instances are gracefully shutdown and do not result in lost or dropped sessions/transactions.

By taking advantage of the cloud and virtualization, downtime can be mitigated, and in some cases, eliminated, and the procedures can be made more robust through automation making it feasible to perform software upgrades anytime, rather than only during maintenance windows. Note that nonservice-impacting upgrade preparations and postwork may be required before or after the single maintenance window when the (potentially service impacting) upgrade action is actually completed.

9.2.2 Maintenance Windows

The purpose of maintenance windows (introduced in Section 8.2) is to arrange in advance for a period when user service may experience service disruptions, degradations, and/or periods of service unavailability with minimal customer impact. The maintenance windows are usually scheduled during times of low traffic (e.g., during the late night hours), encompassing one work shift (e.g., nominally 4–6 hours of activity). For traditional systems, software upgrade is often a user service-impacting operation with many manual procedures and thus is performed during these maintenance windows. Enterprise users are often notified of scheduled maintenance windows when service of critical applications may be disrupted so they can plan accordingly.

Customers prefer to execute very few of these upgrades, since they require these maintenance sessions and possible service disruption.

Agile and other modern development practices have popularized the "continuous deployment" model, in which software builds are automatically completed once a day, installed on a cloud, verified via rich automated test scripts, automatically soaked with a portion of live traffic, and then have all new user traffic migrated to the new build. As build/install/verify/activate cycles happen every day with continuous deployment models, those processes quickly become very reliable with a robust orchestration mechanism. At least some organizations will then shift their install/verify/activate schedule so it occurs during business hours (e.g., starting at 9 a.m. local time) so that developers and other experts are immediately available to debug and correct any delivery problems. This model can

- improve service agility by dramatically shortening deployment time for new and changed features
- improve service quality by rapidly deploying bug fixes, stability improvements, and security patches
- reduce OPEX by shifting release management activities out of expensive (e.g., overtime or double time) work periods to normal business hours
- improve probability of successful upgrades because frequent execution rapidly improves process maturity and reliability. Shifting work from the middle of the night (e.g., midnight to 6 a.m. local time) into normal working hours tends to reduce the risk of human error also, further improving reliability of human/ procedural activities supporting release management.

Thus, traditional maintenance windows for software upgrade may become deprecated—and possibly even unacceptable—for cloud-based applications in the future.

9.2.3 Client Considerations for Application Upgrade

It is important for upgraded applications to maintain the highest degree of compatibility with client software (i.e., software that is requesting service from the application from an interfacing component or external user, such as a user endpoint) to minimize both user service impact and operational expense associated with reconfiguring client software. Application protocols and client software should enable graceful service transitions, such as server-initiated session disconnection or inactivity timeouts and automatic client session reconnection, so that clients can gracefully transition from an old release to a new release with minimal user impact. If compatibility cannot be ensured, then procedures may need to take into account sequencing of upgrades, versioning changes, and deprecating of features in order to address the incompatibilities. Ideally, new software releases support the following requirements:

1. *The upgraded application is 100% protocol compatible with existing interfacing client software, and hence no client software changes are necessary for it to*

successfully interface with the application on the new version. If protocol compatibility is assured, then strategies that require clients to interface with both old and new application versions running at the same time can be implemented.

2. *The upgraded application's client configuration is 100% compatible (e.g., DNS name and/or IP address) so no configuration information used or maintained by client software must be changed.* If client configuration information is changed, then arrangements must be made to execute those configuration changes and push them out to impacted clients; this is likely to both increase the OPEX of a software upgrade and increase the risk of user service impact.

9.2.4 Traditional Offline Software Upgrade

The simplest upgrade strategy (visualized in Figure 9.1) is referred to in this document as **traditional offline upgrade** and has the following basic steps:

- *Take the application instance offline* so that traffic is no longer being served
- *Install the new release (e.g., N + I, where I is one or more releases, presumably with backward compatibility between N and I) software.*
- *Evolve persistent application data.*
- *Soak new release with test calls followed by live customer traffic* to verify proper operation.
- *Activate (commit) the upgraded application instance* and put it back online so that the application instance resumes serving traffic.

Because the application instance is offline during the software upgrade interval, all active sessions are dropped before starting the upgrade, and user service is completely unavailable from the application instance until the upgrade is completed and the application is brought back online.

If installation of the new software or evolution of persistent data fails, or soak testing reveals the release to be toxic, then it is necessary to back out the new release. Note that backout can take place at any point before the commitment of the new release. When sufficient persistent storage is available and the application is properly architected, offline backout/rollback may be as simple as reconfiguring the system to

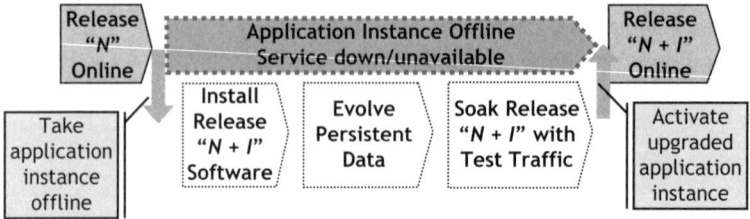

Figure 9.1. Traditional Offline Software Upgrade.

reference the old application's persistent storage (e.g., file system or directory structure) and restarting the application or rebooting the host. Note that any new transactions against the evolved data that occurred on the new release will be lost with the backout/rollback. If insufficient persistent storage was available to retain all release N application software and persistent data, then it will be necessary to reinstall release N software and restore persistent data from backup to complete the backout/rollback.

9.2.5 Traditional Online Software Upgrade

Traditional high availability systems are deployed with sufficient redundant hardware so that no single failure need causes a loss of functionality or capacity. This hardware redundancy creates the opportunity to upgrade software, while the application remains online by splitting the system into two simplex "sides": one side running on the old version of software and the other taken offline to upgrade to the new version. Once the new version side upgrade is complete, a switchover is performed so that traffic is running on the new version. The other side is now upgraded to the new version and activated once the upgrade has completed, thereby returning the system to fully redundant operation. Figure 9.2 illustrates the basic steps of online software upgrade:

1. Take one ***portion*** of the application instance offline (e.g., standby side "B" in Figure 9.2). Note that since the highly available application instance is configured with hardware redundancy, the redundant portion (e.g., active side "A" in Figure 9.2) remains online serving users. However, since the standby component instance (B) is being upgraded, it is not available to rapidly recover service in

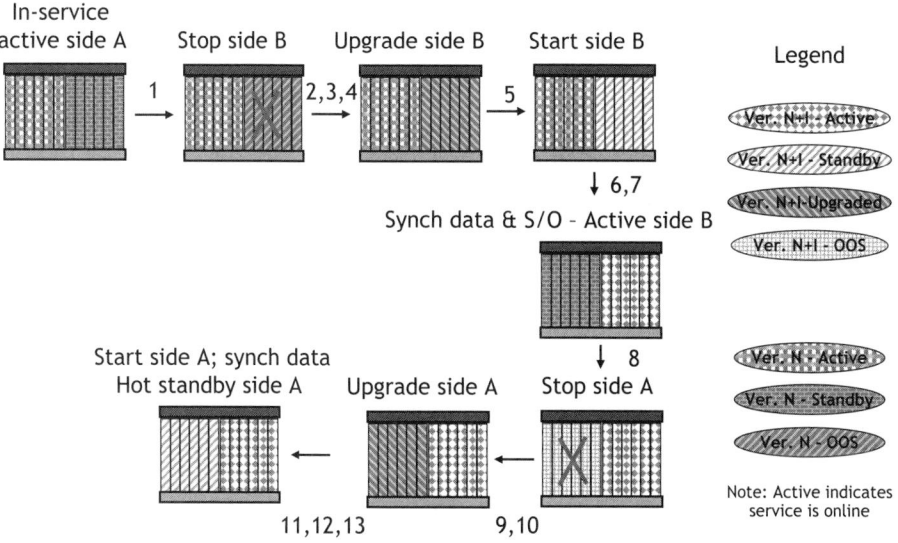

Figure 9.2. Traditional Online Software Upgrade.

the event of a failure of the primary component instance. Thus, the component (and hence the entire application instance) is said to be "simplex exposed" because a single failure of the primary component (A) exposes the system to a prolonged service outage because the high availability mechanism cannot rapidly and automatically recover service to the component being upgraded (B).

2. Install new release software on side B.
3. Evolve persistent data from old release to new.
4. Upload evolved data to side B.
5. Activate new release software on side B.
6. Synchronize (and evolve if necessary) dynamic data between old release A with B.
7. Switchover service so new release B is active component and serves offered load.
8. Take old release component A offline.
9. Install new release on side A.
10. Load or synchronize evolved data on side A.
11. Activate side A.
12. Synchronize dynamic data from side B (note that steps 10 and 12 can be combined).
13. Make side A "hot standby."
14. Optional: Perform a switchover so that side A is back to being the active component to verify that switchover on the new release works.

Soak testing is generally performed after the new release has become active (at step 7) but before the new release has been committed in case a problem is found and a backout is needed. Simplex time is depicted in steps 1–13, entailing most of the software upgrade interval and soak time. Minimizing simplex exposure time is important because a failure of a simplex component is likely to produce a service impacting outage until the failure can be repaired. Some applications require dynamic data that need to be synchronized in order to maintain stable user sessions across the upgrade. If the dynamic data structure has changed, then this too may have to be evolved before it is synchronized, thereby adding more complexity to the procedure.

To rollback in the event of serious problems with the new version after a commit has been performed, the reverse operation would take place, taking the standby side A offline and reloading the old version of software and data (or activating from the old partitions if they still exist), switching over user service to side A, and repeating on the other side. Downtime would typically be similar to the software upgrade, but it could be much longer if the old version of software and application data are no longer available on the system and have to be rebuilt with changes that have occurred since the upgrade. Dynamic data are lost in the event of a backout or rollback. If a problem is found before the new release has been committed, then a backout can be performed at that point. Backouts are generally easier and less service impacting than a rollback.

9.2.6   Discussion

Traditional software upgrade strategies often consist of long procedures with many manual steps that require methodical coordination of changes with multiple systems. Compounding this, large solutions can require weeks of maintenance intervals to individually upgrade the various elements in the solution in a specific sequence that assures the interfaces between the elements function properly. When dependencies exist between different elements within the solution, then solution upgrades become even more complex and may lead to longer simplex exposure periods than are consistent with highly available service. To minimize the risk of failure during upgrade and minimize simplex exposure, the following mitigation techniques are often implemented:

- *Upgrades are performed during low traffic periods to reduce the risk of user service impact*, particularly if there is a failure during the upgrade. Some systems merely indicate to users that the application will be down for a certain amount of time so that the software upgrade can be performed offline.
- *User traffic may be diverted to a (geographically) redundant system instance* to both minimize user service disruption and simplify the upgrade because the application instance can be offline throughout the upgrade.
- *Application elements are configured with sufficient spare disk capacity to store both new version software and evolved data and retain the previous release software and data* so that rollback can be promptly executed, if necessary.
- *Procedures are automated* as much as possible to reduce or eliminate manual operations, thereby both minimizing the risk of human (procedural) errors when executing upgrade procedures and shortening execution time to minimize simplex exposure.
- *Backward compatibility between interfacing solution elements is maintained*, as well as with the clients.

Cloud-enabled software upgrade strategies (considered in Section 9.3) can reduce the complexity and mitigate the risk associated with traditional software upgrade by providing a much more automated, complete management of the software upgrade.

9.3   CLOUD-ENABLED SOFTWARE UPGRADE STRATEGIES

The rapid resource elasticity of cloud infrastructure enables software upgrade of cloud-based applications to adopt radically different strategies because one can allocate sufficient additional resources to install a new and independent instance of the upgraded application and run it alongside the fully redundant previous version. The basic cloud aware strategy is to allocate, install, configure, and soak the new software release instance with minimal disturbance to the existing application instance. There are two general strategies for managing cloud-enabled software upgrade:

- *Type I: Block Party* (Section 9.3.1). Both old and new software releases run in independent VMs simultaneously serving user traffic, and can theoretically continue doing so indefinitely. Some users will be served by the old version, and some users will be served by the new version. This model enables enterprises to enjoy extended soak periods and to minimize user service disruption by letting traffic drain naturally from the old software version. The authors refer to this model as "block party" because software releases can come and go without careful coordination, like the guests at a block party.

- *Type II: One Driver per Bus* (Section 9.3.2). Applications that require tight control of critical resources typically permit one and only one application instance to be active at a time. This strategy is required for application instances, where only a single logical instance is permitted to be in charge at anytime, such as when controlling a database or other resource where strict consistency is required. The authors refer to this model as "one driver per bus," because it logically resembles a city bus, which can carry many people, but only one driver is allowed to steer the bus at a time.

9.3.1 Type I Cloud-Enabled Upgrade Strategy: Block Party

The key characteristic of type I, "block party," software upgrade (pictured in Figure 9.3) is the ability to run both the old and new versions of the virtual application instance at the same time. The new version of software and data is installed into new and independent cloud resources, while the old version is running on cloud resources. The new version is allocated full resources, activated, and some user traffic is directed to the new version while the majority of user traffic is served by the old version. This enables the new release to soak with live traffic for an indefinite period. Once the new release is deemed acceptable, all new traffic can be directed to the new release virtual application. User traffic served by the old release can be allowed to drain away naturally as users routinely log off (and subsequent logon requests are directed to the new release)

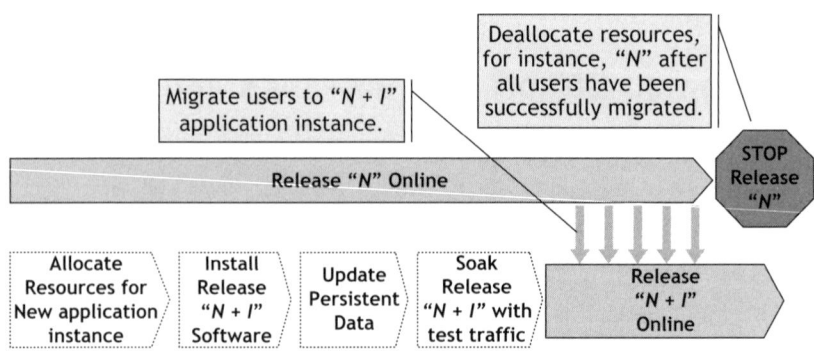

Figure 9.3. Type I, "Block Party" Upgrade Strategy.

so that transactions can complete on the old release and do not have to be applied to the new release, or the application service provider can eventually terminate residual user sessions to the application instance running the old software release. Traffic is controlled by a load balancer or a proxy, which can direct traffic to the new version components. Either way, there is no explicit switchover event so traffic can run to completion on the older version as long as the application service provider would like. Since the old version can run to completion, there is no need to synchronize dynamic data between old and new releases to maintain stable sessions. If there is a need to revert to the old version, then traffic is drained from the new version application instances. Separate IP addresses are needed for the old and new versions since they will be running at the same time; however, a proxy or nonproxy load balancer can expose a single IP address and manage those versions so that it is seamless to the client.

Because type I block party upgrade enables both release "N" and release "$N + I$" to peacefully coexist, Figure 9.4 illustrates how traffic can be gradually redirected from release "N" to release "$N + I$":

1. An application instance is created and activated on release "$N + I$."
2. Some traffic is directed to the "$N + I$" release application instance. When service on the new release is deemed to be successful, all new traffic is directed to the new release.
3. As traffic increases on the new release, capacity is grown on release $N + I$ and degrown on release "N".
4. Once all activity has ceased on release "N," the application instance is shut down, and resources are deallocated.

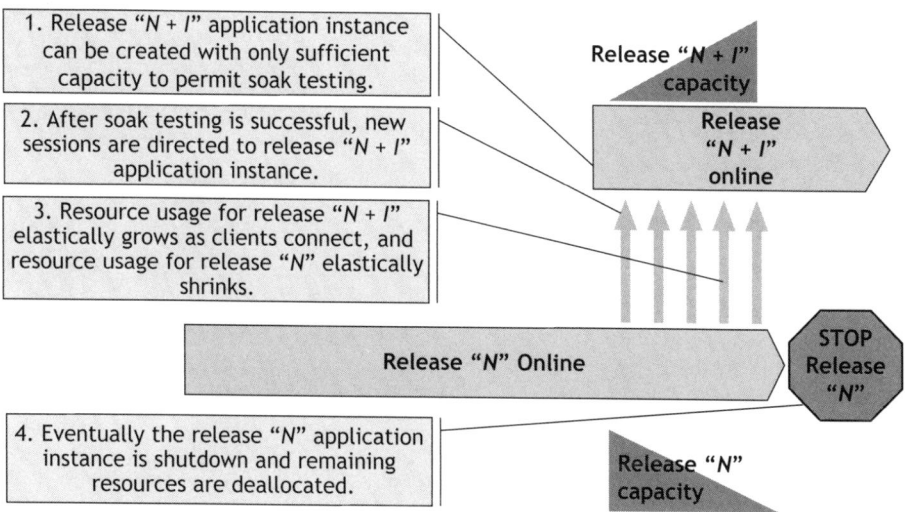

Figure 9.4. Application Elastic Growth and Type I, "Block Party" Upgrade.

Note that it is possible for type I, block party, upgrades to complete with no user impact if traffic is allowed to naturally drain from old application instance "*N*" and new traffic is directed to new application instance "*N + I*." If the enterprise cannot wait for all traffic to naturally drain from the old instance, then application-specific actions can be taken to coerce the traffic from the old instance to the new instance. While this migration period may be prolonged, it is important to note that both the old and new application instances remain fully redundant and at no time is either application instance simplex exposed.

Continuous delivery models of software work well with type I, block party, upgrade that has been enhanced to include automated regression tests to verify release sanity before directing any user traffic to the new release. This ability to support continuous delivery of software directly supports the Open Data Center Alliance (ODCA) cloud awareness "extensible" attribute discussed in Section 3.7, "Cloud Awareness."

Since multiple versions can be running at the same time, type I software upgrade provides the opportunity to install a special version of the application and only direct a select set or number of users to trial it. Once the trial is over, the version can be grown or removed.

9.3.2   Type II Cloud-Enabled Upgrade Strategy: One Driver per Bus

Type II, "one driver per bus," software upgrade (illustrated in Figure 9.5) is a strategy in which only one application instance version is providing user service at any time. This strategy is appropriate when data or resource constraints preclude multiple application instances from sharing access to one or more common resources. The strategy entails the following:

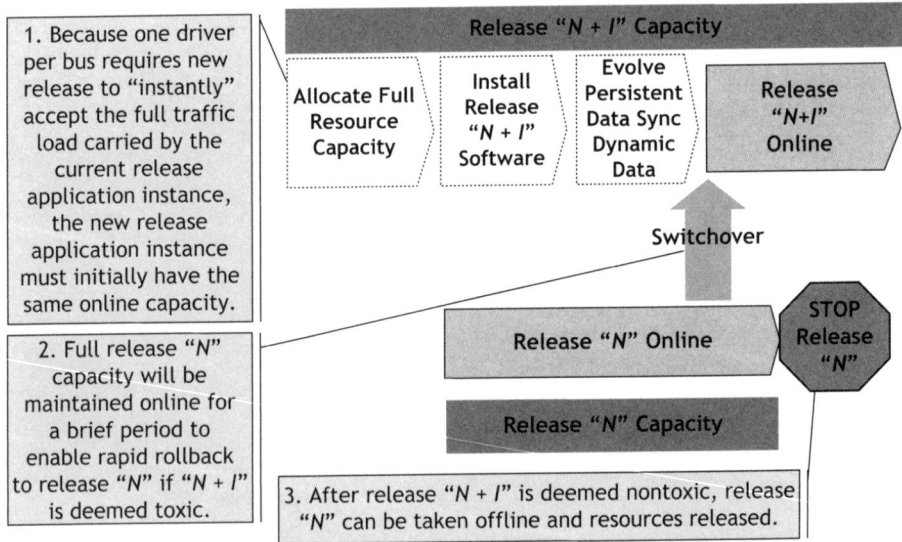

Figure 9.5. Type II, "One Driver per Bus" Upgrade Strategy.

1. Creation of an application instance on the new release "$N + 1$" with sufficient resources to manage equivalent capacity of that of the old release "N." New release software is installed, and persistent data are evolved from the old release to the new release. Dynamic data are evolved (if needed) and synchronized.

2. The new release "$N + 1$" application instance is activated, and traffic is directed to the new release.

3. Once the new release "$N + 1$" is determined to provide acceptable service, the application instance on release "N" is deactivated and its resources are deallocated.

The key characteristic of type II, one driver per bus, software upgrade is that *only one version is actively service users at a time*. As a result, interfacing components do not have to manage supporting both application version instances simultaneously. IP addresses can be reused and moved from the old application instances to the new version virtual application instances. In order to maintain user sessions across the upgrade, user sessions that were still running on the old version at the time of switchover must be assumed by the new application instance with a copy of the associated dynamic data. There is potential user impact during the switchover time, particularly if the dynamic data cannot be synchronized or otherwise accessed by the new version so that needs to be kept to a minimum. If there is a need to roll back to the old version, then the same steps are repeated for the old version: disconnecting resources from the new version and reconnecting on the old, switchover to the old version, including moving of the IP addresses, and traffic redirected to the old version. There is potential user service impact during the switchover interval.

9.3.3   Discussion

Type II software upgrade is similar to the traditional online strategy in that only one version is running at a time, and has the challenge of synchronizing volatile data across active members of the old and new versions. For many traditional applications, this strategy will be the easiest to adopt without major design changes, particularly if there is no volatile data that need to be preserved or if the volatile data can be maintained by the client. Downtime is associated with the transition time needed to move from the old release appliance instances to the new release appliance instances. There is also a potential reliability impact during the transition time, particularly if there are dynamic data that are not replicated.

Type I represents a very different strategy than traditional upgrade as it entails managing multiple versions of application instances executing concurrently. There may need to be architectural changes for an application to adopt this model, including the addition of enhancement of proxy load balancers to manage the routing of service to the appropriate application instances, as well as the mapping of the data. Type I can feasibly upgrade with no user service downtime and no loss of dynamic data, since traffic is being served at all times by at least one of the virtual application instances, assuming traffic is gracefully drained from the old version. With type I, a percentage of traffic could be routed to the new version appliances during the soak period to test it before rerouting all of the traffic as is done with type II. Rollback with type I again can feasibly be performed without downtime since it will be a matter of pausing or suspending the new version and directing all of the traffic to the old version.

Section 15.7, "Release Management Impact Effects Analysis," will provide an assessment of the software upgrade mechanisms and types to help architects determine the best strategy for a given application.

9.4 DATA MANAGEMENT

Persistent application data need to be maintained (e.g., no loss of user records) during the software upgrade process, and the data schema may also need to be evolved if there are any schema changes between releases. In addition, since any upgrade may cause breakage, it must be possible to back out (before the commit) or roll back (after the commit) from an upgrade to return the application to a stable and fully operational state. There also needs to be a mechanism to clean up persistent data when a release is shutdown and removed.

For type I, "block party," a separate copy of the evolved data can be created for the new version application instance. There are several possible approaches for data changes during the upgrade:

- Block provisioning requests after the initial data dump is performed and do not allow any changes until the new release is active.
- Allow provisioning to continue to occur on the old version but log all changes or transactions to be evolved later and stored into the new version database.
- Allow provisioning to continue to occur on the old version and do a real time sync of the data between the old and new versions.
- Use a combination of the items above: allow provisioning to continue to occur on the old version but block provisioning just before the final activation of the new version, and later evolve the old version data changes and store them in the new version database.

Once the old application version is ready to be removed, the old version database resources can also be deallocated and removed as well. A rollback is accomplished by taking the new version instance offline and directing all new traffic to the old version instance. As long as a release is maintained, its data must be backed up and able to be restored if necessary.

For type II, one driver per bus, an evolved copy of the data is created for the new application version. Prior to the switchover, the new application release instance's data are synchronized with the old release instance to make sure the new instance has the latest copy. This synchronization can be done through a journaling type operation to update the recently changed data entries. Note that some applications may choose not to allow changes to persistent data during the upgrade to avoid this final synchroniza-tion step. At the time of the switchover, only the new version of the data schema is used, so there is no need to keep both versions up to date as in type I. If there is a rollback, then updates since the activation of the new version instance should be reapplied to the old version schema as part of the rollback process if possible. Software upgrades may be rolled out to users faster with type II as they do not wait for traffic to drain on the old release; however, there is a greater potential for loss of existing user sessions.

Regardless of the type of upgrade, separation of data (both persistent and dynamic) from the application facilitates migration of virtual machines (VMs) among hosts. An example of data separation is the case where a master copy of the data is kept on virtual storage and is compatible across multiple versions of the software. An application instance can then retrieve the data it needs from the master copy and cache it locally. Updates to the data are only made to the master copy. Version specific access, update, and synchronization functions can be provided to "proxy" the data to older releases if needed. If separation of data is not possible, then software upgrade procedures must include the proper sequencing of data evolution and synchronization of the both persistent and dynamic data to ensure that data are not lost as a result of the upgrade.

9.5 ROLE OF SERVICE ORCHESTRATION IN SOFTWARE UPGRADE

Service orchestration based on a methodical management of tasks and components can be crucial for software upgrade to assist in meeting its service quality requirements for availability, reliability, and retainability. Service orchestration entails the linking together of architecture, tasks, and tools necessary to initiate and automatically manage a service. In the cloud environment, service orchestration includes linking together and automating tasks based on work flows, measured data, and policies with the purpose of providing a service. For software upgrade, service orchestration involves automating the processes for installation and configuration of the new software, allocation and initialization of resources to instantiate the new release, the evolution of persistent data and evolution and synchronization of any needed dynamic data, and transitioning from the old to the new release with a graceful draining of the traffic on the old release and retraining of traffic to the new release. In addition, other components may need to be updated with new IP addresses. All of these activities need to be carefully coordinated and monitored, providing for pauses and backouts if unsuccessful in a way that ensures service availability (i.e., no user downtime) and service reliability and retainability (i.e., maintenance of stable sessions and transactions).

For example, in type I, block party, software upgrade, service orchestration would be responsible for creating and installing the new application version; evolving and synching the persistent data; updating domain name system (DNS), front end distributors, and firewalls to include the new version appliance instance IP addresses or fully qualified directory numbers (FQDNs); and routing configurable amounts of traffic to both the new and old version appliance instances while managing a graceful shutdown of the old version. For type II, "one driver per bus" software upgrade, service orchestration would also be involved in synchronizing dynamic data (if applicable), and performing the switchover of old version appliance instances to new version appliance instances.

For both types I and II, service orchestration would also assist in performing the roll-back if needed.

Load balancers are key components in the orchestration process responsible for directing client traffic to the correct release application instance. There are two main options for this role, although variations may also be designed:

- Client traffic is directed to a proxy load balancer that will send the traffic to the appropriate server instance. The load balancer keeps track of which application instances are managing a particular client session. During software upgrade, messages associated with existing sessions on the old version are still directed to those application instances supporting that old version and a designated portion or all of the new registrations, and messages associated with new sessions are directed to application instances on the new version.
- Client traffic continues to go to the old version application instances via a non-proxy load balancer (e.g., DNS). A proxy that is integrated with the application is invoked to direct traffic associated with registrations or new sessions to the new version application instances. Messages associated with existing sessions on the old version application instance continue to be processed by the old version instance. In this case, the proxy may only be needed during the transition phase and may be deactivated once the old version application instances have been taken out of service. Once all old version traffic has been drained and the old version is no longer needed, the nonproxy load balancer can be updated to address the new version application instance, and the temporary proxy can be disabled.

The role of the proxy load balancer could be enhanced to work based on policies managed by service orchestration, such as defining a certain percentage of new traffic to be directed to the new version server instances to soak the new version for a period. This would also allow multiple versions to run for a chosen period of time—as determined by the customer.

9.5.1   Solution-Level Software Upgrade

Solution-level upgrade introduces another level of complexity to the software upgrade process as it entails a sequencing of virtual application upgrades across the impacted elements in the solution (i.e., all of the elements that require software upgrades). That sequencing requires an understanding of the dependencies and release compatibilities between the various elements in the solution to determine which elements need to be upgraded first and which can be upgraded in parallel. In addition, data distribution among the solution elements needs to be understood and included in the service orchestration procedures so that proper data synchronization is performed between those elements as part of the solution software upgrade process. Obviously, this complexity can be mitigated by ensuring release compatibility for interfaces between elements and ability to perform upgrades in parallel instead of in sequence, but that may not always be possible to ensure.

Service orchestration mechanisms should be implemented to automate and manage this complexity, ensuring the ordering of the upgrades, validating the successful completion of one before starting another upgrade, and synchronizing data among the elements. To facilitate orchestration, software upgrade strategies (e.g., block party and one driver per bus) must be clearly defined for all elements with well-documented interfaces for the management of the virtual applications and data that can be translated into procedures implemented by service orchestration. The procedures manage not only the software upgrade of each of the corresponding elements in the proper sequence, but also the sequencing of the rerouting of traffic between the newly upgraded elements, graceful shutdown of old version instances and eventual deallocation of resources, and deletion of old version instances. As with individual application upgrades, it must be possible to back out the upgrade of one or all of the upgraded application elements. Service orchestration should be able to support the back outs as well.

9.6 CONCLUSION

Both type I, "block party," and type II, "one driver per bus," software upgrade strategies improve the service quality of cloud-based applications compared with traditional software upgrade architectures. Type I, "block party," can offer higher user service quality than type II by supporting the old and new version application instances at the same time so there is no longer the complexity and user service risk of abruptly transitioning from one version to another. With type I, service can be slowly drained from the old version, and active user sessions do not necessarily have to be forcibly migrated to the new version. A portion of the traffic can be directed to the new version as a way to soak it while the rest is still running on the old version. This can also be used to enable limited user trials or testing. If there is a need to roll back the new version, it is just a matter of disabling that version and directing all traffic to the old version. At the solution level, service orchestration can be implemented to manage and coordinate the upgrade of the various applications, taking into account any interface incompatibilities and dependencies.

10

END-TO-END CONSIDERATIONS

End users experience cloud-based applications via their smartphone, tablet, laptop, or other device, and that experience aggregates the service impairments of the cloud-based application, the cloud infrastructure, the wide area and access networks, and the user's device itself. Section 10.1, "End-to-End Service Context," frames the context and general consideration for service quality actually experienced by end users. Section 10.2, "Three-Layer End-to-End Service Model," offers a simple model for analyzing end-to-end service impairments. Section 10.3, "Distributed and Centralized Cloud Data Centers," considers the service quality implications of obtaining service from smaller, nearby cloud data centers compared with larger but more distant regional data centers. Section 10.4, "Multitiered Solution Architectures," considers complex solutions that rely on resources in multiple cloud data centers. Section 10.5, "Disaster Recovery and Geographic Redundancy," considers georedundancy and disaster recovery of cloud-based applications.

10.1 END-TO-END SERVICE CONTEXT

As shown in Figure 10.1, the service quality experienced by an end user in a simple end-to-end application service model is vulnerable to five broad classes of impairment:

Service Quality of Cloud-Based Applications, First Edition. Eric Bauer and Randee Adams.
© 2014 The Institute of Electrical and Electronics Engineers, Inc. Published 2014 by John Wiley & Sons, Inc.

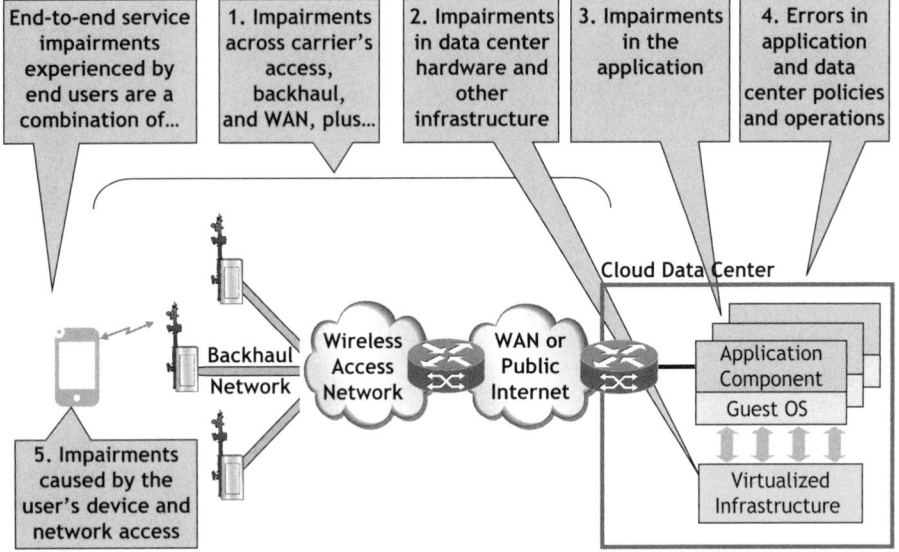

Figure 10.1. Simple End-to-End Application Service Context.

1. IP service quality and *impairments across the access and wide area networking infrastructure and facilities*, such as packet loss, packet latency, and packet jitter.

2. *Impairments within the cloud service provider's infrastructure and data center*, including service quality problems with the cloud data center's compute, storage, network, and service infrastructure (discussed in Chapter 4, "Virtualized Infrastructure Impairments"). This category also covers catastrophic events that render some or all of the cloud service provider's data center unavailable or inaccessible; mitigating catastrophic events is discussed in Section 10.5, "Disaster Recovery and Geographic Redundancy."

3. *Impairments of Application Software and the Underlying Guest OS.* The application software, guest OS, and technology components used by the application are vulnerable to residual software and architectural defects.

4. *Impairments Due to Human Error, Faulty Policies, and So On of Cloud Consumer and Cloud Service Provider.* Procedural or human errors have traditionally contributed significant service downtime; [TL_9000] offers the following canonical examples of traditional procedural errors:

      Examples of a procedural error include but are not limited to
    a. Removing the wrong fuse or circuit pack
    b. Not taking proper precautions to protect equipment, such as shorting out power and not wearing ESD strap
    c. Unauthorized work
    d. Not following methods of procedures (MOPs)
    e. Not following the steps of the documentation
    f. Using the wrong documentation

g. Using incorrect or outdated documentation
h. Insufficient documentation
i. Translation errors
j. User panic response to problems
k. Entering incorrect commands
l. Entering a command without understanding the impact
m. Inappropriate response to a network element alarm.

    While automation can minimize the risk of wrong human actions, there is still the risk of faulty operational policies, such as flawed policies for activating elastic growth or failure to check out newly grown application capacity before directing live traffic to the newly grown components.

5. *Impairments due to end user's device* (e.g., dead battery) *or network access* (e.g., standing in a wireless dead spot) also impact the end user's service, but these impairments are generally attributed to the user rather than to the service quality of the application itself. In addition, the technical characteristics of the device's hardware (e.g., speaker, microphone, and display) and software (e.g., codec implementation) set practical upper limits on the end user's quality of experience. For example, the quality of experience for video rendered to a full-sized high-definition TV is inherently superior to the video rendered to the small screen of a handheld smartphone.

Section 2.2, "Service Boundaries," introduced both the application's customer facing service boundary and the application's resource facing service boundary. Figure 10.2 overlays the service boundaries from Section 2.2 on the end-to-end service context of Figure 10.1.

To analyze end-to-end service, it is useful to define several logical measurement points. Figure 10.3 expands the four measurement points of [Bauer12] by clarifying that measurement point one (MP1) is equivalent to the application's *customer facing service* boundary and referring to the application's *resource facing service* boundary as

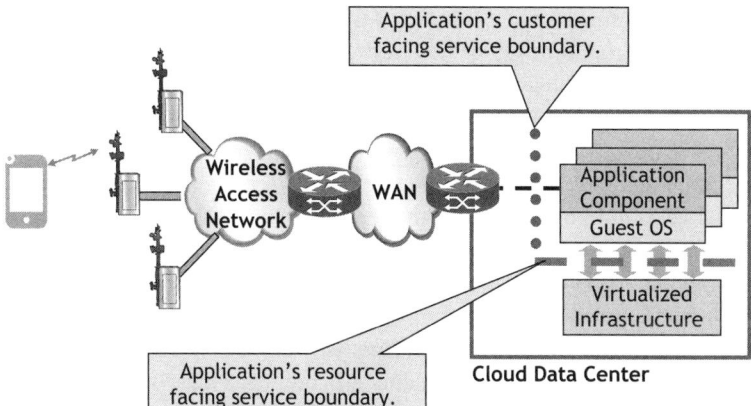

Figure 10.2. Service Boundaries in End-to-End Application Service Context.

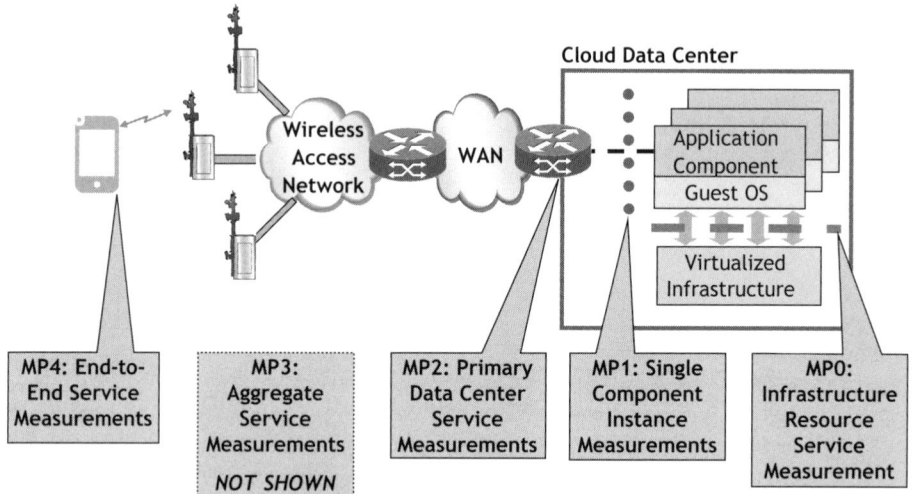

Figure 10.3. Measurement Points 0–4 for Simple End-to-End Context.

measurement point zero (MP0). Figure 10.3 overlays these measurement points onto Figure 10.2:

- MP0—**infrastructure measurements**—is the application's resource facing service boundary to the cloud service provider's virtualized infrastructure. Chapter 4, "Virtualized Infrastructure Impairments," considered the primary service risks across the measurement point.
- MP1—**component instance measurements**—is the application's customer facing service boundary. Service across this boundary is subject to application (or technology component)-specific service quality measurements, such as service reliability and service latency (see Section 2.5, "Application Service Quality"). Different types of application and technology component instances are likely to have different key service quality measurements. For example, session-oriented components may include some application-specific retainability measurements while nonsession oriented components would not.
- MP2—**data center service measurements**—measures the service delivered by an entire suite of application and technology component instances in a single availability zone or data center that deliver a higher level solution service. This measurement integrates the application components, supporting technology components, and operations systems with the cloud data center infrastructure and facilities.
- MP3—**aggregate service measurements**—captures the service benefit of intelligent load distribution and balancing arrangements that manage user workloads across two or more cloud data centers or availability zones, including disaster recovery mechanisms. MP3 is not shown in Figure 10.3.

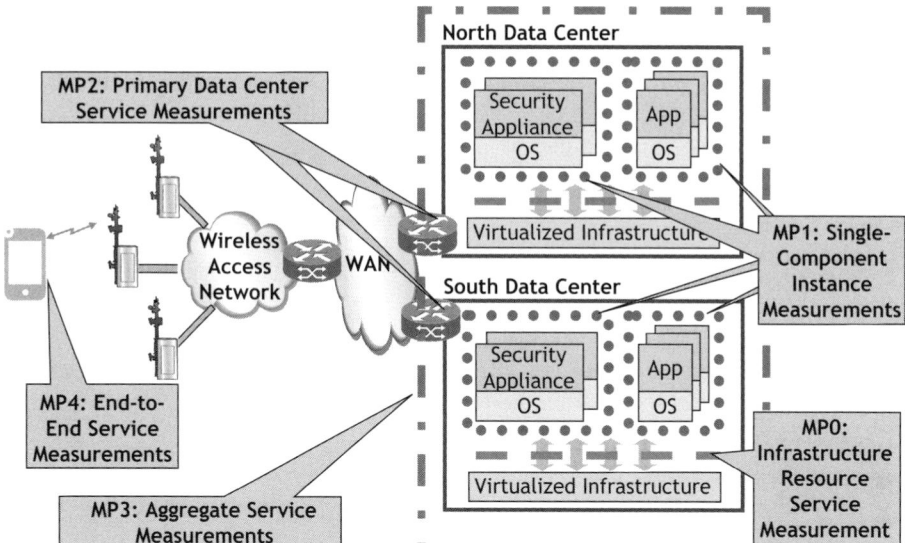

Figure 10.4. End-to-End Measurement Points for Simple Replicated Solution Context.

- MP4—**"end-to-end service measurements"**—aggregates the service impacts experienced by the end user of the aggregate service measurement MP3 and the access and wide area network (WAN) IP transport.

Figure 10.4 places a security appliance in front of the application instance of Figure 10.3 and replicates that application-plus-security-appliance solution to two cloud data centers to highlight two key points:

- *Multiple Component Instances.* Real cloud-based solutions are usually comprised of multiple discrete application and technology component instances. Each of these components provides distinct primary functions that together enable the application solution to deliver acceptable service to end users. Figure 10.4 shows two distinct component instances to illustrate this point: an application instance and a security appliance that protects the application instance from illegitimate traffic (e.g., distributed denial of service [DDoS] attack). Both of these components are required to be fully operational to deliver user service that is feasible and likely to both meet users' expectations for service quality and the enterprise's need for security. Each of these components has fundamentally different role in the overall solution, and thus has rather different key quality indicator (KQI). Real solutions would likely include many more discrete application or technology component instances offering functions such as database functionality, application logic, and network management. The quality characteristics of each of these application or technology component instances can be measured separately, often with somewhat different application component instance (MP1) metrics.

- *Multiple Data Centers.* Critical applications are routinely deployed to multiple data centers to both mitigate the risk of catastrophic failures and to boost service availability. Figure 10.4 shows the same application being deployed to both the "North data center" and the "South data center." MP2 (data center measurement) can logically be made at the service demark between each of these data centers and their respective connections to the public internet (WAN). Thus, the application's MP2 for North data center (or the South data center) would characterize user service delivered across the North (or South) data center's demark to the public network. MP3 characterizes the aggregate cloud service availability seen by users across the pool of data centers. For example, if the cloud consumer takes the application instance in the North data center offline for several hours to perform routine maintenance, then the cloud consumer could gracefully drain application user traffic from the North data center prior to the planned maintenance event and restore user traffic after the maintenance action had successfully completed. Thus, MP2 (data center measurement) for the North data center would reflect several hours of service downtime during the applicable measurement period, but MP3 (aggregate service measurement) for the period would not be impacted because all users were successfully served by the application solution running in the South data center.

Figure 10.5 illustrates the typical service monitoring points.

1. *Application software, operating system, library, and technology components* routinely include performance monitoring mechanisms that record key performance

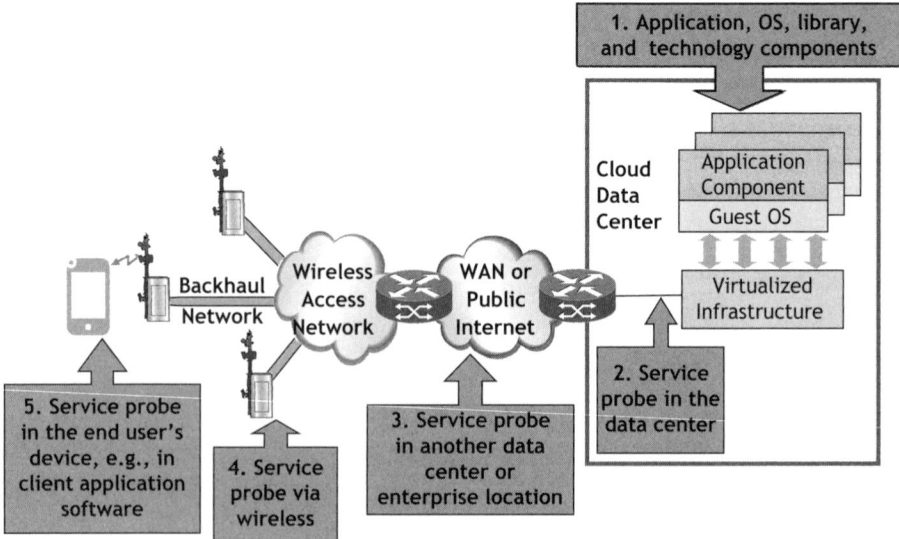

Figure 10.5. Service Probes across User Service Delivery Path.

data and make it available to service assurance and management systems in near real time. While traditional performance monitoring mechanisms are a useful starting point, Internet scale and other factors encourage adoption of cloud friendly performance monitoring tools, such as Dapper [Sigelman]. Note that individual network elements will routinely monitor appropriate performance management metrics which range from generic measurements (e.g., IP packets sent) to protocol-specific messages (e.g., types of specific protocol requests processed successfully). Analysis of these measurements gives insight into performance of an individual network element instance, but less insight into the application service experienced by end users.

2. *Application service can be monitored from within the data center hosting the service.* This probe point eliminates all impairments attributable to access and wide area networking, but may not include all edge routers, security appliances, and other IP infrastructure that service to real end users must traverse. This can accurately measure a single application or component instance (MP1) hosted within a target data center, and can take primary data center measurements (MP2).

3. *Service probes can be installed in one or more locations serviced by wireline internet connections,* such as another cloud data center or the cloud consumer's business office(s). These service probes should characterize the likely service performance experienced for users accessing the service via wireline IP connections. This can approximate MP2, "primary data center service measurements," or MP3, "aggregate service measurements," depending on the behavior and operation of the service probe.

4. *Wireless service probes* can be used to characterize performance of fixed or mobile wireless users. This measurement can roughly approximate MP4 performance experienced by end users via wireless access. While wireless service providers routinely execute the so-called drive testing to identify and correct coverage holes, most cloud consumers have too little control over the wireless access used by the end users to make this measurement generally useful.

5. *Service probes in the end user's device or client application* can easily monitor service impairments, such as late and lost packets, throughput and accessibility and retainability failures. These performance measurements can be made remotely accessible so that the cloud consumer's operations and support teams can retrieve these statistics to better understand the nature of service impairments being experienced by end users. This service probe can capture MP4, "end-to-end service measurements."

10.2 THREE-LAYER END-TO-END SERVICE MODEL

To better analyze end-to-end service risks, it is convenient to decompose this simple model of Figure 10.1 into three logical layers, as shown in Figure 10.6:

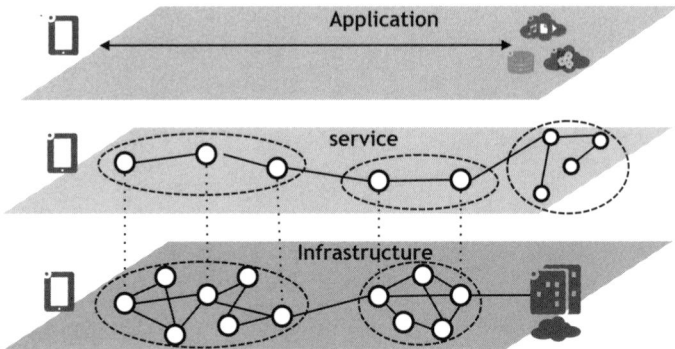

Figure 10.6. Three Layer Factorization of Sample End to End Solution.

1. *Infrastructure layer* for the physical devices, equipment, and facilities that transport IP packets and support application processing. The physical infrastructure layer includes the following:
   • User's device
   • Wireless base station and transmission path (or wireline access equipment and facilities)
   • Access network infrastructure and facilities
   • Wide area networking infrastructure and facilities
   • Access infrastructure and facilities to the cloud data center's demark point
   • Cloud service provider's routers, networking, compute, memory and storage infrastructure, and data center facility.
2. *Service layer* for the logical enabling services, such as IP network service and cloud infrastructure as a service (IaaS). The service layer includes the following:
   • Networking software running on the end user's device
   • IP networking service provided by the end user's wireless service provider
   • Virtual private networking (VPN) services
   • IaaS and associated any as-a-Service (XaaS) offerings (e.g., load balancing as a service) supporting the cloud consumer's application.
3. *Application layer* integrates application software offerings with enabling services from the service layer, all supported by elements of the physical infrastructure layer. The application layer includes
   • Application software running on the end user's device
   • Cloud consumer's application software, policies, and data that are built on XaaS offerings from the service layer
   • Integration with VPN and other networking services.

Each individual network element and facility across the infrastructure should have its own performance measurements (key performance indicators [KPIs]). Providers of

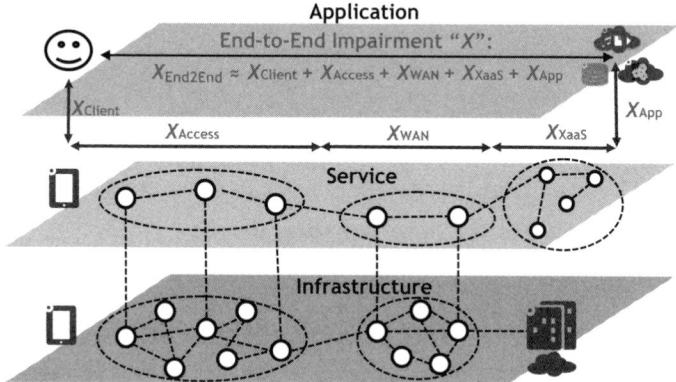

Figure 10.7. Estimating Service Impairments across the Three-Layer Model.

each service across the service layer should methodically manage the service quality delivered between the provider's demark points. For example, enterprise VPN service providers routinely commit to service availability, packet loss, latency, and jitter performance between their demark points, thereby shielding enterprise customers from operation and practical complexity of VPN service. The end-to-end service across the application layer experienced by end users is the focus of this chapter.

10.2.1 Estimating Service Impairments via the Three-Layer Model

Figure 10.7 shows how application service impairments accumulate across the end-to-end service delivery path. As shown in Equation 10.1 (estimation of general end-to-end service impairments), basic service impairment "X" (e.g., typical service latency) experienced by the end user can generally be estimated as the sum of

1. Impairment in the client's device and application (e.g., X_{Client})
2. Impairment in the client device's access network (e.g., X_{Access})
3. Impairment across the WAN and cloud service provider's access network (e.g., X_{WAN})
4. Impairment across the various cloud service provider's services that are used by the cloud consumer's application, such as IaaS, load balancing as a service, and database as a service (e.g., X_{XaaS})
5. Impairment of the application software itself (e.g., XApp).

$$X_{\text{End2End}} \approx X_{\text{Client}} + X_{\text{Access}} + X_{\text{WAN}} + X_{\text{XaaS}} + X_{\text{App}}. \tag{10.1}$$

This impairment model is *composable* in that impairment contributors can be decomposed into "white box" component impairments or composed into aggregate "black box" impairments. For example, the aggregate or black box impairment of

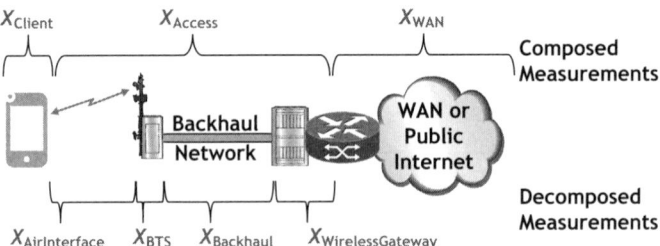

Figure 10.8. Decomposing a Service Impairment.

wireless access (X_{Access}) could be decomposed into smaller black boxes, as shown in Figure 10.8 for deeper analysis into:

- $X_{AirInterface}$. Propagation impairment across the wireless air interface
- X_{BTS}. Impairment due to the wireless base station
- $X_{Backhaul}$. Impairment due to backhaul equipment and facilities
- $X_{WirelessGateway}$. Impairment due to interworking gateway and facilities between the wireless carrier's network and the public Internet.

These impairments could be further decomposed if appropriate, such as factoring $X_{Backhaul}$ into impairments for equipment in the backhaul path and propagation latency across physical transmission lines. Likewise, if IP traffic flows across multiple carriers, then X_{WAN} could be decomposed into the contributions from each of those IP carriers.

10.2.2   End-to-End Service Availability

As discussed in Section 2.5.1, "Service Availability," service availability is driven by service downtime. When an end user accesses application service from a particular application instance in a data center (logically MP2), the components in the end-to-end service delivery path are logically arranged in series; thus, service downtime of each component should logically be summed across the service delivery path to estimate end-to-end service downtime, as given in Equation 10.2 (estimation of end-to-end service downtime). Note that not all of this end-to-end downtime may actually be attributed to the application. For example, if the end user's device is unavailable because they used it to the point of battery exhaustion so Downtime$_{Client}$ is logically impacted; this downtime is usually attributed to the end user rather than the cloud-based applications, and thus can be excluded from application consideration.

$$\text{Downtime}_{End2End} \approx \text{Downtime}_{Client} + \text{Downtime}_{Access} + \text{Downtime}_{WAN} +$$
$$\text{Downtime}_{XaaS} + \text{Downtime}_{App}. \tag{10.2}$$

Assuming that all of the component downtime values were expressed as minutes of service downtime per year (i.e., annualized downtime per system), then Downtime$_{End2End}$

will be given in minutes of downtime per year. This enables one to estimate the end-to-end service availability via Equation 10.3:*

$$\text{Availability}_{End2End} \approx \frac{525,960 - \text{Downtime}_{End2End}}{525,960}. \tag{10.3}$$

Sophisticated client applications and service provider operations can enable user service to be recovered to a redundant application instance, generally in a different availability zone or data center, if the primary instance fails. MP3 captures the benefit of these redundant application instance recovery actions. Estimating the service availability benefit of multiple redundant application instances can often be done via the client-initiated recovery model of [Bauer11].

10.2.3   End-to-End Service Latency

As discussed in Section 2.5.2, "Service Latency," service latency has two key figures of merit: typical (nominally 50th or 90th percentile value) and tail (nominally 99.99th or 99.999th percentile value). The law of large numbers enables one to estimate typical end-to-end service latency ($\text{Typical}_{End2End}$) by summing the typical latencies (e.g., Typical_{App}) across the service delivery path, as shown in Equation 10.4 (estimation of end-to-end typical service latency). As the application service latency (Typical_{App}) may be rather different for different classes of application operations, one typically focuses on measuring one specific application operation, such as call setup, starting a streaming movie, and displaying the first screen of search results. Applications with operations that have materially different latency characteristics for different key functions (e.g., account creation, user logon, or completing a purchase transaction) can measure and optimize each metric separately.

$$\text{Typical}_{End2End} \approx \text{Typical}_{Client} + \text{Typical}_{Access} + \text{Typical}_{WAN} + \text{Typical}_{XaaS} + \text{Typical}_{App}. \tag{10.4}$$

Note that end user operations often include a request message sent by the user, which is served via a response message from the application, so end-to-end service latency should often consider both the upstream packet flow from the user's device to the application, as well as the downstream packet flow from the application back to the user's device. For example, both wireless and xDSL access networks often have asymmetric performance characteristics, so one cannot generally assume that uplink (i.e., user to cloud) service latency will be identical to downlink (i.e., cloud to user) latency. Likewise, WAN traffic flows are often carefully engineered so packets flowing from point B to point A may not simply reverse the path taken by packets from point A to point B.

---

* 525,960 is the number of minutes per *average* year, which is the product of 365.25 days per average year (considering both leap and nonleap years), 24 h/d and 60 min/h.

The shape of tail latency is driven by the throughput of the particular service component, the offered workload, and the queuing/scheduling mechanism and policy. Fundamental differences in the nature of specific services, components, and facilities across the end-to-end service delivery path will produce different tail shapes. While typical latencies can be summed across the end-to-end service delivery path, the tail latencies arithmetically sum across the end-to-end path only when the tail variances are independent. If the long tail (i.e., high variance) events are not independent, then the end-to-end service latency tail will likely be worse than the mathematical sum. Bandwidth reservations should reduce the tail variance compared with ordinary operation (i.e., without resource reservations) because the reservation should enable elements and facilities along the path to minimize the risk that application data will be forced to remain queued due to congestion waiting for resource bandwidth.

10.2.4 End-to-End Service Reliability

As discussed in Section 2.5.3, "Service Reliability," service reliability is conveniently expressed as defective (i.e., failed) operations per million (DPM). Wireless access can have packet loss rates high enough to cause transactions to exhaust timeout and retry mechanisms resulting in outright transaction failure. Failures of networking equipment (e.g., routers) or facilities (e.g., breakage of an optical transmission fiber), and some transient events (e.g., lightning) can cause brief disruptions of access or WAN service that will cause an end user's transaction or operation to fail. Fortunately, robust networking equipment and facilities should recover service promptly (e.g., failover to redundant component or alternate path) so operations retried by the user moments later should succeed. Note that network congestion can also cause packets to be materially delayed or even dropped and that will impact service reliability experienced by end users. Unfortunately, the service reliability impairments due to wireless access degradation and network congestion are likely to vary based on network utilization, wireless transmission path, and other factors, so it is hard to make a generalized service reliability estimate. Thus, the defect rate contributed by each component in the end-to-end service delivery path may change based on the time of day (e.g., traffic load), physical location of the wireless device, and other factors. Nevertheless, Equation 10.5 (estimation of end-to-end service defect rate) gives a useful starting point for estimating end-to-end service reliability, where

- DPM_{App} gives the steady state service reliability of the application.
- DPM_{XaaS} gives the incremental service reliability impact of typical XaaS operation, such as due to virtual machine (VM) stalls and hiccups. DPM_{XaaS} is likely to vary by cloud service provider based on their operational policies and other factors.
- DPM_{Access} gives the impact of the user's wireless and wireline access network.
- $DPM_{NetworkFailures}$ gives the average impact of acute network failure events.
- $DPM_{NetworkTransients}$ gives the average impact of chronic and transient events.
- $DPM_{NetworkCongestion}$ gives the average impact of congestion on the access and backhaul network serving the user (assuming that it is not included in $DPM_{NetworkTransients}$).

$$DPM_{End2End} \approx DPM_{App} + DPM_{XaaS} + DPM_{Access} + DPM_{NetworkFailures}$$
$$+ DPM_{NetworkTransients} + DPM_{NetworkCongestion}. \qquad (10.5)$$

Note that service reliability is not generally affected by having applications deployed across multiple cloud data centers because user devices will typically send each request to an application instance in a single data center and await a response. Theoretically, the user's device could launch concurrent redundant requests to different cloud data centers, but this is rare today.

10.2.5 End-to-End Service Accessibility

As discussed in Section 2.5.4, "Service Accessibility," service accessibility captures the probability that an arbitrary end user will be able to successfully complete application service access, such as logging on to a secure service, starting a streaming movie, or establishing a voice or video call within a maximum acceptable time. These complex operations typically require availability of the entire service delivery path, as well as the service reliability of supporting application operations. As shown in Equation 10.6 (estimation of end-to-end service accessibility), the rate of accessibility failures (inaccessibility) can be estimated by summing the end-to-end unavailability in parts per million* and the failure rate for all required actions by the application and enabling cloud infrastructure.

$$InaccessibilityDPM_{End2End} \approx UnavailabilityDPM_{End2End} + \sum_{RequiredActions}$$
$$(DPM_{App} + DPM_{XaaS}). \qquad (10.6)$$

Like service availability, service accessibility can be improved by deploying redundant application instances across the WAN. Estimating the accessibility benefit of redundant application instances must consider the client application's automatic failure detection and recovery architecture and performance. If the mechanism is fast enough, then it is possible that unavailability of the primary application instance can be detected and service recovered to a redundant application instance fast enough that the end user does not perceive the original service access attempt to the primary application instance to have failed before service was delivered via a redundant application instance. More often, failure of the primary application instance will cause the client's first access after application failure to fail, which triggers clients to direct future requests to a redundant application instance. When the end user retries the failed operation, the client should send that request to a redundant application instance so that operation should succeed. If the client was unable to switch away from the failed primary application instance (e.g., because there was no redundant application instance configured), then all service

---

* Availability (actually unavailability) can be expressed as DPM by multiplying the percentage of unavailability (e.g., 99.999% availability means 0.001% unavailability) times 10,000 (i.e., 0.001% unavailability becomes 10 DPM). Note that the multiplier of 10,000 is used rather than 1,000,000 because a percentage value already includes a factor of 100.

access attempts would fail until the primary application instance was returned to service.

10.2.6   End-to-End Service Retainability

As discussed in Section 2.5.5, "Service Retainability," service retainability character-izes the probability that an end user's service session (e.g., streaming movie, telephone call, and online game) will continue to deliver acceptable service quality until normal session termination (i.e., end of movie or game and user disconnection of telephone call). Service retainability failures are likely to be caused by the following:

1. *Failures of simplex access network components.*
2. *Slow automatic recovery* of components in the service delivery path. For example, if streaming video freezes or a telephone call goes silent for more than a few seconds, most users will abandon the session and restart the movie, redial the call, and so on, rather than waiting tens of seconds or minutes for service to recover (or not). If the user does not have to cancel or abandon an unacceptably slow session, then ideally, the service will automatically begin a reestablished session at or near the point of session loss so the user is not further inconve-nienced by having to manually seek to the point of disconnection to restore their session context.
3. *Unsuccessful automatic recovery* of components in the service delivery path, such as due to loss or inconsistency of session data across redundant components.

Service retainability impairments can be estimated by summing the rate of retain-ability failures per user session minute via Equation 10.7 (estimation of end-to-end service retainability [as DPM]), where each DPM value estimates the rate of failures per million minutes of operation.

$$
\begin{aligned}
DPM_{End2End} \approx{} & DPM_{App} + DPM_{XaaS} + DPM_{Access} + DPM_{NetworkFailures} \\
& + DPM_{NetworkTransients} + DPM_{NetworkCongestion}.
\end{aligned}
\tag{10.7}
$$

Service retainability is generally addressed via redundancy *within* an application instance. When service is recovered to a different (e.g., geographically redundant) application instance, then some user sessions are typically impacted because volatile session data are not generally replicated between distinct application instances.

10.2.7   End-to-End Service Throughput

As discussed in Section 2.5.6, "Service Throughput," application service throughput is not an "end-to-end" metric per se because it captures the aggregate throughput delivered to all end users. The throughput available to an end user typically is the minimum guaranteed service throughput across their end-to-end service delivery path. As a practi-cal matter, an end user's service throughput is often limited by either their (wireless) access network or by their client device.

10.2.8 End-to-End Service Timestamp Accuracy

Timestamp accuracy (Section 2.5.7) is not generally an end-to-end service quality measurement experienced by end users because they typically see only timestamps from applications and from their client device, and most users are not likely to expect precise time synchronization between their device and universal time. Moreover, absolute service timestamps (e.g., exactly when a business transaction was executed) are implicitly relativistic in that they are assumed to be relative to the server's frame of (time) reference rather than to the client's frame of (time) reference. While the server's frame of reference and the client's frame of reference are roughly synchronized, few user devices even attempt to report their local time reference with precision beyond seconds.

10.2.9 Reality Check

The three layer model and the simplified end-to-end impairment estimates are tools to help understand and analyze impairments; they are not a replacement for judicious measurement of user service KQIs and appropriate KPIs across the end-to-end service delivery path. The end-to-end view also sets cloud-related impairments into context. For example, the user service impact of virtualized infrastructure clock event jitter (Section 4.6, "Clock Event Jitter") may be dwarfed by jitter caused by the user's wireless access network or may be the dominant source of end-to-end jitter for users connected via wireline access networks. Thus, cloud consumers should consider the service of the end users experienced at their device, and focus on mitigating service impairments that are most likely to impact the service experience rendered at the end user's device.

10.3 DISTRIBUTED AND CENTRALIZED CLOUD DATA CENTERS

As shown in Figure 10.4, many cloud-based applications are likely to be deployed to multiple data centers to

- *Improve end user service latency* by reducing typical IP packet transmission latency between the data center hosting the application and the end user
- *Improve service resilience* for disaster events (detailed in Section 10.5, "Disaster Recovery").

Once the decision has been made to deploy application instances to multiple data centers that are geographically separated for business continuity and disaster recovery, one must balance the strategy of deploying the target application to a small number of big regional cloud data centers that are likely to be far from end users, or deploying to a larger number of smaller, distributed cloud data centers that can be geographically closer to more end users. This section considers the service trade-offs of deploying service to more (often smaller) local cloud data centers or fewer (often much larger) regional cloud data centers. Section 10.3.1, "Centralized Cloud Data

Centers," considers large, warehouse-scale regional data centers, and Section 10.3.2, "Distributed Cloud Data Centers," discusses small, local cloud data centers.

10.3.1 Centralized Cloud Data Centers

To reduce operating expenses, many cloud service providers have created a small number of warehouse scale centralized cloud data centers that are capable of serving huge geographic regions. Instead of populating these massive data centers with racks or rows of computer equipment, warehouse scale data centers may be filled with entire shipping containers of computer equipment. Thousands of servers are preinstalled in each shipping container in a factory, and the shipping containers are easily transported and installed in the warehouse scale facility.

Warehouse scale data centers are typically arranged to efficiently and conveniently connect to several internet service provider's (ISP's) backbone networks to enable massive traffic volumes across huge populations of users to be efficiently aggregated and offered as load to the massive centralized cloud data center. In the "big cloud" option, where a tiny number of warehouse scale cloud data centers are used, end user traffic flows from their user device across a wireless or wireline access network into their ISP's core network. As shown in Figure 10.9, in many cases, the traffic will flow across a long haul transport network, and perhaps one or more ISPs' networks in order to reach one of the few massive data centers operated by the particular cloud service provider.

10.3.2 Distributed Cloud Data Centers

The logical alternative to a small number of centralized warehouse scale cloud data centers is a large number of smaller, distributed cloud data centers (illustrated in Figure 10.10), in which cloud computing data centers are deployed as close to the end users' edge of the network as practical, perhaps even in the central office terminating the ISP's access or even collocated with wireless base stations. In the distributed cloud case, most users could be served from cloud computing resources installed in either their local access office or from a data center accessible from the ISP's metropolitan area network

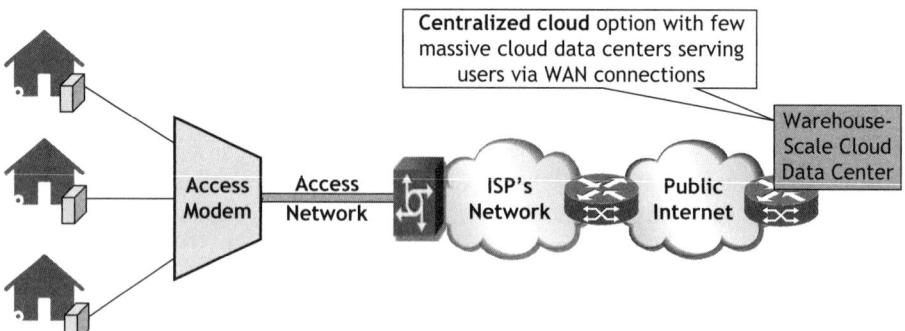

Figure 10.9. Centralized Cloud Data Center Scenario.

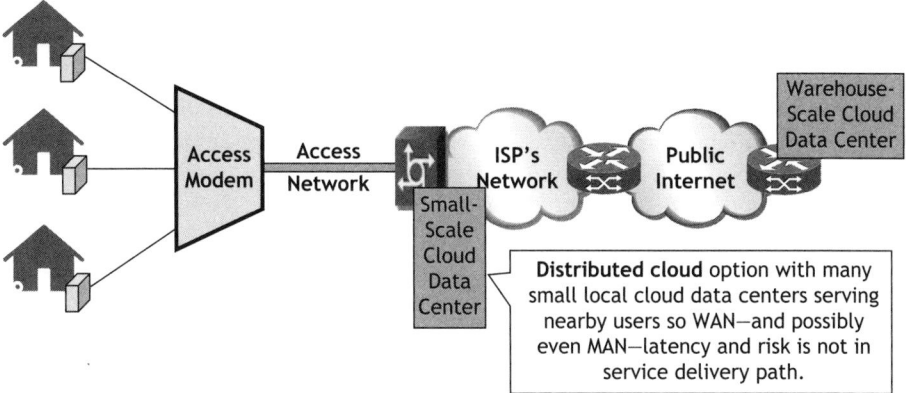

Figure 10.10. Distributed Cloud Data Center Scenario.

(MAN), so that their IP traffic need not traverse a WAN. This reduces both the physical distance of transport facilities (i.e., miles of optical fiber) and number of transport, routing, and security devices that IP traffic must traverse, thereby reducing end-to-end service latency. Note that while this may materially shorten the end-to-end IP latency when a user is connected via a wireline access network, elimination of WAN latency may be small compared with wireless access latency. Local distributed cloud data centers can save WAN bandwidth as well as improve latency by storing data close to where it is being consumed.

Small distributed cloud data centers can also be pushed toward the edge of wireless networks by collocating distributed data centers where wireless IP traffic first becomes accessible. A content delivery network (CDN), which caches content for end users, is an example of an application that benefits from deploying to more local data centers because that arrangement both reduces WAN traffic for the Internet access service provider and improves the end users' quality of experience.

10.3.3 Service Availability Considerations

Given Equation 10.2 in Section 10.2.2, "End-to-End Service Availability," the service availability question becomes: is there likely to be any increase in service downtime with distributed data centers to offset the availability benefit of eliminating Downtime-$_{WAN}$ from the service delivery path? Let us methodically consider the factors that drive service availability (introduced in Chapter 5, "Application Redundancy and Cloud Computing"):

- *Outage Rate.* Outage rate is a function of the following:
  - *Critical Failure Rate.* How frequently do service impacting failure events occur? The authors assume (without data) that the rate of critical failures within a cloud data center (e.g., software crashes and hardware failures) is independent of whether myriad of VM instances are running on containerized hardware in a massive centralized warehouse data center or a small number

of VM instances are running on rack-mounted hardware in a small distributed cloud data center. After all, cloud service providers are accountable for shielding each VM instance from every other VM instance, so the presence of a larger number of VM instances in a massive centralized data center should neither increase nor decrease the risk of the target application's VM instances or supporting infrastructure failing.

  ○ *Probability of Successful Automatic Failure Detection.* How likely is it that a service impacting failure will be automatically detected and correctly isolated fast enough to prevent a prolonged outage? Assuming that the same software surveillance and high availability infrastructures are used, the effectiveness of automatic failure detection mechanisms should be independent of cloud data center size.

  ○ *Probability of Successful Automatic Recovery.* How likely is it that the recovery action initiated by the system will successfully mitigate the user-visible impact of failure, thereby eliminating the need for time consuming—and outage prolonging—manual recovery actions? Assuming that the same high availability platform(s) and infrastructure(s) are used, the probability of successful automatic recovery should be independent of cloud data center size, provided the application and cloud data center are engineered with sufficient online or near-line spare/capacity that service can be recovered within the original data center rather than having to burst to a different data center.

• *Outage Duration.* Assuming similar levels of automation and sophistication of operational policies, outage durations should be comparable for critical failures in both centralized and distributed cloud data centers. The authors assume that all cloud data centers will maintain sufficient spare hardware capacity that non-catastrophic hardware failures can be addressed by (offline) migration of applications from failed hardware to "spare" hardware capacity within the data center, so applications can be restored to full-service redundancy in minutes rather than requiring slower manual hardware replacement or repair to restore full application redundancy (thereby mitigating window of simplex exposure risk). If data centers do not include sufficient spare online service capacity in the local cloud data center, then there may be additional latency to shift recovery traffic to an alternate data center. The real difference in outage duration may arise in the rare case when there is insufficient online redundancy, and remote access is not available or sufficient requiring manual, hands-on troubleshooting or repair actions to reseat a circuit board or replace a failed field replaceable (hardware) unit (FRU) before service can be resumed. Robust virtualization/hypervisor platforms, hardware management infrastructure, and adequate online/near line excess hardware capacity should make hands-on manual service recovery actions (vs. nonemergency repair actions) vanishingly rare.

• *Outage Extent.* The perceived business impact of service outage extent (e.g., number of impacted users) is often nonlinear. Unsurprisingly, service providers are very keen to reduce the risk that outage events can be impactful enough to make the news or move the stock price, and they are also eager to reduce the risk of high impact individual events. More small application instances deployed across many small cloud data centers are inherently at less risk of large outage events that trigger external attention or internal escalations.

Fortunately, service outage events of applications hosted in small local data centers should not impact users beyond the local vicinity served by the impacted application instance; in contrast, events impacting a regional application instance in a big warehouse scale data center can potentially impact a massive number of users, and thus are much more likely to draw negative attention to the application service provider.

10.3.4 Service Latency Considerations

Distributed cloud data centers attached to the users' access network have the following **inherent service quality and latency advantages** over regional warehouse scale cloud data centers accessed via MAN and WAN:

- *Less One-Way Service Latency.* Users who are physically farther away from a data center are likely to experience higher service latency due to the following:
  - *Transmission Latency.* Light takes more than 5 μs to travel a mile, so transmission latency accumulates for each mile of fiber, coaxial cable, twisted pair, or air that data must travel between the user's device and the cloud data center.
  - *Equipment Latency.* Every router, switch, repeater, and interworking element in the transmission path between the user's device and the application adds packet latency.
- *Shorter Dejitter Buffers Are Possible.* Both client and server applications routinely have dejitter buffers for streaming media to mask the effects of network congestion and other impairments. Positioning data centers physically closer to the end user may enable shorter dejitter buffers because less jitter may be introduced across the end-to-end path because of the following:
  - *Less Opportunity for IP Packets to Take Different Routes across the WAN* between end user and application instance, thereby experiencing different transmission latencies.
  - *Less Opportunity for Packet Resequencing.* Eliminating MAN and WAN equipment and facilities reduces the risk of individual IP packets taking different routes and thus arriving out of sequence.
  - *Less Opportunity for Packet Jitter.* IP traffic traverses fewer aggregation or choke points where traffic may encounter congestion and queuing, thereby introducing packet jitter.

Note that the one-way transport latency benefit of using distributed cloud data centers physically close to end users may be small compared with the latency of end users' wireless access.

10.3.5   Service Reliability Considerations

Service reliability impairments typically arise from the following causes:

- *Subcritical Application Software Failures.* A software bug, buffer overrun, contention for critical resource, application switchover, or a similar event causes isolated service requests to fail. The authors assume (without data) that the service reliability (DPM) of applications is independent of the size (e.g., number of VM instances) in a particular application instance. This means that the rate of failed transactions is independent of whether a large application instance (e.g., 100 VMs) is serving a large pool of active users (e.g., tens of thousands or hundreds of thousands) or a small application instance (e.g., 3 VMs) is serving a small pool of active users (e.g., tens to hundreds).
- *Networking Failures and Impairments.* Packet loss, delay, and other impairments can take time to detect and time to recover, which increases the risk that the maximum acceptable service latency time will be exceeded so the operation will be deemed unsuccessful and thus impact service reliability metrics. The more networking facilities (e.g., miles of fiber) and the more network elements (e.g., routers and security appliances), the greater the likelihood that some transaction latencies will exceed the maximum acceptable service latency.

Thus, end-to-end service reliability may be slightly worse from distant regional data centers than from local data centers due to impairments from WAN equipment and facilities.

10.3.6   Service Accessibility Considerations

End-to-end service accessibility may be slightly better for local distributed data centers because end-to-end service is unaffected by WAN (and perhaps MAN) impairments.

10.3.7   Service Retainability Considerations

End-to-end service retainability should be slightly better for applications deployed to local distributed data centers because the service delivery path does not include the WAN (and perhaps MAN) networking equipment and facilities, and thus is exposed to less risk of service impacting failure events.

10.3.8   Resource Distribution Considerations

The scale of the cloud data center impacts the probability that resources requested by cloud consumers will be "in stock" at the data center, rather than requiring outgrowth to fulfill the resource allocation request. Of the four resources offered by IaaS providers (processing, volatile storage, persistent storage, and networking), three of these resources—processing, memory, and networking—are essentially fungible, and thus there is freedom in selecting particular resources to allocate to a particular application because identically configured resources are essentially interchangeable. In contrast, allocated persistent storage is often not fungible because one application's user data are not interchangeable with another application, and often one user's data are not inter-changeable with another user. A trivial example is e-mail or voice mail: a user needs access to their *personal* mailbox; after all, successfully connecting to an e-mail or voice mail system to learn "*your mailbox is currently unavailable*" is an unsatisfactory user experience. Thus, service availability requires that appropriate fungible processing, memory, and network resources to be brought together with nonfungible persistent storage to correctly serve user requests.

The size of persistent storage indirectly impacts the mobility and accessibility of that data. While it may be feasible to download and cache relatively small user-specific persistent data (e.g., user profile information) to a different data center on the fly, it is infeasible to download a multiterabyte database to another cloud data center on the fly. Thus, for data centric applications, it is often most practical to collocate the fungible processing, memory, and networking resources with the massive, nonfungible (and not easily transportable) persistent storage, while applications with less user-specific persistent storage can often be pushed to whichever data center is most convenient. The alternative to collocating persistent data with processing and memory resources is to deploy a multitiered solution architecture, which is considered in Section 10.4, "Multitiered Solution Architectures."

10.4 MULTITIERED SOLUTION ARCHITECTURES

Section 10.1, "End-to-End Service Context," considered a simple solution architecture in which all application server components and data are collocated in a single data center, so a user's service request flows from the user's device to that single data center and a response flows back. Many solutions will be deployed, with more complex architectures relying on two or more tiers of data centers in the service delivery path. For example, an enterprise may rely on compute resources in a public cloud to directly serve end users but retain enterprise data in a private data center on an enterprise location. In this case, the end-to-end service delivery path would flow from the end user's device across access and WAN networks to the public cloud data center (Tier I) where the application logic resides, and then across access and WAN networks to the private cloud data center (Tier II) where the enterprise's data resides.

The end-to-end service delivery path in this two-tiered architecture can be modeled as logically appending additional access and WAN networks and a second data center to the end-to-end model of Section 10.1, "End-to-End Service Context." Figure 10.11 visualizes a sample two-tiered configuration. Logically, the end-to-end path is extended by adding

- $TierII_{WAN}$ for networking between the Tier I and Tier II data centers
- $TierII_{XaaS}$ for the second data center's cloud infrastructure services
- $TierII_{App}$ for the application (e.g., database server) in the Tier II data center.

The end-to-end service availability, latency, reliability, accessibility, retainability, timestamp accuracy, and throughput (discussed in Sections 10.2.2–10.2.7) should be

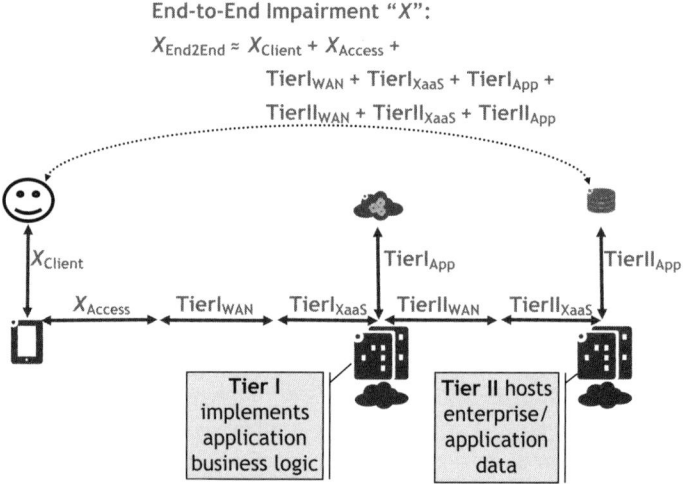

End-to-End Impairment "X":

$X_{End2End} \approx X_{Client} + X_{Access} +$

$Tierl_{WAN} + Tierl_{XaaS} + Tierl_{App} +$

$TierII_{WAN} + TierII_{XaaS} + TierII_{App}$

Figure 10.11. Sample Multitier Solution Architecture.

the same with additional impairments included for the application access, WAN, and data center.

10.5 DISASTER RECOVERY AND GEOGRAPHIC REDUNDANCY

Disaster recovery plans methodically address the restoration of key business services following a disaster event, such as an earthquake or fire, that renders a data center unavailable. Disaster recovery time objective (RTO) and recovery point objective (RPO) are the KQIs for disaster recovery, and are discussed in Section 10.5.1. Geo-redundant architectures are discussed in Section 10.5.2, and service quality considerations of georedundancy are considered in Section 10.5.3. Architectural considerations for assuring RPOs are met are covered in Section 10.5.4, and availability zones and disaster recovery are discussed in Section 10.5.5. Note that two disaster recovery analysis methodologies are also given in Part III: Recommendations: Section 15.8, "Recovery Point Objective Analysis," and Section 15.9, "Recovery Time Objective Analysis."

10.5.1 Disaster Recovery Objectives

Best practice and fiduciary responsibility direct that enterprises establish business continuity plans to assure that critical business systems and data can be recovered following disasters or catastrophic events that render a data center unavailable. Business continuity expectations for information systems are defined via two key performance indicators, shown in Figure 10.12:

- RTO is the time required to recover user service following a disaster event. When manually initiated disaster recovery is used, RTO is often defined as the

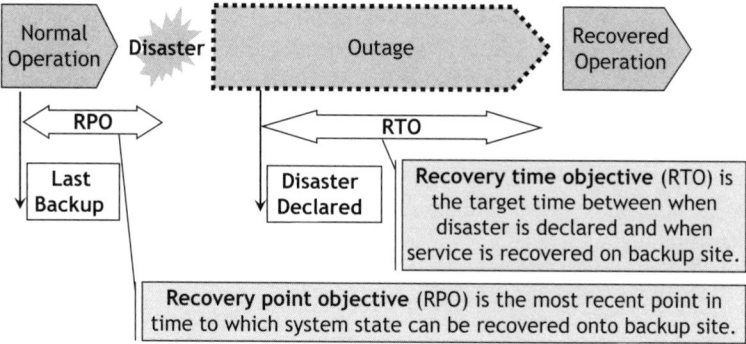

Figure 10.12. Disaster Recovery Time and Point Objectives.

time from when the disaster was formally declared by a business leader, and thus the disaster recovery plan was formally activated, to the time when a specified portion of users (e.g., 90%) have recovered service. When automatic disaster recovery mechanisms are used, RTO may be specified as from the time user service is impacted by the disaster event to the time when a specified portion of users have recovered service. RTO targets were traditionally measured in hours and days, but many critical systems have RTO targets measured in minutes.

- RPO is the amount of data changes that can be lost when service is recovered from (offsite) data (e.g., backup, mirror, and replica). For example, if database changes are replicated to a geographically distant data center every 15 minutes, then the RPO should be about 15 minutes because only slightly more than 15 minutes of database changes could be lost between the last backup and the disaster event (see worst case scenario example in Section 15.8, "Recovery Point Objective Analysis"). Different applications will have different RPO targets. For example, while losing 24 hours of social networking updates on disaster recovery may be acceptable; losing 24 hours of sales, inventory changes, or financial transactions may compromise a business's ability to survive after the disaster event.

In any case, it is important to test and practice disaster recovery procedures periodically, particularly on critical applications, to ensure that procedures are well understood and correct and that the recovery objectives can be met.

10.5.2 Georedundant Architectures

While traditional high availability architectures carefully manage redundant resources *within* a logical system to mitigate ordinary (single point) failures, events can occur that simultaneously impact many components of a single system instance, such as a disaster event that impacts or disables a data center, can overwhelm a single application instance's ability to mitigate user service impact. To mitigate these types of events, a fully independent system instance is deployed at a geographically distant site that can be used to recover the traffic for the impacted applications.

Geographically redundant—or georedundant—architectures feature fully independent application instances located at geographically distant sites to enable business continuity following a disaster event. In the event of a disaster (e.g., earthquake and fire), user traffic will automatically or manually be rerouted to a georedundant site, which is engineered to serve the impacted workload indefinitely. Georedundant recoveries often have a longer RTO and RPO than traditional (intrasystem) redundancy architectures, and thus georedundant recovery is typically only used when normal (intrasystem) redundancy does not succeed (e.g., because ordinary redundancy mechanisms have been overwhelmed).

There are three fundamental options for recovering impacted client devices via georedundancy:

- *Manually Activated Georedundant Recovery.* Traditional disaster recovery plans are manually activated via an appropriate enterprise executive making a formal disaster declaration.
- *Server-Driven Georedundant Recovery.* Georedundant application (server) instances can monitor (aka heartbeat) each other, and if a nominally active server instance becomes unavailable or inaccessible from the specific application's point of view, then a georedundant application instance can automatically promote itself and begin serving user impacted traffic.
- *Client-Initiated Georedundant Recovery.* The application's client instances can control the decision of which application server instance they use. If an individual client instance deems their primary server to be unavailable or inaccessible, then it will select and connect to an alternate (georedundant) application instance.

These three strategies have rather different operational behaviors, with manually activated georedundancy generally having the most explicit human visibility and controllability, and client-initiated georedundant recovery having the least explicit human visibility and controllability.

10.5.3 Service Quality Considerations

Figure 10.13 shows a simplified service impairment model for a georedundant disaster recovery arrangement. While the client device and the client's access networking remain constant, disaster recovery replaces the WAN, XaaS access, and infrastructure to the primary application instance with the WAN, XaaS access, and infrastructure to an alternate application instance. As client devices are generally assigned to the application instance in the physically closest data center, the data center hosting the alternate application instance is likely to be geographically further from the client, and thus WAN impairments, especially transport latency, are likely to be greater for end user service delivered from the alternate application instance. Service impairments of the alternate XaaS access network and infrastructure are likely to vary based on the XaaS service provider's offering. If the same XaaS service providers are used for both the primary and alternate cloud data centers, then service impairment characteristics attributed to

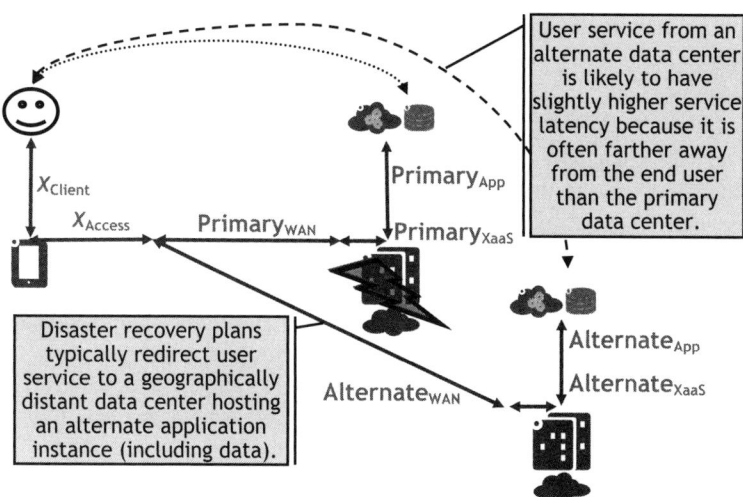

Figure 10.13. Service Impairment Model of Georedundancy.

the XaaS service provider are likely to be equivalent, but if different XaaS providers or different service offerings (e.g., a disaster-recovery-as-a-service offering) are used, then these impairments could be different. Likewise, the service impairment attributable to the alternate application instance should be similar to the impairments attributable to the primary instance if the configuration and workload on the two applications are comparable. Note that user service during the period when service for end users is being recovered to the alternate site may be temporarily degraded due to extremely heavy offered load (e.g., due to re-registration at the alternate site), so one should compare service impairments between primary and alternate sites during stable operational periods (i.e., after service recovery actions have completed).

10.5.4 Recovery Point Considerations

For cost and performance reasons, volatile application and state information are not generally replicated across a WAN between georedundant application instances. Fortunately, many applications and users will tolerate the loss of volatile data and at least some loss of persistent data (i.e., a nonzero RPO) on georedundant (disaster) recovery, so georedundant service recovery generally has more user visible impact than either traditional redundant or concurrent redundancy architectures. From an end user's perspective, georedundancy often is a less desirable alternative to traditional high availability or redundant compute strategies for most failure events, including those associated with VM impairments, particularly for stateful applications, because they are likely to experience greater service disruption due to loss of at least some volatile data. Nevertheless, georedundancy is a common strategy that is highly effective at mitigating impact of catastrophic events including total loss or serious degradation of network resources.

Common data replication strategies (roughly in descending order of consistency) are as follows:

- *Synchronous Data Replication between Mates.* Data changes—particularly volatile data changes—are fully synchronized between mates. This means that requests served by one application instance do not complete until changes are executed successfully on replicated copies of data.

- *Asynchronous Data Replication between Mates.* Data changes are replicated between mates after the data change has occurred. Whenever data are modified on the primary server due to client requests, the primary server sends updates to the alternate server so that the alternate is prepared to immediately take over service and preserve active requests if the primary fails. Often, the primary might wait until a request has reached a relatively stable state or the length of a request has exceeded a threshold before backing up the request's state data.

- *Data Stored in the Client.* User data (e.g., state and context information) are stored in the client itself, so that if the primary server fails, then the client explicitly sends the correct data to the alternate server instance. If the interface between the client and server is HTTP (e.g., a web server), then the servers can store and retrieve data in the client using cookies (assuming that the data itself are appropriately replicated and shared by server instances).

- *Data Backup to Networked Vault.* Persistent data can be backed up to a remote networked storage device. While there is likely to be a small logistical delay in initiating a restoration from a networked backup, the bandwidth to the networked backup device will limit how quickly the entire dataset can be downloaded, thus limiting RTO. Backups can be taken more frequently when using a networked storage device, such as once an hour, which may be fast enough to support volatile data for some applications.

- *Data Backup on Physical Media.* A backup of the persistent data is generated periodically (usually once a day) and stored on physical backup media. The backup should be in a remote location, so that if the primary server's location is lost due to a disaster, the data can still be recovered at another site. Since the backup is on physical media, there is inherently a logistical delay in transporting the physical backup media to the target system.

- *None.* Volatile data are not replicated or synchronized between elements or backed up at all. This is generally acceptable for applications that process short-lived requests that can be retried, such as the print jobs spooled by a print server. While it is theoretically possible to back up all print jobs, their transient nature and the overall unreliability of the printing process itself (e.g., paper jams and image quality issue) mean that users are likely to be prepared to resubmit failed or lost jobs rather than expecting those jobs to be restored from backups.

Section 15.8, "Recovery Point Objective Analysis," gives a methodology that is useful when designing an application's data replication architecture.

10.5.5   Mitigating Impact of Disasters with Georedundancy and Availability Zones

Force majeure events (e.g., hurricanes, earthquakes, and fires) or catastrophic events (e.g., load balancing misconfiguration) can impact some or all infrastructure equipment and facilities at the physical location that it affected. The traditional mitigation for the risk of catastrophic and site disasters is to implement a disaster recovery plan to recover service to an alternate data center with sufficient resources that is sufficiently far away from the primary site that it is unlikely that a single event would impact both sites. Availability zones are a lighter weight disaster recovery option in which fully independent data center infrastructure "zones" are maintained in a single region. By creating and maintaining independent application instances in separate availability zones, applications can contain catastrophic *application* failures, regardless of whether the availability zones are collocated or geographically dispersed across several regions. In theory, the impact of fire or similar event should be contained to a single availability zone. However, true force majeure events, such as earthquakes, could affect more than one availability zone in a single data center. Thus, enterprises should carefully weigh the risk of relying on separation using availability zones within the same region rather than more geographically distributed sites in different regions for disaster recovery and business continuity.

RECOMMENDATIONS

This part of the book covers the following:

- *Chapter 11, "Accountabilities for Service Quality."* The application's resource facing service boundary toward cloud infrastructure is somewhat different from traditional deployment models. This chapter methodically reviews how roles, responsibilities, and accountabilities evolve with cloud deployment.
- *Chapter 12, "Service Availability Measurement."* End users are likely to expect cloud-based applications to deliver equivalent service quality as traditionally deployed applications. This chapter explains how traditional service availability measurements can be applied to cloud deployments.
- *Chapter 13, "Application Service Quality Requirements."* Rigorous architectural, design, and validation diligence requires clear and quantified service quality requirements so methodical analysis and testing can verify that it is feasible and likely that the application's customer facing service expectations will consistently be met. This chapter offers sample service quality requirement for cloud-based applications.
- *Chapter 14, "Virtualized Infrastructure Measurement and Management."* This chapter reviews strategies for measuring quality delivered by the infrastructure

Service Quality of Cloud-Based Applications, First Edition. Eric Bauer and Randee Adams.
© 2014 The Institute of Electrical and Electronics Engineers, Inc. Published 2014 by John Wiley & Sons, Inc.

across the application's resource facing service boundary. High level strategies for mitigating impairments are also reviewed.

- *Chapter 15, "Analysis of Cloud-Based Applications."* This chapter presents a suite of analysis techniques to rigorously identify and mitigate service quality risks during application design.
- *Chapter 16, "Testing Considerations."* This chapter considers testing of cloud-based applications to assure that service quality expectations are likely to be met consistently despite inevitable virtualized infrastructure impairments.
- *Chapter 17, "Connecting the Dots."* This chapter discusses how to apply the recommendations of Part III to both new and evolved applications.

11

ACCOUNTABILITIES FOR SERVICE QUALITY

Cloud consumers, cloud service providers, suppliers, and end users all want the quickest and most effective resolution of any service impairments and failures that may arise. Fast and effective problem resolution requires rapid and accurate problem attribution so that the correct party can determine the true root cause and take effective corrective actions. Cloud deployment subtly shifts roles, responsibilities, and accountabilities compared with traditional deployments, so it is important to reconsider the implications of these revised roles in advance to avoid problems arising around responsibility and accountability gaps across the service delivery chain. This chapter reviews traditional deployment accountabilities as a baseline, and then analyzes how cloud service delivery impacts those traditional accountabilities.

11.1 TRADITIONAL ACCOUNTABILITY

Accountability for application service outages and other impairments is traditionally (per [TL_9000]) factored into three broad categories:

1. Product (or supplier) attributable outage is defined by [TL_9000] as "*an outage primarily triggered by*

Service Quality of Cloud-Based Applications, First Edition. Eric Bauer and Randee Adams.
© 2014 The Institute of Electrical and Electronics Engineers, Inc. Published 2014 by John Wiley & Sons, Inc.

  a. The system design, hardware, software, components or other parts of the system,
  b. Scheduled outage necessitated by the design of the system,
  c. Support activities performed or prescribed by [the supplier] including documentation, training, engineering, ordering, installation, maintenance, technical assistance, software or hardware change actions, etc.,
  d. Procedural error caused by the [supplier],
  e. The system failing to provide the necessary information to conduct a conclusive root cause determination, or
  f. One or more of the above."

2. Customer attributable outage is defined by [TL_9000] as "an outage that is primarily attributable to the customer's equipment or support *activities triggered by*
  a. Customer procedural errors,
  b. Office environment, for example power, grounding, temperature, humidity, or security problems, or
  c. One or more of the above."

3. External attributable outage is defined by [TL_9000] as "outages *caused by natural disasters such as tornadoes or floods, and outages caused by third parties not associated with the customer or the* [supplier] *such as commercial power failures, third-party contractors not working on behalf of the* [supplier] *or customer.*"

Accountability for service quality impairments is thus relatively straightforward; problems are either attributable to the product's supplier, to the "customer" (e.g., the IT organization that purchased and operates the equipment), or to external issues beyond control of either the supplier or the customer. Figure 11.1 illustrates this traditional accountability by overlaying these outage attributability definitions across an expanded 8i + 2d (eight ingredient plus data plus disaster) model (see [Bauer12] for a full description of the expanded eight ingredient model).

11.2 THE CLOUD SERVICE DELIVERY PATH

Cloud computing impacts the traditional accountability model of Section 11.1 by explicitly decoupling the application software from the physical compute, memory, storage, and networking infrastructure that supports it. Further confusing accountability, the application "consumer" (customer of the application supplier, not the end user of the application) also consumes Infrastructure-as-a-Service (IaaS), and perhaps other services (e.g., Database-as-a-Service), from a cloud service provider. The cloud service provider, in turn, is a customer of infrastructure equipment suppliers. The additional service boundary between the cloud consumer and the cloud service provider(s), as well as the new boundary with cloud infrastructure and platform services, increases the risk of interface-related failures and accountability breakdowns.

Figure 11.2 illustrates the simplified critical service delivery path for a cloud-based application; the cloud consumer in this case offers e-mail as a service to end users. The

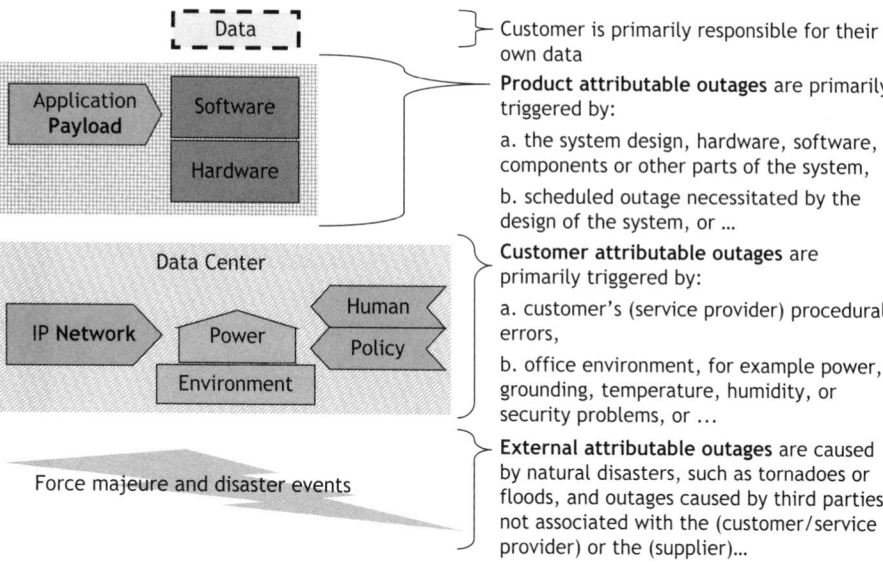

Customer is primarily responsible for their own data

Product attributable outages are primarily triggered by:

a. the system design, hardware, software, components or other parts of the system,

b. scheduled outage necessitated by the design of the system, or ...

Customer attributable outages are primarily triggered by:

a. customer's (service provider) procedural errors,

b. office environment, for example power, grounding, temperature, humidity, or security problems, or ...

External attributable outages are caused by natural disasters, such as tornadoes or floods, and outages caused by third parties not associated with the (customer/service provider) or the (supplier)...

Figure 11.1. Traditional Three-Way Accountability Split: Suppliers, Customers, External.

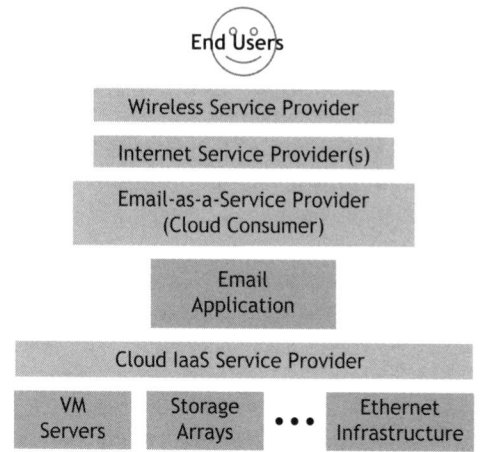

Figure 11.2. Example Cloud Service Delivery Chain.

cloud consumer configures the e-mail application software that they purchased from a supplier onto VM instances and virtualized storage offered by the cloud IaaS provider that the cloud consumer has selected. The IaaS provider's service is physically implemented via VM servers, storage arrays, Ethernet infrastructure, and other equipment that the IaaS provider acquired from equipment suppliers. Some end users of the e-mail service access the cloud consumer's e-mail application instance via a wireless service provider and one or more internet service providers, who haul IP traffic between the

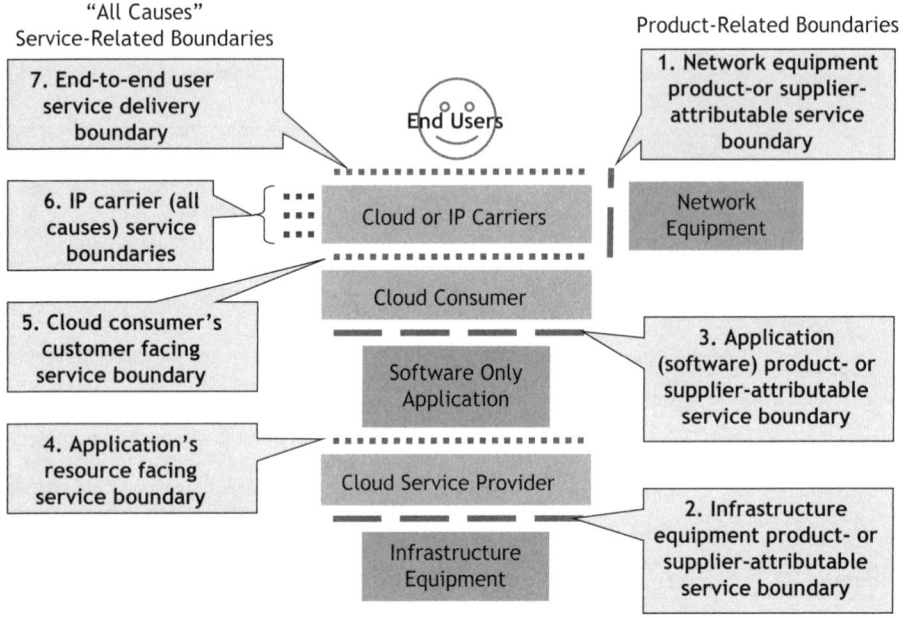

Figure 11.3. Service Boundaries across Cloud Delivery Chain.

end user's device and the cloud service provider's data center that hosts the cloud consumer's application software instance.

The example service delivery path of Figure 11.2 can be generalized as Figure 11.3. Of the seven logical service boundaries in Figure 11.3, three are product-related boundaries between product/equipment/application suppliers and the customers who own and operate those products, and the other four are between service consumers and service providers. The three product suppliers to customer interfaces (shown in dashed lines in Figure 11.3) are the following:

1. *Equipment Supplier to Cloud Carrier (e.g., Selling Networking Infrastructure to IP Network Operators such as Long Haul Transmission Gear).* These quality measurements are covered by TL 9000 Measurement Handbook and product categories today.
2. *Equipment Supplier to Cloud Provider (e.g., Selling VM Servers and Controllers to Cloud Service Providers).* This should be covered by TL 9000 via existing and new product categories.
3. *Application Supplier to Cloud Consumers.* This is the product-attributable service quality of the application's customer facing service (e.g., TL 9000 product-attributable service downtime).

The four service provider to service consumer interfaces (shown as dotted lines in Figure 11.3) are the following:

4. *Application's Resource Facing Service Boundary.* The primary service risks across this boundary were considered in Chapter 4, "Virtualized Infrastructure Impairments."

5. *Cloud Consumer to Cloud (IP) Carrier.* IP traffic passed from the cloud provider's data center to the IP network service providers who haul the cloud consumer's traffic. This is the cloud consumer's customer facing service boundary.

6. *IP Carrier Service Boundaries.* There may be multiple IP network service providers, including wireless providers, in the packet delivery flow, and thus similar service demarcation points will exist between each of those providers.

7. *End to End User Service Boundary.* This is the logical demarcation point between the cloud-based service and the end user. The specifics of this demarcation depend on the service details, including responsibility for the device rendering service to the end user and responsibilities for networking to that device. For example, service impact of device failure if the end user dropped their wireless device on a concrete floor and broke it would probably be deemed user attributable, but hardware failure of a set top box might be attributable to the service provider who bundled the box with television service. Of course, the television service provider would probably cascade accountability to the supplier of the failed set top box across the equipment supplier to cloud provider (or consumer) service boundary.

Clear and measurable service boundaries benefit consumers, providers, and the ecosystem at large because of the following:

1. Standard service measurements enable fair side-by-side comparisons of historic service performance and quality. While historic behavior is no guarantee of future performance, it does provide an excellent estimate of likely performance.

2. It simplifies fault isolation across complex multivendor solutions.

3. It enables clear interfaces with other products and services that implement and use those service measurement standards

4. It enables efficient service quality tracking of globally deployed products and services.

5. It simplifies service level agreement (SLA) negotiations with customers by focusing on quantitative performance levels based on the service measurements rather than having to define and negotiate service measurements themselves.

11.3   CLOUD ACCOUNTABILITY

Accountabilities in the cloud deployment ecosystem are quite different from the service quality accountabilities in the traditional deployment ecosystem. Cloud IaaS fundamentally shifts the traditional accountability model in two ways:

- Customers (now called "cloud consumers") purchase or rent software-only applications from software suppliers, rather than purchasing software bundled with physical hardware (e.g., embedded systems or software bundled with rack mounted servers).
- Customers (now cloud consumers) lease use of virtualized compute, memory, storage, and networking from IaaS (or any as-a-service [XaaS]) cloud service providers. IaaS implicitly includes all aspects of the physical data center hosting the virtualized infrastructure, such as power, grounding, and environmental control.

As a result, neither application suppliers nor cloud consumers have direct control or accountability for the physical hardware infrastructure that their application executes on. In fact, the physical infrastructure hosting the application is probably controlled by one or more cloud service providers who are separate and distinct from the cloud consumer who purchased and operates the application software. Figure 11.4 illustrates the high level responsibilities for cloud-based applications by role via the 8i + 2d model [Bauer11].

- The **cloud service provider** is responsible for the physical hardware and enabling software that supports the virtualized compute, memory, storage, and networking service delivered to application software. The cloud service provider is also responsible for the physical data center environment hosting the hardware, including maintaining acceptable temperature (i.e., cooling), humidity, physical security, and other environmental parameters. The cloud service provider is also

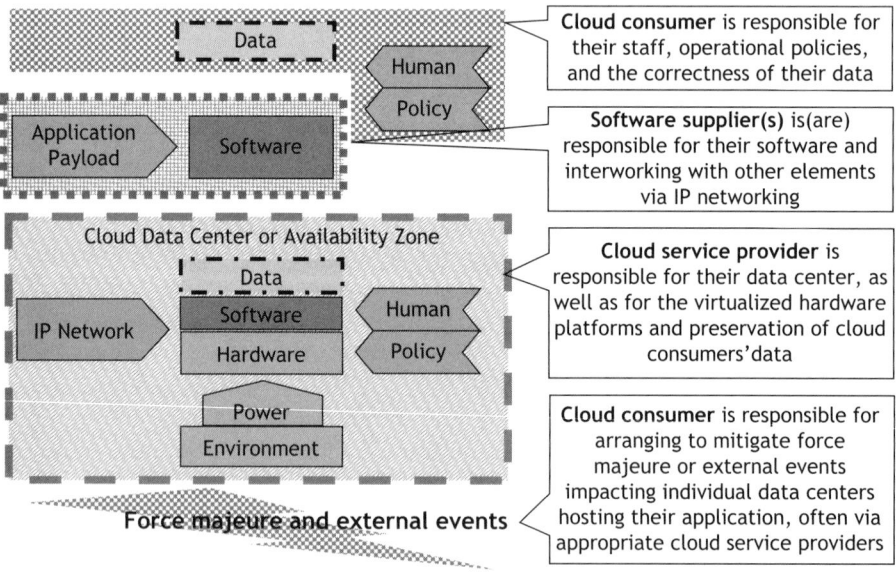

Figure 11.4. Functional Responsibilities for Applications Deployed on IaaS.

responsible for IP networking within the data center and interworking with cloud carriers who haul IP traffic to and from end users. Cloud service providers rely on human staff and operational policies to continuously deliver acceptable service quality to applications that they host. Specifically, cloud service providers' responsibilities include

- Consistently providing high quality virtualized compute, memory, storage, and network resources to host cloud consumer's applications
- Providing service orchestration mechanisms that dynamically manage application resource allocation/deallocation requests, subject to cloud service provider policies; this includes determining where to instantiate the VMs (e.g., within data center, outside data center) and how to balance the load to the application instances
- Enforcing the cloud consumer's affinity and anti-affinity/no single point of failure rules
- Operations, administration, billing, maintenance, provisioning, and billing of all infrastructure hardware, firmware, software, equipment, and facilities.

- The **application software supplier's** responsibilities include
  - Delivering application software that consistently meets applicable functional and nonfunctional requirements
  - Delivering correct installation, configuration, and operational guidance for cloud consumers
  - Providing application resource and configuration information (for initial installation as well as expected growth) to the cloud consumer, including recommended affinity and anti-affinity/no single point of failure rules
  - Providing application mechanisms for fault detection and recovery from programming errors, data integrity problems, process failures, and protocol errors
  - Providing procedures for application maintenance operations, such as software upgrade and disaster recovery
  - Supporting root cause analysis of application-related service impairments/outages.

- The **cloud consumer's** responsibilities include
  - Defining service requirements, architecture, and design of their application solution
  - Selecting application suppliers and products
  - Selecting cloud service provider(s)
  - Mitigating risks associated with gaps or overlaps between cloud service providers and application software suppliers
  - Ensuring the correctness of their application data
  - Establishing, correctly executing, and enforcing operational policies related to operations, administration, maintenance, and provisioning of application service
  - Creating and maintaining disaster recovery plans, which often rely on services offered by one or more cloud service providers.

Technology components offered "as a service" by Platform-as-a-Service (PaaS) suppliers, such as Load Balancing-as-a-Service (LBaaS) or Database-as-a-Service, shift accountability slightly compared with "shrink–wrapped" technology component offerings. The technology-component-as-a-service "product" from a PaaS supplier is a fully operational instantiation of the shrink–wrapped technology component that might be offered and managed by a software supplier. Practically, this means that most or all of the accountability for "customer procedural errors" that would be carried by the customer if they were using the shrink–wrapped technology component is now carried by the technology-component-as-a-service provider and supporter. This accountability is likely to extend to cover both capacity management and release management of the technology component if those services are supported by the technology component supplier. Customers should carefully negotiate accountabilities related to technology component as-a-Service offerings in SLAs with their providers to minimize the risk of errors due to misunderstandings of the exact roles and responsibilities of both the PaaS and IaaS service provider and the cloud consumer.

11.4 ACCOUNTABILITY CASE STUDIES

The commercial alternating current (AC) power infrastructure is now mature and standard enough that assigning accountability for electricity-related service impairments is simple: consider the example of an electric toaster. Residential electric service in North America is nominally 120 V AC so many home appliances are engineered to operate properly for voltage ranges from 110 to 130 V AC at the electrical outlet. Thus, if the appliance does not produce properly toasted bread when the AC voltage at the kitchen electrical outage is between 110 and 130 V AC, then the toaster is probably faulty. But if the voltage at the kitchen electrical outage is, say, 90 V AC, then the root cause of unacceptable toast is probably the commercial AC service, the interior wiring, or the electrical outlet itself. It took time for the electrical power ecosystem to standardize all the physical and electrical expectations and accountabilities necessary to rapidly isolate service failures to the accountable party: either the toaster, the interior wiring including electrical outlet and household circuit breakers, or the local electric power utility. It will inevitably take the cloud computing ecosystem time to agree on standard service boundaries and expectations to enable rapid and accurate assignment of accountabilities for service impairments and outages.

By considering the roles, responsibilities, and accountabilities of the different parties in these case studies, one gains a deeper understanding of the subtle shift that comes with cloud computing and will be better prepared to determine accountabilities surrounding their applications until industry bodies and commercial agreements standardize accountabilities. Undoubtedly, standards from bodies will ultimately adopt accountability rules that are somewhat different from the authors' example in this section, so this is offered merely as illustrative examples. This section considers the following scenarios:

- Accountability and Technology Components (Section 11.4.1)
- Accountability and Elasticity (Section 11.4.2).

11.4.1 Accountability and Technology Components

Cloud Platform-as-a-Service providers offer technology components as services to be integrated with application software to deliver valuable services to end users, such as load balancers, security appliances, and databases. Fortunately, standard quality measurement principles detailed in [TL_9000] enable one to easily establish accountability for service outages based on the primary functionality delivered by the technology component offered as-a-Service. Consider an application server (perhaps a web server) operated by a cloud consumer that is configured to use a cloud service provider's load balancer (i.e., LBaaS) to distribute the workload across application server component instances, as shown in Figure 11.5. The primary function of the application server instances ("S1" and "S2") is to serve clients' application protocol requests (e.g., HTTP GET and PUT for a web server); the primary function of the load balancer (LBaaS) is to distribute client requests across the pool of application server component instances based on business rules.

Figure 11.6 illustrates the simplified [TL_9000] service outage accountability for this configuration:

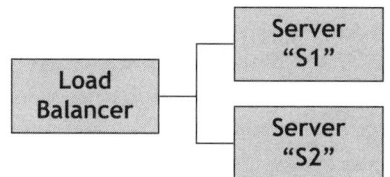

Figure 11.5. Sample Application.

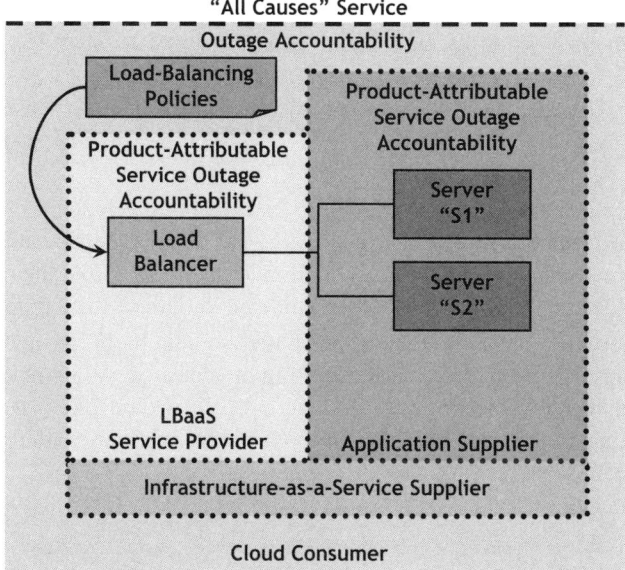

Figure 11.6. Service Outage Accountability of Sample Application.

- The server application supplier retains "product-attributable" service outage accountability for their software-only application component instances (S1, S2).
- The LBaaS service provider retains "product-attributable" service outage accountability for the load balancing technology component, including failures of the load balancer software application itself. While the supplier of the load balancer software may be accountable for product attributable service outages to the LBaaS service provider, the LBaaS service provider is fully accountable for all aspects of the load balancing components operation to the cloud consumer.
- The IaaS cloud service provider is responsible for delivering virtualized compute, memory, storage, and networking services to both the cloud consumer's application software and the LBaaS's load balancer virtual application. Logically, these infrastructure services are generally packaged as VMs that can be modeled like traditional field replaceable units (FRUs)* hardware. Just as traditional FRUs are expected to have a nonzero failure rate which is measured by early life failures (e.g., early return index [ERI]), working life failures (e.g., yearly return rate [YRR]), and long term reliability (e.g., long-term return rate [LTR]), VM instances should have failure rate metrics as well. While it is obviously silly to talk about "return rates" of failed VM instances because VMs are not repaired like failed circuit boards are, it is still worth tracking and carefully managing VM failure rates. VM failure rates are discussed in Section 12.4, "Evolving Hardware Reliability Measurement."
- The cloud consumer retains overall ([TL_9000] "all causes" SO2) outage accountability for the load-balancing **policies** that they configure and which are properly implemented by the load-balancing technology component.

The implications of this sample accountability model are understood by considering likely accountability of several failure scenarios:

- User service outage attributed to a software failure of service instance S1 or S2 would be product attributable service downtime against the server application supplier.
- User service outage downtimes due to excessive (e.g., epidemic) failures of VM compute, memory, storage, or networking are probably attributable to the infrastructure service provider. The IaaS provider is likely to hold their infrastructure equipment supplier accountable for epidemic failure of that equipment.
- User service outage downtime attributed to failure of a single application server instance (e.g., S1) that was not rapidly detected and mitigated via service failover to redundant server instance (e.g., S2) would likely be attributed to LBaaS, assuming that LBaaS was responsible for automatic failure detection and failover.

---

* [TL_9000] defines "field replaceable unit" as "*a distinctly separate part that has been designed so that it may be exchanged at its site of use for the purposes of maintenance or service adjustment.*"

- User service outage downtime attributed to failure of the load balancer would be service downtime against the LBaaS service provider; the LBaaS service provider would then likely hold the supplier of the load balancer virtual application software accountable.
- User service outage downtime attributed to faulty integration between application servers S1, S2, and LBaaS would probably be attributable to the cloud consumer.
- User service outage downtime due to a rare single-point failure of VM compute, memory, storage, or networking provided to a *high availability* application would probably be attributed to the application because highly available applications are expected to mitigate rare single point hardware failure events. However, if the cloud consumer failed to configure the application as recommended by the supplier (e.g., with sufficient online redundancy), then outages that would have been prevented by proper application configuration are accountable to the cloud consumer.

11.4.2 Accountability and Elasticity

As discussed in Chapter 8, "Capacity Management," elasticity of online applications when applications are carrying a workload at or near the application's online capacity is inherently more risky than traditional growth. Elastic growth of online application capacity is a complex process that carries the risk of producing user service downtime. Figure 11.7 illustrates how elastic growth might be supported for our sample application of Figure 11.6. The elastic growth process includes the following logical steps:

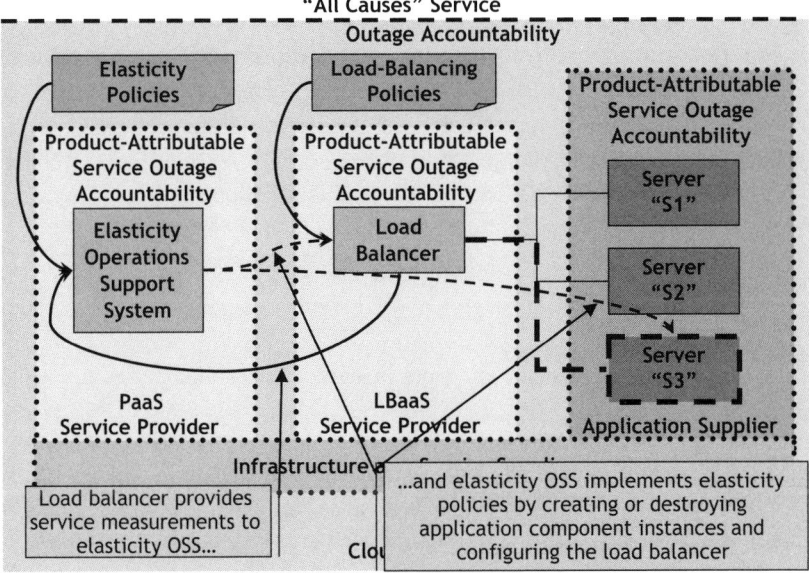

Figure 11.7. Application Elasticity Configuration.

- Some operations support system (OSS) is actively monitoring how well the application instance is serving the offered workload, such as by measuring service latency and throughput reported by the load balancing component
- When the service latency, throughput, or other applicable factors cross threshold(s) defined by the cloud consumer's elastic growth policy, the elasticity triggering functionality in the OSS directs the elasticity management functionality of the OSS to initiate an appropriate elastic capacity growth action.
- The elasticity management function (e.g., elasticity OSS) then
  1. Acquires additional resources from the cloud service provider on behalf of the cloud consumer.
  2. Configures new resources and initializes application component (S3).
  3. Verifies proper operation and full readiness of the new application component S3 (sometimes called a "warm-up" period).
  4. When new application component (S3) is ready for service, the elasticity management function reconfigures the load balancer to include new server S3 in its pool for distribution of workload.
- The elasticity management function is responsible for detecting failures of any of these steps and taking appropriate corrective actions, such as retrying failed requests and cleaning up stranded or lost resources.

As roles and responsibilities related to rapid elasticity are not yet standard enough to offer general rules, the authors offer a list of failure scenarios for readers to consider when defining roles and responsibilities for specific application deployments. Sample elasticity failure scenarios to consider include

- Cloud consumer's elasticity growth trigger criteria are faulty.
- Performance measurements are faulty (e.g., resource utilization is not reported correctly).
- IaaS service provider fails to deliver requested resources promptly.
- IaaS service provider returns faulty resources (e.g., virtual local area network [VLAN] connectivity to allocated resource is not properly configured).
- Application fails to start properly with allocated resources.
- Application component testing during warm-up period fails.
- Elasticity manager fails to properly configure load balancer to include new resources.
- Load balancer fails to distribute work load over newly allocated component (e.g., server S3).

Cloud consumers should assure that roles and responsibilities for parties across their application's service delivery chain are clear so that inevitable service impairments can rapidly be isolated to the proper accountable party so that party can drive prompt service restoration.

11.5   SERVICE QUALITY GAP MODEL

The service quality gap model of [Parasuraman] and [Zeithami] provides a useful framework for rigorously analyzing service, considering how service quality perceptions form and can be managed. Figure 11.8 uses the service quality gap model to separate the perspective of the service consumer and the service provider, and highlights where service quality gaps can arise between what the service consumers expect and the perception of the service they receive. The primary potential service quality gaps of Figure 11.8 are as follows:

• *Gap 1: Customers' Expectations versus (Provider's) Management Perceptions.* Essentially, is the service provider focusing on the key quality indicators (KQIs) that the customers care most about?
• *Gap 2: (Provider's) Management Perceptions versus Service Specifications.* Are the KQI targets set by provider's management aligned with the expectations of customers?
• *Gap 3: Service Specifications versus Service Delivery.* Does the provider's service design make it feasible and likely that KQI targets will be met?
• *Gap 4: Service Delivery versus External Communication.* Has the service provider communicated appropriate service quality expectations to the consumer?

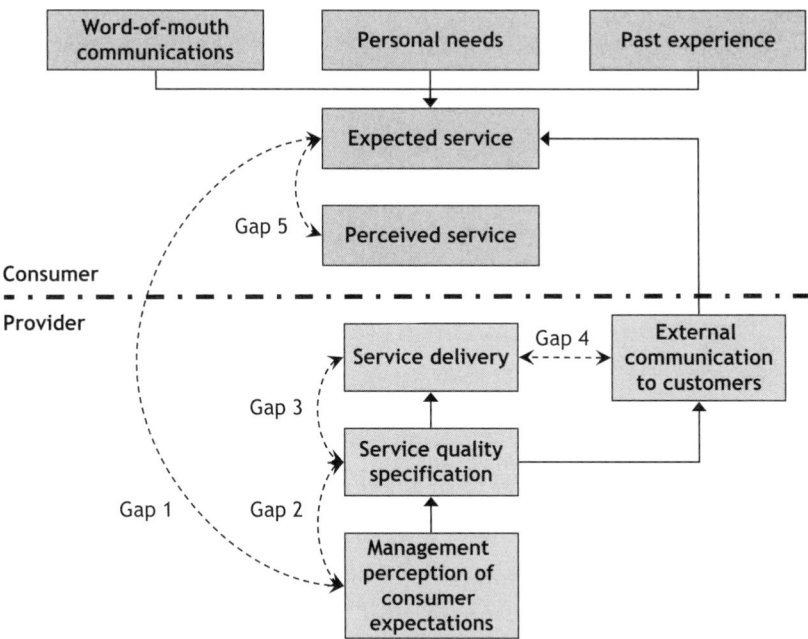

Figure 11.8. Service Gap Model.

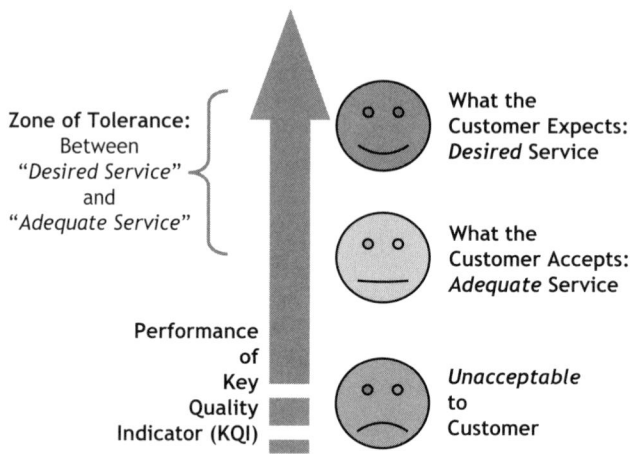

Zone of Tolerance:
Between
"Desired Service"
and
"Adequate Service"

What the
Customer Expects:
Desired Service

What the
Customer Accepts:
Adequate Service

Performance
of
Key
Quality
Indicator (KQI)

Unacceptable
to
Customer

Figure 11.9. Service Quality Zone of Tolerance.

- *Gap 5: Discrepancy between Customer Expectations and Their Perceptions of the Service Delivered.* Does the service perceived by the customer meet their expectations? This is the key perception gap that drives customers' perceptions of service quality.

The goal for all service providers should be to deliver service in the customers' zone of tolerance (see Figure 11.9, that is, at least what the customer accepts and hopefully exceeds what the customer expects, especially for *Gap 5: Perceived Service versus Expected Service*).

Section 11.5.1 applies the service gap model to the application's resource facing service boundary (measurement point zero [MP0]) in which the cloud service provider is the "provider" and the cloud consumer is the "consumer." Section 11.5.2 applies the service gap model to the application's *customer facing service* boundary in which the cloud consumer is the provider and the end user is the consumer.

11.5.1 Application's Resource Facing Service Gap Analysis

The cloud service provider delivers virtualized compute, memory, storage, and networking services, and possibly technology component (PaaS) services, to the cloud consumer. This section considers potential service gaps across the cloud consumer to cloud service provider service boundary, visualized in Figure 11.10.

Each of the five gaps is considered separately:

1. *Gap 1: Customers' Expectations versus Management Perceptions.* Cloud-based applications rely on the virtualized compute, memory, storage, and networking service rendered by the cloud provider to VM instances executing software on the consumer's behalf to meet the consumer's needs. Thus, cloud consumers and application suppliers have expectations regarding the maximum tolerable service

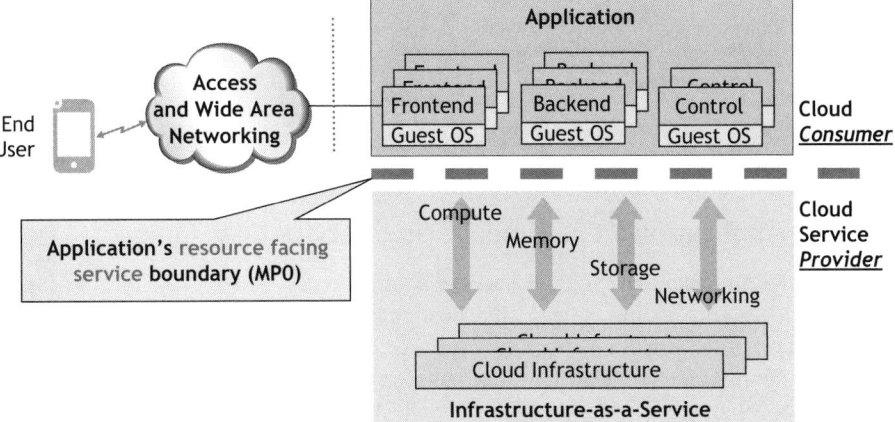

Figure 11.10. Application's Resource Facing Service Boundary.

impairments of the virtualized infrastructure offered by the cloud service provider; these typical impairments were discussed in Chapter 4, "Virtualized Infrastructure Impairments":

- VM Failure (Section 4.2)
- Nondelivery of Configured VM Capacity (Section 4.3)
- Delivery of Degraded VM Capacity (Section 4.4)
- Tail Latency (Section 4.5)
- Clock Event Jitter (Section 4.6)
- Clock Drift (Section 4.7)
- Failed or Slow Allocation and Startup of VM Instance (Section 4.8).

2. *Gap 2: Management Perceptions versus Service Specifications.* Having explained which infrastructure impairments the cloud consumer's applications are most sensitive to, it is essential to agree on the maximum acceptable level of infrastructure impairment that will enable the cloud consumer's applications to deliver acceptable service to end users.

3. *Gap 3: Service Specifications versus Service Delivery.* The cloud service provider must put facilities, equipment, architectures, processes, and procedures in place that make it feasible and likely that acceptable service will consistently be delivered to the cloud consumer's application instances.

4. *Gap 4: Service Delivery versus External Communication.* Cloud service providers should provide cloud consumers with accurate and timely information on service performance, trouble status, estimated times to repair, root cause analysis, and corrective action plans. While cloud service providers may be reluctant to proactively notify cloud consumers of major service impairments, many consumers would prefer prompt trouble notification by their cloud service provider so that they can initiate appropriate mitigating actions rather than be forced to discover the true nature and extent of a major cloud service provider impairment via troubleshooting myriad end user service complaints.

5. *Gap 5: Discrepancy between Customer Expectations and Their Perceptions of the Service Delivered.* Prudent application suppliers and cloud consumers will deploy mechanisms and procedures for monitoring and managing virtualized infrastructure performance (see Chapter 14, "Virtualized Infrastructure Measurement and Management") to assure they have an accurate view of current and historic cloud service performance compared with consumer expectations.

11.5.2 Application's Customer Facing Service Gap Analysis

This section considers the logical service boundary between the cloud consumer's application instance at the edge of the hosting cloud service provider's data center and the cloud or IP network service provider as a proxy for the end user service boundary. This simplification enables us to focus on the differences between traditional application deployment and cloud-based application deployment because we assume that the end user's device, access, and wide area networking are identical, and thus can be excluded from consideration. This logical service boundary is highlighted in Figure 11.11.

Each of the five gaps is considered separately for the customer facing service gaps:

1. *Gap 1: Customers' Expectations versus Management Perceptions.* As discussed in Chapter 2, "Application Service Quality," different applications have rather different application-specific key quality indicators, but usually include at least one of the following:
   - Service Availability (Section 2.5.1)
   - Service Latency (Section 2.5.2)
   - Service Reliability (Section 2.5.3)

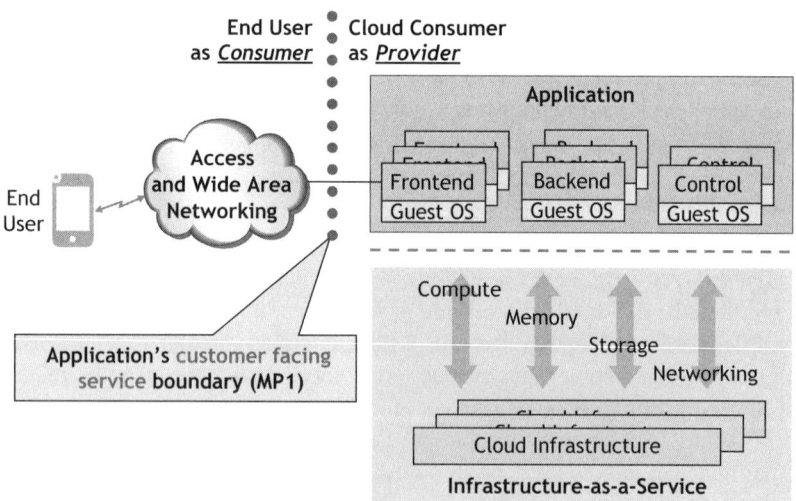

Figure 11.11. Application's Customer Facing Service Boundary.

- Service Accessibility (Section 2.5.4)
- Service Retainability (Section 2.5.5)
- Service Throughput (Section 2.5.6)
- Service Timestamp Accuracy (Section 2.5.7)
- Application-Specific Service Quality Measurements (Section 2.5.8).

2. *Gap 2: Management Perceptions versus Service Specifications.* Having selected the right set of application service KQIs, the cloud consumer should quantify and characterize the minimum acceptable performance on all customer-facing service quality KQIs. Ideally, the cloud consumer will pick target KQI values to increase the probability that end users will be fully satisfied with the application's service quality. Best practice is to budget application service KQI impairments across at least the cloud consumer's application deployment, and ideally across the entire end to end solution (e.g. using the three-layer model of Section 10.2, "Three-Layer End-to-End Service Model"). For example, services that have strict end to end service latency requirements (e.g., interactive communications, and gaming) should be carefully engineered to keep actual end-to-end latency impairments experienced by end users acceptably short.

3. *Gap 3: Service Specifications versus Service Delivery.* The cloud consumer must architect their solution so that it is feasible and likely that application service quality delivered to end users will consistently meet or exceed minimum accept-able KQI performance. To do this, the cloud consumer must understand the sensitivity of application's customer facing service KQI performance to likely virtualized infrastructure impairments and other impairments across the user service delivery path (see Chapter 10, "End-to-End Considerations"). Having set KQI impairment budgets for critical application components, the cloud consumer (or application supplier) should characterize the performance expectations of the underlying virtualized infrastructure that is necessary to make it feasible and likely that application components will meet their targets. The cloud consumer then uses these performance targets when selecting a cloud service provider. If the selected cloud service provider is unlikely to consistently achieve these per-formance targets, then the cloud consumer's architecture should be revised to minimize service sensitivity to the virtualized infrastructure impairments most at risk.

4. *Gap 4: Service Delivery versus External Communication.* Cloud consumers should communicate openly with end users about expected service performance, service troubles, and estimated times to restore service.

5. *Gap 5: Discrepancy between Customer Expectations and Their Perceptions of the Service Delivered.* Distributed (including cloud-based) applications carry risks with gap 5 because application service is usually rendered on a device owned and operated by the end user (e.g., smartphone, tablet, laptop, and gaming console) and service is carried over an access network selected by the end user. This variation in both end user device and specific access network can materially impact the end user's quality of experience. For example, the application service rendered via a laptop that is wired via Ethernet to the user's broadband modem

may be superior to the application service rendered to a smartphone via commercial wireless networking when the end user is riding in a bus or a train. Fortunately, end users are fully aware of the variable nature of wireless data service (e.g., dead zones, contention for finite bandwidth in popular locations), so they are likely to ascribe at least some of their observed service impairments to their wireless access provider or their own actions (e.g., being in a location with poor wireless coverage).

11.6   SERVICE LEVEL AGREEMENTS

"Satisfaction guaranteed or your money back" is the de facto SLA of respectable retailers. This simple rule works well for commercial off-the-shelf (COTS) products to reduce the consumer's risk of traditional take-it-or-leave-it purchase decisions. Customized offerings, such as information systems, are not generally delivered "as is," and thus a simple binary take-it-or-leave-it decision is not ideal for either the consumer or the supplier because a "leave it" decision leaves the consumer with no information system and the supplier with no revenue. Clear SLAs enable consumers and suppliers to agree in advance what the service quality expectations are and how service quality issues will be addressed so a binary take-it-or-leave-it decision can be avoided.

Successful SLAs help both suppliers and consumers meet their business objectives by

1. *Defining the scope and performance expectations* of contracted service
2. *Unambiguously defining expectations and obligations* for both supplier and consumer
3. *Defining remedies if expectations are not met* such as prompt service recovery or an option for the consumer to prematurely terminate the contract
4. *Bounding liabilities* so both consumer and supplier can better manage their business risks.

An agreement should meet the service quality and business needs of both the supplier and the consumer. If the agreement is too heavily biased against one party, then their business may fail or they may breach the agreement for business reasons, which could plunge the counterparty into chaos. Just as "good fences make good neighbors," well-crafted SLAs between providers and consumers can produce more satisfactory relations because of the following:

- Measurable and quantified key quality indicators of delivered service are rigorously specified.
- KQI measurement and reporting arrangements are agreed in advance.
- Accountabilities for service impairments to those KQIs are clearly stated upfront.

- Remedies for failure to meet KQI targets are agreed in advance so that if one or more failures prevent contracted service levels from being consistently delivered, then the expectations and accountabilities for restoration of acceptable service are clear.

Individual SLA commitments should include

- *Definition of a quantitative service metric*, such as one or more service measurements from Chapter 4, "Virtualized Infrastructure Impairments," or Section 2.5, "Application Service Quality"
- *Quantitative service performance targets or objectives*, such as less than 50 failed calls per million attempts or less than one supplier-attributable critical severity trouble ticket created per month
- *Clear measurement accountability and exclusion rules*, such as who is responsible for measuring performance, and exactly how impairments will be normalized
- *Remedy for failing to meet the service performance targets*, such as providing a written root cause analysis within 30 days, the customer's option to terminate the contract early, and service purchase credits.

SLAs generally progress through the following lifecycle phases:

- *Offer.* A service provider decides what service performance targets and assurances to offer to consumers.
- *Discover.* Consumer discovers the service levels offered by various suppliers.
- *Select.* Consumer selects a service offering from a particular supplier.
- *Agree.* Service provider and consumer agree to specific terms of service.
- *Provision.* The consumer's service is provisioned and turned up by the service provider.
- *Use.* The consumer uses the service during the period of agreement.
- *Terminate.* Eventually, the period of agreement ends or the agreement is terminated.

Traditionally, this lifecycle was executed by human beings over weeks, months, or years. As the cloud ecosystem matures and service measurements, terms, and conditions are standardized across the industry, the service level management lifecycle is likely to become more automated.

Keep in mind that SLAs are business mechanisms designed to minimize risk; they are not quality mechanisms that fundamentally increase the feasibility and likelihood of committed service levels actually being achieved. Thus, SLAs are not a replacement for diligent research and careful consideration prior to selecting a supplier. While financial remedies may appear large when reading them in a contract, they are likely to be miniscule compared with the cost to the enterprise of having to change suppliers if the selected supplier proves incapable of consistently delivering acceptable service quality.

SLAs for cloud services remain a popular topic for standardization organizations, research, and trade publications, so readers should leverage the wisdom and experiences (e.g., [ODCA_SUoM], [ODCA_CIaaS], [TMF_TR197]) captured in this growing body of work prior to negotiating an SLA.

12

SERVICE AVAILABILITY MEASUREMENT

Well-designed service measurements can gracefully evolve from one generation of technology to another. Service availability of networked applications is a rigorous service measurement that can be evolved from traditional deployments to cloud-based deployments. This chapter lays out service availability measurement evolution as follows:

- *Parsimonious Service Measurements* (Section 12.1). Illustrates how well-designed service measurements have evolved across significant technology shifts.
- *Traditional Service Availability Measurement* (Section 12.2). The telecommunications industry's TL 9000 "SO" service outage measurement standards are offered as an example of rigorous traditional service availability measurement. Service availability measurements in other industries are likely to be similar to the telecommunications industry's service availability measurements, albeit perhaps less rigorous.
- *Evolving Service Availability Measurements* (Section 12.3). Offers a simple and parsimonious adaptation of traditional service availability measurement of Section 12.2 to a sample cloud-based application.

Service Quality of Cloud-Based Applications, First Edition. Eric Bauer and Randee Adams.
© 2014 The Institute of Electrical and Electronics Engineers, Inc. Published 2014 by John Wiley & Sons, Inc.

- *Evolving Hardware Reliability* (Section 12.4). Since hardware failures can directly impact user service, enterprises have traditionally applied rigorous measurements and management to hardware failures. This section describes traditional hardware reliability measurements and evolves them to apply to virtual machine instances.
- *Evolving Elasticity Service Availability Measurements* (Section 12.5). Traditional applications supported manual capacity growth and degrowth procedures; this section parsimoniously evolves service availability measurements of traditional growth and degrowth procedures to cover elastic capacity management actions of cloud-based applications.
- *Evolving Release Management Service Availability Measurement* (Section 12.6). Traditional applications supported traditional software upgrade procedures; this section evolves service availability measurements for traditional software upgrade procedures to cover software upgrade of cloud-based applications.
- *Service Measurement Outlook* (Section 12.7). This section reviews the broader benefits of parsimonious evolution of traditional service measurements to cloud-based applications.

12.1 PARSIMONIOUS SERVICE MEASUREMENTS

Well-defined service measurements are often technology independent, and thus can be applied to give suppliers, customers, and end users better insight into actual service performance of multiple technology and supplier options. End users, customers, and suppliers are generally best served by parsimoniously applying existing service measurements rather than inventing alternative measurements, or not even bothering with service measurements at all. Consider the example of passenger transportation: trip duration and schedule adherence are fundamentally the key service quality criteria. Trip duration and schedule adherence are obviously applicable to airline travel, but also apply to railroad and intercity bus travel. Concern for trip duration and schedule adherence is certainly not new; one imagines that steamship and stagecoach passengers cared about both of these service qualities just as modern travelers do.

As technology improves, one often has to refine service measurement *details* to make them more precise, but the fundamental service measurement notion remains the same. For example, while "departure time" and "arrival time" are fairly obvious for trains, buses, steamships, and stagecoaches, operational aspects of aircraft travel means that those traditional common sense notions of "departure" and "arrival" become ambiguous. Specifically, aircraft "departure" could reasonably be applied to any one of the following events:

a. When the boarding gate closes
b. When the aircraft door closes
c. When the aircraft pushes back from the gate

d. When the aircraft is airborne (i.e., all wheels have left the ground)

e. When the aircraft has successfully retracted the landing gear after takeoff.

Since there are likely to be several minutes between each of these events and aircraft travel time is measured in hours and minutes, it is best for travelers, airlines, and the industry to agree on exactly which events are used to define "departure time," "arrival time," and "flight duration" so that all parties can make fair comparisons of service performance across different airlines and flight itineraries. By standardizing these measurement details, end users can easily compare performance of different airlines. In addition, the fundamental alignment of duration and schedule adherence measurements across airline and railroad travel enables travelers to intelligently decide between taking an intercity railroad trip or a regional flight.

Note that service *measurements* (e.g., trip duration and schedule adherence) are very different from service *expectations*, and those expectations may shift from one technology to another. Consider aircraft travel compared with railroad travel: end users are typically willing to accept the benefit of shorter airline travel times for long trips while accepting more risk on schedule adherence because airlines are more sensitive to weather conditions; however, on shorter trips, business travelers may prefer intercity railroad travel because of much-better schedule adherence. Similarly, end users overwhelmingly accepted the lower voice quality of wireless telephony as a price for mobility, and longer television channel change (or "zap") time with digital cable and IP-TV (compared with analog cable TV) as a price for a vastly larger selection of channels. Thus, if a cloud-based application delivers a material benefit (e.g., service is free to end users) beyond traditional deployment, then end users may accept lower service quality performance, otherwise end users will generally expect service quality performance of cloud-based applications to be at least equivalent to native service quality performance.

12.2 TRADITIONAL SERVICE AVAILABILITY MEASUREMENT

While *"service impact outage downtime"* measurements ([TL_9000] SO2 and SO4) used by the telecommunications industry may be more rigorous than those used in other industries, the same measurement principles are likely to apply for service availability to myriad applications across all enterprises and organizations and thus can serve as a useful example for analysis. While some enterprises will use the actual number of users (e.g., measuring impact of failure events as *"1234 user-minutes of service impact"* or *"5678 user sessions impacted"*), those absolute metrics make it harder to put service impact into context; for instance, is 1234 user-minutes of service impact during a 1-month measurement period excellent performance or disastrous? Since many enterprises will deploy multiple instances of a particular application, and each instance can serve multiple users, one generally normalizes service availability to better characterize the overall service impact. Typically, service availability is normalized *per system instance per year*, and partial capacity loss outages are prorated. For example,

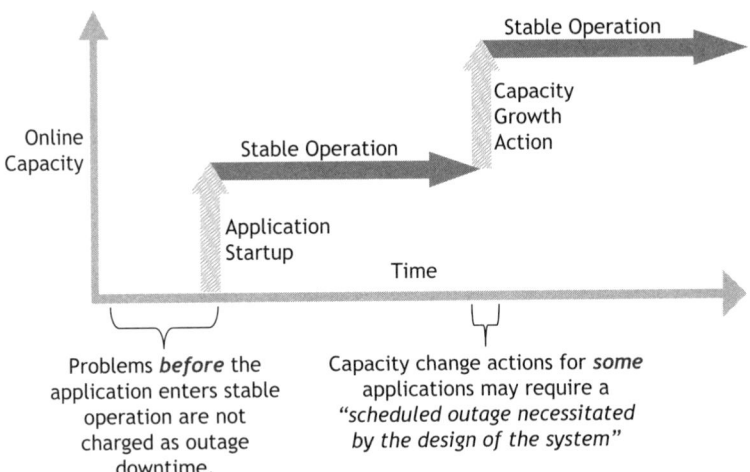

Figure 12.1. Traditional Service Operation Timeline.

"five 9s" service availability translates to 5.26 minutes per system per year of prorated user service impact downtime.

Figure 12.1 gives a simplified operational timeline for an application to make three points:

1. Service outage measurements apply only *after* the application has entered stable operation. Failures that prevent the application instance from originally installing, starting up, and delivering acceptable service to end users are generally considered installation problems rather than being attributed to outage downtime service measurements.
2. Service outage measurements apply during normal (i.e., stable) operation.
3. From time to time, the online capacity, configuration, or software release of an application instance will change. This action can complete either while the application instance is offline (e.g., as "scheduled downtime" for maintenance) or while the application instance is online. If the event occurs while the application instance is online and actively serving user traffic, then any user service impact during that maintenance action is potentially chargeable as outage downtime.

Service availability measurement in the stable operation phase is covered in Section 12.3 and availability measurements during capacity management events are covered in Section 12.5. Release management events are routinely executed to patch, update, upgrade, or retrofit application software or the underlying guest OS; service availability measurement of release management events is considered in Section 12.6.

12.3   EVOLVING SERVICE AVAILABILITY MEASUREMENTS

Figure 12.2 illustrates a sample application deployed on cloud that exposes enterprise data to end users subject to business rules enforced by application logic modules. The application includes a pair of load balancing components that distribute user workload across a pool of application logic components, and the application logic components are supported by a pair of database servers. The load balancer components are protected by a pair of security appliances, and all of the software components are hosted in virtual machine instances furnished by an Infrastructure-as-a-Service provider.

The first step in applying traditional service availability measurements to the sample application of Figure 12.2 is to define exactly what is within the "application instance" perimeter and thus is covered by the application's service availability measurement. TL 9000 typically normalizes service outage measurements by either network element or system, defined as:

- *Network Element.* "*A system device, entity, or node, including all relevant hardware and/or software components located at one location. The Network Element (NE) must include all components required to perform the primary function of its applicable product category. If multiple FRUs, devices, and/or software components are needed for the NE to provide its product category's primary function, then none of these individual components can be considered an NE by themselves. The total collection of all these components is considered a single NE*" [TL_9000].

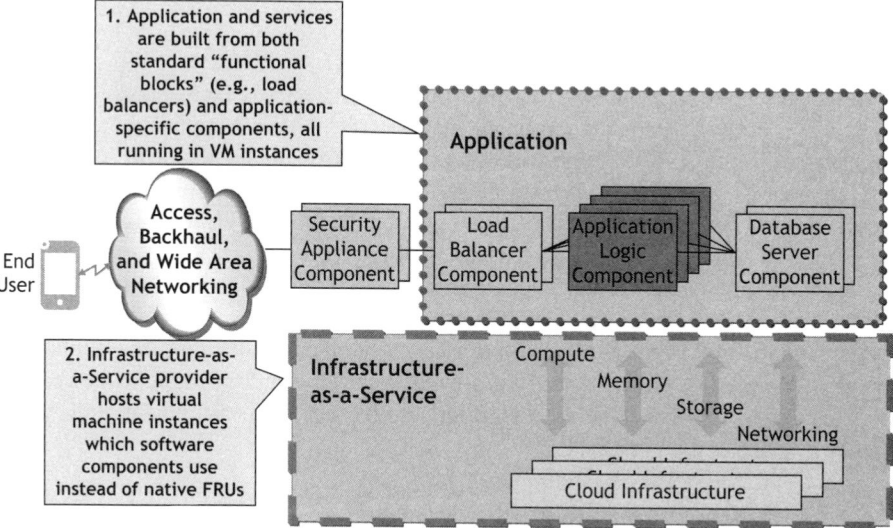

Figure 12.2. Sample Application Deployment on Cloud.

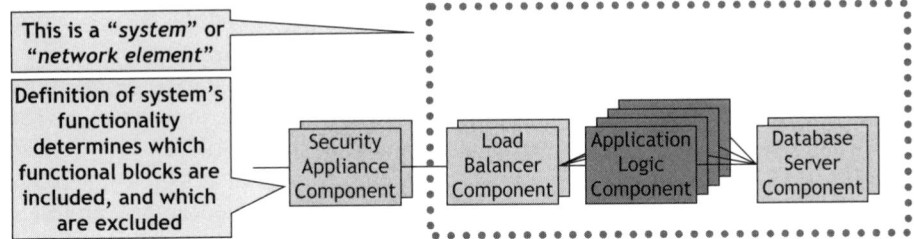

Figure 12.3. "Network Element" Boundary for Sample Application.

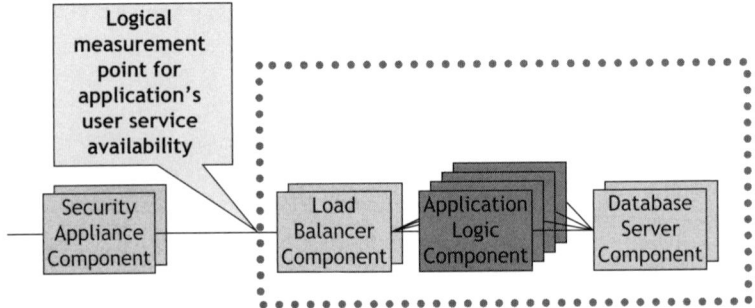

Figure 12.4. Logical Measurement Point for Application's Service Availability.

- *System.* "*A collection of hardware and/or software items located at one or more physical locations where all of the items are required for proper operation. No single item can function by itself*" [TL_9000].

As protecting the application from illegitimate traffic, DDoS attack, and other external security threats is not a primary function of the sample application, a separate security appliance is added to protect the application from external attack. As the security appliance is separate from the application itself, it is outside of the application's perimeter, as shown in Figure 12.3. Thus, the application's service availability should measure performance presented to end users at the logical edge of the application; in this case, the application instance's customer facing service boundary is in front of the load balancer components but behind the security appliance, as shown in Figure 12.4. Service availability and quality of the security appliance protecting the application should certainly be measured, but those measurements should be against the security appliance itself rather than being aggregated into the service measurement of the application instance being protected.

12.3.1 Analyzing Application Evolution

Reliability block diagrams (RBDs) are a useful visualization for analyzing and understanding the service availability risks and behaviors of an application. Figure 12.5 gives

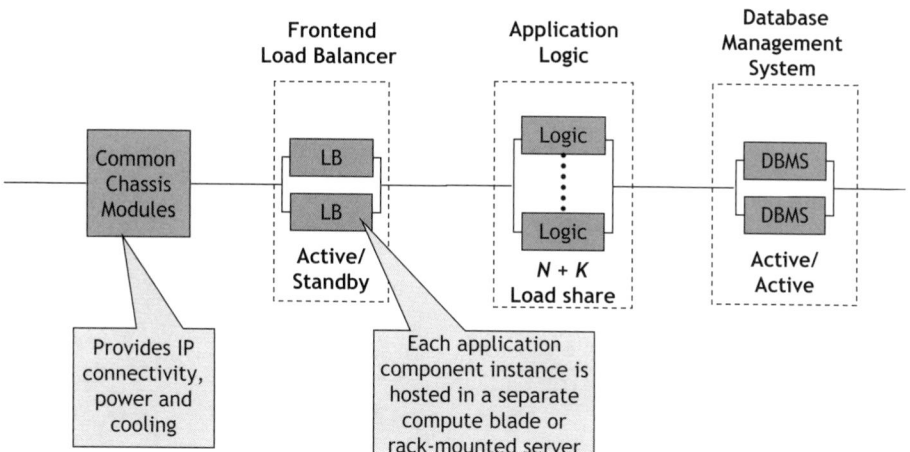

Figure 12.5. Reliability Block Diagram of Sample Application (Traditional Deployment).

an RBD of the sample application of Figure 12.2 deployed on traditional hardware architecture. Each application component instance (e.g., frontend load balancer, application logic, and database management system) is deployed onto a separate compute blade or rack mounted server, and all of those blades or servers are installed in a chassis or rack with IP connectivity between application instances, as well as electrical power and cooling, which are represented as the block labeled "Common Chassis Modules."

Figure 12.6 visualizes how the RBD of Figure 12.5 maps onto cloud:

- Each compute blade or rack mounted server hosting an application component instance is replaced by a virtual machine instance
- The IP connectivity between each of those VM instances is provided by the Infrastructure-as-a-Service provider and can be considered a logical element referred to as "Connectivity-as-a-Service."

As shown in Figure 12.7, the RBDs of the sample application of Figure 12.5 can be evolved to cloud by replacing the traditional chassis or rack-mounted Ethernet switching infrastructure with virtual "Connectivity-as-a-Service" to represent the IP connectivity between VM instances, as well as chassis power distribution and cooling infrastructure.

Figure 12.8 shows side-by-side RBDs for traditional and cloud deployments of the sample application highlighting the two points for alignment between the deployments.

As explained in Chapter 11, "Accountabilities for Service Quality," cloud deployment complicates accountabilities for failures and impairments by potentially attributing service impairments to either the cloud consumer (customer), application software supplier, or XaaS cloud service provider(s). Figure 12.9 gives a chassis-like visualization of the sample application deployed on a cloud to explicitly connect the

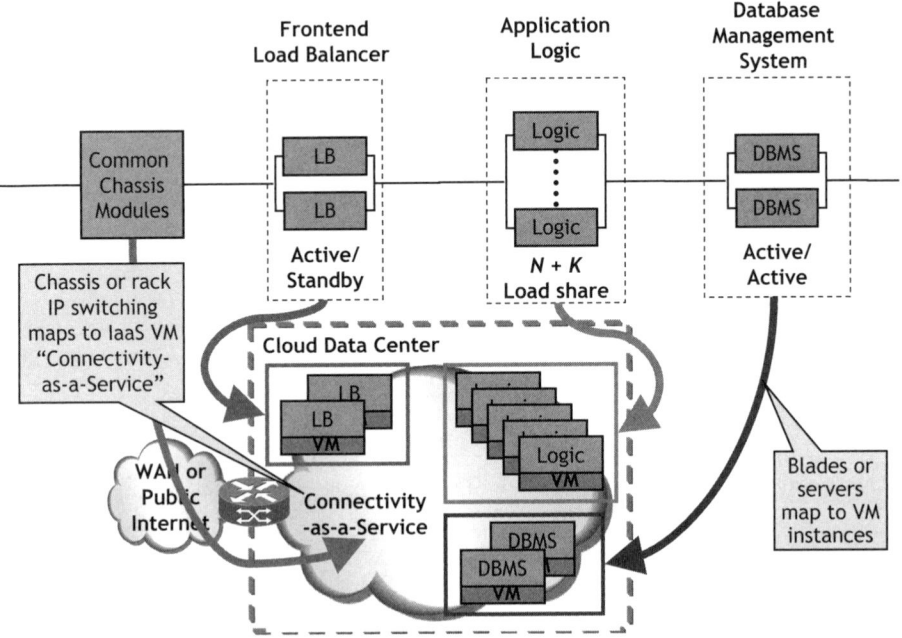

Figure 12.6. Evolving Sample Application to Cloud.

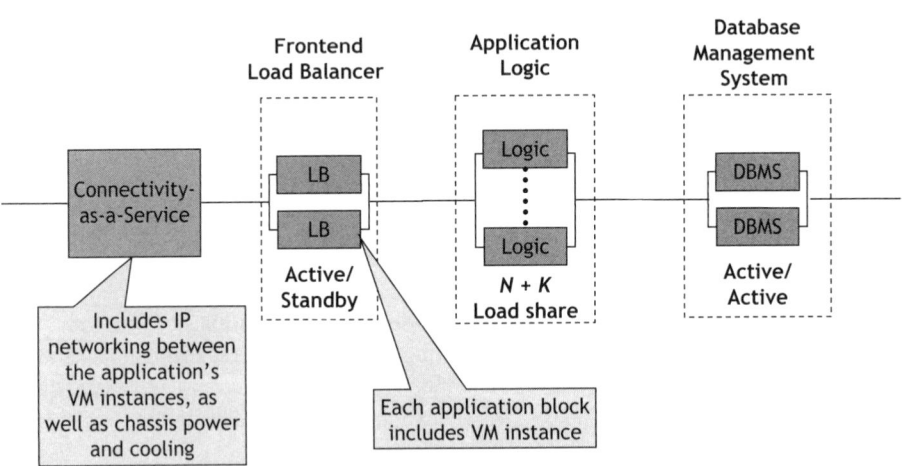

Figure 12.7. Reliability Block Diagram of Sample Application on Cloud.

measurement discussions of this chapter with the accountability discussions of Chapter 11. The dotted box of Figure 12.9 shows the logical perimeter of the sample application instance; traditionally, this is the perimeter of the chassis that would host all of the application's blades. As with traditional system architectures, this perimeter encloses a suite of application components (e.g., load balancers, application logic modules and database server components), and each of those component instances

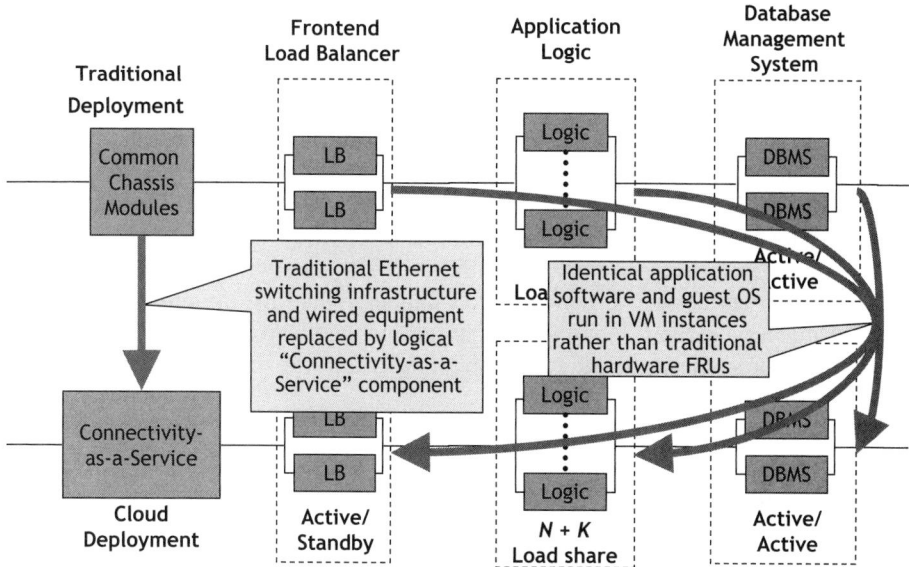

Figure 12.8. Side-by-Side Reliability Block Diagrams.

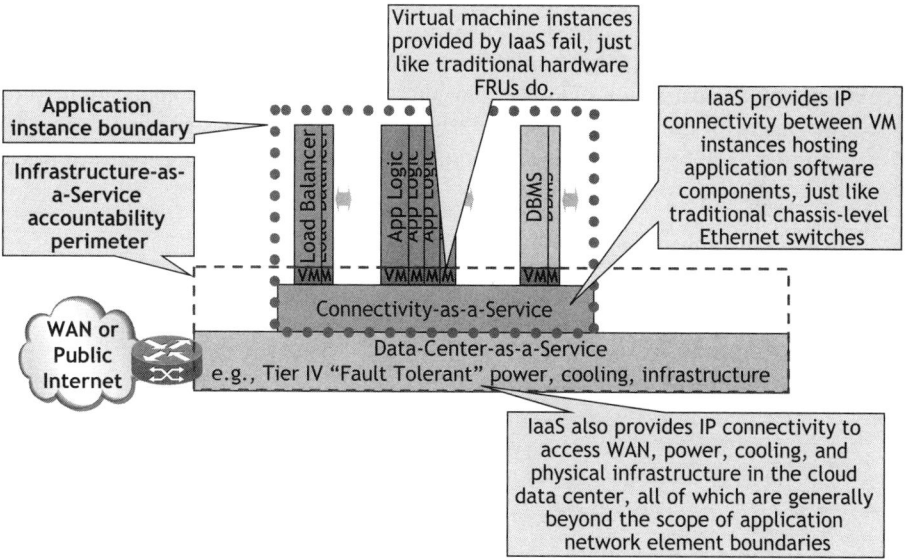

Figure 12.9. Accountability of Sample Cloud Based Application.

executes in a distinct virtual machine instance. All of these virtual machine instances are networked together via a logical "Connectivity-as-a-Service" notion that emulates the IP infrastructure that traditionally connects the blades or rack-mounted servers within a traditionally deployed application instance. This application instance physically exists within an Infrastructure-as-a-Service provider's data center.

The dashed box on Figure 12.9 visualizes the accountability perimeter of the IaaS provider in the context of our sample application:

- *VM Instances Hosting Application Component Instances.* These VM instances host the application software and guest operating systems for all application components. Inevitably these VM instances will occasionally experience failures (e.g., VM reliability impairments, per Section 12.4, "Evolving Hardware Reliability Measurement"). Just as hardware suppliers are expected to analyze failures of their equipment to identify the true root cause of field failures and deploy appropriate corrective actions to continuously improve the reliability of their hardware products, high-quality IaaS providers should assure that VM failures are appropriately analyzed and corrective actions are deployed to continuously improve VM instance reliability.

- *"Connectivity-as-a-Service" Providing IP Connectivity between the VM Instances Hosting Application Component Instances.* This emulates the IP switching within a traditional application chassis or rack, which enables highly reliable and available communications between application components with low latency. Just as architects traditionally engineer application configurations with minimal IP switching equipment and facilities between application components to maximize application performance and quality, IaaS providers will apply affinity rules and intelligent resource placement logic to assure that all of an application's VM instances and resources are physically close together without violating the application's anti-affinity rules. Connectivity-as-a-Service captures the logical abstraction of the IP connectivity between all of an application's VM instances. As shown in Figure 12.10, Connectivity-as-a-Service can also be viewed as a logical nanoscale VPN offered by the IaaS that connects each of the

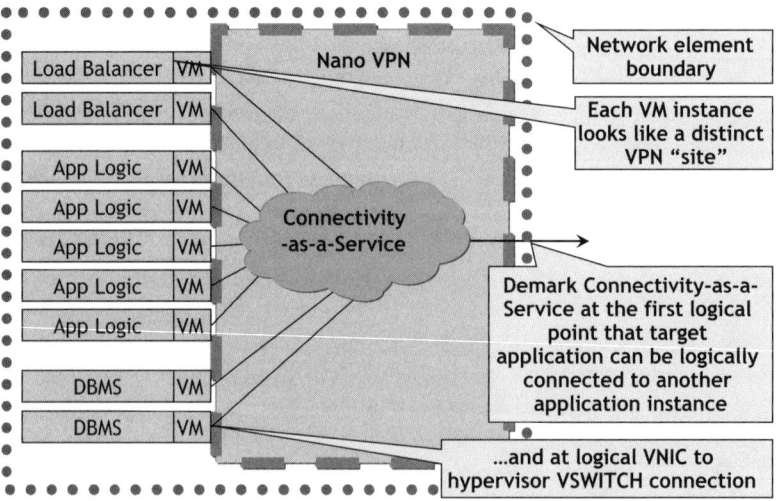

Figure 12.10. Connectivity-as-a-Service as a Nanoscale VPN.

application's VM instances in a virtual private network, regardless of where each VM instances is actually placed.

- *Logical "Data-Center-as-a-Service"* that provides a secure and environmentally controlled physical space to host the virtual machine servers that host the applications VM instances' along with electrical power, cooling, and wide-area IP connectivity. Typically, the availability expectations of the Data-Center-as-a-Service are characterized by the Uptime Institute's taxonomy [UptimeTiers]: Tier I basic; Tier II redundant components; Tier III concurrently maintainable; or Tier IV fault tolerant. Data-Center-as-a-Service outages are traditionally excluded from traditional application service availability estimates and measurements, so they often can be excluded from service availability estimates and measurements for cloud deployments. Logically speaking, Connectivity-as-a-Service supports IP communications within the perimeter of the application instance, while Data-Center-as-a-Service provides IP communications from the edge of the application instance's perimeter to the demark point between the IaaS service provider and the cloud carrier, including connectivity to any other application instances in the service delivery path (e.g., connectivity between the security appliance on Figure 12.2 and the application's load balancer components).

12.3.2 Technology Components

Platform-as-a-Service offers technology components or functional blocks that applications can use to:

- *Shorten time to market* because they are already written
- *Improve quality* because they should be mature and stable
- *Simplify operations* because PaaS provider handles operations and maintenance of the technology component.

Both load balancing and database management systems are technology components that are offered "as-a-Service"; let us consider Database-as-a-Service (DBaaS) in the context of the sample application of Figure 12.2. Architecturally, the application's pair of active/active database management system component instances of Figure 12.5 can be replaced with a blackbox representing Database-as-a-Service as shown in Figure 12.11. The blackbox abstraction is appropriate because the DBaaS provider explicitly hides all architectural, implementation, and operational details from both the cloud consumer and the application supplier, so DBaaS truly is an opaque—or black—box.

As technology components such as Database-as-a-Service offer well-defined functionality to applications, it is conceptually easy to know whether that functionality is available to the sample application (i.e. "up") or not (i.e., "down"). With appropriate application and component instrumentation, one can thus measure technology component downtime via service probes or other mechanisms. As application service relies on the technology components that are included in the architecture, service downtime of included technology components cascades directly to user service downtime of the

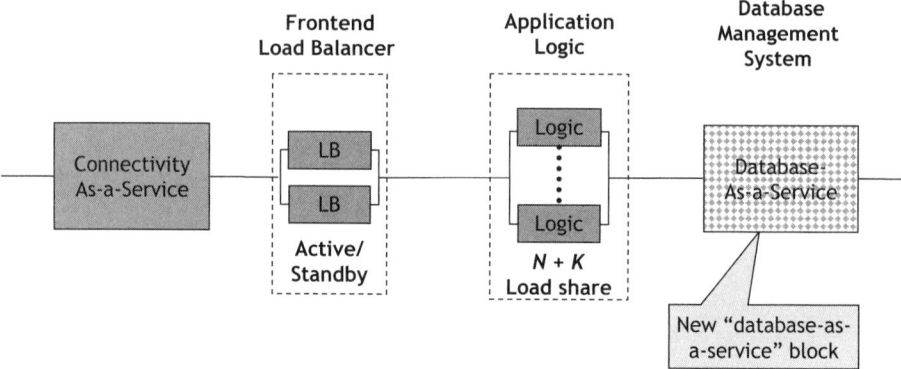

Figure 12.11. Sample Application with Database-as-a-Service.

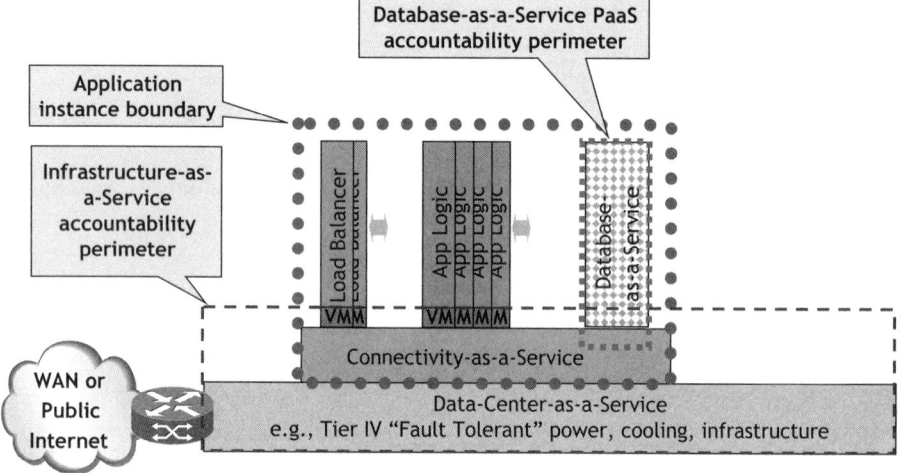

Figure 12.12. Accountability of Sample Application with Database-as-a-Service.

application. Replacing the application's DBMS component with DBaaS changes the accountability visualization of Figure 12.9, Figure 12.10, Figure 12.11, and Figure 12.12. Application suppliers may budget for reasonable and customary technology component downtime (e.g., based on the availability estimated by the technology component PaaS provider), but excess service downtime attributed to that technology component is generally attributable to the technology component PaaS provider rather than the application supplier.

12.3.3   Leveraging Storage-as-a-Service

Physical servers or compute blades—as well as virtual machine instances—routinely offer mass storage via a local hard disk that is sufficient for many application component instances. However, for some application architectures, it is better to rely on shared—and often highly reliable—mass storage for some application data. For example, application data that would be stored on a RAID array in native application deployment would generally be configured onto a Storage-as-a-Service offering for cloud deployment. The addition of "outboard" RAID storage array to host application data evolves the sample application RBD of Figure 12.7, Figure 12.8, Figure 12.9, Figure 12.10, Figure 12.11, Figure 12.12 and Figure 12.13.

When the sample application is deployed to cloud, the outboard RAID storage array of Figure 12.13 can be replaced by a Storage-as-a-Service offering, as shown in Figure 12.14. Figure 12.15 modifies the accountability diagram of Figure 12.9 to include Storage-as-a-Service. Note that Figure 12.15 shows the Storage-as-a-Service

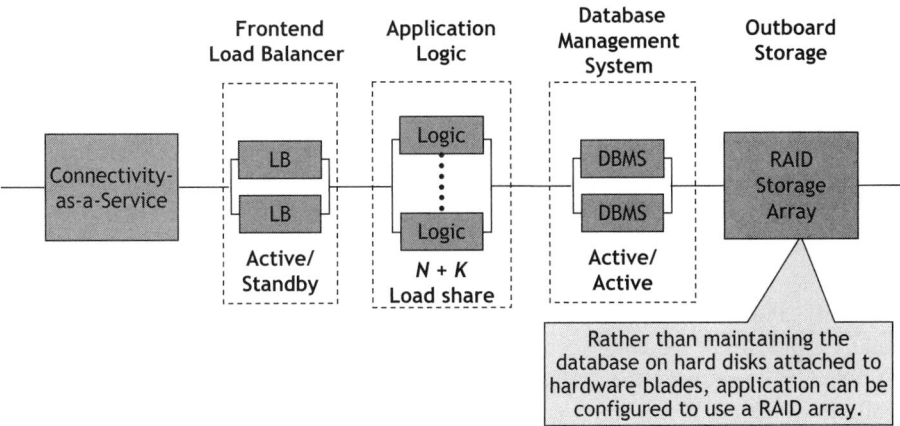

Figure 12.13. Sample Application with Outboard RAID Storage Array.

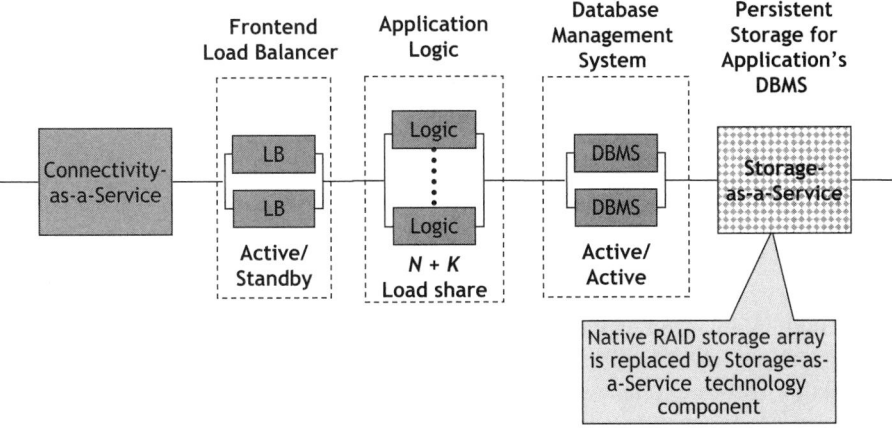

Figure 12.14. Sample Application with Storage-as-a-Service.

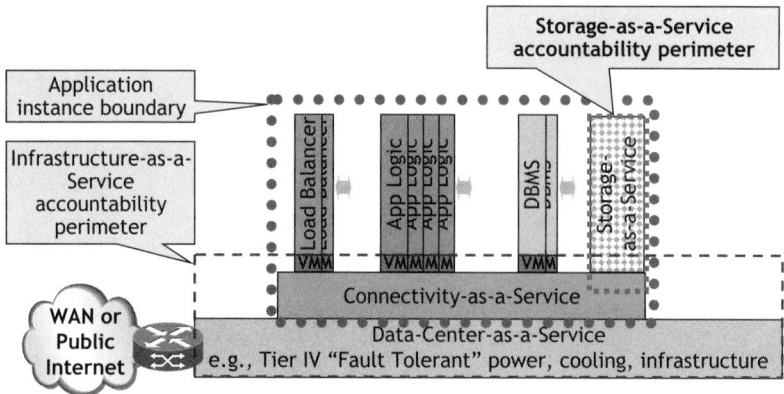

Figure 12.15. Accountability of Sample Application with Storage-as-a-Service.

component within the application instance's perimeter, but some applications, consumers, and cloud service providers will deem Storage-as-a-Service as a distinct element that is measured separately.

12.4 EVOLVING HARDWARE RELIABILITY MEASUREMENT

Hardware reliability of ICT components has improved so that mean time between failures (MTBF) of repairable or replaceable units often stretches to tens of thousands of hours or more; nevertheless, hardware still fails for well-known physical reasons. Failures of physical hardware, as well as failures of hypervisors and host operating systems inevitably impact application software components hosted in virtual machines executing on impacted infrastructure. The infrastructure or application must detect the underlying hardware failure and take corrective actions, such as by redirecting workload to a redundant application component and allocating and configuring a replacement VM instance to restore full application capacity. As both the failure events themselves and the failure detection and recovery actions impact service quality experienced by application users, VM failure events should be measured to drive corrective actions to manage and minimize this user service quality risk.

12.4.1 Virtual Machine Failure Lifecycle

Traditionally system software is hosted on hardware field replaceable units (FRUs) defined as "*a distinctly separate part that has been designed so that it may be exchanged at its site of use for the purposes of maintenance or service adjustment*" [TL_9000]. Virtualized application components execute in virtual machine instances that are effectively virtualized FRUs. Just as a hardware FRU failure triggers high availability software to recover service to a redundant FRU, failure of a VM instance often triggers recovery to a redundant VM instance. The failed VM instance is likely to be "repaired" via a new VM instance that is allocated and configured as a replace-

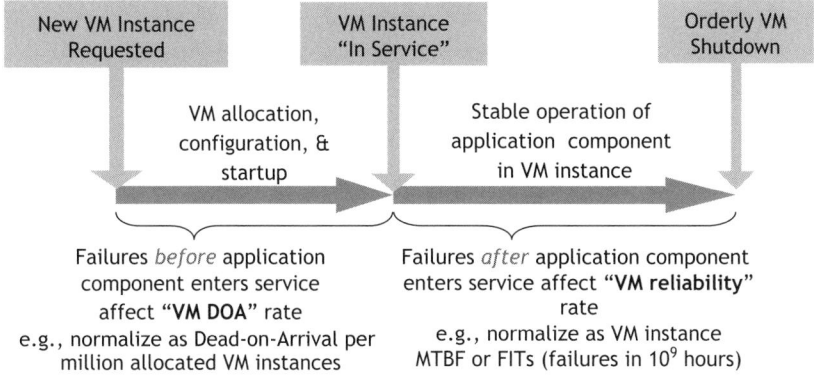

Figure 12.16. Virtual Machine Failure Lifecycle.

ment by an automated Repair-as-a-Service or self-healing mechanism (see Section 5.3, "Improving Infrastructure Repair Times via Virtualization"); the failed VM instance is likely to ultimately be destroyed rather than returned for repair (as a hardware FRU might be).

Virtualization technology and IaaS operational policies should decouple VM instance failure patterns from the underlying hardware reliability lifecycle so measurements based on traditional hardware reliability lifecycle phases should not be directly applicable. For example, at the moment an arbitrary VM instance is allocated to a cloud consumer's application, the underlying physical hardware is not necessarily any more likely to be in the hardware's early life phase (with a higher failure rate) than it is to be in the useful life phase (with a lower steady state failure rate). Thus, the authors propose the simplified virtual machine failure measurement model of Figure 12.16.

Let us consider the two measurements of Figure 12.16 carefully:

- *VM "Dead on Arrival" (DOA).* "Dead on arrival" is *"a newly produced hardware product that is found to be defective at delivery or installation (usage time = 0)"* [TL_9000]. Just as hardware FRUs are occasionally nonfunctional when they are first removed from factory packaging and installed (aka an "out of the box" failure), occasionally newly created VM instances do not startup and function properly because they have been misconfigured or are otherwise nonfunctional. VM DOAs can be expressed as defects (i.e., DOA events) per million VM allocation requests (DPM), or as a simple percentage of VM allocation requests. VM DOA explicitly measures cases in which the IaaS presents a VM instance to the application that is misconfigured (e.g., VLAN not set up properly, wrong software loaded, and application's persistent data are inaccessible) or otherwise not fully operational so the application component instance nominally hosted in the DOA VM is unable to begin serving application users with acceptable service quality. As VM DOAs are likely to prolong the time it takes for application capacity to be elastically grown (because DOA VMs must be detected, disengaged from the application and replacement VM instances allocated and configured), minimizing VM DOA rate should improve the predictability and consistency of elastic growth actions.

- *VM Reliability.* Failures after an application's component instance has successfully started delivering service count as VM instance failures. VM instance failure rate can be expressed as mean time between failures (MTBF) or normalized as failures per billion hours of operation (FITs) as traditional hardware failure rates are. VM reliability should explicitly cover hypervisor failures and failures of the underlying hardware and infrastructure. For example, an infrastructure failure that broke network connectivity for a VM instance would count as a VM reliability impairment because service offered by the application component instance would be impacted. As discussed in Section 4.2, "VM Failure," the authors propose that any event that prevents a VM instance from executing for more than some maximum VM stall time be deemed a chargeable VM reliability impairment unless the event is attributed to one of the following excluded causes:
  - ○ Explicit request by the cloud consumer (e.g., request via self-service GUI)
  - ○ Explicit "shutdown" request by the application instance itself
  - ○ Executed by IaaS provider for predefined policy reasons, such as nonpayment of bill or executing a lawful takedown order.

VM DOA and VM reliability should be back-to-back measurements so that all VM failures are covered by one and only one VM quality measurement. The exact dividing point between VM DOA (nominally "accessibility") and VM instance failure rate (nominally "retainability"), as well as specific failure counting and normalization rules should ultimately be defined by industry standards bodies so that cloud consumers, service providers, and suppliers can rigorously measure and manage these critical infrastructure quality characteristics.

12.5 EVOLVING ELASTICITY SERVICE AVAILABILITY MEASUREMENTS

Growth of traditional systems is usually driven by long-term forecasting of capacity utilization and is not used to support short-term spikes in traffic. Short-term increases in traffic are managed through overload control mechanisms that throttle or refuse traffic that exceeds the application capacity until the offered load falls within the engineered capacity. If traffic is refused or dropped due to workloads exceeding engineered capacity, then no product attributable outage accrues because the application is performing per specification. Per [TL_9000]: *"Use of a product beyond its specifications would be a customer procedural error and an outage resulting from that misuse would be classified as customer attributable."*

Cloud-based systems offering elasticity provide the ability to dynamically grow (and degrow) capacity and thus can be employed to add or remove VM instances to manage online service capacity to address increases (or decreases) in traffic. Although growth can be automated and triggered by policies (e.g., offered load exceeding some

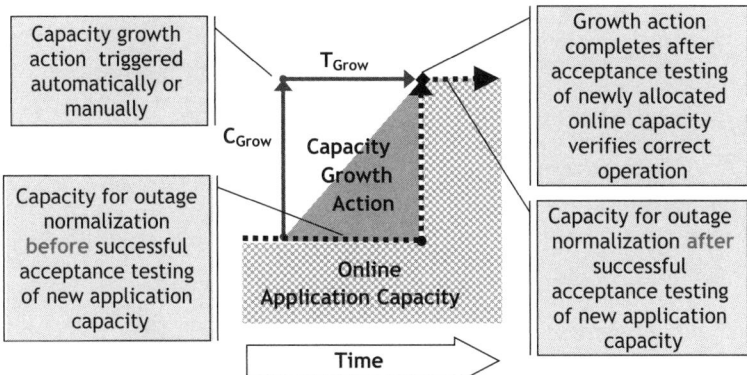

Figure 12.17. Elastic Capacity Growth Timeline.

capacity threshold), elastic growth is neither instantaneous nor flawless, so it does not eliminate the need for overload control mechanisms to manage the traffic until the additional VM's have been activated and integrated into the system.

As explained in Section 3.5.2, "Provisioning Interval," cloud elastic growth actions take a finite time (T_{Grow}) to add a finite increment of application capacity (C_{Grow}). Figure 12.17 highlights that, as with traditional capacity growth actions, the additional capacity is not considered to be "in-service" until the acceptance testing of the elastically grown capacity has confirmed that the new IaaS capacity was not DOA (see Section 12.4, "Evolving Hardware Reliability Measurement") and that the capacity has been properly integrated with the active application instance and is thus fully ready to serve users with acceptable quality. Note that if the cloud consumer elects to bring the elastically grown capacity into service without completing the recommended suite of acceptance tests, then any service impact due to unsuccessfully added service capacity may be customer attributable, just as it would be if a customer elected to omit recommended testing for traditional, manual system capacity growth procedures. If the growth of the VM instances is too slow or fails and is unable to mitigate the workload that has exceeded engineered capacity, then the overload control mechanisms should continue to manage the traffic, just as with traditional systems.

12.6   EVOLVING RELEASE MANAGEMENT SERVICE AVAILABILITY MEASUREMENT

Just as with growth, software release management (including software patch, update, upgrade, and retrofit) is considered a planned maintenance activity and any required downtime would be considered planned or scheduled. Some customers require that software upgrade of critical applications be completed with no user service downtime or service impact. If the software upgrade operations are not successful and cause service impact or exceed the agreed-upon planned outage period, service

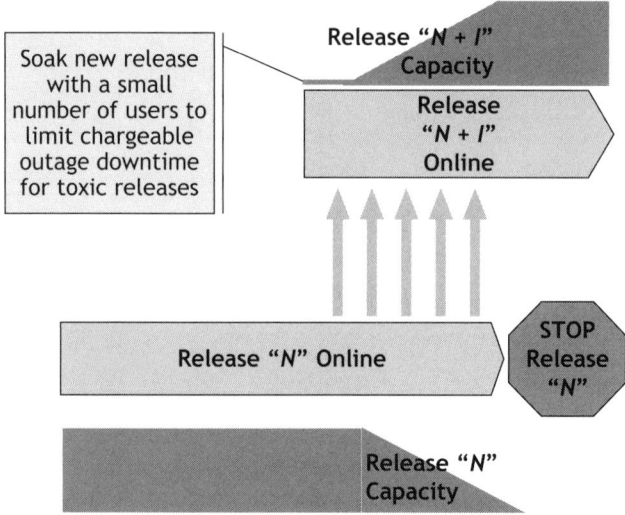

Figure 12.18. Outage Normalization for Type I "Block Party" Release Management.

downtime may accrue. As the user service impact of release management of cloud-based applications will appear the same to end users, the same service outage measurement rules should apply.

Normalization of any user service impact event during release management is impacted by the release management model. Chapter 9, "Release Management," factored cloud-based release management actions into two broad types:

- *Type I: Block Party* (see Section 9.3.1). Both old and new software releases of software run in VMs simultaneously serving user traffic, and can theoretically continue doing so indefinitely. Some users will be served by the old version and some users will be served by the new version. As shown in Figure 12.18 (modified version of Figure 9.4), each release (i.e., Release "N" and Release "$N + I$") appears as distinct and independent application instances, so following successful acceptance testing of Release "$N + I$," service outages are normalized for each application instance separately based on the configured capacity of each instance. Note that sophisticated customers will generally soak a new release with a small enough set of users that the impact of a toxic release does not produce a chargeable outage event.
- *Type II: One Driver per Bus* (see Section 9.3.2). In this case the active application instance is explicitly switched at a particular instant in time, so outage measurements are directly applied to the active application instance. As shown in Figure 12.19, at any instant in time, only one release is nominally in service (like traditional deployments), so outage events are normalized just as they would be for traditional application deployment.

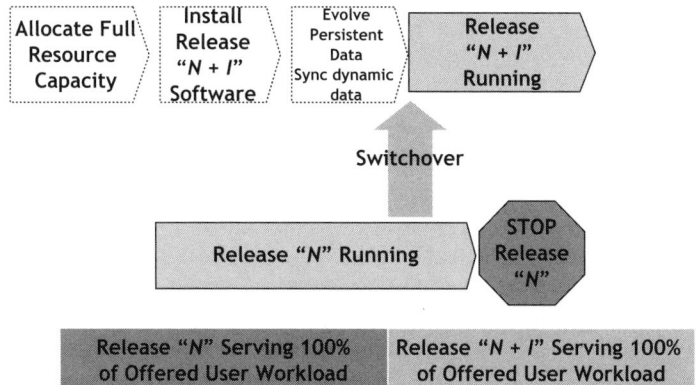

Figure 12.19. Outage Normalization for Type II "One Driver per Bus" Release Management.

12.7   SERVICE MEASUREMENT OUTLOOK

Traditional service availability measurements can be gracefully adapted to cover existing applications that run on cloud computing infrastructure. One can generally also apply traditional application service reliability, latency, accessibility, and retainability measurements to cloud deployments. Applying traditional service measurements to cloud-based applications enables end users, customers, and suppliers to easily compare service performance for both traditional and cloud deployments to drive root cause analysis and corrective analyses necessary to enable cloud deployment meet and then exceed service quality of traditional application deployments. Tracking and analyzing service measurements by software releases enables insights into quality of the development, validation, and deployment processes used for each release. Likewise, tracking and analyzing service measurements of application instances hosted by different cloud service providers and supported by different operations teams enables useful side-by-side comparisons.

13

APPLICATION SERVICE QUALITY REQUIREMENTS

Rigorous definition and quantification of key service performance characteristics enables methodical analysis, architecture, design, and verification to assure the feasibility and likelihood of those requirements being consistently met in production deployment. The key service quality requirements for a target application should be specified with clear definitions for unambiguous measurement and quantified minimum expectations. The highest level service quality requirements should characterize key aspects of the end user experience rather than focusing on behaviors of individual components or APIs. The fundamental application service quality performance requirements for application instances from Section 2.5, "Application Service Quality," are considered separately:

- Service Availability Requirements (Section 13.1)
- Service Latency Requirements (Section 13.2)
- Service Reliability Requirements (Section 13.3)
- Service Accessibility Requirements (Section 13.4)
- Service Retainability Requirements (Section 13.5)
- Service Throughput Requirements (Section 13.6)
- Timestamp Accuracy Requirements (Section 13.7).

Service Quality of Cloud-Based Applications, First Edition. Eric Bauer and Randee Adams.
© 2014 The Institute of Electrical and Electronics Engineers, Inc. Published 2014 by John Wiley & Sons, Inc.

The following requirements categories are also considered: ·

- Elasticity Requirements (Section 13.8)
- Release Management Requirements (Section 13.9).

13.1   SERVICE AVAILABILITY REQUIREMENTS

Service availability is the most fundamental quality requirement because if the application is not available to serve users then little else matters. The identification of the primary functionality of the application is critical because loss of primary functionality of a system is deemed an outage, while loss of a nonprimary function is merely a problem (albeit perhaps a serious problem). Primary functionality is typically specified by the highest level requirements and product documents should identify which of an application's functions are considered primary.

Beyond specifying the primary functionality of the application that is covered by availability requirements, service availability requirements should define:

1. *Maximum Acceptable Service Disruption.* Different applications, especially when accessed via different clients, may render application service disruptions somewhat differently. For example, decoders of streaming media often include lost packet concealment algorithms, such as replaying the previous audio packet rather than rendering a moment of silence so that occasional late, lost, or damaged media packets can be concealed from end users. A more extreme example are streaming video clients that include huge buffers that prefetch 10 seconds or more of content which enable the client to automatically detect and recover from myriad application and networking problems with no perceptible impact to user service. The maximum tolerable service disruption period entails how long application service delivery to the client device can be impacted before creating an unacceptable service experience. Application and infrastructure architectures and configurations (e.g., settings of guard timers and maximum retry counts) are engineered to successfully deliver service within some maximum acceptable service window. If a service impacting failure cannot be detected and recovered within this maximum acceptable service disruption time, then the service is generally deemed to be "down" and service availability metrics are impacted. For example, [TL_9000] stipulates that "*all outages shall be counted that result in a complete loss of primary functionality for all or part of the system for a duration of greater than 15 seconds.*" Note that the maximum acceptable service latency for an individual transaction is often shorter because a service outage requires more than one failed transaction. Readers will be familiar with this behavior from their experiences with web browsing: a "stuck" or hung webpage load will generally prompt them to "cancel" and "reload" the page; if the first—or perhaps second—reload succeeds, then the failed page load is counted as a failed transaction and should impact the web site's service reliability metrics. But if reloads for at least the maximum acceptable service disruption period are unsuccessful,

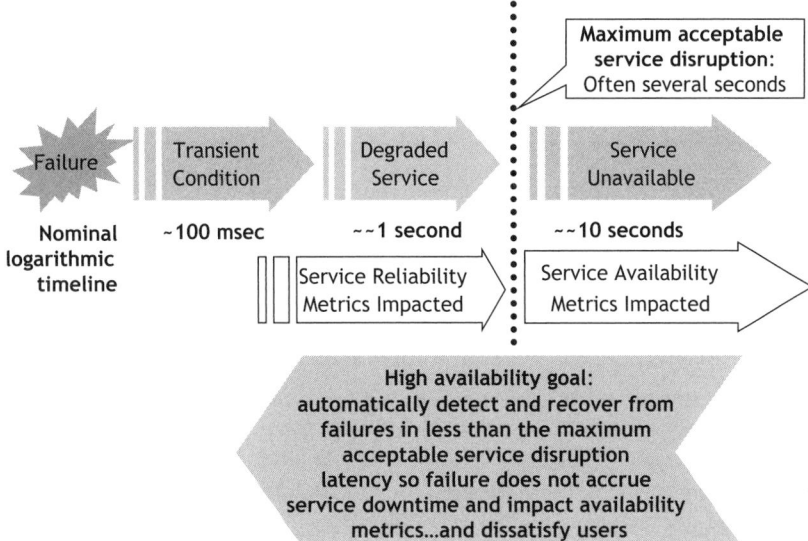

Figure 13.1. Maximum Acceptable Service Disruption.

then the website is deemed unavailable (at least to the user). This is visualized in Figure 13.1.

2. *Prorating Partial Capacity Loss.* Large and complex multiuser applications have myriad failure modes, often with different impacts on user service capacity. While a failure that critically impacts all users is deemed a total outage, if an event impacts only a single user when tens, hundreds, or thousands of users enjoy normal access to the application, then the problem is not generally deemed to be a service outage. For example, painfully slow rendering of a webpage to a handful of users might not qualify as a chargeable service outage, but it may prompt the impacted users to abandon the site and turn to a competitor. The question becomes how much user service capacity must be impacted before the event is deemed a partial capacity loss service outage. It is customary to prorate partial capacity loss outages by the percentage of users impacted. As this calculation is often rather complicated in practice, especially when applications support elastic capacity, it is useful to agree on partial capacity loss prorating rules in advance. For example, application service providers might have operational policies regarding incident reporting and management, with events impacting at least 10,000 users receiving immediate executive attention, events impacting 50–9999 users receiving immediate directors' attention, events impacting 10–49 users receiving supervisory attention, and events impacting 1–9 users being directly worked by maintenance engineers with normal priority; this policy encourages failures to be contained to no more than 9 users, then no more than 49 users, and then no more than 9999 users.

TABLE 13.1. Service Availability and Downtime Ratings

Number of 9s	Service Availability (%)	Annualized Down Minutes	Quarterly Down Minutes	Monthly Down Minutes	Practical Meaning
1	90	52,596.00	13,149.00	4383.00	Down 5 weeks per year
2	99	5259.60	1314.90	438.30	Down 4 days per year
3	99.9	525.96	131.49	43.83	Down 9 hours per year
4	99.99	52.60	13.15	4.38	Down 1 hour per year
5	99.999	5.26	1.31	0.44	Down 5 minutes per year
6	99.9999	0.53	0.13	0.04	Down 30 seconds per year
7	99.99999	0.05	0.01	—	Down 3 seconds per year

3. *Prorating Partial Functionality Loss.* Failures often impact partial system functionality. For example, Netflix's "Rambo architecture" [Netflix] is explicitly designed to continue delivering at least primary functionality to end users despite failures. Thus, it is useful to agree in advance if and how partial functionality loss events will be charged. For example, the following traditional partial functionality prorating rules of [TL_9000] include:

   a. *Total loss of one or more operation, administration, and maintenance (OA&M) functions (default weight is 5%)*

   b. *Total loss of visibility from the Element Management System (EMS) (default weight is 10%).*

4. *Maximum Quantified and Normalized Service Downtime.* Table 13.1 gives maximum annualized prorated service downtime per system for common service availability expectations. Note that the smaller the maximum allowable downtime per measurement period (e.g., monthly down minutes), the more important it is to rigorously define the maximum acceptable service disruption, the minimum chargeable capacity impact, and the prorating rules for partial capacity and functionality loss events.

Availability requirements should be fully aligned with the outage measurements that will be used when the application is deployed and in production so that architects, developers, and testers understand the quantitative service downtime impact that any particular failure event will likely accrue. Clear alignment on the quantitative downtime impact of any particular failure event and mitigation architecture enables architects, developers, testers, and others to have richer conversations about improving service availability.

As practical test campaigns are unlikely to exercise an application release for long enough to characterize the likely service downtime per system per year with high statistical confidence, mathematical modeling is often used to verify high service availability requirements. Typically, architecture-based availability models consider the likely rate of system failures, the success probability and timing of service recovery actions and other factors to estimate the feasible and likely long-term service availability of the system in production deployment. While construction of architecture-based service availability models are beyond the scope of this work, architecture-based models reflect key behaviors and characteristics of the system, so it is possible to construct quantified and verifiable requirements for at least some of these key application characteristics, such as:

- Application startup and restart time
- Failure detection latencies
- Latency for service recovery actions (e.g., switchover and failover)
- Probability of successful switchover or failover.

As many key application characteristics are not accurately known in the architecture and design phase, development teams will often estimate target values for all input parameters initially, then measure the actual values during testing, and update the architecture-based availability model with actual values for input parameters to create a better availability prediction prior to test complete. Best practice is to set quantitative requirements for key availability input parameters to assure the each value is carefully measured during testing, but less rigorous approaches can be acceptable.

13.2   SERVICE LATENCY REQUIREMENTS

End users typically experience an application one transaction (e.g., web page click, call setup, and channel change) at a time, and the latency between the user's action and the application service's response is a critical service quality characteristic. The maximum acceptable transaction service latency specifies the upper limit beyond which many or most users will abandon the request (e.g., cancel the web page load). Transactions that complete slower than this maximum acceptable latency are deemed failures and thus are counted as service reliability impairments (covered in Section 13.3, "Service Reliability Requirements").

As discussed in Section 4.1, "Service Latency, Virtualization, and the Cloud," service latency is best thought of as a statistical distribution rather than a single value that can crisply be measured. A simple specification technique is to frame a service latency distribution requirements via two points, like the maximum acceptable latency at both the 90th percentile (slowest 1 in 10 transactions) and the 99.999th percentile (slowest 1 in 100,000 transactions). These requirements can then be verified by inspection of a latency CCDF to verify that the distribution does not exceed the 10^{-1} (i.e., 90th percentile point) or the 10^{-5} value (i.e., the 99.999th percentile point).

13.3   SERVICE RELIABILITY REQUIREMENTS

Service reliability requirements specify the probability that a logically, syntactically, and semantically correct service request will produce a correct response within the maximum acceptable service latency (from Section 13.2, "Service Latency Requirements"). Service reliability requirements are most conveniently specified as defective (or failed) operations per million attempts, or DPM. Historically, some have expressed service reliability via a number of 9s, but this format is difficult for most people to manipulate and evaluate, so the authors recommend DPM. One should also specify the maximum acceptable transaction latency; transactions that exceed that latency are deemed unsuccessful because the user would likely have canceled or abandoned transactions that slow. Common percentage-based service reliability expectations map easily to DPM values as follows:

$$99.9\% \text{ service reliability} = 1000 \text{ defective operations per million (DPM)}$$

$$99.99\% \text{ service reliability} = 100 \text{ DPM}$$

$$99.999\% \text{ service reliability} = 10 \text{ DPM}$$

$$99.9999\% \text{ service reliability} = 1 \text{ DPM}.$$

As shown in Equation 13.1 (DPM via operations attempted and operations successful), Equation 13.2 (DPM via operations attempted and operations failed), and Equation 13.3 (DPM via operations successful and operations failed), DPM is easily computed either from any two of: operations attempted, operations successful, and operations failed.

$$\text{DPM} = \frac{(\text{Operations Attempted} - \text{Operations Successful})}{\text{Operations Attempted}} * 10^6 \qquad (13.1)$$

$$\text{DPM} = \frac{\text{Operations Failed}}{\text{Operations Attempted}} * 10^6 \qquad (13.2)$$

$$\text{DPM} = \frac{\text{Operations Failed}}{(\text{Operations Successful} + \text{Operations Failed})} * 10^6. \qquad (13.3)$$

Note that different transaction types may have different DPM and maximum transaction latency requirements even for the same application. For example, users may expect simple query operations to be fast and reliable (e.g., <10 DPM in <500 milliseconds), but tolerate slower logon times (e.g., <50 DPM in <5 seconds); and complex tasks like provisioning new application users may have even more generous requirements due to even greater complexity (e.g., <100 DPM in <20 seconds).

13.4 SERVICE ACCESSIBILITY REQUIREMENTS

While service *availability* requirements consider the impact of events that affect *large* numbers of users, service *accessibility* metrics consider the probability than any *indi-*

vidual user can successfully acquire service on demand. Service accessibility is conveniently specified as a maximum DPM, and the requirement should stipulate one or more accessibility scenarios, such as:

- The ability to successfully logon to a service and have the correct home screen displayed (e.g. *user logon followed by home screen display shall be accessible within 10 seconds with no more than 100 failures per million attempts [<100 DPM]*)
- The ability to begin streaming a particular movie with acceptable video and audio quality (e.g., *video and audio will begin rendering to the end user within 5 seconds of pressing "play" with no more than 50 failures per million attempts [<50 DPM]*)
- The ability to establish a telephone call and receive ring back (e.g., *ring back shall be returned within 4 seconds of pressing "send" with no more than 20 failures per million attempts [<20 DPM]*).

13.5   SERVICE RETAINABILITY REQUIREMENTS

Service retainability is an application specific metric for session-oriented applications, such as the probability that a streaming movie plays to the end with no perceptible visual or audible impairments or a telephone call continuously delivers acceptable service quality until it is explicitly terminated by one of the callers. For practical purposes, one may specify a nominal test case to be used (e.g., streaming a 2-hour movie or holding a 3-minute telephone call). Service retainability requirements may be quantified as application sessions per million (DPM) that were prematurely terminated or experienced (unacceptable) service impairments.

Note that accessibility and retainability are often meant to be back-to-back metrics for session oriented services, so application setup failures are generally counted as accessibility impairments while service defects after service is properly established with acceptable service quality are counted as retainability impairments. Thus, one should consider an application's accessibility requirement along with the application's retainability requirement to assure that together these requirements adequately specify the quality of experience expectations for individual end users.

13.6   SERVICE THROUGHPUT REQUIREMENTS

Throughput requirements typically specify a minimum rate of correct transactions per second or batch operations per hour. Best practice is to pair service throughput requirements with service reliability requirements, such as "*Application shall deliver a minimum throughput of 5000 operations per hour with a fallout rate of less than 1 failure per 10,000 operations (<100 DPM).*"

13.7 TIMESTAMP ACCURACY REQUIREMENTS

Timestamp accuracy requirements are typically framed either in terms of the maximum acceptable difference (e.g., in microseconds or milliseconds) between the recorded timestamp and the universal time (UTC) that an event actually occurred. For example, *"No more than 50 records per million will have timestamps that are inaccurate by more than 100 milliseconds."*

13.8 ELASTICITY REQUIREMENTS

An application's elasticity architecture, design, and analysis (see Sections 8, "Capacity Management," and 15.6, "Elasticity Analysis") should be driven by verifiable requirements for the applications elasticity metrics (see Section 3.5, "Elasticity"):

- *Density* (Section 3.5.1, "Density"). Density requirements should frame the maximum user workload that can be served by a particular resource configuration while consistently meeting all application service quality requirements. Density varies based on performance characteristics of the cloud service provider's infrastructure, so it may be impractical to specify general density requirements per virtual machine instance. While desirable, it is also impractical to directly specify an application's density requirements in financial cost of applicable IaaS resources (e.g., $X of monthly IaaS charges per Y subscribers served). Instead, density requirements can be addressed via one or both of the following:
  1. Specify density when application executes on a specific reference IaaS configuration, such as *"maximum user density shall be at least X active users per VM instance."*
  2. Specify service quality criteria for determining maximum acceptable density, such as *"maximum user workload per VM instance should be configured so that slowest one in 10^6 query transactions take no more than 100 milliseconds."*
- *Scale Up* (Section 3.5.4, "Scaling In and Out"). The nominal capacity of the largest application instance should be specified, such as maximum simultaneous user sessions or pending transactions.
- *Agility* (Section 3.5.6, "Agility"). The nominal units of capacity growth and degrowth should be specified.
- *Provisioning Interval* (Section 3.5.2, "Provisioning Interval"). The maximum provisioning intervals for all elastic growth actions should be specified, often as an increment of time beyond what is required by the cloud service provider to complete their allocation action.
- *Slew Rate* (Section 3.5.7). The expected rate of sustained capacity growth should be specified, such as *"application shall elastically grow service capacity for at least 5000 users per hour from the smallest (scale in/scale down) configuration to the largest (scale out/scale up) configuration."*

- *Elasticity Speedup* (Section 3.5.8 "Elasticity Speedup"). The application's architecture document should explain if and how any elasticity speedup is supported; if elasticity speedup is supported, then the minimum acceptable speedup should be specified, as well as the speedup benefit (i.e., as a function of increased resource consumption).

Release interval is nominally the lower bound for how fast unneeded resources can be gracefully released from an application instance. As resource charges are generally fairly modest and are often charged by the hour, release interval (Section 3.5.3, "Release Interval") is not usually an important key quality indicator, so it is generally acceptable not to specify quantified release interval requirements.

13.9 RELEASE MANAGEMENT REQUIREMENTS

Application release management requirements typically specify the following:

- Total interval required to perform the software upgrade or data migration (e.g., <4 hours)
- Service downtime allowed, if any, for each release management event (e.g., <15 seconds).
- Service impact on new and existing sessions (e.g., maintain all stable sessions)
- Percentage of traffic directed to a particular release during soak testing
- Dependencies or ordering of application or VM instance upgrades

Metrics on service downtime and number of dropped sessions should be collected to prove compliance to the exact requirements specified.

13.10 DISASTER RECOVERY REQUIREMENTS

An application's recovery time objectives should be quantitatively specified, including exactly when recovery is deemed complete, such as when 90% of impacted users have been successfully recovered.

An application's recovery point objective should quantitatively specify the maximum window size of acceptable data loss. If any persistent application or user data is not protected by disaster recovery mechanisms, that potential loss of data should be clearly specified (e.g., in SLAs) to assure that the limits of disaster recovery are fully understood.

14

VIRTUALIZED INFRASTRUCTURE MEASUREMENT AND MANAGEMENT

Timely identification and accurate attribution of service impairments is essential to both rapid restoration of acceptable user service quality and corrective action to resolve the true root cause of the problem. Correcting the true root cause of service-impacting problems is at the heart of continuous quality improvement. To enable timely identification of virtualized infrastructure impairments, cloud consumers and application suppliers should assure that adequate service measurements of virtualized infrastructure service quality are in place. This chapter considers service quality measurements across the MP0 service boundary (MP0 from Section 10.1, "End-to-End Service Context"). As shown in Figure 14.1, performance of virtualized compute, memory, storage, and networking resources delivered by a cloud service provider across the application's resource facing service boundary (MP0) to a cloud consumer's application component instances running in virtual machines directly impacts the application's service quality delivered to end users. Service performance across the application's resource facing service (MP0) boundary can be measured "below" the boundary by the infrastructure service provider, but that presents risks considered in Section 14.1, "Business Context." Infrastructure service performance across MP0 can also be measured by the application, which is considered in Section 14.2, "Cloud Consumer Measurement Options." Section 14.3, "Impairment Measurement Strategies," considers techniques to measure each of

Service Quality of Cloud-Based Applications, First Edition. Eric Bauer and Randee Adams.
© 2014 The Institute of Electrical and Electronics Engineers, Inc. Published 2014 by John Wiley & Sons, Inc.

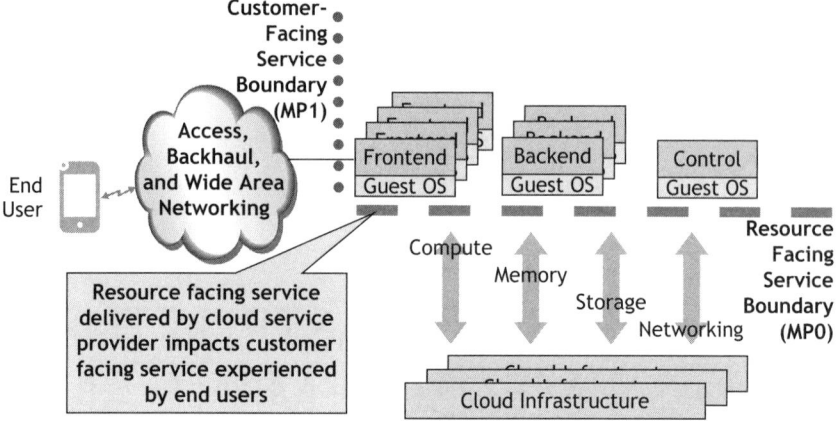

Figure 14.1. Infrastructure impairments and application impairments.

the virtualized infrastructure impairments discussed in Chapter 4, "Virtualized Infrastructure Impairments." Section 14.4, "Managing Virtualized Infrastructure Impairments" reviews the tactical and strategic mitigations that cloud consumers can take if infrastructure performance is below expectation.

14.1 BUSINESS CONTEXT FOR INFRASTRUCTURE SERVICE QUALITY MEASUREMENTS

While the cloud service provider should have access to detailed performance data from the hypervisors and other components that serve virtualized resources to cloud consumers' application instances running in VMs, cloud service providers may be reluctant to candidly share that detailed performance/quality information with cloud consumers for reasons, including:

- *Protecting Proprietary Business Information.* Just as few retailers voluntarily disclose detailed cost and sales data to their customers and competitors, cloud service providers are often reluctant to expose detailed data on performance of individual and specific VM instances.
- *Minimizing SLA Liability.* Even if a cloud service provider has knowledge that performance of infrastructure has breached performance levels contractually committed in service level agreements with cloud consumers, financial remedies (e.g., service credits) might only be triggered if the cloud consumer explicitly reports the performance breach and explicitly requests SLA remedies. As cloud consumers might not otherwise be aware of the true duration or impact of an SLA breaching event, volunteering those details potentially exposes the service provider to larger remedies than consumers might otherwise have requested.

- *Nonstandard Measurements.* As industry standards do not yet exist for quantifying virtualized infrastructure impairments, measurements available to cloud service providers are likely to be product specific and thus may be hard to stitch together into clear stories about what performance is actually delivered to individual VM instances. For example, different hypervisor suppliers may expose different performance management data to the cloud service providers. An additional problem is that infrastructure elements may not track performance characteristics to specific cloud consumers, applications or VM instances, so it may be difficult to map performance data from infrastructure components back to individual VM instances associated with specific cloud consumer's application instances.

Thus, cloud service providers may not routinely provide sufficiently detailed performance management data to enable cloud consumers to accurately characterize the true performance of virtualized resources and implement aggressive application performance management.

The alternate solution is for cloud consumers and their application instances to monitor the performance of virtualized infrastructure resources delivered to each VM instance and include these data along with the other performance management information that is recorded and analyzed for each of the application's component instances. Ideally, these data will be rich enough to clearly differentiate application service performance impairments that are attributable to the cloud service provider's virtualized infrastructure not meeting expectations from problems with application software component instances and other factors. Once the root cause of a service impairment is known, then appropriate actions can be taken to correct the true root cause of the impairment and/or to make the application more robust to future impairment events.

14.2 CLOUD CONSUMER MEASUREMENT OPTIONS

Cloud consumers have two fundamental options for assuring that the cloud service provider delivers acceptable infrastructure service performance to their application component instances:

1. *Rely on (IaaS) Cloud Service Provider's Best Effort.* The cloud consumer can simply rely on the good faith effort of the cloud service provider and make no effort to measure actual virtualized resource service delivered to their application software. Crudely put, this is trust-but-don't-verify the cloud service provider.
2. *Enhance Application Software to Measure Actual Infrastructure Performance.* Sophisticated applications generally feature performance monitoring mechanisms coupled to a management and control infrastructure that affords external visibility and controllability of the application instance. This function can be enhanced to directly or indirectly measure performance of VMs and virtualized infrastructure on an application component instance by instance basis.

Application software can deploy several measurement strategies:

- *Poll Hypervisor and Infrastructure Measurements.* Useful performance measurement data may be exposed by hypervisors and/or cloud service providers. Unfortunately, the specific performance data that were exposed to applications and cloud consumers, as well as the programmatic interfaces to that data, may vary from cloud service provider to service provider and from hypervisor to hypervisor.

- *Active Service Probes.* Application or middleware software can proactively probe infrastructure performance, such as by periodically executing performance benchmark routines within the application's VM instances. Active service probes should be configured so that they add no more than a small incremental workload to the target application so that the probe itself does not materially impact the service performance enjoyed by the application's software. For example, if network throughput is actively probed by running a network performance benchmark routine, then when that benchmark routine is actively using network I/O, less network capacity is available for the application components running in the same VM instance. Note that active service probes can be configured to run when the application itself is idle or lightly loaded to minimize application service impact, but this may not accurately characterize infrastructure performance when the application is under load.

- *Loopback Mechanisms.* Loopback mechanisms (shown in Figure 14.2) can give insight into virtualized infrastructure behavior by characterizing the latency for a request to actually reach a target virtualized component instance, and by comparing the loopback latency and consistency to the service latency, one can gain insight into the virtualized infrastructure's contribution to overall service latency and consistency.

- *Minimally Intrusive (VM Instance) Monitoring.* Application, middleware, and/ or guest OS software can be enhanced to directly or indirectly characterize performance of virtualized infrastructure delivered to the specific component

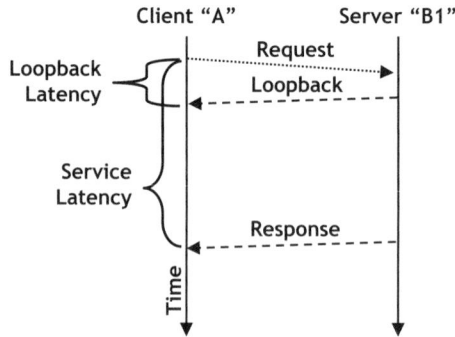

Figure 14.2. Loopback and Service Latency.

instance. For example, clock event jitter can be measured by reading the time when an application's routine clock event is set to compute the time when the event should fire and later reading the time when the event actually does fire. The predicted and actual event times are compared to characterize clock event jitter.

- *Repurpose Traditional Measurements.* Traditional operating systems, utilities, and applications often include rich performance measures that are designed for native deployments. Some of these traditional measurements can be used to gain insight into the true performance of the virtualized infrastructure. While these measurements often do not give directly useful information because hypervisors effectively mask the full effects of virtualization from the guest OS, careful analysis and correlation of traditional measurements can be useful.

14.3   IMPAIRMENT MEASUREMENT STRATEGIES

Strategies for measuring each of the virtualized infrastructure impairments given in Chapter 4, "Virtualized Infrastructure Impairments," are discussed separately:

- Measurement of VM Failure (Section 14.3.1)
- Measurement of Nondelivery of Configured VM Capacity (Section 14.3.2)
- Measurement of Delivery of Degraded VM capacity (Section 14.3.3)
- Measurement of Tail Latency (Section 14.3.4)
- Measurement of Clock Event Jitter (Section 14.3.5)
- Measurement of Clock Drift (Section 14.3.6)
- Measurement of Failed or Slow Allocation and Startup of VM Instance (Section 14.3.7).

As performance management data is often recorded every 15 minutes and data on virtualized infrastructure impairments should be recorded individually on a per VM instance basis, it is important to be frugal on the amount of performance management data actually recorded to avoid hugely increasing the volume of data to be analyzed and stored.

14.3.1   Measurement of VM Failure

Section 12.4, "Evolving Hardware Reliability Measurement," introduced the notion of VM instance reliability measurements as MTBF or FITs. While it is infeasible for a failing VM instance to reliably record its own failure event, complex applications often include a monitoring and control mechanism that manages high availability and/or operations, administration, and management of each component instance, and this mechanism routinely monitors the health of application components. Heartbeat messages exchanged between the application's monitoring and control component and individual application components do not reliably characterize VM instance failure rates because critical failures of application or guest OS software could prevent heartbeat messages from being correctly acknowledged. Those causes must be excluded from consideration to accurately identify VM failure events. VM failures can be differentiated from nondelivery of configured VM capacity events, such as live migration of a VM instance, by appropriately configuring guard timers and maximum retry counts for heartbeat messages. Differentiating catastrophic application OS software failures from underlying VM failure can be inferred via:

1. Requiring application instances to explicitly record orderly VM termination request events before initiating graceful VM termination.
2. Probing availability of the VM instance's operating system (e.g., via ping).
3. Checking status of the VM instance hosting the nonresponse application component instance via a cloud service provider mechanism (e.g., API) to see if the VM instance is reported to be operational.

Applications will generally wish to retain individual VM instances for hours, days, weeks, or even longer; thus, VM premature release rate must include a time component in the metric to capture the probability that an arbitrary VM will continuously deliver acceptable service over a fixed time period. Hardware failure rates have traditionally been normalized as failures in 10^9 hours (a.k.a., FITs), so the authors propose that VM failure rates be normalized as premature VM releases in 10^9 hours (i.e., VM FITs). Equation 14.1 gives the formula for computing VM FITs, where:

- NumPrematureVMReleases is the whole number of VM failures or abnormal terminations that were not triggered by one of the three normal termination triggers given in Section 4.2, "VM Failure," and repeated here for the reader's convenience:
  1. Explicit request by the cloud consumer (e.g., request via self-service GUI)
  2. Explicit "shutdown" request by the application instance itself
  3. Explicit execution by IaaS provider for predefined policy reasons, such as non-payment of bill or executing a lawful takedown order.
- HoursVMInServiceTime is the total number of hours VM instances were in service during the measurement period. Nominally, the VM "in service" clock begins when the VM is stable after allocation and initialization, but the clock can begin as early as the instant the VM allocation request was received. Time that the VM instance is suspended does not count as being in service because the VM is not executing and thus should not be vulnerable to failure.

$$\text{VM\_FITs} = \frac{\text{NumPrematureVMReleases}}{\text{Hours VMInServiceTime}} * 10^9. \qquad (14.1)$$

FITs can easily be converted to Mean Time Between Failures (MTBF) in hours via Equation 14.2:

$$\text{MTBF}_{\text{Hours}} = \frac{10^9}{\text{VM\_FITs}}. \qquad (14.2)$$

This metric should be computed monthly.

14.3.2   Measurement of Nondelivery of Configured VM Capacity

Nondelivery of VM CPU capacity can be measured via tools like jHiccup [jHiccup]. Comparing time stamps of high frequency regularly scheduled events allows the application to easily isolate intervals in which the VM did not run. Nondelivery of network capacity can be measured by comparing output queues with transmit data statistics. An increase in queue depth without a corresponding increase in transmitted bits may indicate a network nondelivery condition. A similar technique can be applied to storage if queue and I/O statistics are available for storage devices.

14.3.3   Measurement of Delivery of Degraded VM Capacity

Delivery of degraded resource capacity is hard because hypervisors explicitly make virtual machine instances believe that they have full and dedicated access to the underlying physical resources. Growing work queues when the volume of offered work remains stable may indicate that the virtualized infrastructure is delivering less resource capacity. Likewise, an increase in IP packet retransmissions or lost packets suggests that cloud networking infrastructure may be congested and thus is discarding packets. Analysis of performance counters from the guest OS or the hypervisor can offer insights into the quality of infrastructure service delivered by the cloud service provider.

14.3.4   Measurement of Tail Latency

As discussed in Section 4.1, virtualized and cloud infrastructure is often subject to materially longer tail latencies for resource (e.g., CPU) access, which results in materially longer tail latencies for user service response times. Applications can potentially measure mean and variance for application service latencies across the application's resource facing service boundary to the infrastructure (e.g., disk I/O latency).

The traditional way to monitor and characterize that service latency would be to build latency performance complimentary cumulative distribution functions (CCDF) or histograms (see Section 2.5.2.2, "Characterizing Service Latency"). While histograms or CCDFs yield deep insight into latency behavior, they require an array of 10, 20, or more buckets for each measurement interval for each latency measurement being tracked. A larger challenge is that determining the optimal size of measurement buckets is a function of actual behavior and thus is too complex to configure in advance. For reasons detailed in Section 4.1, "Service Latency, Virtualization, and the Cloud," latency is far more variable with cloud computing so it is important to monitor latency on a regular basis (e.g., every 5 or 15 minutes) and to record the results for offline analysis. Unfortunately, histograms typically require sizeable data arrays for bucket counters. Fortunately latency can be characterized more simply with the mean latency (i.e., the average latency) and some variance measurement (e.g., root of mean of squared latency). The first-order statistic (mean latency) and a second-order statistic (root of mean of squared latency) compactly characterize service latency performance, including the latency tail. As an optimization, one can often employ sampling techniques (e.g., measuring and recording only every Nth sample) to reduce incremental measurement overhead.

14.3.5 Measurement of Clock Event Jitter

Real-time applications often rely on clock event interrupts to regularly service isochronous traffic, like streaming interactive media for video conferencing applications. Typically, these applications will include real-time components that rely on timer interrupts every few milliseconds to assure that traffic promptly flows through the application with bounded latency. In these cases, one can measure the mean and variance latency between when each clock event was requested to trigger (e.g., 1000 μs from now) and when the timer service routine was actually executed (e.g., 2345 μs later). Clock event jitter can also be probed using software that periodically fires events and measures response latency like RealFeel (http://elinux.org/Realtime_Testing_Best_Practices#RealFeel).

14.3.6 Measurement of Clock Drift

Conceptually, drift in a virtual machine instance's clock is easy to characterize by measuring the periodic corrections to a VM's clock to resynchronize with a reference clock (e.g., time.nist.gov) via a well-known mechanism like Network Time Protocol (NTP RFC 5905) or Precision Time Protocol (PTP IEEE 1588). Time synchronization programs, such as NTP daemon, can be configured to log the clock adjustments they make, and analysis of these adjustment logs enables one to characterize the nature and magnitude of clock drive experienced by each VM instance.

14.3.7 Measurement of Failed or Slow Allocation and Startup of VM Instance

It is infeasible for a VM instance being allocated and started to know that its allocation and startup was slow or faulty, and thus these impairments must be monitored from another, preexisting VM instance. If the application's monitoring and control component explicitly initiates VM instance allocation for application startup and growth actions, then that monitoring and control component can measure the response latency and status of the allocation and startup of VM instances. It is useful to record at least the following details for each VM allocation request:

- Time of allocation request
- Characteristics of VM being requested (e.g., number of CPU cores and RAM allocation)
- Time of allocation response
- Final status of allocation request (e.g., success or error code).

This information should be recorded for each VM allocation request, and it can be analyzed offline to characterize overall characteristics of IaaS performance.

14.3.8 Measurements Summary

While acute infrastructure impairments—such as simultaneous failure of many VM instances—may be relatively easy to diagnose, chronic user service quality impairments impacting several transactions or sessions per hundred, thousand, or more transactions or sessions are often much harder to diagnose to true root cause. Appropriate monitoring of virtualized infrastructure performance can help determine whether user service impairments are attributable to the application, the virtualized infrastructure, end-to-end networking, or some combination of those and/or other factors.

Figure 14.3 visualizes a sample cloud consumer's rich infrastructure impairment measurement strategy:

- Software in the application's VM instances monitors: nondelivery of configured VM capacity; delivery of degraded VM capacity; tail latency; clock event jitter; and clock drift.
- The application's management and control function monitors: VM failure rates; and perhaps failed or slow allocation or startup of VM instances.
- The cloud OSS monitors: VM failure rates; failed or slow allocation or startup of VM instances; and other infrastructure and technology component failures and service impairments.

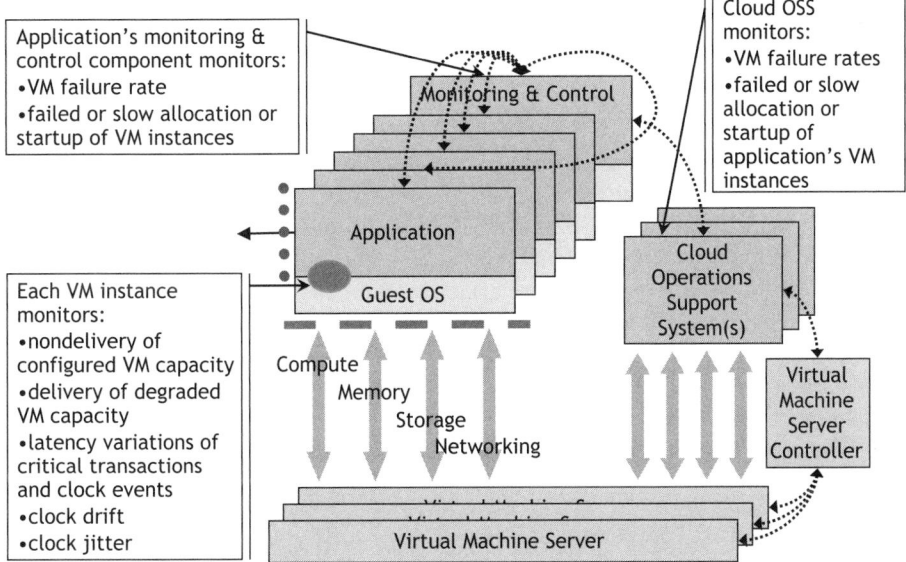

Figure 14.3. Simplified Measurement Architecture.

Threshold crossing alarms can be configured to alert the cloud consumer when infrastructure performance drops below specific targets, and this data can be analyzed over days, weeks, and months to characterize IaaS service quality.

14.4 MANAGING VIRTUALIZED INFRASTRUCTURE IMPAIRMENTS

If performance of virtualized infrastructure drops below expectations, then the cloud consumer can mitigate the impairment with a combination of technical and business mitigations. Technical mitigations that enable short-term mitigation of poor infrastructure performance include one or more of the following:

- Minimize Application's Sensitivity to Infrastructure Impairments (Section 14.4.1)
- VM-Level Congestion Detection and Control (Section 14.4.2)
- Allocate More Virtual Resource Capacity (Section 14.4.3)
- Terminate Poorly Performing VM Instances (Section 14.4.4).

Chronic infrastructure service impairments may require nontechnical business mitigations, such as:

- Accept Degraded Performance (Section 14.4.5)
- Proactive Supplier Management (Section 14.4.6)
- Reset End Users' Service Quality Expectations (Section 14.4.7)
- SLA Considerations (Section 14.4.8)
- Changing Cloud Service Providers (Section 14.4.9).

14.4.1 Minimize Application's Sensitivity to Infrastructure Impairments

Recognizing that virtualized infrastructure is vulnerable to service impairments beyond what applications experience on native hardware, architects should explicitly design their application to minimize the application's sensitivity to likely infrastructure impairments. An IaaS Impairment Effects Analysis (see Section 15.2) should be completed to methodically characterize residual sensitivities that can be architecturally mitigated or which can drive minimum performance expectations for virtualized infrastructure service. Some mitigations are as simple as adjusting configurable parameters to tolerate a wider range of infrastructure performance, such as widening the time window for fault/alarm event correlation. More profound architectural changes, such as deploying concurrent redundancy (see Section 5.5 "Sequential Redundancy and Concurrent Redundancy"), are required to fundamentally reduce an application's sensitivity to infrastructure impairments.

14.4.2 VM-Level Congestion Detection and Control

Cloud deployment introduces more performance variability between application component instances than would traditionally be experienced on native deployments.

Relatively consistent performance of natively deployed application components may have enabled applications to sample workload levels at a few points in the application and then estimate workload levels across all application components. Cloud computing is potentially very different because even if the application uniformly distributes the workload across application component instances, the cloud service provider may not uniformly schedule virtualized compute, memory, storage, and networking resources to each of the VM instances hosting those application components, so the throughput and application service performance may vary dramatically between those application component instances. Thus, congestion controls must assess the throughput and backlog of each of the application's VM instances separately. Knowing that a single VM instance is congested should cause the impacted application component to activate congestion control mechanisms that trigger application or solution mechanisms to shift workload to one or more component or application instances with spare, high-quality infrastructure capacity. As discussed in Chapter 6, "Load Distribution and Balancing," proxy load balancers can efficiently distribute workloads across a pool of serving components to effectively mitigate virtualized infrastructure impairments. Nonproxy load balancers (e.g., DNS) are often used to distribute workloads across application instances, but nonproxy mechanisms do not offer the same degree of performance monitoring and workload distribution control as proxy load balancers because they are not positioned in the critical service delivery path.

14.4.3 Allocate More Virtual Resource Capacity

If the virtualized resources delivered to one or more application component instances are unacceptable, then the application can horizontally grow another application component instance and hope to serve the workload with acceptable application service quality across a larger pool of poorer performance VM instances. If the application instance is at or near maximum engineered capacity or the infrastructure impairments are impacting multiple application components, then the application can outgrow a new application instance, possibly to another availability zone or data center.

14.4.4 Terminate Poorly Performing VM Instances

After a VM instance has delivered unacceptable service impairments for a period of time, it may be appropriate to simply terminate the poorly performing VM instance and rely on the application's high availability mechanisms to recover service for impacted users. Note that terminating VM instances is not appropriate when infrastructure impairments are not narrowly isolated to a single individual VM instance. After all, the more widespread the infrastructure impairment event is, the greater the probability that the redundant VM component instance that recovers service will also be affected by that impairment.

14.4.5 Accept Degraded Performance

In some cases, end users will temporarily accept degraded application service quality. For example, if application service quality is disrupted for a disaster or external event beyond the cloud consumer's reasonable control, then customer goodwill may limit damage to the consumer's reputation as a supplier of high-quality application service.

14.4.6 Proactive Supplier Management

Cloud consumers can work with their cloud service providers to characterize the most troubling infrastructure impairments, provide necessary data to enable service provider to drive true root cause analysis, and insist that appropriate corrective actions be promptly deployed.

14.4.7 Reset End Users' Service Quality Expectations

If virtual infrastructure impairments impact the feasibility and likelihood of achieving end users' expectations for service quality, then cloud consumers can attempt to lower end users' expectations. As service quality expectations are generally a core attribute of a product's or service's brand experience, resetting the expectations of that brand to a lower level may be a complex business problem that must be carefully managed.

14.4.8 SLA Considerations

If the cloud consumer has infrastructure service quality SLAs in place with the cloud service provider, then financial or nonfinancial remedies may be due as compensation for performance impairments. Typically, these SLAs are in the form of modest service credits (e.g., crediting the cloud consumer for the cost of the resources that were not delivered with acceptable service quality), so these remedies may not cover the cost of the financial and/or nonfinancial remedies that the cloud consumer may be obligated via SLA to provide to *their* end users. After all, unlike insurance products, SLAs are not meant to make the consumer "whole" after a loss event.

14.4.9 Changing Cloud Service Providers

The ultimate business mitigation of unacceptable virtualized infrastructure performance is to change cloud service providers. Cloud consumers should require that their contracts with cloud service providers give them the option to prematurely terminate their relationship with a cloud service provider if the infrastructure performance delivered by the service provider fails to meet specified service levels. As changing cloud service providers is often an expensive and time-consuming task for cloud consumers, it is wise to diligently research potential service providers and select a service provider that is extremely likely to consistently deliver acceptable infrastructure service quality. Note that using standard rather than proprietary cloud interfaces and services will make it easier to change cloud service providers, thereby making this option more practical.

15

ANALYSIS OF CLOUD-BASED APPLICATIONS

Reliability engineering diligence for critical applications routinely includes activities such as reliability block diagrams (RBDs), failure mode effects analysis (FMEA), single point of failure analysis, and architecture based availability (downtime) modeling. As discussed in Chapter 4, "Virtualized Infrastructure Impairments," and throughout Part II: Analysis, virtualization and cloud deployment present new challenges to application service quality; thus, new engineering diligence is appropriate to assure that it is feasible and likely that application architectures will mitigate the user service impact of these new challenges. This chapter offers the following analysis methodologies to consider when evolving or architecting applications that will be deployed on virtualized and cloud platforms:

- Reliability Block Diagrams and Side-by-Side Analysis (Section 15.1)
- IaaS Impairment Effects Analysis (Section 15.2)
- PaaS Failure Effects Analysis (Section 15.3)
- Workload Distribution Analysis (Section 15.4)
- Anti-affinity Analysis (Section 15.5)
- Elasticity Analysis (Section 15.6)

Service Quality of Cloud-Based Applications, First Edition. Eric Bauer and Randee Adams.
© 2014 The Institute of Electrical and Electronics Engineers, Inc. Published 2014 by John Wiley & Sons, Inc.

- Release Management Impact Effects Analysis (Section 15.7)
- Recovery Point Objective Analysis (Section 15.8)
- Recovery Time Objective Analysis (Section 15.9).

15.1   RELIABILITY BLOCK DIAGRAMS AND SIDE-BY-SIDE ANALYSIS

Reliability block diagrams (RBDs) are a convenient way to analyze the service availability risks and redundancy mitigations for an application. While RBDs for new cloud applications can be created from scratch, when evolving existing applications or architecting new applications that will run both on cloud and native hardware, it is useful to perform a side-by-side analysis of both native/traditional and cloud deployments. As discussed in Chapter 12, "Service Availability Measurement," side-by-side analysis begins with reliability block diagrams for both native/traditional and cloud deployments that are actually laid side by side, such as Figure 15.1 (identical to Figure 12.8). Any components that are present in one RBD but absent in the other, or other differences in the RBDs, should be explained. The architecture of the application's cloud deployment may actually be quite different—especially if technology components as-a-Service and other cloud centric architectures are used. Nevertheless, a side-by-side comparison of traditional and cloud deployment can be useful when analyzing service risks, setting performance targets and so on.

If PaaS technology components replace traditional components, then that will be highlighted in the side-by-side analysis, like how common chassis module components

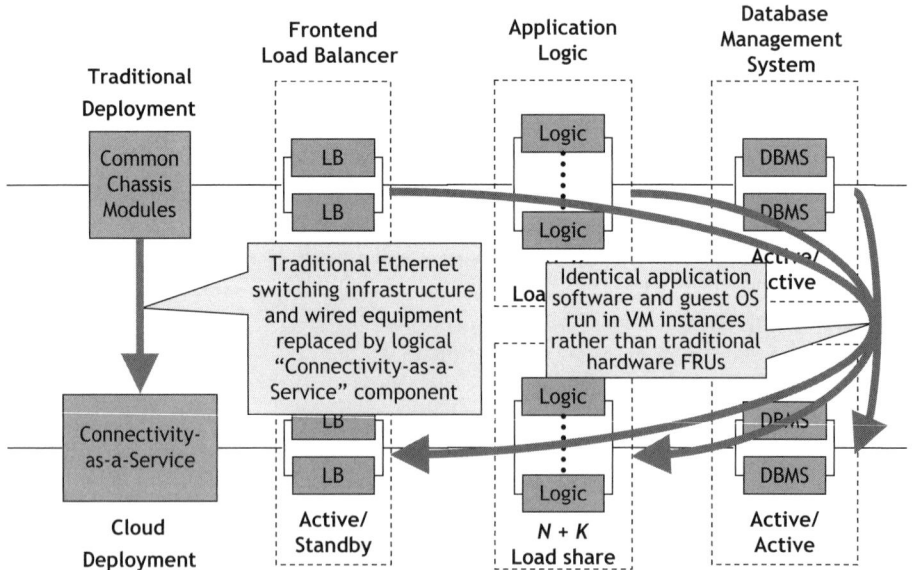

Figure 15.1. Sample Side-by-Side Reliability Block Diagrams.

in traditional deployment are logically replaced by "Connectivity-as-a-Service" in cloud deployment in Figure 15.1. If there is a difference in the functionality supported in cloud deployment compared with traditional deployment (e.g., because a more functional PaaS technology component is used in cloud deployment compared to the native technology component), then this can also be highlighted.

As architecture-based service availability models generally align with reliability block diagrams, carrying side-by-side RBD analysis through to side-by-side architecture based service availability (i.e., downtime) modeling should be straightforward. Given side-by-side service availability (i.e., downtime) predictions from an architecture-based mathematical model, one can construct side-by-side downtime targets and budgets for each application module and technology component. Downtime budgets for individual technology components (e.g., database-as-a-service, discussed in Section 12.3.2, "Technology Components") can be useful for setting requirements when selecting a PaaS supplier.

15.2   IAAS IMPAIRMENT EFFECTS ANALYSIS

The fundamental service quality question that application teams and decision makers should be concerned with is: is it feasible and likely that the application will consistently meet its service quality requirements in production deployment on cloud infrastructure? Infrastructure-as-a-Service impairment effects analysis (IIEA) identifies qualitative risks to achieving the application's service quality requirements. This knowledge enables application teams and decision makers to take actions to mitigate identified risks. Logically, the analysis is a matrix with the application's key service quality indicators (per Section 2.5, "Application Service Quality") arranged as rows, virtualized infrastructure impairments (per Chapter 4 "Virtualized Infrastructure Impairments") arranged as columns, and cells of the table indicating the application's sensitivity. Having identified the most sensitive points in the design, architects can focus on both application mitigations (e.g., refining redundancy arrangements and retransmission/ retry strategies) and infrastructure mitigations (e.g., IaaS supplier evaluations, IaaS performance monitoring, and aggressive IaaS supplier management).

IIEA methodology has the following steps:

1. *Enumerate Applicable Application Service Quality Metrics.* In this step, one should enumerate the exact service quality metrics that are applicable to the target application. In many cases, some or all of these metrics will directly or indirectly be included in the application service provider's own quality performance measurements, perhaps even including the service performance measurements that impact bonus payments for management and staff. These measurements may also appear in the application service provider's RFPs with suppliers and service-level agreements (SLAs) with their customers. Section 2.5, "Application Service Quality," gives general service quality measurements:
   - Service Availability (Section 2.5.1)
   - Service Latency (Section 2.5.2)

- Service Reliability (Section 2.5.3)
- Service Accessibility (Section 2.5.4)
- Service Retainability (Section 2.5.5)
- Service Throughput (Section 2.5.6)
- Service Timestamp Accuracy (Section 2.5.7).

    Note that classes of applications and industries often have tailored service quality measurements that use or modify one or more of the earlier-mentioned service quality measurements. For example, the telecommunications industry uses failed call attempts as the primary service accessibility metric and dropped calls as the primary service retainability metric.

2. *Characterize Sensitivity of Virtualized Infrastructure Impairments on Application's Service Quality Metrics.* Individually consider the likely impact to each application service measurement from step 1 on the virtualized infrastructure impairments from Chapter 4, "Virtualized Infrastructure Impairments":
   - Virtual Machine Failure (Section 4.1.3)
   - Nondelivery of Configured VM Capacity (Section 4.3)
   - Degraded Delivery of Configured VM Capacity (Section 4.4)
   - Excess Tail Latency on Resource Delivery (Section 4.5)
   - Clock Event Jitter (Section 4.6)
   - Clock Drift (Section 4.7)
   - Failed or Slow Allocation and Startup of VM Instances (Section 4.8).

       Operationally, one can consider the impact of each virtualized infrastructure impairment on each type of virtual machine instance used by the application (e.g., frontend component, backend component, and management and control component). While some virtualized infrastructure impairments may have negligible impacts (e.g., clock drift is unimportant for application components that do not use absolute timestamps), other impairments (e.g., nondelivery of configured VM capacity) may have complex impacts on application service quality. Note that at this step, one focuses on describing the *qualitative* user service impact; ranking and classifying application service impacts is the next step.

3. *Summarize the Infrastructure Impairment Impacts.* The result of step 2 is a rich description of expected user service impact resulting from IaaS service impairments. Note that these impacts may be nonlinear, such as when nondelivery of VM capacity (aka stall) events are so long that client retry mechanisms timeout and present a failure indication to the client. Service vulnerability estimates the likelihood that the application's target service quality requirement will not consistently be met when the target infrastructure is delivering minimally acceptable service (i.e., maximum acceptable infrastructure impairment). High vulnerability means that the application's service quality requirement is unlikely to be met when the infrastructure is impaired. To enable application teams and decision makers to comprehend the risk and prioritize corrective actions from the complex results of step 2, the impacts can be categorized via a color coded heat map table with application service metrics as rows, virtualized infrastructure impairments as columns, and cells colored according to simplified risks:

- *High Risk (Red).* Application service quality metric is ***highly vulnerable*** to this IaaS service impairments
- *Medium Risk (Yellow).* Application service quality metric is ***somewhat vulnerable*** to this IaaS service impairments
- *Low Risk (Green).* Application service quality metric is ***not vulnerable*** to this IaaS service impairment

4. *Detection at Scale.* Verify that mechanisms exist so that if these impairments impact a single VM instance when the application is scaled out to the maximum configuration then the faulty VM instance can be promptly identified.

5. *Recommend Mitigations.* Specific actions to drive all of the high risk (highly vulnerable) and medium risk (somewhat vulnerable) to low risk (not vulnerable) should be offered for project teams and decision makers to consider. Project teams are likely to create a feature plan that maps each of the recommended actions into an appropriate application release.

Note that application test teams should use the IIEA as input when planning application service quality, reliability, and latency testing cases by focusing test cases around the most vulnerable infrastructure impairments (i.e., high risk/red and medium risk/yellow cells from step 3).

15.3 PAAS FAILURE EFFECTS ANALYSIS

In addition to leveraging virtual machine Infrastructure-as-a-Service, cloud-based applications may also leverage Platform-as-a-Service technology components like load balancers, databases, security appliances, and so on. Just as Section 15.2, "IaaS Impairment Effects Analysis," considered the application service impact of IaaS failures or impairments, this section considers the application service impact of PaaS technology component failures. Platform-as-a-Service failure effects analysis (PFEA) has the following steps:

1. *Enumerate the PaaS Technology Components Used by the Application.* All of the PaaS technology components used by the application that are directly or indirectly in the user service delivery path should be enumerated.

2. *Describe How the Application Will Detect PaaS Technology Component Failure or Unavailability.* Like any other software object, technology components can fail slowly and silently, as well as fast and clean, so the application should be prepared to detect and mitigate a range of technology component failures.

3. *Characterize Impact of Technology Component Unavailability.* What is the user service impact of each PaaS technology component's unavailability? For example, if the particular component is unavailable for about 5 minutes per year (as one would expect with a "five 9s" technology component), then is user service unavailable for that time also?

4. *Characterize Impact of Technology Component Failover.* While technology components offered by PaaS service providers are likely to be highly available, technology component instances will inevitably fail and recover service. What is the likely user service impact of technology component failure followed by prompt, successful recovery by the technology component?

5. *Characterize Impact of Technology Component Software Release Management and Planned Maintenance.* Software components inevitably need to be patched, updated, and upgraded, and service providers may not notify cloud consumers of every planned maintenance action of every technology component. What is the likely application user service impact of planned maintenance actions of this technology component?

6. *Summarize the Technology Component Failure Effects Analysis.* PFEA is summarized as a table with: one technology component per row; one column for technology component failover and another column for technology component planned maintenance; cell characterizing the application service impact. Essentially, the same three risk classifications can be used for PFEA as for IIEA:
   • *High Risk (Red).* Application service quality metric is **highly impacted by** failure of this PaaS technology component
   • *Medium Risk (Yellow).* Application service quality metric is **somewhat impacted by** failure of this PaaS technology component
   • *Low Risk (Green).* Application service quality metric is **not impacted by** failure of this PaaS technology component

7. *Recommend Mitigations.* Specific actions to drive all of the high risk (highly impacted) and medium risk (somewhat impacted) to low risk (not impacted) items should be offered for decision makers and project teams to consider.

15.4 WORKLOAD DISTRIBUTION ANALYSIS

As discussed in Chapter 6, "Load Distribution and Balancing," load distribution becomes more complex with cloud, and it is very important that load distribution functions are robust and positively contribute to the service quality of the application. Workload distribution analysis entails a review of the load balancing mechanisms and policies to assure they are meeting the application's expectations. Workload distribution analysis for proxy load balancers used by an application should complete the following analyses:

   • Service Quality Analysis (Section 15.4.1)
   • Overload Control Analysis (Section 15.4.2).

If analysis indicates that it is not feasible or likely to achieve the application's workload distribution expectations or the likely user service impact is deemed unacceptable, then the application's architecture and/or load balancing policies can be reworked and the analysis repeated until results are satisfactory.

15.4.1   Service Quality Analysis

Service quality analysis will involve the following steps:

1. Describe how the proxy load balancer supports **service availability and service accessibility**:
   - How does the load balancer monitor and detect failures of application component instances?
   - How does the load balancer rebalance the workload based on failures?
   - How long is the interval of fault detection and traffic redistribution?
   - Is failure detection and traffic redistribution faster than the minimum chargeable outage duration so that no chargeable outage event occurs on component failure?
   - Does the load balancer buffer or resend messages based on server instance availability?
2. Describe how the proxy load balancer supports **service latency**:
   - What data does the proxy load balancer collect on application component instance service latency?
   - How does the load balancer use performance data in load distribution decisions to manage user service latency?
3. Describe how the proxy load balancer supports **service reliability**:
   - How does the proxy load balancer monitor and detect service reliability performance of application component instances?
   - How does the proxy load balancer alter load distribution based on service reliability performance data?
   - How quickly does the load balancer modify load distribution?
4. Describe how the proxy load balancer supports **service retainability**:
   - How are requests redirected if the service component that was previously handling a session fails before the session has completed?
5. Assess whether the described methods and techniques will ensure compliance with the application's user service quality requirements. If the analysis indicates that compliance to the requirements is not likely to be met, then recommend mitigations to address the gaps.

15.4.2   Overload Control Analysis

To analyze the service quality risks of managing overloaded application instances, one should:

- Describe how the load proxy load balancer detects overload of individual application server components.
- Describe how the load distribution policy changes based on individual server component overload of failure.
- Describe how the load balancer determines whether individual application server component instance overload events have cleared or resulted in the instantiation

of a new application server component to replace the failed overloaded component.

- Describe what actions the load balancer takes to mitigate overload of most or all of a server component pool
- Describe how the load balancer determines that overload of a pool of components has cleared.

Any gaps in functionality identified during the assessment and overload testing should be addressed through work items or new features and roadmapped appropriately to meet product service requirements.

15.5 ANTI-AFFINITY ANALYSIS

To boost performance, IaaS providers often try to consolidate all of an application's VM instances onto the same virtualized host, rack or row of equipment to minimize latency between the application's interworking components and minimize bandwidth utilization within the cloud data center. The IaaS provider may even try to consolidate all of an application's virtual machine instances onto a single chassis or a single virtual machine server, which makes that virtual machine server a single point of failure that impacts total application service capacity.

To prevent IaaS providers from collocating VMs so aggressively that an application's high availability mechanisms are defeated by putting them into the same failure group (e.g., active and standby components running on the same virtual machine server), anti-affinity rules (see Section 7.2.3, "Affinity and Anti-Affinity Considerations") are used to instruct the IaaS which virtual machines should not be put into the same failure group. The purpose of an anti-affinity analysis is to assure that the application is likely to promptly recover service following infrastructure failures. The anti-affinity analysis steps are:

1. *Construct a Reliability Block Diagram (RBD) of Application Virtual Machine Instances.* Each block on the RBD maps to a type of application virtual machine instance.

2. *Determine the Minimum Number of Virtual Machine Server Hosts that Can Meet the Application's Anti-affinity Rules.* Logically, start from the assumption that all of the application's VM instances will be collocated on a single hypothetical, infinitely large VM server, and then apply the anti-affinity rules such that the smallest number of VM instances are moved from the hypothetical VM server onto the smallest number of alternate VM server hosts.

3. *Pick Colors or Other Identifiers for the Minimum Number of Virtual Machine Servers from Step 2.* For example, if the minimum number of VM server hosts expected to support the smallest application configuration while meeting anti-affinity rules is three, then one can use red, blue, and green.

4. *Color RBD Blocks of Step 1 Using Colors of Step 3 ONLY for Blocks Explicitly Covered by Specified Anti-affinity Rules.* Blocks (i.e., VM instances) not explic-

itly covered by specified anti-affinity rules are NOT colored. If the assumed minimum number of VM server hosts from step 2 is incorrect, then define additional colors.

5. Assume that all uncolored VM instances are then assigned to one of the color groups (e.g., red), and consider:
   A. Is the user service impact of that color group failure (e.g., red) acceptable (i.e., does not violate the application's service quality requirements)?
   B. Is the user service impact of failure of one of the alternate color groups (e.g., blue) acceptable?
   C. Will user service recover automatically within the application's maximum acceptable service recovery time following (individual) failure of each color's VM server host?

6. Repeat step 5 with uncolored VM instances all assigned to other color groups.

7. *Recommend Mitigations.* If the footprint of failure from steps 5 and 6 is too great, then rework anti-affinity rules. If automatic application recovery is expected to take too long for any permitted VM consolidation arrangement in step 4 or step 5, then refine anti-affinity rules, make application recovery mechanisms more robust, or both. Repeat analysis as necessary. Note that a chaos monkey can be used to extend the recovery time in order to determine the impact of the delay on service.

As complex anti-affinity rules are harder to specify correctly, more challenging for cloud service providers to implement, and may overconstrain application deployment, one should parsimoniously apply anti-affinity rules. Note that application's anti-affinity rules are designed to mitigate likely single (VM server host) point failures, and more extreme or multipoint failure scenarios will be mitigated via disaster recovery mechanisms (e.g., failing over service to one or more alternate application instances in different availability zones or data centers). Thus, application architects may plan to activate disaster recovery plans if a VM server hosting too many application VM instances fails.

15.6 ELASTICITY ANALYSIS

Rapid elasticity of cloud-based applications introduces new service risks that should be carefully analyzed and managed in the architecture and design phases. Two general elasticity analyses are completed:

- *Online Service Capacity Elasticity Analysis* begins by cataloging all of the application's supported elastic service capacity growth actions (Section 15.6.1, "Service Capacity Growth Scenarios"). The service risk of each of the growth actions will be considered in Section 15.6.2, "Service Capacity Growth Action Analysis." Risks associated with capacity degrowth are considered in Section 15.6.3, "Service Capacity Degrowth Action Analysis."
- *Storage Capacity Elasticity Analysis* begins by cataloging all of the application's supported storage capacity growth actions (Section 15.6.4, "Storage Capacity

Growth Scenarios"). Then the service risk of each cataloged action will be considered separately for (1) each supported storage capacity growth action (Section 15.6.5, "Online Storage Capacity Growth Action Analysis") and for each supported storage capacity degrowth action (Section 15.6.6, "Online Storage Capacity Degrowth Action Analysis").

If analysis indicates that it is neither feasible nor likely to achieve the application's elasticity expectations or requirements (see Section 13.8, "Elasticity Requirements") or if the likely user service impact is deemed unacceptable, then the application's design can be reworked and the analysis repeated until results are satisfactory. Results of this analysis should be used as input when planning elasticity test cases for the application (Section 16.4.5, "Application Elasticity Testing").

15.6.1   Service Capacity Growth Scenarios

Enumerate the supported capacity growth strategies of the application's elasticity architecture:

1. If **horizontal growth** of service capacity is supported, then:
   - What are the units of horizontal capacity growth, such as pairs of VM instances?
   - What is the minimum horizontal scale down configuration and service capacity?
   - What is the maximum horizontal scale up configuration and service capacity?
2. If **vertical growth** is of service capacity supported, then
   - What are the units of vertical service capacity growth?
   - What is the minimum vertical scale down?
   - What is the maximum vertical scale up?
3. Regarding **outgrowth** of service capacity:
   - If outgrowth is supported by creating an independent application instance, then how are the independent application instances federated?
   - If outgrowth is supported by integrating resources with a preexisting application instance, then how does that integration work?

15.6.2   Service Capacity Growth Action Analysis

Having identified the specific growth actions for online service capacity supported by the application, one should methodically consider the following for each supported action:

1. *Provisioning Interval Analysis.* Construct a timeline to estimate the likely provisioning interval for the online elastic capacity growth action, including a soak interval to run test traffic.
2. *Decoupling from Overload Control Mechanisms.* Verify that the application's overload control mechanisms will not impact elastic growth actions, for example,

elasticity-related actions will not fail within the application instance TOO BUSY errors or other overload control mechanisms.

3. *Robust Operation on Degraded Infrastructure Platform.* Verify that the elastic growth operation is robust and relatively insensitive to the degraded performance of virtualized infrastructure resources and other application components that may be heavily loaded while the elastic growth action is executing.

4. *Robust Integration with Overload Control Triggers.* Verify that overload control triggers are promptly reevaluated when additional service capacity comes online so that traffic is not rejected by congestion control mechanisms after additional application capacity has been brought online.

5. *Concurrency Control.* Verify that robust concurrency control mechanisms are implemented so that growth or degrowth requests posted before a growth action has completed will not compromise the pending elastic growth operation and that elasticity management functions consider the expected capacity after that change completes so capacity doesn't materially overshoot offered load.

6. *Rainy Day Analysis.* Verify that if any of the elasticity failure scenarios of Section 8.11, "Elasticity Failure Scenarios," occur, then the application will continue to operate (presumably activating overload controls, as necessary) at the current capacity indefinitely.

15.6.3   Service Capacity Degrowth Action Analysis

To analyze the service quality risks of elastic capacity degrowth of each supported action, one should do the following:

1. Describe the degrowth procedure, including the technique for draining user traffic from the resources to be released.

2. Characterize the service impact of gracefully draining traffic served by the targeted resource.

3. Describe the procedure to forcibly drain user traffic from the targeted resource if graceful drainage is not fast enough and characterize the user service impact of forcibly draining traffic.

4. Estimate the likely and worst case release interval.

5. Explain how a service capacity growth action that is requested while a release action is pending will be served.

Any supported elastic growth actions that are not complemented by matching elastic degrowth actions should be highlighted, and a brief explanation for why the elastic degrowth action is not supported should be given.

15.6.4   Storage Capacity Growth Scenarios

In addition to conducting an analysis of elasticity of online application capacity, architects should also consider elasticity of all persistent storage for the application. Architects should classify all persistent application data into one of three categories:

- *Online Elastic Storage.* These data stores can be elastically grown with the application instance online and delivering service to end users.
- *Offline Reconfigurable Storage.* The size of these data stores can be reconfigured (e.g., grown) via an offline maintenance action, such as restarting or reinstalling the application instance. Identify the applicable MOP and tool(s), and summarize the procedures. The user service impact of these offline elasticity options should be summarized (e.g., same service impact as installing a new software release).
- *Inelastic Storage.* The size of this data store cannot be changed in the field. The practical constraints (and mitigations) of inelastic storage allocations should be clearly explained, such as requiring another application instance to be created. Identify the most likely (perhaps extreme) scenario that would exhaust this inelastic resource, and what the user visible service impact of that resource exhaustion would be.

15.6.5   Online Storage Capacity Growth Action Analysis

For each supported online elastic storage growth action, one should:

1. Characterize the growth strategy as horizontal, vertical, or outgrowth.
2. Give the unit(s) of storage growth (e.g., disk volume), as well as the minimum scale down and maximum scale up limits.
3. Describe the storage growth procedure.
4. Estimate the typical provisioning interval.
5. Summarize the user service impact on successful storage growth actions.
6. If storage capacity growth actions can be triggered automatically, then what conditions and policies are likely to trigger the action?
7. Explain detection and recovery strategies for failures during elastic storage growth.

15.6.6   Online Storage Capacity Degrowth Action Analysis

For each online elastic storage growth scenario identified, one should explain if a symmetric degrowth action is supported. If a symmetric degrowth action is not supported, then one should explain why not. For supported online degrowth actions, one should:

1. Explain the storage capacity degrowth procedure.
2. Estimate the typical case release interval.
3. If storage capacity degrowth actions are expected to be triggered automatically, then what conditions and policies are likely to trigger the action.
4. Explain how an elastic storage capacity growth action triggered during a release interval will be handled.

15.7 RELEASE MANAGEMENT IMPACT EFFECTS ANALYSIS

For applications that support online release management actions, it is essential to analyze and minimize the service impact to users who are online when the patch, update, upgrade, or retrofit action is executed.

15.7.1 Service Availability Impact

In order to assess the impact of release management actions on service availability:

1. *Describe the procedures defined for software upgrade*, including the time intervals required to accomplish each task. How long are the intervals in which service is not available to the clients (e.g., during the redirecting of traffic from old version to new version) for a successful software upgrade? Is a health check done to make sure there are sufficient resources available for the new release instances?
2. *Describe the procedures defined for backing out or rolling back a software release*, including database schema and content rollback. How long are the intervals in which service is not available to the clients (e.g., during the redirecting of traffic from new version to old version) for a successful backout/rollback?

15.7.2 Server Reliability Impact

Verify that data records and other resources will be fully available so that no service requests are failed due to "resource temporarily unavailable" conditions. If any requests cannot be successfully served at any point in the release management process, then document the exact nature and duration of service impact.

15.7.3 Service Accessibility Impact

If service will not be continuously accessible to all users throughout the entire release management process, then characterize the likely duration and nature of that service inaccessibility.

15.7.4 Service Retainability Impact

If any preexisting user sessions may be disrupted or dropped during the release management process, then characterize the likely service impact. Verify that the draining process effectively retains user sessions until they are officially terminated.

15.7.5 Service Throughput Impact

Data evolution often puts a heavy load onto application databases, and this additional workload may impact service throughput. Analyze if data evolution or any other aspect of release management is likely to impact service throughput and characterize the nature and duration of that impact.

15.8   RECOVERY POINT OBJECTIVE ANALYSIS

Recovery point objective (RPO) analysis considers: how stale might the recovered data be or what is the maximum window of data loss? For example, how many seconds, minutes, hours, or days of user provisioning actions, inventory changes, sales, or other transactions might be lost on disaster recovery?

As shown in Figure 15.2, the worst case recovery scenario is when a catastrophic failure occurs the instant before a periodic backup completes, so one must recover to the last fully completed backup, which is the sum of:

    a. the periodic backup interval ($T_{Periodic}$), such as 24 hours for daily backups plus up to the time required to successfully execute

    b. the time to execute a backup to a geographically distant site ($T_{Archive}$).

The best case RPO (shown in Figure 15.3) is when the catastrophic event occurs the instant after the archive to a geographically distant site completes.

Methodical RPO analysis includes the following steps:

    1. *Enumerate all persistent data repositories that are archived* and have been periodically updated to a geographically distant data center and will be restored as part of disaster recovery procedures, such as:
        • Inventory database
        • Sales database
        • Configuration database

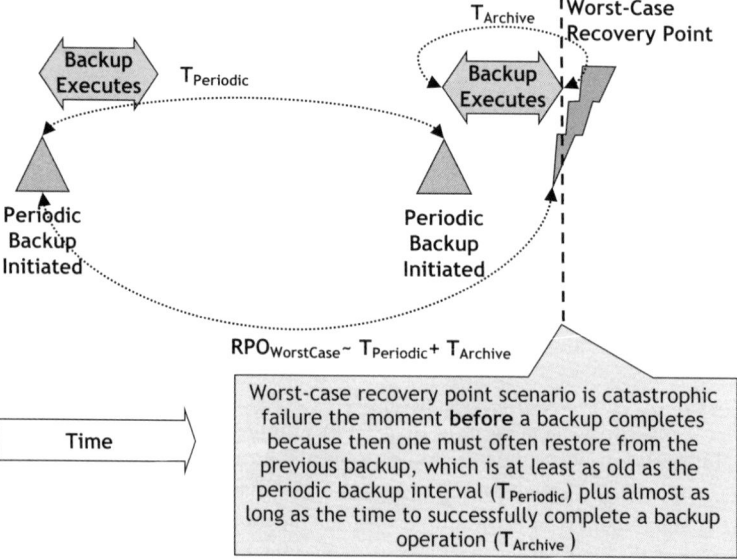

Figure 15.2. Worst-Case Recovery Point Scenario.

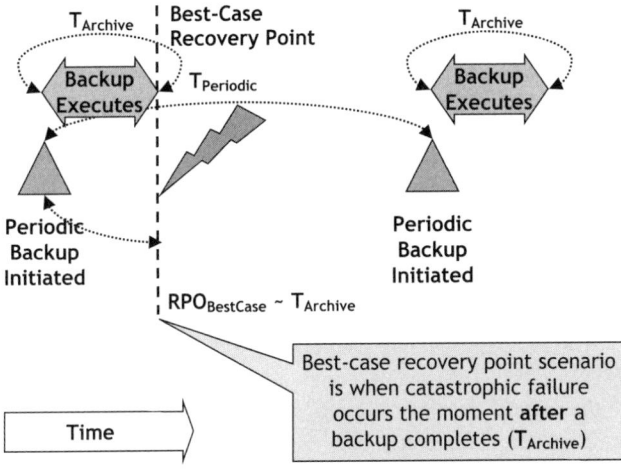

Figure 15.3. Best-Case Recovery Point Scenario.

- Security logs
- Event logs.

2. *Enumerate volatile and persistent data classes and repositories that are NOT archived* to geographically distant data centers and hence will be lost on disaster recovery, such as:
   - Active user sessions, registrations, and all pending and previous transactions associated with those active sessions
   - Performance management data.

3. *Summarize user and overall visible impact of recovering service when nonarchived data is abruptly lost* (e.g., following unexpected disaster event), such as:
   - Active user sessions are abruptly terminated, and when users recover service to DR site, there is no trace of anything that occurred during the abruptly terminated session.
   - All performance management data not pushed to service assurance product is permanently lost.

4. *Summarize visible and overall impact of recovering archived data that are "RPO" time old.* Explain the practical impact of losing "RPO" seconds/minutes/ hours/days of data changes since the last backup for each of the persistent data repositories that are archived, such as:
   - All inventory changes less than RPO minutes old are completely lost when inventory database is recovered.
   - All sales less than RPO minutes old are completely lost when sales database is recovered.
   - All configuration changes less than RPO minutes old are completely lost when the configuration database is recovered.

- All security events less than RPO minutes are completely lost when security log is recovered.
- All alarm events less than RPO minutes are completely lost when event log is recovered.
  For each, indicate whether the data have also been sent to an OSS or another component where it can be recovered.

5. *Give the default (or recommended) periodic backup interval ($T_{Periodic}$) for each persistent data store* that is archived and restored as part of disaster recovery action, such as:
   - Periodic backups (i.e., $T_{Periodic}$ = 4 hours) of persistent data is recommended for: inventory database, sales database, configuration database, security logs, and event logs.

6. *Estimate the typical time to complete a periodic backup ($T_{Archive}$) to a geographically distant data center,* such as:
   - Daily backups of inventory database, sales database, configuration database, security logs, and event logs to geographically distant recovery site typically complete in 2 hours (i.e., $T_{Archive}$ ~2 hours)

7. *Estimate the worst case time to complete a periodic database backup* ($T_{Archive}$).

8. *Summarize the likely range of RPO values from* $T_{Periodic}$ *to* $T_{Periodic}$ + $T_{Archive}$, such as:
   - Actual recovery points are likely to be between 2 hours ($T_{Archive}$ ~2 hours) and 26 hours ($T_{Periodic}$ of 24 hours plus $T_{Archive}$ ~2 hours).

15.9   RECOVERY TIME OBJECTIVE ANALYSIS

Recovery time objective (RTO) analysis estimates the actual recovery time if a disaster occurs when the system is running at nominally full capacity by summing the times required to complete all applicable recovery activities.

1. *Disaster Detection Time.* For automatically activated disaster recovery mechanisms, time must be included for some offsite system to deem that a catastrophic failure has occurred and activate the disaster recovery mechanism. For manually activated disaster recovery plans, time to make the decision to formally declare a disaster and activate the disaster recovery plan should be included in the recovery time estimate.

2. *Select Disaster Recovery Site(s).* Some disaster recovery architectures have all impacted workload served by a single recovery site; other disaster recovery architectures distribute the impacted workload across two or more recovery sites. If any aspects of this site selection decision are made on the fly, then time must be allocated to gather necessary data, select disaster recovery site(s), and communicate that selection to all applicable sites and systems. Time to notify the selected disaster recovery site, support personnel, and others involved in recovery actions are included in this time.

3. *Allocate and Bring Online Sufficient Virtualized Resources to Serve Impacted Workload at Recovery Site(s).* If sufficient spare capacity was not previously allocated and maintained online and "hot" at the recovery site to serve the impacted workload redirected to the recovery site, then additional virtual machines, networking, storage, and other infrastructure resources must be allocated, configured, and activated.

4. *Locate and Restore Application Data from the Last Recovery Point.* Data saved from the impacted site must be restored and/or resynchronized to the application instance(s) that will recover the impacted workload. Depending on the data backup/replication strategy, it may be necessary to import one or more database backups and then apply a series of incremental updates to rebuild a usable image of the application data at the last recovery point. If archived data are stored at a location other than the recovery site, then surging additional WAN capacity at both the archive site and the recovery site might shorten time required to retrieve archived data. Depending on the size of the backup data, the number of different sets of data, and where that backup data are stored (e.g., collocated with recovery application instance or geographically separated), significant time could be required reading data back from persistent storage, compressing it for transmission, transmitting data across wide area networks, and decompressing it at the recovery site.

5. *Recovering Sufficient User Service Capacity.* Well-written RTO requirements often explicitly specify a percentage of impacted users for whom service has become available before a disaster recovery action is deemed complete. Authenticated and session-oriented applications may experience unusually high logon volume, as all impacted clients automatically attempt to restore service quickly. This simultaneous spike in logon traffic may be far higher than the normal logon and authentication workload that the application serves. After all, during a normal day, users are likely to attempt to access the system across a range of hours (e.g., 7:30–9:30 a.m. on weekdays for business systems), but a disaster event will impact all users served by the impacted site to be impacted simultaneously, and thus all users are likely to attempt to initiate recovery actions more or less simultaneously when the recovery site comes online. Nearly simultaneous recovery by all impacted clients is likely to push the recovery application instance into overload, so congestion control mechanisms or backoff algorithms are likely to activate to enable impacted users to be authenticated and served in an orderly fashion. Depending on the online capacity of the recovery application instance, the efficiency of the applications congestion control mechanisms and the configuration of clients' retry mechanisms, it could take tens of minutes or longer for the stipulated percentage of impacted users to be fully restored to service.

Notes:

a. Depending on the disaster recovery architecture and readiness of the standby site, some activities may be omitted from consideration.

16

TESTING CONSIDERATIONS

Deploying applications on cloud infrastructure adds service quality risks due to impairments in service delivered by virtualized infrastructure (see Chapter 4, "Virtualized Infrastructure Impairments") and from cloud operational characteristics such as rapid elasticity (see Chapter 3, "Cloud Model"). This chapter considers the incremental testing appropriate to assure that application service quality meets expectations when deployed on cloud infrastructure. This chapter begins by framing the context of this testing, then discusses testing strategy, simulating virtualized infrastructure impairments and test planning.

16.1 CONTEXT FOR TESTING

Service quality testing of applications is what ISO 9000 would consider a qualification process "*to demonstrate the ability to fulfill specified requirements*" [ISO_9000]. Verification means "*confirmation, through the provision of objective evidence that specified requirements have been fulfilled*" [ISO_9000] and answers the question "***have we built the system right***?" Validation means "*confirmation, through the provision of objective evidence, that the requirements for a specific intended use or application have been*

Service Quality of Cloud-Based Applications, First Edition. Eric Bauer and Randee Adams.
© 2014 The Institute of Electrical and Electronics Engineers, Inc. Published 2014 by John Wiley & Sons, Inc.

fulfilled" [ISO_9000] and answers the question "***Have we built the right system?***" This chapter focuses on verification that the service quality requirements (see Chapter 13) are properly implemented; validation that the "right" system has been developed is not considered in this work.

These confirmations are typically done via

- *Test*, meaning "*determination of one or more characteristics according to a procedure*" [ISO_9000].
- *Inspection*, meaning "*conformity evaluation by observation and judgment accompanied as appropriate by measurement, testing or gauging*" [ISO_9000].
- *Review*, meaning "*activity undertaken to determine the suitability, adequacy and effectiveness of the subject matter to achieve established objectives*" [ISO_9000].

While resource usage measured by an application may be an important factor that directly impacts the cloud consumer's operational expenditure (OPEX), characterizing the application's resource usage is not considered in this chapter.

16.2 TEST STRATEGY

Cloud computing explicitly decouples application software from the underlying infrastructure hardware because the cloud service provider that operates and maintains the cloud infrastructure is often organizationally separate from the cloud consumer who operates the application software. The application virtual machine (VM) instances that are coresident on VM servers and share storage arrays and network infrastructure can vary, and the application's specific configuration will change over time as capacity is elastically grown and shrunk, and so on. Thus, it is unrealistic to expect that application teams can test service quality on the "exact" deployment architecture because neither the application supplier nor the cloud consumer has strict control over the actual placement of application components across the cloud service provider's physical infrastructure, and that exact configuration will likely change over time. As a result, application suppliers must design applications to be tolerant of the variations that will be experienced when the application is deployed across different cloud service providers' infrastructures, where both the physical configuration and the quality of virtualized resources available to the application's VM instances will vary across time as overall data center workloads shift and cloud service provider operations and maintenance actions are executed. This configuration variability leads one to consider several strategy topics when framing service quality test plans:

- Selection of cloud platform to use as a test bed (Section 16.2.1, "Cloud Test Bed")
- How much cloud test bed capacity should be used for testing (Section 16.2.2, "Application Capacity under Test")
- How many transactions should be executed to adequately characterize service quality and latency (Section 16.2.3, "Statistical Confidence")

- How to measure service disruption time (Section 16.2.4, "Service Disruption Time").

16.2.1 Cloud Test Bed

The fundamental test strategy question when considering verification of a cloud-based application is if the application will be verified on the target production cloud infrastructure or on some reference or convenient (e.g., most cost effective) cloud infrastructure. If an application is developed to execute on a single cloud service provider's infrastructure, then it makes sense to test the application on that cloud service provider's infrastructure. However, if an application will be deployed onto many cloud service providers' infrastructures, then it may make sense to either pick a "reference" cloud environment to test on or to simply pick the most cost-effective cloud infrastructure to test on. This flexibility is an advantage of cloud testing over traditional configurations that required verification of the specific deployment environment. Business considerations may suggest a hybrid testing arrangement in which the majority of testing is completed on a reference or cloud of convenience, and a subset of the test campaign (e.g., verifying service quality performance) is repeated on specific customers' target cloud infrastructures. While the choice of clouds may have little impact on ordinary functional testing, the results of service quality testing may be highly influenced by the normal behavior and typical impairments of the specific cloud infrastructure. Thus, it may be difficult to accurately extrapolate the likely application service quality characteristics of execution on clouds other than the one actually tested on. To manage this risk of varying application performance across different clouds, one should plan to test with the simulated infrastructure impairments that the application is most sensitive to. As different hypervisors have different operational characteristics, at least some testing should be executed on different hypervisors that are supported by the application software.

As part of continuous delivery, a canary release version of the software can be instantiated and made active for a small number of users in order to test service quality in a live environment. Data gathered from this can be used to determine whether changes need to be made to the application or whether the release is stable enough to increase the traffic load directed to that version.

16.2.2 Application Capacity under Test

Testing of traditional applications was often limited by capital constraints because the development organization had only finite capital for test bed hardware, software licenses, and user load generating capacity. Thus, the maximum workload a test team could place on a system under test was often practically constrained by their capital budget. Just as cloud computing morphs capital expenditure (CAPEX) into OPEX for cloud consumers, test organizations can also reengineer their operations to potentially shift from being CAPEX constrained to being OPEX constrained. Rather than having to purchase infrastructure to host application configurations under test and user load simulators, test organizations can configure their test beds (including user load simulators) on public clouds, which potentially have sufficient infrastructure resource capacity to create the largest supported application configuration and simulate an arbitrarily large user workload. However, as this cloud capacity is likely to have usage based pricing, the OPEX per test run becomes much more tangible, so a test run with 50,000 simulated users is likely to have a somewhat higher cost than a test run with 5000 simulated users, and an endurance test run for several days with perhaps a billion transactions has a higher cost than a test run for a few hours with perhaps millions of transactions.

More interestingly, this flexibility can potentially allow testers to reengineer test activities so that massive cloud test bed infrastructure resources are brought online to shorten test execution time. With sufficient test automation of user workload and cloud capacity, one can shorten the time required to execute an application's test campaign by executing many test plans in parallel on independent cloud test beds simultaneously. While it may be impractical to actually execute all test plans in parallel because a handful of bugs or misconfiguration may cause numerous test cases to fail, and each failed test case requires engineering effort to analyze and determine the root cause, judicious use of parallel test execution (e.g., for daily regression testing) can shorten an application's overall development intervals.

16.2.3 Statistical Confidence

Service reliability, latency, accessibility, retainability, and throughput are fundamentally statistical in nature: thousands, millions, or billions of operations must be completed to verify statistical requirements with confidence. In lieu of applying rigorous mathematical analysis to compute the number of test case iterations required to achieve a quantified statistical confidence level, testers should plan to include enough iteration to produce statistically significant results. Practically, this means including at least an order of magnitude more iteration than are nominally necessary to successfully meet the requirement with a single failure, so if the requirement is for no more than 1 in 100,000 transactions to fail (10 DPM [defects per million]), then at least 1,000,000 transactions should be executed ($10 \times 100,000$).

16.2.4 Service Disruption Time

As explained in Chapter 5, "Application Redundancy and Cloud Computing," different application architectures, guard timeouts, and maximum retry counts can yield different user service impacts on failure. To accurately characterize the user service impact for high performance sequential, concurrent, and hybrid redundancy architectures, one needs appropriately high resolution test tools.

Figure 16.1 illustrates a conceptual measurement of service disruption latency experienced by client "A" due to a failure of an application "B." Client "A" normally sends requests to "B" to which "B" promptly issues a response. A robustness test case produces a critical failure of some component of "B" that precludes "B" from responding to requests for a period of time ("disruption latency") during which requests 2–6 fail, and finally request 7 succeeds when "B" promptly returns a correct response to client "A"'s request.

Figure 16.2 illustrates how the time between client requests quantizes the resolution of the disruption latency because while service latency can be precisely measured

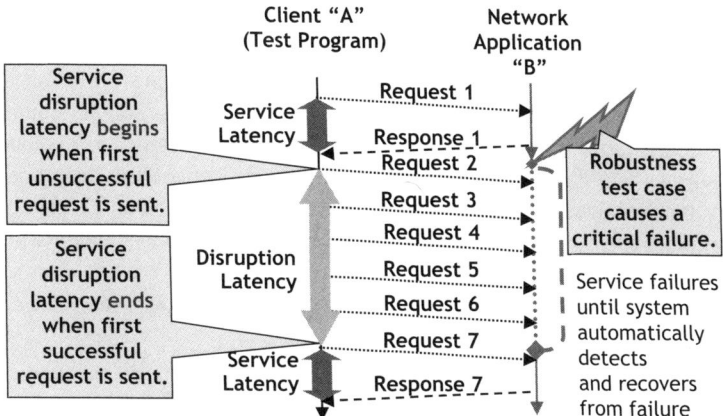

Figure 16.1. Measuring Service Disruption Latency.

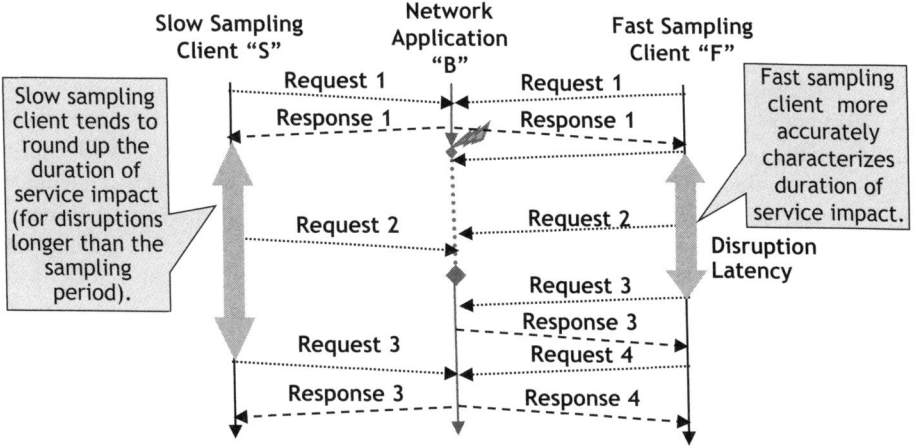

Figure 16.2. Service Disruption Latency for Implicit Failure.

by computing the time between when a request was sent and when the corresponding reply was received, service disruption time often must be probed to estimate when the system stopped successfully serving requests and when it resumed serving requests. Thus, sampling time of service probing should be no more than one-tenth of the maximum acceptable service disruption duration to accurately characterize duration of service impact.

16.3   SIMULATING INFRASTRUCTURE IMPAIRMENTS

As discussed in Chapter 4, "Virtualized Infrastructure Impairments," virtualization introduces a suite of infrastructure impairments that can impact the customer facing service quality delivered by cloud-based applications. Testing of cloud-based applications should verify that application service quality remains acceptable even when the application instance is confronted with degraded infrastructure performance. The ability to simulate specific levels of virtualized infrastructure impairments on demand enables testing to characterize an application's service quality sensitivities to cloud impairments. Section 15.2, "IaaS Impairment Effects Analysis," enables architects and testers to identify the impairments that are likely to be most impactful to service quality, so simulation mechanisms for those impairments in an environment modeled after a production system should be a priority.

Simulating virtualized infrastructure impairments raises two challenges:

1. *Characterizing maximum level of infrastructure impairments*, the application can endure and still deliver acceptable service quality. Sophisticated cloud consumers may have quantitative requirements for maximum allowable infrastructure impairments that they use when selecting cloud service providers, and those same expectations may be appropriate to be used by application suppliers.

2. *Creating tools or procedures to simulate the maximum acceptable level of infrastructure impairments on a cloud test bed*, as described in this section. VM failures can be simulated by suspending or destroying a VM instance. Nondelivery impairments can be simulated by pausing VM instances and reactivating them after the simulated nondelivery interval has elapsed. Slow or failed VM allocation can be simulated by hooking the VM allocation request and either delaying it before passing it to the cloud operations support system (OSS) or returning a simulated failure to the caller. Simulating degraded delivery of configured resource capacity, tail latency degradation, clock event jitter, and clock drift should be feasible with appropriate test tools and procedures.

16.4 TEST PLANNING

An application's test campaign will include test plans to verify acceptable behavior, characteristics, and performance. Best practice is for the service quality test campaign for a cloud-based application to include aspects of most or all of the following test types:

- Service Reliability and Latency (Section 16.4.1)
- Impaired Infrastructure Testing (Section 16.4.2)
- Robustness Testing (Section 16.4.3)
- Endurance/Stability Testing (Section 16.4.4)
- Application Elasticity Testing (Section 16.4.5)
- Upgrade Testing (Section 16.4.6)
- Disaster Recovery Testing (Section 16.4.7)
- Extreme Coresidency Testing (Section 16.4.8).

16.4.1 Service Reliability and Latency Testing

Basic service quality testing verifies that service reliability requirements (Section 13.3) and service latency requirements (Section 13.2) are met when application virtualized infrastructure is delivering typical or nominal performance and the application is running at or below engineered capacity. Concretely, this means that none of the virtualized infrastructure impairments of Chapter 4 are significant. If the test tools are properly instrumented, then service reliability and service latency can be characterized from the same test run(s). The application load generation tool should generate a consistent stream of properly formed transactions, and the responses should be monitored to both check return codes and results, and monitor transaction latency. In addition to recording the count of each request type sent, the test tool should do the following:

- *Explicitly Count and Record Successful (e.g., "200 OK") and Unsuccessful (Anything Else) Responses.* This enables service reliability to be evaluated.
- *Record Service Latency Counts in Enough Measurement "Buckets" to Produce Useful Results.* While two measurement buckets (less than maximum acceptable service latency and greater than maximum acceptable service latency) are minimally sufficient to determine rate of unacceptably slow transactions, it is best to use at least 10 and ideally 20 or more measurement buckets. There should be at least two measurement buckets above the maximum acceptable service latency (one to capture "slightly" longer than maximum acceptable service latency and another to capture significantly longer than maximum acceptable service latency), and the majority of measurement buckets should cover the range of acceptable service latency times. Nonuniform bucket sizes can be used (e.g., smaller buckets around the 50th and 90th percentiles and bigger buckets in the "tail" approaching the maximum acceptable service latency value). Less than 20% of samples should be in any single bucket. The data should be plotted as a statistical distribution for easy analysis.

As discussed in Section 16.2.3, "Statistical Confidence," sufficient iterations of each request type should be sent to characterize performance with reasonable confidence. Test results should be summarized by key function/operation and as follows:

- "Typical" service latency, such as median (50th percentile) or 90th percentile, and a tail latency point, such as the 99.999th (slowest 1 in 100,000). A complementary cumulative distribution figure is best.
- The rate of transactions that are unacceptably slow is reported; generally as per million attempts, as in *"0.3 DPM (too slow)."*
- The overall rate of failed transactions is reported, as in *"3.2 DPM (overall)"*
- Service latency tail is characterized, such as via a complementary cumulative distribution figure.

Service reliability and latency testing should also be performed during the following:

- *Production.* Service reliability, latency, and disruptions should be monitored on live releases to determine how well the application is performing with actual traffic. This is particularly useful for canary releases, as discussed in Section 16.4.11, "Canary Release Testing."
- *Cloud Service Provider's Operations, Administration, Maintenance and Provisioning (OAM&P).* Service reliability, latency, and disruptions should be monitored when likely cloud service provider maintenance actions are executed (e.g., during live migration, provisioning, and growth).

16.4.2 Impaired Infrastructure Testing

Section 15.2, "IaaS Impairment Effects Analysis," qualitatively characterized the expected application service impact of virtualized infrastructure impairments. Impaired infrastructure testing simulates the maximum acceptable infrastructure impairments to verify that user service impact is acceptable. While impairment test cases should focus on the impairments that IaaS impairment effects analysis (IIEA) indicated were highest risk, cases should be included for all classes of impairments to verify that the application is no more sensitive to infrastructure impairments than the analysis indicated. The test plan should identify the tools and techniques to be used to simulate infrastructure impairments (see Section 16.3, "Simulating Infrastructure Impairments").

16.4.3 Robustness Testing

Robustness testing verifies that no single failure event causes service impact greater than the maximum acceptable service disruption period (discussed in Section 13.1, "Service Availability Requirements"). Logically, robustness testing should verify that user service impact of failures is no more severe than what is documented in the application's failure mode effects analysis (FMEA). Robustness testing should also verify that failure of all Platform-as-a-Service (PaaS) technology components used by the application (e.g., load-Balancing-as-a-Service, Database-as-a-Service) are no worse than estimated in the PaaS failure effects analysis (PFEA) (see Section 15.3).

To assure that an acceptably broad robustness testing campaign is planned, the authors suggest that testers consider test cases from each of the following categories. The relevant test cases should be automated and also used as regression tests for validation of software changes as part of the release management activity:

- *VM Instance Failures.* Fail all types of application VM instances individually and simultaneously.
- *Technology Component "as-a-Service" Failures.* Individually fail each PaaS technology component used by the application.
- Noisy neighbor and variable resource latency failures:
  - Bursty VM scheduling (excessive scheduling latency)
  - High IP packet loss
  - Slow disk access
  - Slow database access
  - High clock event jitter.

- Service orchestration errors:
  - VM activation failure
  - VM dead on arrival (DOA)
  - Slow VM startup
  - Slow VM live migration.
- Real-time clock skewing:
  - High clock drift between VMs hosting application component instances
  - Clock time appearing to run backward in some VM instances.
- Application programming errors:
  - Memory leak or exhaustion (including excessive fragmentation)
  - Shared resource conflict
  - Tight or infinite loop
  - Remote execution failures and "hangs," including remote procedure call failures
  - Thread stack or address space corrupted
  - Reference uninitialized or incorrect pointer
  - Logic errors
  - Nonmemory resource leaks
  - Process abort, crash, or hang
  - Thread hang or abort.
- Data errors:
  - File system corruption, including from disorderly disk write on power down
  - Database corruption, including from disorderly disk write on power down
  - Database mismatch between active and standby versions
  - Record corrupted
  - Disk partition or file system full
  - Persistent storage failure or corruption
  - Shared memory corruption (e.g., checksum error)
  - Linked list breakage
  - File not found
  - File corrupted
  - Database upgrade failed.
- Redundancy errors:
  - Failed recovery
  - Failure of application's high availability process(es)
  - Failed VM repair.
- Networking errors:
  - Failure or unreachability of adjacent or supporting network elements
  - Dropped IP packets
  - Corrupted IP packets
  - IP packets out of sequence.
- Application protocol errors:
  - Invalid protocol syntax
  - Invalid protocol semantics

- ○ Unexpected or illegal message sequences
- ○ Out-of-range parameters, including illegal command codes
- ○ Malicious messages.

Netflix has popularized a suite of automated robustness test tools that together are called the Simian Army [Netflix11], and include the Chaos Monkey [Netflix12] that randomly kills component instances to verify that automatic failure detection and recovery mechanisms operate properly. While operators of critical applications are not likely to have the same freedom to unleash a Simian Army on their production environment as Netflix does, one can use a separate application test bed in the cloud and unleash automated robustness test tools such as Chaos Monkey to verify the speed and effectiveness of an application's robustness mechanisms without risking service to end users. There are also monkeys that can introduce network traffic delays and corruption that can be unleashed in the test bed to verify the application's handling of the network issues.

16.4.4 Endurance/Stability Testing

Best practice is to execute endurance or stability tests to verify that applications remain completely stable under long sustained workloads that simulate production usage patterns. Cloud enables stability testing to evolve from traditional time bound (i.e., 72 h) stability testing of a static application configuration into workload bound testing of a dynamic application configuration where more transactions can be executed against an elastic application configuration. In particular, stability testing of cloud-based applications can include the following:

- Elastic growth operations early in the endurance test run as workload grows at the maximum growth rate supported by the application and cloud service provider configuration.
- Millions or billions of transactions executed when the application runs at or near maximum engineered capacity for hours.
- A cloud consumer operations phase when database backup and other OAM&P activities are run while application serves user workload at or near maximum engineered capacity
- (If possible) a cloud service provider operations phase when the application's VM instances are live migrated individually and Ethernet switches are rebooted to simulate routine cloud service provider operations
- Adversarial phase in which VMs are "randomly" killed to verify rapid automatic recovery under heavy sustained workload
- Elastic degrowth when workload drains at the end of the endurance test run.

Figure 16.3 visualizes a sample endurance test case for a cloud-based application. This sample test case includes the following phases:

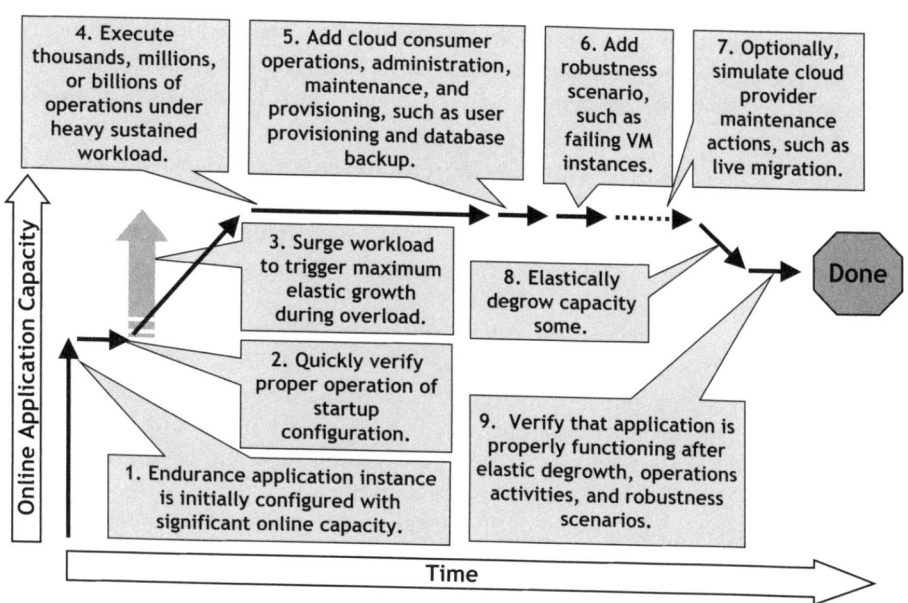

Figure 16.3. Sample Endurance Test Case for Cloud-Based Application.

1. Application under test is instantiated with somewhat less than maximum supported online capacity.

2. "Warm up" verification of application functionality at startup is completed to verify that the application instance is sufficiently functional to proceed with the endurance test and to baseline service key quality indicators (KQIs).

3. Workload surges significantly above the online application capacity to push the application into overload and activate automatic elastic growth. Maintain elevated workload to verify that the application can rapidly grow its way out of overload.

4. With nominally full application capacity online, execute prolonged user service KQI testing runs, completing millions or billions of transactions to characterize service quality performance with high confidence.

5. Cloud consumer operations, administration, maintenance, and provisioning operations (e.g., database backup; adding, modifying, and deleting user accounts) are introduced and KQI performance of both the application and OAM&P operations is measured.

6. Adversarial scenarios are introduced, such as individually killing VM instances to verify automatic recovery actions and briefly pausing VM instances to simulate infrastructure impairments. KQIs are measured throughout this adversarial phase, and the extent of degraded performance is noted.

7. Optionally, cloud service provider OAM&P actions, such as live migration, can be executed while monitoring application KQIs to verify that those actions will neither destabilize the application nor significantly impact application KQI performance.

8. Application capacity is elastically degrown to verify that no material impact on user KQIs is observed during degrowth.

9. A final "cool down" phase verifies all KQIs to assure that performance has not degraded from the warm up and full capacity test phases.

The sample endurance test case of Figure 16.3 should be tailored for individual applications based on the application's usage profile, sensitivities, vulnerabilities, and quality history. For example, a period of traffic overload when the application is configured at maximum capacity could be added. Automated test cases to mimic traffic patterns that had caused field failures in a previous release could be added to verify that the application is at least as stable as previous releases.

Service reliability and latency of all operations are measured separately for each endurance test phase. While stability testing is not necessarily a replacement for service latency or service reliability testing, stability testing should record service reliability (DPM) data and service latency data when possible. The DPM results from stability testing should be comparable with the focused service reliability testing; if not, then the cause of variation should be investigated.

16.4.5 Application Elasticity Testing

Application elasticity functionality and requirements (Section 13.8, "Elasticity Requirements") are verified via several test scenarios:

1. Verifying that elasticity requirements (see Section 13.8, "Elasticity Requirements") are met for all supported elastic growth and degrowth actions for service and storage capacity.

2. Verifying that application service gracefully recovers from elasticity failure scenarios discussed in Section 8.11, "Elasticity Failure Scenarios."

3. Verifying that user service quality requirements are met throughout elastic service capacity and storage growth, provided the workload does not rise so quickly as to activate the application's overload control mechanisms.

4. Verify that user service quality requirements are met throughout supported elastic degrowth operations.

5. Verify that when the application is driven into overload, rapid elasticity mechanisms operate properly to eventually mitigate the offered load (provided that the offered load is less than the application's maximum scale up capacity).

6. Verify that traffic surges which occur while elastic capacity degrowth actions are underway are appropriately managed.

7. Verify that component failure during elastic capacity growth actions are appropriately managed.

8. Verify that component failure during elastic capacity degrowth (shrink) actions are appropriately managed.

Note that distributed denial of service (DDoS) attacks are likely to be far more dramatic than ordinary traffic swings as attacks flood many times more than the normal workload at an application instance. Applications are frequently deployed behind security appliances, such as firewalls or deep packet inspection (DPI) engines, and those security devices should absorb the brunt of a DDoS attack. DDoS and other security attack scenarios should be explicitly verified as part of security testing.

16.4.6 Upgrade Testing

Although each software upgrade strategy requires testing to validate and measure any downtime or loss of sessions or data during the upgrade, there are some tests associated with each particular strategy.

For type I, "block party" software upgrade (see Section 9.3.1, "Type I Cloud-Enabled Upgrade Strategy: Block Party") testing, one must verify the following:

- Installation and initialization of new release instances do not impact traffic running on the old release.
- There is a strategy to configure and direct traffic to particular release instances.
- Traffic can run on multiple releases at the same time.
- Data added, updated, or deleted for one release do not impact data integrity of another release.

For type II, "one driver per bus" software upgrade (see Section 9.3.2, "Type II Cloud-Enabled Upgrade Strategy: One Driver per Bus") testing, one must verify the following:

- Target release software and data can be instantiated without disrupting the current release application service.
- Traffic can be drained from the originating release and redirected to the target release within the maximum acceptable service disruption time (see Section 13.1, "Service Availability Requirements").

16.4.7 Disaster Recovery Testing

Catastrophic events that simultaneously impact all consumer applications running in a single cloud data center should be simulated periodically to activate disaster recovery plans to verify that observed recovery objectives are consistent with recovery point analysis (Section 15.8, "Recovery Point Objective Analysis") and recovery time analysis (Section 15.9, "Recovery Time Objective Analysis"). Testing should measure actual service impact of the following:

1. Unplanned site failure (i.e., no orderly preparation)
2. Orderly site switchover (i.e., taking an active site offline before initiating major maintenance actions at that site)

3. Orderly georedundant switch back (i.e., gracefully restoring service to a site that was offline for repair, following a disaster event or major maintenance action).

16.4.8   Extreme Coresidency Testing

As discussed in Section 7.3, "Extreme Solution Coresidency," extreme coresidency means that multiple application components are consolidated onto a single virtualized infrastructure so that a failure of a VM server can simultaneously impact multiple solution components. Because neither cloud consumers nor application suppliers have explicit control over exactly how cloud service providers distribute application component instances across the cloud service provider's virtualized infrastructure, applications must be prepared to recover from any possible extreme coresidency configuration. Thus, various extreme coresidency failure scenarios should be tested to verify that user service is not unacceptably impacted. Special configuration procedures may be required to coerce a solution into an extreme coresidency configuration and then to simulate an infrastructure failure.

16.4.9   PaaS Technology Component Testing

As discussed in Section 15.3, "PaaS Failure Effects Analysis," PaaS technology components may be included in the solution. Failures of these components may have an impact on application service; therefore, applications must be prepared to deal with these failures. PaaS technology component testing includes the PaaS component failure scenarios identified in the PFEA to verify that user service impact is acceptable when faced with the failures. A complete set of regression tests, as discussed in Section 16.4.3, "Robustness Testing," should be run with an emphasis on the failure scenarios corresponding to the impairments that PFEA indicated were highest risk.

16.4.10   Automated Regression Testing

To ensure that no new problems are introduced with a software or configuration change, a set of automated regression tests should accompany the delivery to be run on the production environment to further validate the change. This is particularly important when supporting continuous delivery to ensure that the introduction of new software does not negatively impact the active system. Examples of possible tests are included in Section 16.4.3, "Robustness Testing."

16.4.11   Canary Release Testing

A canary release provides an opportunity to monitor the quality of the application in a production environment with a small set of early adopter users. Service reliability and latency tests, as discussed in Section 16.4.1, "Service Reliability and Latency Testing," should be run, and KQIs monitored and analyzed to determine the quality of the release and whether enhancements to the application need to be made before the number of users is increased.

17

CONNECTING THE DOTS

Part I of this book considered the resource facing service impairments introduced by virtualization and cloud that risk degrading the customer facing service offered by cloud-based applications. Part II methodically analyzed those risks, and Part III offered recommendations to mitigate the end user service impact of those risks. This chapter summarizes the key points from these three parts.

17.1 THE APPLICATION SERVICE QUALITY CHALLENGE

Since end users do not generally care whether an application is deployed on a traditional infrastructure or on cloud infrastructure, one routinely assumes that customer facing service quality requirements are the same for both deployment options. Unfortunately, cloud deployment introduces additional impairments (discussed in Chapter 4, "Virtualized Infrastructure Impairments") across the application's resource facing service boundary compared with deployment on nonvirtualized hardware configurations. As shown in Figure 17.1 (identical to Figure 4.1), these impairments include the following:

Service Quality of Cloud-Based Applications, First Edition. Eric Bauer and Randee Adams.
© 2014 The Institute of Electrical and Electronics Engineers, Inc. Published 2014 by John Wiley & Sons, Inc.

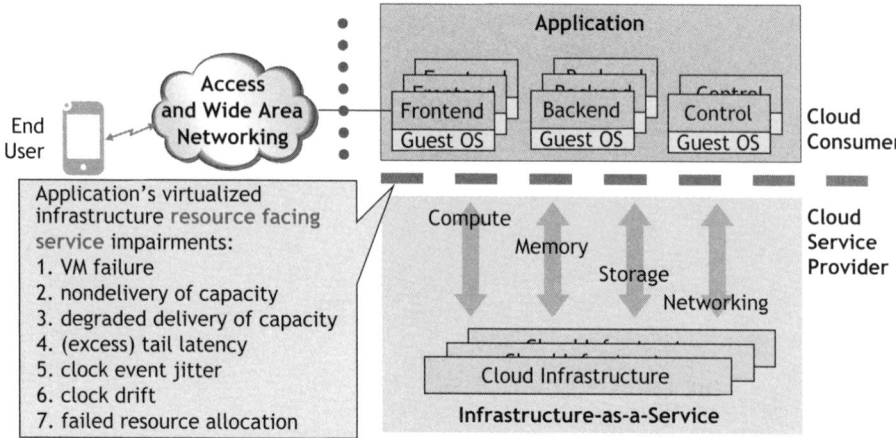

Figure 17.1. Virtualized Infrastructure Impairments Experienced by Cloud-Based Applications.

- *Virtual Machine Failure* (VM) (Section 4.2). Such as traditional hardware, VM instances can fail.
- *Nondelivery of Configured VM Capacity* (Section 4.3). For instance, VM instance can briefly cease to operate (aka "stall").
- *Degraded Delivery of Configured VM Capacity* (Section 4.4). For instance, a particular VM server may be so congested that some application IP packets are discarded by the host OS or hypervisor.
- *Excess Tail Latency on Resource Delivery* (Section 4.5). For instance, some application components may occasionally experience unusually long resource access latency.
- *Clock Event Jitter* (Section 4.6). For instance, regular clock event interrupts (e.g., every 1 ms) may be tardy or coalesced.
- *Clock Drift* (Section 4.7). Guest OS instances' real time clocks may drive away from true (UTC) time.
- *Failed or Slow Allocation and Startup of VM Instances* (Section 4.8). For instance, newly allocated cloud resources may be nonfunctional (aka dead on arrival [DOA]).

As shown in Figure 17.2, the challenge is to create an application that is robust enough that customer facing service quality metrics (discussed in Section 2.5, "Application Service Quality"), such as service availability, service latency, and service reliability, are insensitive to impairments of the application's resource facing service delivered by the cloud service provider.

The quality of the resource facing service delivered by the infrastructure fundamentally drives the architectural choices of the applications that execute on that infrastructure. For example, two-wheel drive is more efficient for vehicles that operate on

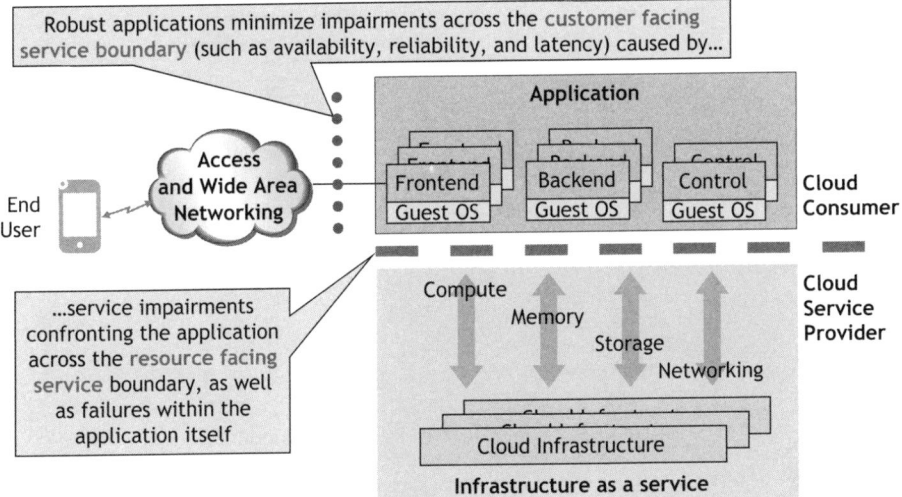

Figure 17.2. Application Robustness Challenge.

well-maintained paved roads, but vehicles that use unpaved roads often require all wheel drive and heavy-duty suspension systems to negotiate obstructions and impairments in the terrain being traversed. Similarly, one should consider the likely cloud infrastructure impairments when selecting an application architecture to assure that it is feasible and likely that customer facing service quality expectations can be met despite expected infrastructure impairments.

17.2   REDUNDANCY AND ROBUSTNESS

The plentiful, flexible, and elastic resources offered by cloud enable applications to consider a broader range of redundancy options to increase service robustness. Fundamentally, there are four redundancy models which can be deployed by application components:

- *Simplex.* A single component instance is serving one or more users, and if that instance fails, then the impacted component must be repaired prior to user service recovery. Virtualization and cloud-enabled rapid automatic Repair-as-a-Service (see Section 5.3, "Improving Infrastructure Repair Times via Virtualization") mechanisms can dramatically improve the service availability of simplex architectures by reducing the time to restore service following failure from hours to minutes or less.
- *Sequential Redundancy.* Redundancy adds alternate component instances, which can serve users without first requiring a failed (simplex) component to be repaired. In sequential redundancy (see Figure 17.3), each request is served by

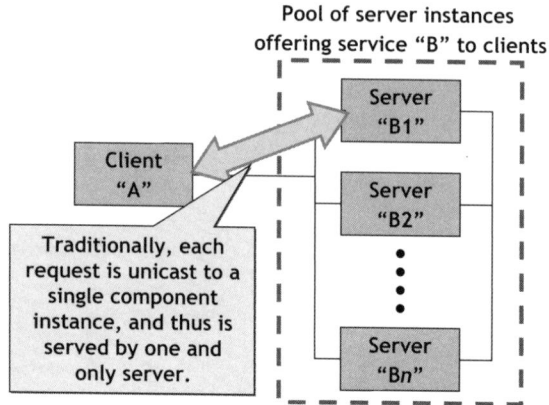

Pool of server instances
offering service "B" to clients

Figure 17.3. Sequential (Traditional) Redundancy.

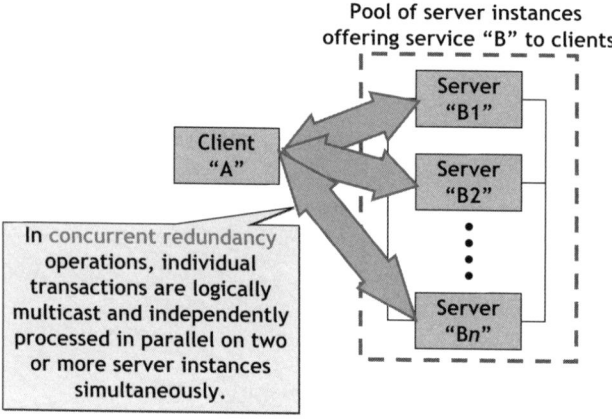

Pool of server instances
offering service "B" to clients

Figure 17.4. Concurrent Redundancy.

a single component instance, but if that component instance fails, then user service fails over to a redundant component instance with minimal user service impact. This redundancy arrangement potentially puts failure detection and recovery from failure of a serving unit "B1" in the critical path of user service delivery since failures are fundamentally mitigated by first detecting the unavailability of the nominally serving component ("B1") before the request can be redirected to a redundant online component instance (e.g., "B2").

- *Concurrent Redundancy (Figure 17.4).* Each client request is logically multicast to several online server component instances simultaneously so redundant copies of each client request are processed concurrently. Client "A" logic is more complex in this arrangement than with traditional redundancy, as it must simultaneously multicast requests to several server component instances and then select a response to use from those returned. Server instances must be architected to efficiently deal with synchronization challenges that arise when several component instances process the same request in parallel. Concurrent redundancy architectures mitigate component failures more effectively compared with sequential redundancy architectures because failure detection and recovery are no longer in the critical service delivery path. Even if there is a failure of one of the component instances, there will likely be at least one successful response by an operational component instance promptly received by client "A" that it can use rather than having to wait to detect the failure of a component instance and then retrying the request to another component instance. In addition to this service availability benefit, concurrent redundancy architectures can effectively mitigate some virtualized infrastructure impairments, such as nondelivery or degraded delivery of virtualized resources (aka VM hiccups or stalls) since it is likely that at least one component instance is fully operational and can return a prompt successful response to the client.

- *Hybrid Concurrent Redundancy (Figure 17.5).* Rather than logically multicasting copies of each request for simultaneous processing by multiple serving components in concurrent redundancy, the client can send a request to a single serving instance and await a prompt reply. If the selected serving instance does not respond in less than guard time $T_{Overlap}$ (perhaps the 99th percentile latency time), then the request is sent to another serving instance, and the client uses whichever response is received first. This hybrid concurrent approach mitigates the service impact of failure and infrastructure impairments better than sequential redundancy by shortening the failure detection time. While hybrid concurrent redundancy potentially delivers somewhat longer user service latency than concurrent redundancy during both normal and failure operation, hybrid concurrency consumes far less resources, because the overwhelming majority of client requests are processed only once compared with processing each request multiple times with "full" concurrent redundancy.

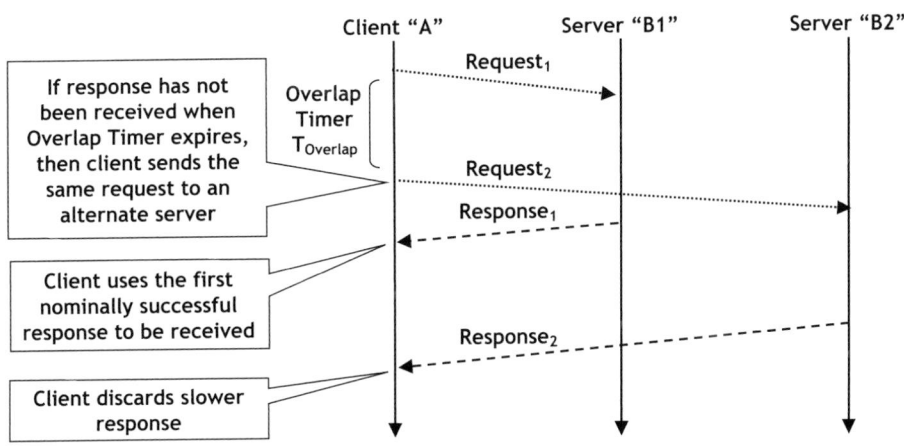

Figure 17.5. Hybrid Concurrent with Slow Response.

Cloud-based applications that cannot tolerate the user service impact of simplex component failures or the outage duration while Repair-as-a-Service mechanisms operate should deploy redundant architectures. Hybrid concurrent redundancy can deliver better service quality than sequential redundancy because it effectively mitigates tail latency events. Concurrent redundancy offers the robustness benefits of hybrid concurrent redundancy plus improving service latency, albeit with much higher resource utilization.

17.3   DESIGN FOR SCALABILITY

Rapid elasticity enables applications to bring additional resources online to serve an increased offered load. As discussed in Chapter 8, "Capacity Management," designing weakly coupled components facilitates efficient horizontal growth and degrowth. As discussed in Chapter 6, "Load Distribution and Balancing," load balancers can facilitate workload distribution across elastic pools of serving components. Moving application state information out of serving component instances into a highly available registry for volatile data that are shared by all of the application instance's pool of serving components can improve the scalability for stateful applications.

As discussed in Chapter 7, "Failure Containment," virtualization decouples VM resources from the underlying physical resources. Thus, application components can be engineered to run in VM instances that are sized to scale by appropriate units of capacity growth and to limit the footprint of impact of a VM instance failure to meet business service quality requirements.

17.4   DESIGN FOR EXTENSIBILITY

Virtualization and elasticity enable software upgrade of cloud-based applications to adopt radically different strategies because one can allocate sufficient additional resources to install a new and independent instance of the upgraded application and run it alongside the (fully redundant) current version. As discussed in Chapter 9, "Release Management," the preferred strategy, which the authors call type I "block party" (see Section 9.3.1, "Type I Cloud-Enabled Upgrade Strategy: Block Party," and Figure 17.6), is to allocate, install, configure, activate, and soak the new/upgraded application instance with test or a small portion of user traffic with minimal disturbance to the existing application instance until user service migrates completely over to the new instance.

Block party not only facilitates continuous delivery of software, it also enables cloud consumers to easily experiment with their service. For example, an application release can be modified to trial a slightly different webpage layout or architectural optimization, deploy it to a small portion of live user traffic, and make A/B comparisons of application key quality indicators (KQIs) to assess the value of the change under test.

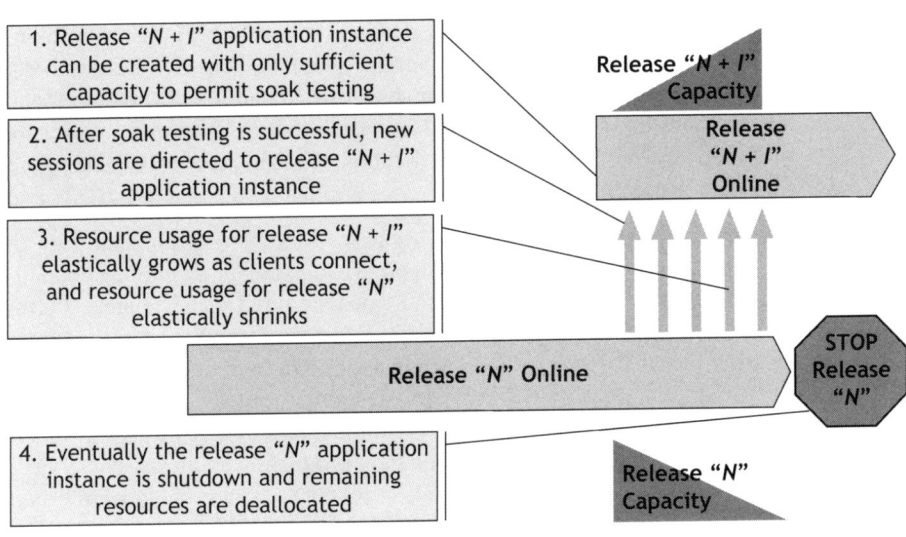

Figure 17.6. Type I, "Block Party" Upgrade Strategy.

17.5 DESIGN FOR FAILURE

VM instances will fail more often than native hardware because hypervisors and additional cloud software is inserted in the critical path between the application's virtualized machine instances and the underlying hardware. In addition, complex software systems and operational policies deployed by cloud service providers to support the virtualized infrastructure environment can fail in ways that impact VMs hosting application components. Thus, application components should be prepared for more frequent critical failure events than with traditional deployments.

The basic design for failure principles that suppliers and consumers of cloud-based applications should consider are the following:

- *Design for Failure Containment.* Inevitable failures should be automatically contained so failure cascades are prevented (see Chapter 7, "Failure Containment").
- *Design for Failure Detection.* Applications should be engineered to rapidly detect failures and activate recovery mechanisms as quickly as possible to minimize the risk of silent or sleeping failures. Cloud consumers should never be forced to rely on end users to detect and notify them of application failures.
- *Design for Service Availability.* The user service impact of failure can be minimized via rapid and automatic failure detection and service recovery. Automatic service recovery to online redundant components is inevitably faster than with simplex arrangements, even when automatic Repair-as-a-Service mechanisms are used (see Chapter 5, "Application Redundancy and Cloud Computing").

- *Design for Application Repair.* To mitigate the impact of a more frequent failure rate (of VMs vs. traditional hardware) from increasing the cloud consumer's operational expenditure (OPEX), automatic VM Repair-as-a-Service or self-healing mechanisms should be used (see Section 5.2, "Improving Software Repair Times via Virtualization," and Section 5.3, "Improving Infrastructure Repair Times via Virtualization").

By definition, failure events are messy because the system is plunged into an unpredictable state. Thus, extensive testing is appropriate to assure that failure containment, detection, recovery, and repair mechanisms operate rapidly and reliably. Fortunately, cloud makes it practical to create test beds to run extensive robustness tests against application instances with no risk of impacting live user traffic. Services that can tolerate the risks of robustness testing on production systems can benefit from frequent validation of robustness mechanisms on production systems using test tools such as the Simian Army that Netflix deploys on their production applications. Services that can tolerate only very limited verification on product systems should limit their testing on production systems to periodic disaster recovery drills.

17.6 PLANNING CONSIDERATIONS

As discussed in [Carr], cloud represents a "big switch" in the information and communications technology (ICT) sector that will ultimately impact how enterprises use information technology. [TOGAF] gives four types of architecture: business, application, data, and technology. All four of these architectures will evolve as the needs of the enterprise, customer and market demands, and technologies and ecosystems evolve. Thus, business leaders must plan the evolution of these related architectures so that application, data, and technology architectures support the needs of the business with acceptable service quality while adhering to schedule and cost constraints. As a result, cloud awareness for applications (see Section 3.7, "Cloud Awareness") is more likely to be an evolving process than a single big bang event. When considering new, written from scratch applications for cloud, one should set aside traditional architectural assumptions and start from cloud friendly architectural principles, such as those described in works such as [Birman], [CCPP], [ODCA_DCCA], and [Varia].

The following actions are recommended to assure the feasibility and likelihood of cloud-based applications consistently achieving their service quality expectations:

- *Explicitly Define Service Quality Requirements.* Methodical architecture, analysis, design, and testing requires qualitative and quantitative requirements. Baselining verifiable application service quality requirements (see Chapter 13, "Application Service Quality Requirements") is a key foundation for any high service quality application.
- Architect and design applications to:
  - Contain, detect, recover, and repair inevitable failures (see Chapter 5, "Application Redundancy and Cloud Computing," and Chapter 7, "Failure Containment")

- ◦ Smoothly grow and shrink online capacity (see Chapter 8, "Capacity Management," and Chapter 6, "Load Distribution and Balancing")
- ◦ Support block party release management (see Chapter 9, "Release Management")
- ◦ Monitor virtualized infrastructure performance to facilitate proper root cause analysis of service failures or impairments (see Chapter 14, "Virtualized Infrastructure Measurement and Management").
- • *Analyze Application's Architecture to Assure the Feasibility and Likelihood of Consistently Meeting Service Quality Requirements in Production Deployment.* Complete analysis methodologies detailed in Chapter 15, "Analysis of Cloud-Based Applications":
  - ◦ Reliability Block Diagrams and Side-by-Side Analysis (Section 15.1)
  - ◦ IaaS Impairment Effects Analysis (Section 15.2)
  - ◦ PaaS Failure Effects Analysis (Section 15.3)
  - ◦ Workload Distribution Analysis (Section 15.4)
  - ◦ Anti-affinity Analysis (Section 15.5)
  - ◦ Elasticity Analysis (Section 15.6)
  - ◦ Release Management Impact Effects Analysis (Section 15.7)
  - ◦ Recovery Point Objective Analysis (Section 15.8)
  - ◦ Recovery Time Objective Analysis (Section 15.9).
- • *Test Application Software on Cloud.* Chapter 16, "Testing Considerations," discusses the incremental testing beyond what is done for traditional deployments that is appropriate to assure that applications deployed to cloud deliver acceptable service quality. In addition to functional testing, the application's test campaign should include (where applicable)
  - ◦ Service Reliability and Latency (Section 16.4.1)
  - ◦ Impaired Infrastructure Testing (Section 16.4.2)
  - ◦ Robustness Testing (Section 16.4.3)
  - ◦ Endurance/Stability Testing (Section 16.4.4)
  - ◦ Application Elasticity Testing (Section 16.4.5)
  - ◦ Upgrade Testing (Section 16.4.6)
  - ◦ Extreme Coresidency Testing (Section 16.4.8).
- • *Drive Continuous Quality Improvement.* Design for failure is an appropriate principle for cloud computing, but this should be accompanied by continuous quality improvement. The service impact of failure will generally be far less severe when the system automatically detects and recovers from failure events, but often one or more users are impacted directly by each failure event. When properly deployed, design for failure should enable failure events that might otherwise have produced acute outages with major service impact to be addressed automatically with minimal service impact. Note that minimal service impact is not necessarily the same as no service impact. Often, the minimal service impact of a failed transaction here and a painfully slow transaction there blends into the background of chronic service impairments. After acute service impairments, such as outages, are under control, leading enterprises will work to drive their

level of chronic or background service impairments to best in class. This effort to drive chronic impairments to best in class generally relies on the classic quality improvement approach as follows:

1. Measure service performance.
2. Do Pareto analysis of service impairments.
3. Perform a deep root cause analysis of primary service-impacting problems.
4. Deploy corrective action to prevent recurrence of service problems.
5. Repeat.

17.7 EVOLVING TRADITIONAL APPLICATIONS

This section considers the challenge of taking an existing or traditional application (see Section 3.7, "Cloud Awareness") that is successfully deployed on native hardware configurations to cloud while continuing to deliver at least comparable service quality to end users. Given the complexity of this task and business realities associated with ongoing support of existing customers in a dynamic marketplace, most application suppliers and cloud consumers will adopt a phased transition from traditional (native) deployment to full cloud support over several application releases rather than taking the risk of a single "big bang" release that does everything cloud related all at once. Figure 17.7 illustrates a sample application evolution timeline that begins with phase 0, in which the existing traditional application is deployed only on native hardware and grows to full cloud awareness over several releases.

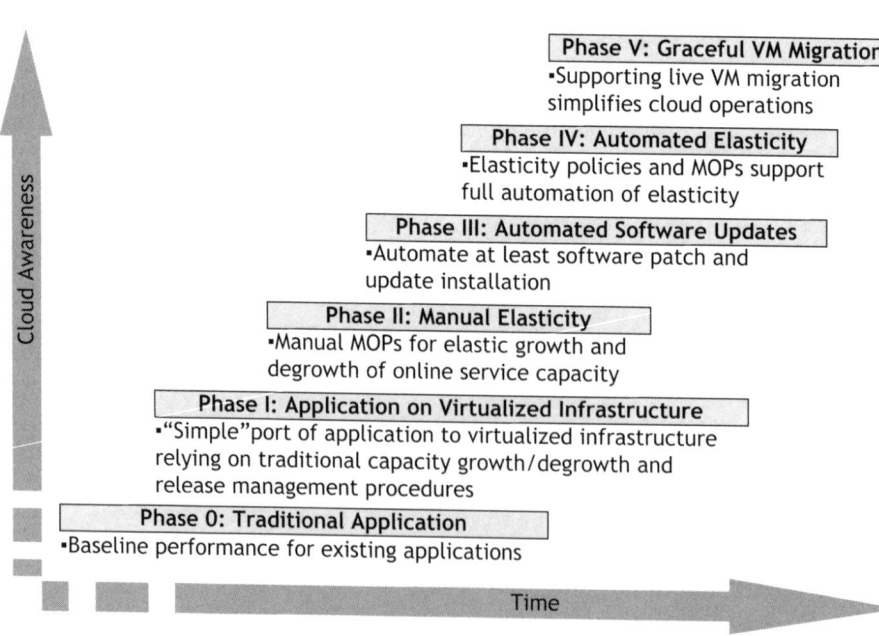

Figure 17.7. Sample Phased Evolution of a Traditional Application.

- *Phase 0: Traditional Application* (Section 17.7.1). One should quantitatively characterize key user service quality metrics of native deployment so application architects, developers, and testers have an accurate performance target to shoot for.
- *Phase I: High Service Quality on Virtualized Infrastructure* (Section 17.7.2). The first step is to assure that the application delivers acceptable service to users when installed on cloud infrastructure.
- *Phase II: Manual Application Elasticity* (Section 17.7.3). Online elastic capacity growth and degrowth are often challenging for traditional applications. Full elasticity of cloud-based applications logically has two pieces:
  A. The procedure to manually expand or contract the application's capacity
  B. The policies, mechanisms, and integration that enable those elastic growth and degrowth procedures to reliably execute automatically without human involvement.
     To minimize the risk of user service impact, many application service providers of critical services will want to manually execute elastic growth and degrowth procedures until the procedures are demonstrated to be sufficiently reliable and deterministic that they can be automated without jeopardizing the application service provider's reputation for quality. Manual application elasticity enables cloud consumers to easily grow application capacity ahead of anticipated loads (e.g., Cyber Monday for eCommerce sites), and to conveniently reduce online capacity when the need has passed. Mechanisms and policies to automatically trigger capacity growth and degrowth events, managing—and possibly forcing—drainage of traffic from resources to be released during degrowth operations, and other details of full automation are deferred to Section 17.7.5, "Phase IV: Automated Application Elasticity."
- *Phase III: Automated Release Management* (Section 17.7.4). Release management actions often include data evolution steps that should be automated in this phase, but suppliers retain the option of requiring that major release upgrades rely on some manual actions, particularly if there are failures during the procedure that require a decision to be made on whether to repair it or continue.
- *Phase IV: Automated Application Elasticity* (Section 17.7.5). Once the elastic growth and degrowth procedures of phase II are demonstrated to be highly reliable, one can focus on automating both activation and execution of those procedures, and then fully integrating them with a cloud elasticity OSS.
- *Phase V: VM Migration* (Section 17.7.6). When graceful VM migration is supported by the application, the cloud service provider can autonomously move application VM instances to perform maintenance actions (e.g., release management of infrastructure components) or consolidate workloads to manage power consumption (e.g., powering down servers during low usage periods) without producing unacceptable service impact for the application's end users.

Readers will recognize that these steps can be resequenced and tailored to meet the needs of specific applications, cloud consumers, cloud service providers, and end users. For example, some application service providers will want automated application capacity (nominally phase IV) deployed before automated release management (nominally phase III).

17.7.1 Phase 0: Traditional Application

A traditional application that consistently delivers acceptable user service is a solid foundation to evolve from. Ideally, the application's customer facing KQIs will be known and used as targets for the cloud deployed application and will be recorded in clear and quantitative service quality requirements, as described in Chapter 13, "Application Service Quality Requirements." Note that many of the application's user facing KQI measurements may exceed users' expectations, so it may be acceptable for cloud deployment to approach rather than equal those targets.

17.7.2 Phase I: High Service Quality on Virtualized Infrastructure

The first phase of evolving a traditional application to cloud is to run it in VM instances served by a hypervisor; this phase has the collateral benefit of increasing the application's hardware independence. Deployment on virtualized infrastructure can enable a degree of server consolidation or application coresidency. Virtualization enables resource sharing, which introduces the risks of those discussed in Chapter 4, "Virtualized Infrastructure Impairments." Note that as there are differences between hypervisors, suppliers generally pick specific hypervisors to focus their support on.

Architects first map the application's software components into VM instances. When appropriate, application architects will consider replacing native application components with technology components offered by the target Platform-as-a-Service provider (e.g., load balancers and database servers). The architects and developers should anticipate imperfect infrastructure and technology components, and complete both IaaS impairment effects analysis (Section 15.2) and PaaS failure effects analysis (Section 15.5). Applications should implement rich monitoring of virtualized infrastructure impairments to enable effective troubleshooting of application service quality problems both in testing and in production deployment. If unacceptable performance is delivered to a single VM instance, then application architects can consider supporting one or more of the following mitigation strategies:

- VM-Level Congestion Detection and Control (Section 14.4.2)
- Terminate Poorly Performing VM Instances (Section 14.4.4).

When elastic growth is supported, applications can consider an additional mitigation: allocate more virtual resource capacity (Section 14.4.3)

Architects should complete an anti-affinity analysis (Section 15.5) to facilitate the writing of anti-affinity rules to explicitly distribute the application's VM instances across sufficient VM server hosts so the application instance can withstand single VM server failures. Note that architects can mitigate VM host failures of extreme coresidency deployments via manual or automatic disaster recovery mechanisms. Recovery point objective analysis (see Section 15.8) and recovery time objective analysis (see

Section 15.9) should be executed to verify that the architecture meets its business continuity and disaster recovery objectives, including recovering from major cloud infrastructure failures that overwhelm the application's high availability mechanisms.

Application installation and release management actions are manual in phase I, and capacity growth and degrowth actions generally follow traditional (i.e., offline) procedures.

In addition to functional testing, the application's test campaign for cloud deployment should include (as applicable) the following:

- Service reliability and latency testing (Section 16.4.1). Note that this should include testing with simulated virtualized infrastructure impairments.
- Impaired infrastructure testing (Section 16.4.2)
- Robustness testing (Section 16.4.3)
- Endurance/stability testing (Section 16.4.4)
- Upgrade testing (Section 16.4.6)
- Disaster recovery testing (Section 16.4.7)
- Extreme coresidency testing (Section 16.4.8).

17.7.3   Phase II: Manual Application Elasticity

Existing applications will undoubtedly support some capacity growth procedures, but they are typically executed when the application is offline (e.g., during a maintenance window) and may require profound changes to the application instance (e.g., reinstalling the application with different settings, such as a larger database). Application teams will decide which aspects of application growth and degrowth should support online operation (e.g., adding user service capacity) and which aspects should remain as offline operations using existing procedures (e.g., growing database capacity). Note that the licensing strategy of both the application itself and included components should be considered to assure that license management is aligned with application elasticity.

The architect determines whether the application's online growth will be performed horizontally or vertically, and designs appropriate mechanisms. The architect will also determine both the units of growth (e.g., individual VM instances or groups of VM instances) and the limits of elastic growth. Elasticity analysis (see Section 15.6) should be used to assure robust elasticity architecture. Appropriate application elasticity testing (Section 16.4.5) should be planned.

17.7.4   Phase III: Automated Release Management

Automated release management enables software patches, updates, upgrades, and retrofits to be efficiently installed by cloud consumers with minimal manual intervention. Chapter 9, "Release Management," gives a detailed discussion of this topic. In addition to reducing the cloud consumer's OPEX, this can boost application service quality by encouraging bug fixes and security or stability patches to be applied rapidly, thus reducing the time window that an application is vulnerable to known risks that have already been patched. Automated release management is required to support continuous delivery, but automated release management is valuable even for periodic release delivery models. Release management impact effects analysis (see Section 15.7) should be used to analyze the application's release management strategy, and upgrade testing (see Section 16.4.6, "Upgrade Testing") should be completed to verify proper operation.

17.7.5 Phase IV: Automated Application Elasticity

Application elasticity was considered in detail in Chapter 8, "Capacity Management." Automation of application elasticity requires application architects to perform the following:

- Determine what application performance indicators should trigger automatic elastic growth and degrowth decisions.
- Develop policies that evaluate performance indicators to appropriately trigger elasticity operations.
- Define automated elasticity procedures that are robust enough to assure acceptable service operation and quality despite inevitable failures and impaired operation.

Architects should be careful to assure that elasticity actions are appropriately connected to the right automated triggers to minimize the risk that an observed performance slowdown or throughput bottleneck triggers growth of the wrong resource so the application ends up with a glut of (unneeded) resource capacity and a performance/throughput issue. Application developers will implement these mechanisms and integrate them with the appropriate elasticity operations support system. Elasticity analysis (see Section 15.6) should be repeated to assure that the architecture and high level design for automated elasticity operations are robust.

Appropriate application elasticity testing (Section 16.4.5) should also be planned, including verification that automated elasticity mechanisms do not interfere with automated failure detection and recovery mechanisms. Upgrade testing (Section 16.4.6) should be repeated to assure that automated elasticity does not adversely impact software upgrade. Endurance/stability testing (Section 16.4.4) should be expanded to include automatic elastic growth (and perhaps degrowth) as a standard part of routine stability testing.

17.7.6 Phase V: VM Migration

Inevitably, it will be convenient or necessary for the cloud service provider to remove an application's VM instance from a particular VM server host to enable the service provider to perform a maintenance action such as release management on the VM server itself or to make a configuration change or repair to the IP infrastructure. The traditional solution to this problem was to schedule those actions into a maintenance window (e.g., between midnight and 4 a.m. local time) when the application could be taken offline or exposed to an extended period of simplex operation. The preferred solution is for applications to support graceful migration of VM instances to other servers so cloud service providers can execute maintenance actions efficiently with minimal service impact to the application's end users, and hopefully minimal incremental OPEX and risk for the cloud consumer. Hypervisors enable VM instances to be paused on one host, to transfer the VM's memory, storage, and network connectivity to another host, and then activate on the VM on the other host to produce a "live" VM migration. The hypervisor, cloud service provider's infrastructure and operational policies, and other factors will determine exactly how long the period of nondelivery of configured VM capacity is (see Section 4.3). If that period is not short enough, application architects should refine migration mechanisms to enable VM instances to be gracefully moved on demand with minimal user service impact.

17.8 CONCLUDING REMARKS

Cloud computing enables enterprises to improve service agility and to reduce capital expenditure (CAPEX) and OPEX compared with traditional application deployment while delivering acceptable service quality to end users. But cloud computing also introduces risks associated with virtualized infrastructure, more complex ecosystems, and new layers of accountability that can impact application service quality delivered to end users. This work methodically delineated and analyzed the risks, and offered concrete recommendations to enable applications deployed to cloud to deliver service quality at least as good as native application deployments and in some cases even better.

ABBREVIATIONS

AC	Alternating current
ACID	Atomicity, consistency, isolation, durability
API	Application programming interface
ASP	Application service provider
BASE	Basically available, soft state, eventual consistency
BAU	Business as usual
BE	Best effort
CAPEX	Capital expenditure
CCDF	Complementary cumulative distribution function
CDF	Cumulative distribution function
CDN	Content delivery network
CFS	Customer facing service
CI	Configuration item
COTS	Commercial off-the-shelf
CPU	Central processing unit
CSP	Cloud service provider
DfR	Design for reliability
DHCP	Dynamic host configuration protocol
DNS	Domain name system
DOA	Dead on arrival
DPM	Defects per million, such as defective transactions per million or defective calls per million attempts
DR	Disaster recovery
DSL	Digital subscriber line, a wireline access technology
EMS	Element management system
EOR	End-of-row Ethernet switch

Service Quality of Cloud-Based Applications, First Edition. Eric Bauer and Randee Adams.
© 2014 The Institute of Electrical and Electronics Engineers, Inc. Published 2014 by John Wiley & Sons, Inc.

ERI	Early return index (nominally the hardware failure rate in first 6 months of service)
FMEA	Failure mode effects analysis
FRU	Field replaceable (hardware) unit
GMT	Greenwich mean time
GPS	Global positioning system
GR	Georedundancy
GUI	Graphical user interface
HA	High availability
IaaS	Infrastructure-as-a-service
ICT	Information and communications technology
IIEA	IaaS impairment effects analysis
ISP	Internet service provider
IT	Information technology
ITIL	IT Infrastructure Library, a suite of IT management processes published by UK government.
KPI	Key performance indicator
KQI	Key quality indicator
LAN	Local area network
LBaaS	Load balancing as a service
LTR	Long-term returns (nominally the hardware failure rate after more than 18 months of service)
MAN	Metropolitan area network
MOP	Method of procedure
MOS	Mean opinion score
MTBF	Mean time between failures
MTRS	Mean time to restore service
MTTR	Mean time to repair
NE	Network element
NFS	Network file system
NFV	Network function virtualization
NIST	U.S. National Institute of Standards and Technology
NSP	Network service provider
NTP	Network Time Protocol
OAM	Operations, administration, and maintenance
OAM&P	Operations, administration, maintenance, and provisioning
ODCA	Open Data Center Alliance
OLTP	Online transaction processing
OOS	Out of service

OPEX	Operational expenditure
OSS	Operations support system
PaaS	Platform-as-a-Service
PIEA	PaaS impact effects analysis
PM	Performance management
PTP	Precision Time Protocol
QoS	Quality of service
RaaS	Repair-as-a-Service
RAID	Redundant array of independent (or inexpensive) discs
RAM	Random access memory
RBD	Reliability block diagram
REST	Representational state transfer
RFC	Request for comment
RFP	Request for proposal
RFS	Resource facing service
RMS	Rack-mounted server
RPO	Recovery point objective
RTO	Recovery time objective
SaaS	Software-as-a-Service
SO4	Annualized product attributable service downtime measurement
SPOF	Single point of failure
TOR	Top-of-rack Ethernet switch
VFRU	Virtual field replaceable unit
VIP	Virtual IP address
VLAN	Virtual local area network
VM	Virtual machine
VMI	Virtual machine instance
VMS	Virtual machine server
VMSC	Virtual machine server controller
VoIP	Voice over IP
VPN	Virtual private network
WAN	Wide area network
XaaS	Any as-a-Service offering
YRR	Yearly return rate (nominally the hardware failure rate in the first 6–18 months of service)

REFERENCES

[Bauer11]   Eric Bauer, Randee Adams and Dan Eustace, *Beyond Redundancy: How Geographic Redundancy Can Improve Service Availability and Reliability of Computer-Based Systems*, Wiley-IEEE Press, 2011.

[Bauer12]   Eric Bauer and Randee Adams, *Reliability and Availability of Cloud Computing*, Wiley+IEEE Press, 2012.

[Birman]   Kenneth P. Birman, *Guide to Reliable Distributed Systems: Building High-Assurance Applications and Cloud-Hosted Services*, Springer Verlag, 2012.

[Carr]   Nicholas Carr, *The Big Switch: Rewiring the World from Edison to Google*, 2013.

[CCDF]   Daniel Zwillinger and Stephen Kokoska, *CRC Standard Probability and Statistics Tables and Formulae*, 32nd edition, CRC Press, 2011.

[CCPP]   Rajkumar Buyya, James Broberg, and Andrzej M. Goscinski (eds), *Cloud Computing: Principles and Paradigms*, John Wiley and Sons, 2011.

[CSA]   Cloud Security Alliance, http://cloudsecurityalliance.org (accessed September 17, 2003).

[Dean]   Jeffrey Dean and Luiz André Barroso,The Tail at Scale, *Communications of the ACM*, Vol. 56, No. 2, pp. 74–80, 2013, 10.1145/2408776.2408794, http://cacm.acm.org/magazines/2013/2/160173-the-tail-at-scale/fulltext (accessed September 17, 2003).

[DSP0243]   Distributed Management Task Force, Open Virtualization Format Specification, DSP0243, version 1.1.0, January 12, 2010, http://www.dmtf.org/sites/default/files/standards/documents/DSP0243_1.1.0.pdf (accessed September 17, 2003).

[FAA-HDBK-006A]   Federal Aviation Administration Handbook: Reliability, Maintainability, and Availability (RMA) Handbook, FAA-HDBK-006A, January 7, 2008.

[Freemantle]   Paul Fremantle Blog-Cloud Native, http://pzf.fremantle.org/2010/05/cloud-native.html (accessed September 17, 2003).

[IEEE610]   IEEE Standard Glossary of Software Engineering Terminology, IEEE Std 610.12-1990(R2002).

[ISO_9000]   Quality Management Systems—Fundamentals and Vocabulary, International Standard ISO 9000:2005(E), February 12, 2008.

[ITIL-Availability]   ITIL® Glossary and Abbreviations—English, 2011, http://www.itil-officialsite.com/InternationalActivities/ITILGlossaries_2.aspx (accessed September 17, 2003).

[ITIL_CM]   http://www.itlibrary.org/index.php?page=ITIL_Service_Transition (accessed September 17, 2003).

Service Quality of Cloud-Based Applications, First Edition. Eric Bauer and Randee Adams.
© 2014 The Institute of Electrical and Electronics Engineers, Inc. Published 2014 by John Wiley & Sons, Inc.

[ITIL_ST]   Cabinet Office, TSO, ITIL® Service Transition 2011 Edition, 2011.

[ITILv3MTRS]   http://www.knowledgetransfer.net/dictionary/ITIL/en/Mean_Time_to_ Restore_Service.htm (accessed September 17, 2003).

[ITILv3MTTR]   http://www.knowledgetransfer.net/dictionary/ITIL/en/Mean_Time_To_ Repair.htm (accessed September 17, 2003).

[jHiccup]   http://www.azulsystems.com/jHiccup (accessed September 17, 2003).

[Keynes]   John Maynard Keynes, *A Tract on Monetary Reform*, London: Macmillan, 1924.

[Merriam-Webster]   http://www.merriam-webster.com/dictionary/whipsaw (accessed September 17, 2003).

[Netflix10]   5 Lessons We've Learned Using AWS, December 16, 2010, http:// techblog.netflix.com/2010/12/5-lessons-weve-learned-using-aws.html (accessed September 17, 2003).

[Netflix11]   The Netflix Simian Army, July 19, 2011, http://techblog.netflix.com/2011/07/ netflix-simian-army.html (accessed September 17, 2003).

[Netflix12]   Chaos Monkey Released into the Wild, July 30, 2012 http://techblog.netflix .com/2012/07/chaos-monkey-released-into-wild.html (accessed September 17, 2003).

[NIST]   http://csrc.nist.gov/publications/PubsDrafts.html (accessed September 17, 2003).

[NoSQL]   NoSQL Relational Database Management System: Home Page, Strozzi.it., March 29, 2010, http://www.strozzi.it/cgi-bin/CSA/tw7/I/en_US/nosql/Home%20Page (accessed September 17, 2003).

[ODCA_SUoM]   Open Data Center Alliance, Standard Units of Measure for IaaS Rev 1.1, http://www.opendatacenteralliance.org/docs/Standard_Units_of_Measure_For_IaaS_ Rev1.1.pdf (accessed September 17, 2003).

[ODCA_CIaaS]   Open Data Center Alliance, Compute Infrastructure as a Service Rev 1.0, http://www.opendatacenteralliance.org/docs/ODCA_Compute_IaaS_MasterUM_v1.0_ Nov2012.pdf (accessed September 17, 2003).

[ODCA_DCCA]   Jan Drake, Arun Jacob, Nigel Simpson, and Scott Thompson, Open Data Center Alliance, Developing Cloud-Capable Applications White Paper Rev. 1.1, November 2012, http://www.opendatacenteralliance.org/docs/DevCloudCapApp.pdf (accessed September 17, 2003).

[P.800]   International Telecommunications Union, P.800: Methods for Subjective Determination of Transmission Quality, August 1996, http://www.itu.int/rec/T-REC-P.800-199608-I/en (accessed September 17, 2003).

[Parasuraman]   A. Parasuraman, Valarie A. Zeithamal, and Leonard L. Berry, A Conceptual Model of Service Quality and its implications for Future Research, Journal of Marketing, Vol. 49, pp. 41–50, Fall 1985.

[RFC2616]   R. Fielding et al., Hypertext Transfer Protocol—HTTP/1.1, June 1999, http:// www.ietf.org/rfc/rfc2616.txt (accessed September 17, 2003).

[RFC4594]   Internet Engineering Task Force, Configuration Guidelines for DiffServ Service Classes, RFC 4594, August 2006, http://tools.ietf.org/html/rfc4594 (accessed September 17, 2003).

[Riak]   http://docs.basho.com/riak/latest/ops/building/benchmarking/ (accessed September 17, 2003).

[Sigelman]   Benjamin H. Sigelman, Luiz André Barroso, Mike Burrows, Pat Stephenson, Manoj Plakal, Donald Beaver, Saul Jaspan, and Chandan Shanbhag, Dapper, a Large-Scale Distributed Systems Tracing Infrastructure, 2010, http://research.google.com/pubs/pub36356.html (accessed September 17, 2003).

[SP800-145] Peter Mell and Timothy Grance, National Institute of Standards and Technology, US Department of Commerce, The NIST Definition of Cloud Computing, Special Publication 800-145, September 2011, http://csrc.nist.gov/publications/nistpubs/800-145/SP800-145.pdf (accessed September 17, 2003).

[SPECOSGReport] SPEC Open Systems Group, Cloud Computing Working Group, Report on Cloud Computing to the OSG Steering Committee, http://www.spec.org/osgcloud/docs/osgcloudwgreport20120410.pdf (accessed September 17, 2013).

[TL_9000] Quality Excellence for Suppliers of Telecommunications Forum (QuEST Forum), TL 9000 Quality Management System Measurements Handbook 5.0, 2012, http://tl9000.org (accessed September 17, 2003).

[TMF_TR197] TM Forum, Multi-Cloud Service Management Pack: Service Level Agreement (SLA) Business Blueprint, TR 197, V1.3, February 2013.

[TOGAF] The Open Group, TOGAF® Standard Courseware V9.1 Edition, http://www.togaf.info/togaf9/togafSlides91/TOGAF-V91-M1-Management-Overview.pdf (accessed September 17, 2003).

[UptimeTiers] Uptime Institute Professional Services, LLC, Data Center Site Infrastructure Tier Standard: Topology, Aug, 2012.

[Varia] Jinesh Varia, Architecting for the Cloud: Best Practices, January 2011, http://jineshvaria.s3.amazonaws.com/public/cloudbestpractices-jvaria.pdf (accessed September 17, 2003).

[Weinman] Joe Weinman, *Cloudonomics: The Business Value of Cloud Computing*, Wiley, 2012.

[Wikipedia-DB] http://en.wikipedia.org/wiki/ACID (accessed September 17, 2003).

[Wikipedia-LB] http://en.wikipedia.org/wiki/Load_balancing_(computing) (accessed September 17, 2003).

[Wikipedia-TI] http://en.wikipedia.org/wiki/Temporal_isolation_among_virtual_machines (accessed September 17, 2003).

[Zeithami] Valarie A. Zeithaml, Leonard L. Berry, and A. Parasuaman, *Delivering Quality Service*, The Free Press, 2009.

ABOUT THE AUTHORS

ERIC BAUER is reliability engineering manager in the IP Platforms CTO of Alcatel-Lucent. He has worked on reliability of Alcatel-Lucent's platforms, applications, and solutions for more than a decade. Before focusing on reliability engineering topics, Mr. Bauer spent two decades designing and developing embedded firmware, networked operating systems, IP PBXs, Internet platforms, and optical transmission systems. He has been awarded more than a dozen U.S. patents, authored *Reliability and Availability of Cloud Computing*, *Beyond Redundancy: How Geographic Redundancy Can Improve Service Availability and Reliability of Computer-Based Systems*, *Design for Reliability: Information and Computer-Based Systems*, and *Practical System Reliability* (all published by Wiley-IEEE Press), and has published several papers in the *Bell Labs Technical Journal*. Mr. Bauer holds a BS in Electrical Engineering from Cornell University, Ithaca, New York, and an MS in Electrical Engineering from Purdue University, West Lafayette, Indiana. He lives in Freehold, New Jersey.

RANDEE ADAMS is a consulting member of technical staff in the IP Platforms CTO of Alcatel-Lucent. She has spent the last decade concentrating on product reliability. She has given talks at various internal forums on reliability. Ms. Adams authored *Beyond Redundancy: How Geographic Redundancy Can Improve Service Availability*, *Reliability for Computer-Based Systems*, and *Reliability and Availability of Cloud Computing*. She originally joined Bell Labs in 1979 as a programmer on the 5ESS switch. Ms. Adams has worked on many projects throughout the company (e.g., software development, trouble ticket management, load administration research, software delivery, systems engineering, software architecture, software design, tools development, and joint venture setup) across many functional areas (e.g., database management, recent change/verify, common channel signaling, operations, administration, and management, reliability, and security). Ms. Adams holds a BA from University of Arizona and an MS in Computer Science from Illinois Institute of Technology. She lives in Naperville, Illinois.

Service Quality of Cloud-Based Applications, First Edition. Eric Bauer and Randee Adams.
© 2014 The Institute of Electrical and Electronics Engineers, Inc. Published 2014 by John Wiley & Sons, Inc.

INDEX

Abbreviations 303
Accessibility 25
Accessibility requirements 238
Accuracy 26
ACID 91
Adversarial testing 280
Agility 42
Analysis 66
Anti-affinity 262
Anycast 99
Application characteristics 15
Application instance 34
Application layer 170
Application model 9
Application service quality
    measurements 17
Application software supplier
    responsibilities 199
Audio-video synchronization 27
Availability 18, 68
Availability ratings 236
Availability requirements 234
Availability zone 44, 102, 104, 114, 189,
    263

Backout 146
BASE 92
Batch type applications 16
Block party upgrade 154, 155
Boundaries 11
Break testing 280

Broad network access 31
Business continuity 184

Canary release 275, 280, 286
Capacity scale down 41
Capacity scale in 40
Capacity scale out 40
Capacity scale up 41
CCDF. *See* Complementary cumulative
    distribution function
C_{Grow} 38
Chaos Monkey 263, 282
Circuit breaker 113
Cloud awareness 45
Cloud computing 29
Cloud consumer 199
Cloud operations support systems 36
Cloud service models 30
Cloud service provider responsibilities
    198
Complementary cumulative distribution
    function (CCDF) 22
Composability 171
Connectivity-as-a-Service 219
Containers 124
Containment 112
Continuous delivery 156
Continuous deployment 149
Coresidency testing 286
Critical criticality 16
Criticality, service 15

Service Quality of Cloud-Based Applications, First Edition. Eric Bauer and Randee Adams.
© 2014 The Institute of Electrical and Electronics Engineers, Inc. Published 2014 by John Wiley & Sons, Inc.

C_{Shrink} 39
Cumulative distribution function (CDF)   22
Customer facing service   11

Data-center-as-a-service   223
Data redundancy   90
Data replication strategies   188
Dead on arrival (DOA)   227
Defective operations per million (DPM) 237
Degraded delivery of VM capacity   57
Delay, packet   17
Density   37
Disaster recovery   184, 189
    testing   285
Disruption time   276
Distributions   23
DNS   98
Downtime ratings   236
DPM. *See* Defective operations per million
Dynamic data   146

Elasticity speedup   44
Elasticity testing   284
Elephants   21
End to end service model   169
Endurance testing   282
Error   112
Essential characteristics of cloud
    computing   31
Essential criticality   16
Extreme coresidency testing   286

Failure   112
Failure containment   111, 112
Failures per billion hours of operation
    (FITs)   248
Fault   112
Field replaceable units (FRUs)   226
FITs. *See* Failures per billion hours of
    operation
Footprint of failure   115
FRUs. *See* Field replaceable units

Georedundancy   189
Goodput   26
Growth density   38

Hardware reliability measurement   226
Hierarchy of failure containment   113

IaaS. *See* Infrastructure-as-a-Service (IaaS)
IIEA. *See* Infrastructure-as-a-Service
    impairment effects analysis
Infrastructure layer   170
Infrastructure-as-a-Service (IaaS)   30
    service impairments   49
Infrastructure-as-a-Service impairment effects
    analysis (IIEA)   257
Inspection   274
Interactive type applications   17
Interactivity   16

Key performance indicators   12
Key quality indicators   12
Keynes, John Maynard   63

Latency requirements   237
Latency tail   21
Latency verification   279
Linearity   43
Lip sync   27
Live VM migration   300
Load balancing   97
Loss, packet   17

Maintainability   69
Maximum acceptable service disruption
    234
Mean Opinion Score   26
Mean Time Between Failures (MTBF)   248
Mean Time to Restore Service (MTRS)
    68
Measured service   33
Measurement, service availability   213
Measurement points   165
MTBF. *See* Mean Time Between Failures
MTRS. *See* Mean Time to Restore Service
Multicast IP addressing   98
Multiservice architecture   80

Negative testing   280
Network element   34
No single point of failure. *See* Single Point of
    Failure
Non-interactive type applications   16
Non-proxy load balancers   98
Non-proxy load distribution   101
Normal type applications   17
Normalization   215

One driver per bus upgrade   156
Operations support systems   36

PaaS. *See* Platform-as-a-Service
Packet delay   17
Packet loss   17
Parsimonious service measurement   214
Part I—Context   7
Patch   145
Persistent data   146
PFEA. *See* Platform-as-a-Service failure
    effects analysis
Platform-as-a-Service (PaaS)   30, 33, 46,
    259, 280, 298
Platform-as-a-Service failure effects analysis
    (PFEA)   259
Proxy load balancers   97, 99

Qualification process   273
Quality requirements   233

Rambo architecture   236
Rapid elasticity   32
Real time applications   17
Reboot   70
Recovery point objective (RPO)
    analysis   268, 270
    testing   285
Recovery time objective (RTO)   184
    analysis 270
    testing   285
Redundancy   66
Redundant architecture   80
Regions   44
Release interval   39
Release management   145
Release management impact effects
    analysis   267
Reliability   24
Reliability block diagrams   116, 218, 256
Reliability verification   279
Requirements   233
Reset   70
Resolve   28
Resource facing service   12
Resource pooling   32
Respond   28
Restore   28
Retainability   25

Retainability requirements   239
Retrofit   146
Review   274
Robustness   13
Robustness testing   280
Rollback   146, 152
Routine criticality   15
RPO. *See* Recovery point objective
RTO. *See* Recovery time objective

SaaS. *See* Software-as-a-Service
Sampling times   276
Scale down   41
Scale in   40
Scale out   40
Scale up   41
Security   28
Self service   31
Service accessibility   25, 175
    requirements   238
Service availability   18, 172
    measurement   213
    ratings   236
    requirements   234
Service boundaries   11
Service criticality   15
Service disruption time   276
Service latency   19, 173
    requirements   237
    verification   279
Service layer   170
Service level agreements   210
Service models   30
Service orchestration   159
Service quality
    measurements   17
    requirements   233
Service reliability   24, 174
    verification   279
Service retainability   25, 176
    requirements   239
Service throughput   25
    requirements   239
Side-by-side analysis   256
Simian army   282
Simple application model   9
Simplex   68
Simulating infrastructure impairments   277
Single point of failure (SPOF)   116

Slew rate   43
Snapshot   70, 131
Soak   147
Software-as-a-Service (SaaS)   30
Software patch   145
Software supplier responsibilities   199
Software upgrade   145, 146
Speedup   44
SPOF. *See* Single point of failure
Stability testing   282
Statistical confidence   276
Statistical distributions   23
Support service   27
System   34

Tail   21
Tail latency   59
Technology, components   200, 223
Test   274
Test bed   275
Test considerations   273
Test planning   278
Test strategy   274
T_{Grow} 37, 38
Three layer service model   169
Throughput   25
  requirements   239

Timestamp accuracy   26
  requirements   240
Tolerance to network impairments   17
Traditional applications   45
Transaction latency   19
T_{Shrink} 39
Type I "block party" upgrade   154
Type II "one driver per bus" upgrade   156

Update   145
Upgrade   145, 146
Upgrade impact effects analysis   267

Validation   273
Verification   273
Virtualization   114
Virtual machine (VM)   9
  DOA   227
  failure   54
  migration   300
  reliability   228
  server controllers   35
  servers   35
  service impairments   49
  snapshot   131

Whipsaw   138